Women, Crime, and Criminal Justice

Original Feminist Readings

Claire Renzetti
St. Joseph's University

Lynne Good stein
Simmons College

New York   Oxford
OXFORD UNIVERSITY PRESS
2009

Oxford University Press, Inc., publishes works that further Oxford University's
objective of excellence in research, scholarship, and education.

Oxford   New York
Auckland   Cape Town   Dar es Salaam   Hong Kong   Karachi
Kuala Lumpur   Madrid   Melbourne   Mexico City   Nairobi
New Delhi   Shanghai   Taipei   Toronto

With offices in
Argentina   Austria   Brazil   Chile   Czech Republic   France   Greece
Guatemala   Hungary   Italy   Japan   Poland   Portugal   Singapore
South Korea   Switzerland   Thailand   Turkey   Ukraine   Vietnam

Copyright © 2001 by Oxford University Press, Inc.

Published by Oxford University Press, Inc.
198 Madison Avenue, New York, New York 10016
http://www.oup.com

Oxford is a registered trademark of Oxford University Press

Library of Congress Cataloging-in-Publication Data

ISBN 978-0-19-532996-4

Contents

Part I:
Connecting Gender and Crime

   Stanko analyzes how the emotion-laden concept of *danger* has
   been used by criminologists to frame discussions of women's
   criminality, fear of crime, and criminal victimization.

   Shattering the silence surrounding girls' delinquency, Chesney-
   Lind examines the problems that bring them to the attention of
   the juvenile justice system and the sex bias that characterizes the
   system.

   More girls today are involved in gangs. The authors describe the
   factors that have led to this increase, as well as girls' gang activity
   and the "double standards" imposed on girl gang members.

Part II:
Crimes Against Women

Part III:
Gender, Law, and Criminal Justice

Preface

It was only about 30 years ago that women were almost completely excluded from criminological research. There were a few exceptions—studies of prostitutes and, occasionally, the homicidal woman—but these works were notable for their rarity as well as for their stereotypical portrayals of female offenders. Little attention, if any, was paid to the victimization of women. Feminism changed all that; feminist criminologists have made the inclusion of gender as a central variable standard practice in most criminological research. Feminist criminologists have become so prolific in their studies of female offending and female victimization that it is difficult for many of their colleagues to keep up with the literature. We are proud to provide in this volume a survey of feminist research on mainstream and cutting-edge topics in the area of women, crime, and criminal justice, presented by some of the world's leading feminist criminologists.

The book is organized into three major sections: Connecting Gender and Crime; Crimes Against Women; and Gender, Law, and Criminal Justice. The chapters in each section were written for this volume and have not been published elsewhere. Readers will find chapters on standard topics covered in criminology courses in general and in gender and crime courses in particular, including juvenile justice, gangs, theoretical explanations of women's crime, crime trends, corrections, and policing. In addition, however, readers will find chapters on topics that are not typically covered in criminology textbooks but that feminists especially have brought to light in recent years—for example: gender, substance abuse, and crime; corporate violence against women; violence

against women as a human rights issue; the intersection of gender and race in criminal offending and criminal justice processing; and battered women charged with crimes. Each chapter opens with a brief summary, so readers have an overview of what the chapter is about. Each chapter ends with a set of discussion questions to encourage critical thinking about the chapter's content and to facilitate classroom discussion.

We are confident this volume will be a useful resource to students interested in the gendered nature of criminal offending, victimization, and criminal justice processes, including the criminal justice professions. That the book has come to fruition is due to the efforts of many more people than ourselves. We wish to thank Claude Teweles, president of Roxbury Publishing Company, for initially suggesting our collaboration and for encouraging us to continue when we doubted we had the time or energy to see the project through to completion. We are especially grateful to Maureen O'Connell, formerly of St. Joseph's University and editorial assistant for the journal *Violence Against Women*, who checked manuscripts for inconsistencies; identified missing references, discussion questions, and biographical statements; and corresponded with authors. Maureen heroically brought order to chaos. We also thank our copy editor, Jackie Estrada, for her efforts in making the chapters consistent and more readable, and Jim Ballinger, our production manager, who patiently and expertly guided the book into print.

We would like to thank the following reviewers for their insightful comments and suggestions: Barbara Bloom (Sonoma State University), Kimberly Cook (University of

Southern Maine), Walter S. DeKeseredy (Carlton University, Toronto), Teresa Donati (Farleigh Dickinson University), Helen Eigenberg (University of Tennessee at Chattanooga), Evelyn Gilbert (Livingstone College), Beth Hess, Christine Rasche (University of North Florida), Nanci Koser Wilson (Indiana University of Pennsylvania), Richard A. Wright (Arkansas State University), and Marjorie S. Zatz (Arizona State University).

Most of all, we thank the contributors, not only for their excellent chapters but also for their commitment to improving the lives of female offenders and victims.

Finally, Claire Renzetti wishes to thank her husband, Dan Curran, and her sons, Sean and Aidan, for their perceptive insights, unwavering support, and disarming sense of humor. Lynne Goodstein wishes to thank Claire Renzetti for her commitment, generosity, and good humor; her sons, Aaron and Zach Shotland, for keeping her grounded; and her husband, Peter Langer, for his support. ✦

About the Editors

Claire M. Renzetti is a professor and chair of the Sociology Department at St. Joseph's University, Philadelphia. She edits the international interdisciplinary journal _Violence Against Women_, coedits the _Violence Against Women_ book series for Sage Publications, and edits the series on gender, crime, and law for Northeastern University Press. She has authored or edited ten books and numerous book chapters and journal articles. She has been honored as an Outstanding Scholar by both the Women and Crime Division and the Critical Criminology Division of the American Society of Criminology.

Lynne Goodstein is the dean of the College of Arts and Sciences and Professional Studies at Simmons College in Boston. For 22 years she was on the faculty of the Pennsylvania State University and served in a number of capacities, most recently as an associate dean of the graduate school and a professor of crime, law, and justice and women's studies. For almost a decade (1986–1995), she served as the director of the Women's Studies program at Penn State. She has authored or edited three books and numerous journal articles and book chapters. Her criminological work deals with inmate adjustment to prison, criminal sentencing, and women in the criminal justice system. Her women's studies research encompasses multiculturalism in general education, curricular issues, and interdisciplinarity. She is currently engaged in research on women's studies faculty, focusing on organizational structure, models of faculty involvement, and knowledge production. ✦

About the Contributors

Julie Allison (Ph.D., University of Kansas, 1991) is associate professor at Pittsburg State University, Pittsburg, Kansas. She has been involved in research in the area of sexual aggression for the past ten years, and is coauthor of *Rape: The Misunderstood Crime.* Her interests also include gender and psychology-and-law issues. She teaches courses in social psychology and offers workshops on various gender issues, including violence against women.

Frances Bernat is an associate professor in the Administration of Justice Department at Arizona State University West. Dr. Bernat's research has been focused on the policy and application of criminal law, and women in the criminal justice system. This scholarship has been largely directed at understanding essential questions that pertain to our constitutional form of government and crime. Dr. Bernat's recent research includes the study of crime and the fear of crime among elder populations, the nature and extent of crime committed by youth, and the degree to which social service programs can reduce recidivism among youthful offenders. In 1998 Dr. Bernat received the following awards: Arizona State Governor's Spirit of Excellence Award; a semi-finalist award for Innovations in American Government from the Ford Foundation and the John F. Kennedy School of Government at Harvard University; and the ASU President's Medal for Team Excellence.

Judith Bessant teaches at the Australian Catholic University in Melbourne, Australia, and her areas of research include social policy, sociology, social theory and youth studies.

Lisa Broidy is an assistant professor of sociology at the University of New Mexico and a network associate for the John D. and Catherine T. MacArthur Network on Adolescent Development and Juvenile Justice. Her research interests center on the etiology of crime and delinquency with a particular interest in gender-based similarities and differences in criminal/delinquent behavior and its correlates. Her current research is rooted in life-course/developmental approaches to the study of crime and focuses on the linkage between chronic disruptive behaviors in childhood and adolescent outcomes (especially offending and depression) among males and females.

Rodney K. Brunson received a master's degree in criminology and criminal justice from the University of Missouri-St. Louis in 1998 and is currently pursuing a Ph.D. in criminal justice at the University of Illinois-Chicago. His research interests are the intersection of race, class, and gender. He is specifically interested in neighborhood processes as they relate to communities' ability to regulate drug activity.

Meda Chesney-Lind, Ph.D., is a professor of women's studies at the University of Hawaii at Manoa. She has served as vice president of the American Society of Criminology (ASC) and president of the Western Society of Criminology (WSC). Nationally recognized for her work on women and crime, her books include *Girls, Delinquency and Juvenile Justice*, which was awarded the American Society of Criminology's Michael J. Hindelang Award for "outstanding contribution to criminology" in 1992, and *The Female Offender: Girls, Women and Crime*, published by Sage in 1998. She was named a fellow of the American Society of Criminology in 1996 and has received the Distinguished Scholar

Award from the Division on Women and Crime of the ASC, the Herbert Block Award for service to the ASC, the Paul Tappan Award for "outstanding contributions to the field of criminology" from the Western Society of Criminology, the Founders Award for "significant improvement of the quality of justice" from the WSC, and the University of Hawaii Board of Regents' medal for excellence in research.

Sandy Cook is a senior lecturer in the School of Law and Legal Studies at La Trobe University. Her research and teaching are in the areas of violence against women, disability studies and criminal justice. Sandy is associate editor of *Violence Against Women* and on the editorial board of *Inclusive Education*.

Kathleen J. Ferraro is the director of women's studies at Arizona State University. She is a scholar-activist who has worked in the area of violence against women for the past 25 years. Her current research focuses on the intersection of victimization and offending in women's lives and the unintended consequences of "getting tough" on domestic violence.

Evelyn Gilbert is an associate professor of criminal justice at Livingstone College. Her research interests include criminal justice education, homicide, and minorities in the criminal justice system. Dr. Gilbert's publications have focused on African-American males and violence, women in prison, and AOD prevention among African-American women.

Nancy C. Jurik is a professor of justice studies at Arizona State University. She has published research on women and crime and on gender issues in the workplace. She coauthored (with Susan E. Martin) *Doing Justice, Doing Gender: Women in Law and Criminal Justice Occupations* (Sage, 1996). Dr. Jurik's current research focuses on women and men in home businesses and on microenterprise loan programs in the United States.

Irene Kollenbroich-Shea is a master's student at Pittsburg State University, Pittsburg, Kansas. Her current research program concerns the cognitive trauma resulting from violence against women. Her interests include violence against women and posttraumatic stress disorder.

Ronald C. Kramer is a professor of sociology and director of the Criminal Justice Program at Western Michigan University in Kalamazoo. He earned his Ph.D. in 1978 from The Ohio State University. His specialty area is corporate and government violence. His recent publications on this topic have appeared in *Social Problems, Social Justice, Humanity & Society, Peace Review,* and *Violence Against Women.* Professor Kramer chairs the Kalamazoo Coalition for the Prevention of Youth Violence and has organized Peace and Justice Education Week at WMU for the past 15 years.

Candace Kruttschnitt is a professor and chair of the Department of Sociology at the University of Minnesota. She has published extensively on the subject of female offenders, including both reviews of research pertaining to gender differences in etiology and primary analysis of criminal court sanctions. More recently, she has been involved in an NSF–funded study that replicates and extends Ward and Kassebaum's research on women's adaptations to incarceration. This research examines both temporal and institutional variations in women's prison experiences in California over a 30-year period.

Richard F. Mancuso holds M.A. degrees in both criminal justice and sociology, the former from the State University College at Buffalo and the latter from the State University of New York at Buffalo. He is currently in the sociology Ph.D. program (ABD) at the University of Buffalo and is a research analyst at the Center for Research on Urban Social Work Practice with an emphasis on mothers' alcohol problems and children's victimization.

Susan E. Martin has been studying women in policing since the 1970s, when her dissertation research resulted in publication of *'Breaking and Entering': Policewomen on Patrol.* While a project director at the Police Foundation in Washington, D.C., one of the studies that she conducted resulted in *On the Move: The Status of Women in Policing*. In 1996 she published *Doing Justice, Doing Gender: Women in Law and Criminal Justice Occupations*, coauthored with Nancy Jurik (which won an award from the Gustavus Myers Center for the Study of Human Rights in North America for Outstanding Book on the subject of human rights in North America, 1997). She currently is a program officer at the National Institute on Alcohol Abuse and Alcoholism and oversees that institute's research on alcohol-related violence, drunk driving, and public policies designed to reduce alcohol-related intentional and unintentional injuries. Dr. Martin's recent publications focus on drinking and driving, the social construction of hate crime, alcohol-related violence, and police work and emotional labor. She also has a forthcoming review article on women in policing in *The Encyclopedia of Women and Crime*. She holds a Ph.D. in sociology from American University.

Brenda A. Miller is a professor in the School of Social Work at the State University of New York at Buffalo and a director at the Center for Research on Urban Social Work Practice. In addition to her research, Dr. Miller is also a consultant with a variety of agencies, including the National Institute on Alcohol Abuse and Alcoholism and the National Institute on Drug Abuse.

Jody Miller is an assistant professor of criminology and criminal justice at the University of Missouri–St. Louis. She is currently completing a study (with Dheeshana Jayasundera) of the commercial sex industry in Sri Lanka, funded by a Fulbright Senior Scholar Award. She is a member of the National Consortium on Violence Research, through which she is currently researching (with Norman White) violence against urban African-American adolescent girls. Her monograph, *One of the Guys: Girls, Gangs and Gender*, will be published by Oxford University Press in 2001.

Susan L. Miller is an associate professor in the Department of Sociology and Criminal Justice at the University of Delaware. She received her Ph.D. in criminology from the University of Maryland. Her research interests include gender and crime, domestic violence, community policing and social control, and criminal justice policy. Her work has been published in various journals, such as *Law & Society Review, Violence and Victims, Justice Quarterly*, and *Women & Criminal Justice*. Her book *Crime Control and Women: Feminist Implications of Criminal Justice Policy* was published in 1998; her most recent book, *Gender and Community Policing: Walking the Talk*, was published in 1999.

Sue Osthoff is the cofounder and executive director of the National Clearinghouse for the Defense of Battered Women, a nonprofit organization that provides technical assistance to both battered women charged with crimes and to their attorneys.

Barbara Owen, a former research analyst with the Federal Bureau of Prisons, received her Ph.D. in sociology from the University of California at Berkeley. Currently a professor in the Department of Criminology, California State University—Fresno, Dr. Owen continues her work in the areas of prisons and social control, specifically gender issues and substance-abuse treatment. Her most recent publication is a monograph on female prison culture, *In the Mix: Struggle and Survival in a Women's Prison* (SUNY Press, 1998). She has also conducted evaluation, survey, and qualitative research on prison drug treatment programs, the gender-specific needs of girls and young women, and descriptions of the adult and youth prison populations in California.

Linda Rynbrandt is an assistant professor in the Department of Sociology at Grand Valley State University. Her research interests include gender and social movements for change, both past and present. She is currently at work on a manuscript for Garland Press that examines the role of women in early sociology and Progressive Era social reform.

Lisa Sanchez, Ph.D., is an assistant professor of criminal justice at the University of Illinois at Chicago. She is interested in urban and cultural studies, gender, sexuality, and critical race theory. She has published articles in *Law and Social Inquiry, Political and Legal Anthropology Review*, and *Studies in Law, Politics and Society* on the growth and regulation of licit and illicit sexual economies in one Northwestern U.S. city. Her current work focuses on the use of public space ordinances, such as drug- and prostitution-free zones, gang-loitering ordinances, and nuisance ordinances, to regulate difference in urban communities.

Elizabeth A. Stanko, a professor of criminology, received her Ph.D. in sociology from the City University of New York, Graduate School in 1977. She worked for thirteen years teaching sociology and women's studies at Clark University (USA), and then moved to London in 1990 to take her position at Brunel University's Law Department. She is the author of *Everyday Violence* (Pandora, 1990), *Intimate Intrusions* (Routledge, 1985), editor of texts on gender and crime (most recently *Just Boys Doing Business: Men, Masculinities and Crime* with Tim Newburn, Routledge 1994), and has published widely on issues of prosecutorial discretion, violence, violence against women and crime prevention. She is the research director of the Economic and Social Research Council's Programme on Violence.

Darrell Steffensmeier is a professor of sociology and crime/law/justice at the Pennsylvania State University. His research interests include courts and sentencing, correlates of crime (age, gender, ethnicity), organized crime and criminal careers, and joint application of qualitative and quantitative methods. ✦

1
Women, Crime, and Criminal Justice—An Overview

Lynne Goodstein

We live in a gendered world. By being born as a boy or girl, in virtually all locations on the planet our life courses will be to some extent differentially determined. These differences in the lives of females and males are shaped to some extent by biological differences between the sexes—hormone levels, body type, body size, and specific roles in the process of reproduction. Yet by far the larger influence on life-course differences comes from how society inscribes sex differences with broad-scale meaning through the social construction of gender. In virtually every society, the concept of gender determines the range of activities deemed appropriate for individuals to perform. Males are assumed to possess certain attributes, be superior in performing certain tasks, be more appropriate to function in certain social situations and organizations than females, and vice versa. The specific attributes, tasks, and settings linked to males or females are not necessarily reflective of biological or physiological differences and vary to some degree from culture to culture and throughout historic periods. In this sense, gender—the prescription of appropriate attributes, behaviors, and social roles to females and males—is socially constructed.

Not only do differential roles result as gender is socially constructed, but feminist scholars have emphasized that differential power is associated with masculine and feminine roles. Historically, and in contemporary life in most cultures across the globe, males hold more power and privilege—both publicly and privately—than females. Men control more of the wealth, hold the highest positions in government and industry, control the military, make more scientific and scholarly discoveries, and are more prominent in sports and entertainment than women. Since the advent of the second wave of the feminist movement, the last several decades have brought better opportunities and some degree of equality for women. Many women have moved into positions in the workplace where they compete with men; some have attained prominence. Yet, profound differences remain in terms of the life courses and opportunities of the average woman and man across the globe. Life courses are also profoundly affected by conditions other than gender, including class, race, sexual orientation, and physical ability.

Patriarchy is the term generally used to describe a society in which there is an unequal distribution of power and privilege between males and females. One mechanism for enforcing patriarchy, according to a number of feminist historians, is the segregation of activities by gender into what are called the public and private spheres. Historically, and to some extent in contemporary life, men have had jurisdiction over both the public sphere—political, economic, and cultural affairs—and the private sphere of the home, whereas women were expected to involve themselves only with the private sphere of the home and the raising of children. Illustrative of the concept of male domination of the public sphere is the fact that for most of the eighteenth and nineteenth centuries, by virtue of their sex, women could not vote, run for public office, or become educated at the nation's most prestigious institutions. Essentially, women had no civic identity separate from that of their husbands or fathers. Moreover, because the public and private spheres were seldom breached, what males chose to do to their "property" behind the closed doors of the home was essentially off limits to the scrutiny of those committed to enforcing justice. Violence committed by men against their wives in the home would not come to the attention of law enforcement. Indeed, the "rule of thumb," a part of English common law for centuries, implied that men could beat their wives with impunity, provided the implement used was no thicker than the man's thumb.

Although most laws and governmental policies that stripped equality from women have long been abolished, there continue to be inequalities between the treatment of men and women in society. In contemporary life, these inequalities are based less on official doctrine and more on informal attitudes and values about appropriate life courses for men and women. It should also be noted that the gains made by the feminist movement of the late twentieth century were not equally distributed across all sectors of women. These gains benefited women particularly at the middle and higher echelons of the working world, and hence were less palpable for poorer and working-class women, a group that is disproportionately comprised of minorities.

Women, Crime, and Justice

It is in this context of patriarchy that any analysis of women, crime, and criminal justice must be carried out. This collection brings together scholarly observations and research findings of some of the most prominent scholars of these subjects in the world today. Each chapter was written expressly for publication in this volume, with a focus on an advanced undergraduate and graduate student readership, although the volume will be valuable to the scholarly community as well. The authors review the most up-to-date scholarship and place in perspective what has been discovered about women offenders, victims, and professionals and the response of the criminal justice system to these groups. The last two decades have witnessed a burgeoning of interest in these topics and

this volume is the beneficiary of this new and exciting scholarship.

Chapter 2 of this volume, Elizabeth A. Stanko's "Women, Danger, and Criminology," sets the stage for what follows in the book. She offers a sophisticated and complex analysis that uses the concept of danger to integrate our understanding of traditional criminological perspectives on male and female crime, the criminal justice system's response to crime, violence against women, and fear of crime. Readers will be well rewarded by reviewing this piece more than once; it exemplifies a gendered approach to criminological theorizing and places much of what will follow in the volume within a feminist perspective.

Stanko's analysis begins by equating criminality and danger—people who are labeled as criminals are viewed by the public and the criminal justice system as deserving to be controlled and as inducing fear of victimization among the law-abiding citizenry. The obverse of this statement, of course, would be that those who are not identified and labeled as criminals are not dangerous and do not need to be feared.

A gendered analysis of danger and criminality carries with it some ironies. As readers will learn from a number of chapters of this book, women offenders generally are involved in less serious types of crime than men. Moreover, in many cases of women committing the most serious crimes (such as murdering their domestic partners), their offenses were committed because they believed their lives, or the lives of their children, were in mortal danger. Yet because women are labeled as criminals they are considered dangerous and are viewed as fair game for incarceration. Stanko also discusses the fact that those considered dangerous—the criminals—are not perceived as people with whom members of the law-abiding public have everyday relationships. The flip side of this assumption is that those persons with whom we interact on a daily basis would not be criminal. Yet, as Stanko notes, many women experience the most serious victimization at the hands of those who are the closest to them—husbands and fathers. Stanko's analysis calls for a "gendered social justice" that takes into account the experiences and realities of women and in which officials responsible for ensuring fairness acknowledge gendered perspectives. Stanko's arguments are echoed in various ways by many of the authors in this volume.

The Gendered Nature of Women's Crime

Much more is known today than even 20 years ago about women and crime. Traditionally, criminology as a discipline has focused on male offending—street crime, violent crime, organized crime, and white collar crime. Most theories of crime have been developed to explain why men commit crime with little focus on the different dynamics that might affect women as criminals. Yet there are some very substantial differences between male and female criminality that virtually scream out for interpretation.

It does not take advanced criminological sophistication to recognize differences between male and female criminality—women commit substantially less crime than do men in virtually every crime category save prostitution. This gender gap in offending is examined in several of the book's chapters. Moreover, several authors explicate how both criminal activity and the criminal justice system's response to such activity is affected by gender, such that a *gendered theory of crime* is called for to adequately understand and explain criminal behavior.

To adequately explain women's criminality and its dramatically lower rates than men's is to recognize the importance of gender in prescribing behavior and how gender interacts with race and class. Darrell Steffensmeier sets the stage for this examination in chapter 13, "Female Crime Trends, 1960–1995," and, with Lisa Broidy in chapter 8, assesses the adequacy of existing theories of crime. In "Explaining Female

Offending," Steffensmeier and Broidy cite a theory of crime that does take gender into account. They review many sociocultural and some biological factors that are likely to contribute to the frequency and patterns of female crime.

Sociocultural factors accounting for women's criminality involve a number of dynamics discussed in various chapters in this volume. First, compared with men and boys, mechanisms of social control keep women and girls more restricted in terms of freedom of movement. Increased surveillance by parents and greater restriction to the private space of the home reduces access to criminogenic settings as part of routine activities. In chapter 6, "Gender and Violence," Candace Kruttschnitt emphasizes this point in accounting for women's lower levels of violent crime. Kruttschnitt also discusses another sociocultural factor, the fact that the women have primary responsibility for child rearing. Saddled with primary child-rearing obligations, women's attention is more likely than men's to be diverted from public settings to those of the home and family relationships. A by-product of this dynamic, as Kruttschnitt notes, is that when women do commit violent crime, there is a higher probability that the targets of their violence will be family members.

Normative differences in acceptable behaviors for women and men are dictated by gender as well, and these differences have an impact on women's and men's criminality. Masculinity involves a certain amount of aggressiveness, and men are valued for their dominance and risk-taking ability. These attributes are compatible with criminal activity, which frequently requires boldness and the ability to dominate others. Women, who are not socialized as a whole toward these behavioral attributes, may be less inclined toward criminal activity. Women's opportunities for engagement in organized criminal activity are also limited by the same factors that account for the glass ceiling in corporate America. Steffensmeier and Broidy note that, if anything, women face even greater occupational segregation in underworld crime groups than women encounter in legitimate businesses. Rodney Brunson and Jody Miller, whose research on gangs is reported in chapter 4, "Girls and Gangs," reinforce these last two dynamics in their analysis of gang activity. They argue that gangs remain male dominated and that girls who do join gangs tend to commit crimes that are less serious than those of their male counterparts.

The gendered theory of crime also points to biological and physiological differences between men and women that may result in different patterns and frequency of crime. Richard F. Mancuso and Brenda A. Miller, in chapter 7, "Crime and Punishment in the Lives of Women Alcohol and Other Drug (AOD) Users: Exploring the Gender, Lifestyle and Legal Issues," focus on women involved in lifestyles of alcohol and other drug usage. In addition to sociocultural factors differentiating male and female offenders involved in these lifestyles, they make several observations about gender and AOD involvement that relate to biological differences between men and women. Because women become addicted more quickly than men, they may be more at risk for drug-related criminal involvement. AOD-involved women also have a biological connection to childbearing and child rearing that results in different consequences than for AOD men: women's involvement in alcohol and drugs may cause harm to their children, both in utero and during the child rearing period. Also, HIV and AIDS are more significant threats to AOD women because of the dual risks of drug involvement and prostitution.

This volume provides rich detail on the lives of female offenders and reviews the theoretical and statistical literature accounting for patterns of female crime. Some of the material may be challenging for readers unfamiliar with general criminological theory, statistical analysis, or feminist theory. The bulk of it should be accessible to any reader, however, and readers particularly interested in women and crime will find a wealth of insightful information.

The Victimization of Women

Our understanding of women and crime is one-sided without a perspective on the victimization of women. *Women, Crime, and Criminal Justice* benefits greatly from the high-quality scholarship that has been conducted on this topic over the past several decades. Until the 1970s, little was known about the crimes of sexual assault, childhood sexual abuse, and wife battering. Historically, law enforcement agencies spent little effort in enforcing the law in these areas relative to the magnitude of the problem. These offenses, perpetrated for the most part by people known to the victims, occurred primarily in the private sphere and did not fit traditional conceptions of "real" crime—that is, crimes committed by criminals who were strangers to the victims.

As a result of the advocacy of feminist activists and researchers working with agents of the criminal justice and legal systems, the conceptualization of what is considered a "crime" has changed in recent decades. Behaviors that in the past may have been overlooked or ignored are now attended to by the police and the courts; the legitimacy of women's victimization by acquaintances and spouses is much more adequately acknowledged.

Stanko underscores the importance of integrating an analysis of gender into our understanding of crimes against women. The notion of "fear of crime," as it is traditionally used by criminologists and criminal justice professionals, generally refers to fear of strangers. Hence, preventive strategies for ensuring safety from crime include improved locks and protection of property, walking in well-lit areas at night, and learning self-defense tactics. While these approaches may have some benefit in reducing or deflecting victimization by strangers, they have limited utility in preventing the type of crime to which many women fall prey—crimes by intimates. For women, the most dangerous location may be the one where traditional crime prevention tactics are least effective—the home.

Several chapters of this volume focus in various ways on the impact of patriarchy on the dynamics of intimate relationships. Offenses committed against women by acquaintances and intimates reflect gender dynamics embedded in a patriarchal system based on male power and control. Julie Allison and Irene Kollenbroich-Shea's chapter 10, "Sexual Assault" and Kathleen J. Ferraro's chapter 9, "Woman Battering: More Than a Family Problem" underscore the important point that violence against women is not simply a reflection of a "sick personality" or "psychological illness," but rather is a reflection of structural gender dynamics, informed by racial and class positions.

At the other end of the continuum from intimate violence is corporate violence against women. Ironically, corporate violence towards women frequently relates to women's sexuality. In chapter 11, "Corporate Violence Against Women," Linda Rynbrandt and Ronald C. Kramer discuss a topic only recently acknowledged by feminist criminologists as falling within the rubric of studies on gender and crime—how decisions made by corporations in the interests of profit may result in harm to women. The chapter examines breast implant surgery and its resultant adverse medical side effects in some women as illustrative of corporate violence against women. Reinforcing media-generated desires among women to be sexually attractive, Dow Corning and other corporations' silicone breast implants were adopted by thousands of women who later developed negative physical reactions. Another instance of corporate victimization of women is the dalkon shield, a contraceptive device that rendered some women infertile.

Over the past two decades, feminist criminologists and scholars have shed light on the prevalence of victimization of women not just within the borders of the United States but throughout the world. Judith Bessant and Sandy Cook explicate issues of violence against women as a human rights issue in chapter 12, "Understanding Violence Against Women: Universal Human Rights and International Law." Bessant and Cook discuss the global prevalence of physical and nonphysical violence against women. They argue that social institutions in most communities across the planet are male centered. Therefore, inequitable power relationships exist among men and women to some degree in most nations and are manifested in customs and practices that are, at times, severely harmful to women. These practices are wide-ranging and include such violations as rape as an instrument of warfare, dowry deaths, genital circumcision, sexual slavery, and economic deprivation. Yet for those attempting to safeguard human rights of women across the globe the challenges are immense due to the wide diversity among women across cultures, nationalities, races, and classes and the difficulties in relying on the concept of "universal human rights" in light of culturally specific violations.

Integrative Perspectives on Women's Criminality and Victimization

Another major contribution of the authors to this volume is in their recognition and detailed description of the complex interrelationship between women's victimization and women's offending. Put succinctly, women and girls commit crime to avoid being further victimized and they experience victimization in the course of committing crime. Perhaps the most significant work outlining the victimization and criminality relationship has been conducted by Meda Chesney-Lind in her lifelong research on adolescent girls and their involvement in the criminal justice system. In chapter 3, " 'Out of Sight, Out of Mind': Girls in the Juvenile Justice System," Chesney-Lind reviews patterns of delinquency among girls and the responses of the criminal justice system to these young women. Her chapter enumerates a fact that is also echoed in several other chapters—that girls are much more likely to be victims of child sexual abuse than are boys. This victimization reflects traditional male attitudes shaped by patriarchy about women as men's sexual property. Chesney-Lind also explicates the role of physical and sexual abuse in girls' delinquency by citing the high proportion of incarcerated girls and women who report prior physical or sexual abuse.

Lisa Sanchez, who conducted an ethnography of women prostitutes, has also provided valuable insights on this dynamic in chapter 5, "Gender Troubles: The Entanglement of Agency, Violence, and Law in the Lives of Women in Prostitution," describing how prostitution functions as part of a complex recursive cycle of victimization to criminality, then back to victimization. She argues that although complex cultural meanings involve sharp boundaries between victims and offenders, women involved in prostitution experience both active participation in criminal activity and subjection to violence. Young women run away to escape sexual or other abuse at home, enter prostitution as a means of livelihood, and encounter victimization as a routine part of the profession. Sanchez poignantly depicts how women working as prostitutes become accustomed to physical violence, threats, and intimidation and how they come to accept this victimization as an unavoidable occupational hazard. Moreover, given their stigmatized status, Sanchez discusses how victims have little recourse through the criminal justice system because they are viewed by many police officers as having abdicated their rights to be considered legitimate victims by their involvement in a criminal lifestyle.

The ultimate example of the victimization and criminality nexus is the case of women who kill their abusers. Kathleen Ferraro ar-

ticulates eloquently the dynamics of woman abuse in domestic situations and sets the stage for an understanding of how victims could become killers. Ferraro situates her analysis within a general feminist framework that attributes violence against women to a patriarchal culture that fosters men's expectations of male privilege and female service and subordination. As Ferraro recounts,

> While most men do not use violence to enforce male privilege, the men who do clearly articulate beliefs in legitimate entitlement to women's obedience and loyalty and the [man's] right to punish infractions.

Ferraro emphasizes that wife abuse reflects a strategy of power and control over the entire life of another human being and occurs on an emotional level to an even greater extent than on a physical one.

Susan Osthoff discusses cases of women who kill their abusers in chapter 16, "When Victims Become Defendants: Battered Women Charged With Crimes." These individuals, she argues, have endured years of mental and physical abuse, frequently having been ignored by the criminal justice system when they had been harmed by their husbands. Although there is no single model, women who kill their domestic partners have come to a point of believing that their, or their children's, lives hang in the balance. It is also noteworthy that although Osthoff focuses on battered women who kill, she also acknowledges another manifestation of the victimization and criminality nexus for women—being forced by batterers to commit other crimes.

Several of the authors in this volume note that women commit other types of crime as well because of coercive relationships with powerful males. In some situations, male partners threaten to enact violence against the woman or her children if she fails to comply with his wishes. In others, simply the level of emotional control is strong enough for the male to achieve the desired result. Steffensmeier and Broidy's chapter reinforces this argument by noting that when women are arrested for more serious crimes (such as robbery) they are more likely to have served as accomplices to men in various capacities (such as driving the getaway car) than to have masterminded the offense.

Perhaps one of the most unfortunate types of crime that abused women are prosecuted for is "failure to protect" their children, as Osthoff describes in her chapter. Abused women may be arrested not because they harmed their children in any way but because they "failed" to intervene or obtain assistance while the person who abused them also abused their children.

Throughout the book readers will find discussions of the connections between victimization and criminality among women. The thread that ties these analyses together is that authors situate violence against women within a societally condoned context of male power and control. As Ferraro argues in her chapter, the social institutions of religion, kinship, the economy, and the media normalize hierarchical gender relations and enforce male power and privilege, leading some males to exercise emotional and physical control through abusive means. In some sense, physical and emotional abuse suffered by women at the hands of men represent a second victimization, the first one being the relegation to second-class citizenship within a patriarchal culture. For the many women who fall into criminal activity as a result of abuse, the consequences of criminality may be viewed as yet a third level of victimization.

The Role of the Criminal Justice System in Responding to and Perpetuating Crime

Women's crime is not only influenced by individual, interpersonal, and sociocultural influences—the responses of the justice system itself also have the potential to shape women's criminal involvement and identities.

In recent years, an increasing proportion of women have been identified as criminals as a result of changes in criminal justice system policy regarding certain behaviors, particularly those that are drug related. In chapter 15, "Women, Race, and Criminal Justice Processing," Evelyn Gilbert focuses on how changes in governmental policy regarding drug offenses have disproportionately affected women, especially minority women, in terms of increased prosecution and incarceration. In the 1980s the federal and many state governments attempted to deal with what they viewed as an increasing problem with drug-related crime by imposing stiffer penalties for relatively low-level drug offenses. In addition, many jurisdictions implemented mandatory prison sentences for certain drug crimes, reducing judges' discretion to mete out alternative sanctions to incarceration. These policy changes reflected a more politically conservative orientation for legislative bodies as well as a specific response to the proliferation of a particularly virulent drug, crack cocaine. Given women's greater susceptibility to drug addiction, especially to crack cocaine, these policy changes rendered dramatic impacts on the involvement of women in the criminal justice system.

Barbara Owen, in chapter 17, "Perspectives on Women in Prison," provides additional data to support Gilbert's arguments about the dire consequences for women following these changes in sentencing policy regarding drug offenses. Owen notes that the number of women in state prisons has tripled within the past two decades, primarily as a result of increased convictions for drug-related offenses. Indeed, as Owen states, the war on drugs appears to have become a war on women. Moreover, as Gilbert notes, this assault on low-level women offenders has not been directed equally but has been especially hard on poor women of color. During this period of increased women's imprisonment, African-American women showed the greatest increase in incarcerations rates of all offender groups.

In chapter 14, "Gender and Law," Frances Bernat reviews gender issues in the treatment of offenders by legal institutions, noting that laws in many jurisdictions that historically meted out harsher penalties for women than for men convicted of similar crimes were found unconstitutional and were rescinded or revised by the end of the 1970s. However, sentencing judges continue to make distinctions on the basis of gender that often operate to the detriment of women offenders. Bernat cites studies demonstrating that women convicted of less serious offenses are sentenced more harshly than their male counterparts. Additionally, judges may consider factors unrelated to the case itself—such as marital status, family background, and the degree to which the defendant is viewed as "respectable"—in making sentencing decisions for women defendants, considerations that are not taken into account in the sentencing of males. Another domain in which women offenders may receive more unpleasant treatment than their male counterparts is their treatment during incarceration. By virtue of the significantly smaller number of women in prison than men, women prisoners receive relatively fewer prison programs, services, and work-release opportunities, may be incarcerated at distances farther from their families, and due to less overcrowding, may end up spending more time in prison because they are not eligible for early release programs.

The Role of the Criminal Justice System and the Public in Responding to and Perpetuating Women's Victimization

When violence against women was considered essentially a private matter, many offenders could commit their crimes with impunity. The last several decades have witnessed progress in this area, and the criminal justice and legal systems should be credited for their efforts to improve the quality of official response and services for victims of violence, regardless of the identities of the perpetrators. Kathleen Ferraro notes this progress in her chapter on intimate violence by citing a number of reforms that have improved official responses to women's victimization. Coordination and communication of the various community and governmental agencies involved in dealing with violence against women have helped victims of violence, as have the shelter movement, the Violence Against Women Act, and other rape reform legislation. Yet these measures have only gone so far, and much of the general public still holds dismissive attitudes regarding women's complicity in their victimization. Moreover, classism and racism often exacerbate public condemnation of women victims who are poor, of color, or both. Osthoff, who directs the National Clearinghouse for the Defense of Battered Women in Philadelphia, Pennsylvania, describes the difficulties of defending women who kill their abusers unless these defendants conform to a rigid construction of the "legitimate victim"—white, deferential, and middle class.

Chesney-Lind's chapter on girls and the juvenile justice system underscores the role of the formal criminal justice system in perpetuating the continued victimization of young women who have suffered abuse at the hands of fathers or other so-called "protectors." All too often, the very strategies abused girls and young women use for their survival—running away from abusive homes—are criminalized. Young women runaways are given the label of status offenders and are either returned to the abusive environments or incarcerated. Moreover, the irony of a double standard exists, in that runaway boys who are less likely to leave home for such extreme self-protective reasons are not as likely as victimized girls to be detained as status offenders.

Reducing Women's Crime and the Treatment of Women Offenders

Several authors address the issue of what can and should be done to reduce women's criminality. Combating the effects of poverty and racism would reduce crime for all offenders, but some issues regarding crime prevention are particularly germane to women. For example, in their discussion of women drug- and alcohol-involved offenders, Mancuso and Miller suggest replacing a crime-fighting approach with one of harm reduction. Rather than focusing on punishment for criminal violations, consideration should be given to the harm that emanates from the AOD lifestyle for the women, their children, and society in general. These harms take many forms, including increased health risks for users, physical and emotional damage to AOD offenders' children, and the increased risk of harm to self and others from criminal behavior. Rather than focusing on punishing offenders, officials may better serve society by viewing and dealing with the AOD lifestyle and its concomitant criminal activity as public health problems.

Discussing incarcerated women, Owen also underscores the importance of designing treatment programs for women offenders that are responsive to their particular situations and needs, not only within the context of gender but also of race and class. Given the less serious nature of the offenses of many women, she argues for community alternatives to prison that speak specifically to women's economic needs, particular substance abuse problems, and societally prescribed roles as mothers and care givers. She recognizes the victimization and criminality nexus for so many female offenders and emphasizes the importance of programs to as-

sist women offenders in dealing with past physical, sexual, and emotional abuse within culturally sensitive contexts.

Challenges to Women in Policing and Corrections

Although the lives of women police and corrections officers may appear far removed from those of women offenders and victims, female professionals also must contend with the gendered nature of the criminal justice system. Popular attitudes regarding appropriate gender roles present challenges to women trying to make it in policing and corrections that are not dissimilar to the challenges faced by women offenders desiring to break into certain criminal organizations.

Two chapters in the volume address issues of women professionals in the criminal justice workplace. In chapter 18, "Gender and Policing," Susan Miller addresses issues of women in law enforcement; Nancy Jurik and Susan E. Martin discuss women in the fields of policing and corrections in chapter 19, "Femininities, Masculinities, and Organizational Conflict: Women in Criminal Justice Occupations."

An analysis of the social construction of gender and its impact in various historical periods is necessary to comprehend fully the roles that women have played—historically and in contemporary life—in criminal justice professions. Jurik and Martin show that women have been full-fledged actors in policing and corrections for a very brief period of time. It was not until the 1970s that women were "allowed" to assume the roles of patrol officer in police forces and corrections officer in male institutions. Moreover, these advances were the result of legislative changes achieved through the civil rights and women's movements of the 1960s and 1970s as well as hard-won court battles by dedicated women who challenged the status quo. Prior to this period, women's involvement in law enforcement and corrections was defined narrowly to fit traditional stereotypes regarding appropriate roles for women. In the nineteenth century, the involvement of women in policing and corrections reflected the interests of upper-middle-class reformers attempting to resocialize "fallen women" and guide and nurture underprivileged children. This "matronizing" approach to women who had violated the law clearly embodied a social work, as opposed to a crime control orientation. During the nineteenth and early twentieth centuries, a small number of women held leadership positions in policing and corrections—some rather prestigious—but always separate and apart from men.

It is one thing to open up the regular ranks of police and correctional organizations to women; it is another for women to be accepted and integrated into those ranks. While court and legislative victories have enabled women to serve alongside males on patrol and in the general population of prisons for men and women, traditional attitudes about the kinds of activities that are appropriate for women—and those that are not—continue to present challenges to women attempting to climb the ladder of success in these male-dominated fields. The chapters by Miller and Jurik and Martin provide analyses of the types of attitudinal, organiza-

tional, and behavioral resistance women face, as well as strategies women use to combat and overcome these sources of resistance.

Women, Crime, and Criminal Justice: An Invitation

It has only been within the past quarter century or so that there have been sufficient knowledge and interest in the field of women and crime to support the publication of textbooks expressly devoted to these topics. In this period, the volume and quality of scholarly work on gender, crime, and criminal justice have increased dramatically. Readers of *Women, Crime, and Criminal Justice* are the beneficiaries of this cutting-edge scholarship.

This volume provides an alternative to much of the content of traditional texts in criminology and criminal justice that focus primarily, and sometimes exclusively, on men. Hopefully, exposure to the perspectives presented by the authors in this volume will help to sensitize readers to a fuller range of issues that must be considered in formulating a comprehensive understanding of crime and justice. ✦

Part I
Connecting Gender and Crime

It is inaccurate to say, as some observers do today, that historically criminologists failed to recognize a relationship between gender and crime. Criminologists have long acknowledged that crime is gendered—and that the gender of crime is masculine. What they ignored was female offending and offenders and, often, female victimization, laboring under the assumptions that women just do not engage in much criminal activity and women's victimization is more limited than that of men. Like many assumptions, these are not completely false. As we will learn in the following chapters, women's crime rates have been and remain significantly lower than men's crime rates. And women are less likely than men to be crime victims, with a few important exceptions. What most criminologists failed to recognize, however, is that when women—and men—commit crimes, their offending is related to their social locations *as women*—and *as men*—in our society. The crimes women typically commit and their motivations for committing these crimes are direct reflections of the gender inequality inherent in our social structure. Gender inequality intersects with other inequalities, including racism and ethnocentrism, social class inequality, ageism, and heterosexism, to increase or decrease women's likelihood not only of offending but also of getting arrested and incarcerated, being victimized, or a combination of these outcomes.

The first eight chapters of this book examine general female crime trends as well as specific types of offenses in which women are involved. A major theme connecting most of the chapters is the interaction between women's victimization and women's offending. Indeed, as the authors point out, women often engage in criminal activity as a survival strategy, in response to physical, psychological, and sexual abuse in their homes and on the streets.

Stanko takes up this theme by focusing on how the concept of *danger* in criminology has not only been associated with women's fear of crime and victimization, but also with women's offending. Chesney-Lind discusses how young women who run away from home and ultimately find themselves in the hands of the juvenile justice system are frequently running away from abusive parents, stepparents, or other intimates. Ironically, the juvenile justice system criminalizes their survival strategies and, invoking the girls' "best interests," sends them back to their abusers.

Brunson and Miller, as well as Sanchez, point out that girls and women may "choose" illegal pursuits (gang activity, prostitution, and sex work) as a way to escape family violence, as a means of social and economic survival, and as a means to develop a supportive network of friends. However, given that the environments in which these girls and women typically live are impoverished, chaotic, violent, and marginalized, one cannot fairly call their offending a "choice" or an "option." Moreover, their involvement in gangs and sex work may put them at further risk of victimization—by male gang members and members of rival gangs, by "johns" and pimps, and by the criminal justice system.

Kruttschnitt focuses specifically on violent crime. She discusses women's lower rates of offending but, at the same time, emphasizes that women's violence is tied to the gender-based social and economic inequality they experience as well as the types of victimization—especially victimization at the hands of intimate partners—they usually encounter.

Kruttschnitt also raises the connection between gender, crime, and substance abuse, but this problem is taken up in greater detail by Mancuso and Miller. Mancuso and Miller point out that women who use alcohol and other drugs (AOD) and who engage in crime are regarded by most people as multiply deviant. Their problems are considered their own "fault," and they are ostracized even within the criminal justice system, making it difficult if not impossible for them to break out of the AOD and crime lifestyle. As Mancuso and Miller show, social rejection, economic isolation, and violent victimization contribute to women's use of AOD as well as their involvement in crime.

Finally, Steffensmeier and Broidy explore a variety of theories that have been proposed to explain female crime, including biological and psychological explanations. In examining these theories in light of available empirical data, Steffensmeier and Broidy make a clear connection to gender inequality in its many manifestations and female offending. In addition to violent victimization by intimates, Steffensmeier and Broidy pay particular attention to how gender-based economic inequality propels many women into criminal activity. They are also quick to point out, however, that women's crime is consistent with gender norms and gendered opportunities.

The authors of these chapters compare women's offending with men's offending to show the gendered nature of crime. Their work makes clear that when women engage in crime, they are not acting like men; they are behaving as women responding to the structural constraints imposed on them by society's hierarchical valuing of their gender, race or ethnicity, social class, age, and sexual orientation. Criminologists must incorporate these intersecting inequalities into their analyses of crime if we are to get a comprehensive understanding of the connection between gender and crime. The chapters in this section provide us with a solid foundation for undertaking such analyses. ✦

2
Women, Danger, and Criminology

Elizabeth A. Stanko

This chapter argues that the elusive concept of danger drives conceptualization in criminology. Through an analysis of the way danger is associated with and through women's criminality, women's victimization, and women's fear of crime, the chapter illustrates how the emotionality of danger serves as the foundation to separate thinking about crime from thinking about women's place in society. This chapter places the concept of danger squarely at the heart of criminology.

Danger is a recurring theme in criminology. Throughout the history of the discipline, criminologists have theorized about the damage to society caused by uncontrollable villains, wreaking havoc among law-abiding citizens. These theorists, alongside policy makers and politicians, have tried desperately to devise the right program or punishment to convince those who cause such unhappiness and insecurity that they have done wrong. The implication is if not for the unwanted intrusion of these dangerous criminals law-abiding folk would live in an idyllic world.

This chapter treats danger—and its relationship to criminology—as a crucial concept through which thinking about women, crime, and justice can be framed. Without such a critical analysis of danger's ubiquitous place in criminology, we would not be able to understand the significance of feminists' challenges to the discipline over the past 25 years. These challenges range from queries about the way women are treated by police or the courts, for instance, to queries

about why assault against women in the home is not treated by criminal justice officials in the same way as assault against women in public.

I shall begin with a process of making visible the tensions in criminology's thinking about women, using the discussions about criminality, victimization, and fear of crime as guideposts. Later, I propose the elevation of danger to a theoretical concept, one that assists us in using contemporary criminology more creatively to highlight women's relationship to crime and justice.

Defining Danger

Danger, strictly defined, means peril and uncertainty. It is linked to risk and being under threat. Its menace lurks throughout the study of criminology. Crime represents a hazard to stability, normality, and safety. Interestingly, danger is also defined as a "natural course" event. Crime makes us anxious because its potential in modern life is almost inevitable, or at least it seems that way. Crime prevention advice demonstrates an acceptance of crime's inevitability, encouraging us to devise practical precautions to avoid it (O'Malley 1992). We are expected to take the necessary steps to keep crime at bay. An undercurrent of emotion drives this state of alert. We may experience heightened states of anxiety if, for example, we somehow forget to take care of ourselves or lock up our possessions. Criminologists have attempted to explain this sense of anxiety through analyses of the concept of "fear of crime." Through my later discussion of this concept in this chapter, I show how women's fear of crime is treated as part of the natural malaise of modern life and is welded to women's place in a society that takes many dangers to women for granted. Indeed, as I show throughout, these notions—peril, unsafety, risk, natural disaster—have become a routine part of the way we think about crime itself (Garland 1996).

So when we think of crime as a routine nuisance—albeit one that also frightens many—we think about ways that we can avoid it without major disruptions to our lives. Treating crime as a routine part of our lives, though, merges our common sense with calculations about risk. We are accustomed to taking avoidance actions daily in order to avert the possible disaster of crime: We lock our houses and cars, carry alarm devices, plan journeys, change the way we dress, and so forth (Stanko 1990). It is this combination of danger and risk that has particular conceptual strength in criminology. It is hard to imagine any debate or discussion about crime without these concepts being part of the backdrop of debates and policy about crime. We wonder, for instance, whether we can predict the dangerousness of individual offenders, when, for example, a parole board considers the release of a prisoner or whether, in the course of our routines, we can eliminate the risk of being a victim of crime.

We also link the competence of criminal justice professionals and our own common sense to the way we make judgments about danger and risk. Our own assessments, as well as those within this so-called scientific discipline of criminology, will be analyzed in relation to thinking about these twin concepts of danger and risk. Using the example of the parole board again, will the board members be considered responsible if they misjudge the dangerousness of a particular offender? And how do our own deliberations about walking down a street rest on notions about how safe we (or others) think the street is? Any assessment about the danger of any particular offender or the safety of any particular street is highly fluid. We may decide, for example, that walking down a particular street is safe during the day but not at night or during certain hours. If we decide to walk the street during the period of time we think it is risky to do so, we may feel more anxious or at the last minute decide to take another route. Will our common sense be questioned if we decide to walk down a particular street at one time of day rather than another?

Just as danger and risk are part of the scientific discipline of criminology, as well as our own lives, so too is the notion of blame, if we, or those criminal justice professionals, somehow get it wrong. An anthropologist, Mary Douglas (1992), speaks about how the nature of risk, danger, and blame is a process informed and framed by our social and world views. If we are found to be acting in a risky manner, for instance, we (and others) may decide that whatever might happen to us is our fault, as we didn't take all necessary safeguards to ward off danger. We might also blame the parole board for releasing an offender who, in committing another crime, shows that the risk of reoffending was not properly assessed. And others do make assessments about whether our judgments are well founded or whether the actions of individual criminals or the decisions of courts or parole boards are to be blamed for disrupting people's lives.

Ted Sasson's (1995) study of the way Bostonians make sense of crime is a good illustration of how ordinary citizens easily speak about the danger of crime, and often attribute blame to individual criminals for endangering their presumed stable and prosperous lives. Of course, not all the public thinks alike. Some people also recognize other contributors to public unsafety that have their foundation in the way society is organized; racism or structural unemployment, some believe, encourage crime. But regardless of who or what people blame for crime, the acceptance of crime as danger to normality has become a barometer for the health of democratic life.

This theoretical coupling in criminology, linking the language of danger with that of risk, has the effect of pushing worry about safety onto the shoulders of individuals or into the arms of criminal justice professionals, yet hiding the way we will quickly blame a calculation that goes wrong. Both categories of people are expected to act as if they can control the danger of criminals and minimize the risk of crime. Given its central importance, danger—as a concept in debates in criminology—needs to be considered more carefully. It is also useful to explore how our thinking about danger illuminates our thinking about gender and justice. I shall argue that this exploration is key to any critical awareness of justice issues. I begin by examining our conceptualization of criminal women.

Criminal Danger of Women: A Modernist Scourge

Danger posed by criminality has been defined through prohibitions found in criminal statute. Real danger, we often still believe, comes from criminals, and those criminals and criminality can be determined through the legal process. Much traditional criminological theorizing about criminality and those who commit it was woven through the belief that containment and eradication of crime are possible and that the science of criminology can aid in the control of crime. Failing to stem the tide of criminality, we are led to believe, endangers the very progress of civilization itself.

There is, of course, active debate about the consequences of thinking of all criminals as dangerous. Throughout the history of criminology, women's law-breaking was portrayed as out of character for normal women (see Klein 1973, for a critique). Women were, according to traditional thinking, passive by nature. With few exceptions even today, criminology textbooks address explanations of women's criminality as being out of character for normal women. Any use of violence by women must be explained by characterizing such women as being more like men. Be they born or environmentally fostered, women criminals are portrayed as the *others* to be feared.

Theoretical explanations of women's crime and criminal indiscretions embrace the difference between law-abiding women and criminal women. Historically (and in some contemporary versions), this difference had its origins in biology (Heidensohn 1985; Klein 1973; Morris 1987). Criminal women, for example, were "hairier" (more masculine) than their law-abiding sisters, and some were seen as driven by their female (or even their male) hormones. Although some of this early work may bring a smile to the reader, highlighting physical—often cast as man-like—anomalies of criminal women assisted criminologists in demonstrating why these women behaved in a criminal manner. Such imagery was (and sometimes still is) considered evidence in explaining why criminal women were heartless, helpless, hopeless, and in need of protection or isolation by the father-state. These women were not *real* women. Their criminal actions endangered the very assumptions that women were by nature compliant and orderly.

Criminal men, too, were characterized as driven by biology or environment. However, men's criminal indiscretions were somehow more understandable. Men who commit crime are not typically portrayed as unnatural. At the same time, men's role as protector of women is a persistent image. Whether men are portrayed as altruistic protectors or savage violators, both categories have been treated by society as real men. Female criminals, on the other hand, have been seen as inherently evil human beings, fallen angels, or masculine women. These women are dangerous *because* the crime they commit is proof of their ability to step beyond what is considered to be the ordinary range of behavior of "real" women.

But why has it been so important to place women's law-breaking outside the boundaries of real womanhood? The danger that criminal women pose is to wider beliefs about women's appropriate place in society. Thinking about women's criminality should lead us to question what promotes women's law-abiding behavior. In general, though, criminal women are not a noteworthy problem for policymakers and for criminologists, because their participation in crime, and especially in violent crime, is less feared than men's. But this does not mean that women who commit crimes do not feel the full wrath of condemnation for stepping outside the boundaries of real womanhood. What I am suggesting, though, is that female criminals are treated as dangerous because they endanger thinking about women's passivity. Confidence in women's law-abidingness is confirmed through people's lack of fear of the clicking of high heels behind them on a darkened street. What would happen if we could no longer *depend* on women's more limited participation in the crime business as part of our strategic planning to reduce crime among such large populations of people? Would this shift force us to think differently about women who do commit crime?

Feminist debates in the 1970s and 1980s about women's criminality placed critiques of traditional assumptions about the so-called character of women center stage. We asked: Why don't women commit crime in the same proportions as men? Is it because women are already obligated to other people through social responsibilities, stemming from, but not limited to, childbearing and child rearing, often shored up by the denial of work and other kinds of opportunities given to men? The contribution of thought about women's—and particularly criminal women's—place in society was also well recognized by many feminist criminologists. Women's civil rights were often secondary to men's. As the second wave of the feminist movement in the 1970s documented women's second-class citizenship, feminist criminologists pointed out how women were expected to behave harmlessly. The danger of female criminals is their ability to threaten ideas about traditional womanhood as well as conventional law-breaking. In the study of female criminality, not surprisingly, feminist research revealed the usefulness of explaining women's crimes through an analysis of

how women were especially bonded to their relationships with men. But this approach did not explain all women's law-breaking, nor did it break the link between thinking about women's criminality and thinking about appropriate womanhood. So when women have committed crimes, they have been cast as potentially dangerous, even more *dangerous* than male lawbreakers.

Today, periodic analyses of the law-breaking by women as indicative of their supposed liberation demonstrates that such thinking is alive and well. We are told that women are becoming drug dealers, fraudsters, and serial or even contract killers, as if doing so says something about women's position in society. The many variations of this kind of thinking link women's law-breaking with the breakdown of conventional controls over all women. But such analyses of female crime, and especially female violence, should be questioned through the evidence we have about women lawbreakers. First, women's crimes are still predominantly those involving petty theft, low-level drug use and sales, minor fraud, and prostitution. There is no equality of opportunity with the men who dominate the crime business. (Of course, some women reach relative positions of power in the illegal markets, as do some women in legal employment markets.) Second, disproportionate numbers of nonwhite women imprisoned for law-breaking show the persistence of how other forms of disadvantage—racism and poverty, in particular—help create conditions in which some forms of criminal behavior are forms of survival. These forms of disadvantage, though, disappear and are subsumed within definitions of who is dangerous. Third, although the majority of women appear to be law-abiding, these women who become caught up in the criminal justice system are much more likely to be institutionalized by medical, psychiatric, or welfare systems than men (Carlen 1992; Daly 1995; Eaton 1986; Worrall 1990). Convicted women, moreover, are ultimately punished with an eye to their role in the family (Eaton 1986; Daly 1995). Women, it seems, are still better controlled here.

Since the intricacies in the way we think about women are invariably woven into the way we look at women's crime, there are many tensions in trying to rethink a way forward, for women do commit crime and stand before the criminal justice system every day. Although we are continually reminded that women do not take an equal part in law-breaking, what do we do about the women who *do* commit crime? To be less dangerous, do criminal women need to be reminded of their duty to *real womanhood*? While this is a crucial question, I fear that we are no longer in a position to debate its implications. Over the past 20 years, the landscape of criminal justice has changed dramatically (Feeley and Simon 1994; Garland 1996). To some extent, social events have overtaken us and have muted the ability of lawmakers to hear, much less understand, feminists' critiques of criminal justice practice and policy. Rather than convince policymakers that women lawbreakers pose a less serious threat to society, leading to a reduction of imprisonment for women, these days there is an explosion of convicted women being sentenced to prison (Chesney-Lind 1997). What is different now is that governments, particularly Western governments, are no longer interested in why people commit crime, nor are they especially willing to intervene in individuals' lives to minimize the potential for law-breaking (Feeley and Simon 1994). What is now important is that as part of a general category—convicted criminals—women belong to a dangerous group that needs *to be managed*. Any differentiation between women's and men's participation in crime becomes irrelevant to wider issues of managing the overall intrusion of criminality in society. Whereas feminist criminologists' work shows that women's crimes and their contribution to danger are different and lesser than men's, the fact that women are criminals places them in the category of the dangerous. This category is meant to be managed by new penal measures: life sentences, mandatory sentences, and punishment formulas that treat all criminals alike.

Any and all criminals are the danger: They threaten our safety, our livelihoods, our freedom of movement. Managing women criminals merely becomes part of the wider apparatus of regulation that administers justice. Nevertheless, we know that in any careful analysis of criminality, gender matters. If it did not, women would break the law in the same proportions as men. But when women become caught up in the criminal justice system, it is increasingly difficult to point out that they pose differential danger to society. Without theorizing about criminal *women*, and dangerous criminal women specifically, women's contribution to law-breaking becomes subsumed within the debates about the scourge of all crime to civilized society. In this way, we have once again sidelined thinking about women's criminality when thinking about crime. Ways to manage prison populations have taken center stage in the debate about crime.

The way women have become marginal to the critiques of social policy concerning criminality and the rise in the prison population is shown in the way in which feminist criminology is ignored for its critique of criminology in general. But more crucially, ignoring women has an untold impact on the treatment of women who find themselves before the eyes of the law. Yet, excluding the impact of social policy on women from public debate (consider the public debate about the dangerous criminal) is part of a larger process that puts what happens to men above what happens to women (Connell 1987, 1995). The celebration or condemnation of bad boys, often to the exclusion of women or bad girls, is underpinned by the assumption that male lawbreakers or deviants are only acting like real men. As a consequence, the three common features of women's crimes noted earlier remain largely invisible in the public debate about crime. When women do appear in the media spotlight as criminals, the double abhorrence of their deeds—and the assumed greater danger to society—is often unquestioned. They are still treated as unnatural women. In many ways it is not surprising that the move to lock up criminals and throw away the key resulted in so many women being behind bars. But this thinking about the danger of crime has also affected our thinking about the so-called normal men who pose the greatest danger to women.

Criminal Danger to Women: Another Modernist Scourge

Addressing women's experiences of psychological, physical, and sexual harm also poses problems to traditional criminology. As historians have shown, women's experiences of violence have always been much more prevalent than official records recognize (see, for instance, Allen 1988; Clark 1988; Gordon 1988). Moreover, men known to women, not the vilified strangers of criminological theorizing, are the greatest threat to women's safety. Yet women report greater fear of the danger of public space than private.

Both officially recorded crime and the vast hidden extent of violence against women suggest that women's assailants are most likely to be known to them. As part of the feminist strategy of naming sexual violence as a form of oppression, feminist researchers set out to document women's experiences of sexual and physical violence. During the late 1960s and early 1970s, the collective voices of women began to tell story after story about men's abuses. There was a keen sense that the traditional ways of asking women about violence had masked much of what happened to them. So feminist researchers began to devise their own questions about violence to better capture what it is like to be female in society. The crime survey, adapted by feminists, served as an important mechanism to expose the high levels of violence in women's lives. Adapted surveys included many questions about women's experiences of men's violence that were rarely classified as criminal offenses, such as receiving obscene phone calls, being followed on the street, or being touched by men while riding on public transport.

The often-cited pioneering research of Diana Russell (1982, 1984), which found that one in two women would confront a rape or attempted rape in her lifetime, with the majority of such sexual attacks being perpetrated by men known to the women, served as a catalyst to expose widespread, yet hidden (to official monitoring) violence against women. Mary Koss and Mary Harvey (1992) later concluded that the cumulative findings of the rape prevalence studies "suggest that 1 in 5 [U.S.] adult women has experienced a completed rape" in her lifetime (p. 29).

The best example of a large-scale survey that focuses exclusively on violence against women is that conducted by the Canadian government. In this extensive nationwide survey, researchers interviewed 12,000 women by telephone, asking them about past experiences of various forms of threat and violence. It found that 39 percent of the women had experienced sexual assault, and one-third had experienced physical threat or assault at the hands of men (Johnson and Sacco 1995).

No doubt, surveys that explore the extent of violence against women in the general population are important in that they consistently demonstrate how widespread it is. However, raising the *potential* of victimization because one is a woman, it seems, may also raise another form of dubious biological determinism. Women, accordingly, are naturally victims. Reconceptualizing danger in situations that jeopardize women's and children's lives, however, demands that we reexamine what constitutes *real crime* to most female victims of violence. The greatest threat to women is within intimate relationships. Feminist research has emphasized the instrumental impact of serial, intentional, and directed violence by men on women in intimate settings (Dobash and Dobash 1979; Hoff 1990). Women are most likely to be injured, to be raped, and to receive medical attention in assaults from known assailants (Mirrlees-Black, Mayhew, and Percy 1996).

Further evidence shows that men do not sustain the same level of serious injuries at the hands of intimates (unless they are killed, often in self-defense, by women they batter). Women (or those acting on behalf of women) ask police for help in 90–95 percent of requests for assistance in domestic violence incidents.

Studies of violence between intimates (or former intimates) argue that it is men's sense of entitlement to women's services that feeds sources of conflict leading to violent events. Rebecca Dobash and Russell Dobash (1992) propose that the nature of relations between men and women, men's consequent demands and expectations of wives, support for the prerogatives and power of husbands, and cultural beliefs that sustain individuals' attitudes of marital inequality combine to such an extent that collectively women are more at risk of violence in intimate relations than in public spaces. Men use violence against women in domestic situations, as most notably the Dobashs (1992) and Martin Daly and Margo Wilson (1988) observe, as (1) a result of men's possessiveness and jealousy; (2) an expectation concerning women's domestic work; (3) a punishment for perceived wrongdoing; and (4) a prop to men's authority.

Yet it is difficult to question such a natural state—heterosexual union—and label it as dangerous. But with woeful regularity in the media and elsewhere, women's experiences of violence are reduced to simple accounts of just being a woman. The heterosexual union—and, in particular, the often unequal power men have over women in many such couples—seldom comes under scrutiny. That women are most likely to be assaulted or killed by known men is still explained as a natural-course event of some intimate relationships. What is not part of the explanation are the findings of many of the feminist-inspired studies: Men's control, not natural conflict, looms large in women's experiences of physical and sexual violence.

Ironically, however, crime prevention advice targets women's use of public space. Despite over 20 years of sustained campaigning, feminist work has not shifted attention in criminology away from thinking about the danger of strangers. We are still being told to be careful when walking on the streets at night. Even highly publicized cases of random murder against women have given rise to media commentary that "no woman alone is safe in public." Observations from feminist commentators, such as Caputi (1987) and Cameron and Frazer (1987), who argue that sexual murder is not just an unfortunate event but part of systematic violence against women, are not to be found in these public comments. The evidence about women, violence, and victimization is overwhelming; its implications about danger are denied. The commonly held belief is that only beasts hurt women; the reality is that most violence against women is perpetrated by "nice guys," not beasts. As the evidence mounts that women lead more restricted lives and use greater caution when out in public, the impact of violence against women must be acknowledged as *a collective harm against all women*.

As we learn more about the danger of known men, feminist criminologists document the hypocrisy of the criminal justice system, accusing it of failing to protect women from men's widespread abuses. Law reforms, it seems, barely touch the conditions that support, maintain, and reproduce gender inequality. Battered women and their advocates angrily and regularly demand better treatment by the police, the courts, and social services. Raped and sexually abused women typically meet the contempt of a legal process that can find no way of proving rape and sexual abuse without routinely humiliating the complainant. While much of this humiliation is now a recognized and largely uncontested part of the criminal justice process, it is extremely difficult to eliminate it from the way criminal justice officials establish the facts of crime during investigations and trials (Roberts and Mohr 1994). Many women who have brought abuse to the attention of the criminal justice system say that the system is as bad as (or sometimes worse) than the abuse itself.

Yet, all the criminological evidence underscores the predominance of women's victimization at the hands of known men. Shifting our understanding of the danger of heterosexual intimacies is still far from social policy on crime: In criminological debates we continue to separate the danger of known men from that of the so-called dangerous stranger. This separation, I believe, is in part supported by the documentation of women's greater worry about safety in public places found so consistently in studies about fear of crime.

Fearing the Danger of Men (Crime)

Although there is no consensus among researchers about a definition of fear of crime, there are basic components upon which many researchers would agree. Generally, fear of crime is taken to represent individuals' diffuse sense of danger about being physically harmed by criminal violence. It is associated with concern about being *outside* the home, probably in an urban area, alone and potentially vulnerable to personal harm.

Typically, the classic fear-of-crime question focuses on danger outside the home. The most popular question on victimization surveys is: How safe do you feel walking alone in your neighborhood [in this area] after dark [or at night]? This is the question used in most large-scale victimization surveys. Individuals may be asked to assess their probability of encountering, say, a burglary, robbery, or rape within the next 12 months. It is from this perspective that an analysis is made of respondents' evaluations of their risk of being a crime victim. Finally, information is collected about actual (that is, reported to the researchers) victimization.

While there have been a number of criticisms about how the concept of fear of crime is constructed, the concept itself and what it is presumed to represent—citizen anxiety about crime and disorder—are now treated as social problems in their own right. Beyond any doubt, the gender differential is the most consistent finding in the literature on fear of crime. Women report fear at levels three times that of men, yet their recorded risk of personal violence, especially assault, is, by all official sources, lower than men's. Indeed, there is a mismatch between women's and men's *reported* risk of violent criminal victimization and their fear of falling victim to such violence. Those who admit feeling safest—young men—reveal the greatest proportion of personally violent victimizations.

Why do women admit more to fearing the potential danger of encountering assailants in public? There have been some attempts to explain why women might harbor such anxiety about their personal safety. Wesley Skogan and Michael Maxfield (1981) suggest that women's fear of crime is fostered by greater physical and social vulnerability. Maxfield (1984), analyzing the 1982 British Crime Survey, found some evidence to suggest it is women's fear of sexual assault that "reduces feelings of safety among young women." Mark Warr (1984) argues that it may well be that for women "fear of crime is fear of rape." Margaret Gordon and Stephanie Riger (1988), extending their earlier work, go further by naming women's fear of rape as "the female fear." Limiting the explanation of women's fear of crime to the fear of rape, as some criminologists have, directs our attention to the worst case scenario of sexual violence, the violent invasion of rape. Categorizing rape as the only understandable, abhorrent sexual intrusion that could reasonably frighten women causes ordinary events, such as receiving sexual comments on the street or from coworkers (which can be experienced as threatening, often private encounters) to be overlooked in most crime surveys, because they are not serious enough (i.e., not crime, or real danger) and, therefore, supposedly do not contribute to women's fear of crime.

If women's fear of crime is related to their fear of rape, how are we to explain such widespread fear in the context of the low number of recorded rapes? What is generally agreed by conventional criminologists is that women feel at greater risk of rape but that this concern is not founded in *actual* experience. Crime against women, however, as most criminologists now agree, is seriously underreported and underrecorded. The oft-cited government-conducted crime surveys have no way of estimating this hidden figure (Stanko 1988). But we cannot fully explain women's fear of crime by examining crime data alone. Taking into account the threats and crime women experience *inside* the home, many feminists have argued over the past 20 years, is important in understanding women's feelings of insecurity.

The study of fear of crime neglects the domestic nature of a vast majority of men's violence to women that may contribute to women's fear and anxiety about their own safety; women are treated as if they fear only the unknown male stranger. As Rachel Pain (1993) found, despite disclosing a variety of domestic and intimate assaults, her interviewees spoke of potential violence as "stranger danger." Such concern about danger begins early in life, suggests Jo Goodey (1994). The schoolchildren she interviewed took safety precautions, especially with strangers; girls took more precautions than boys. My research on safety and violence avoidance strategies of adult women and men illustrates how early lessons in danger become part of a lifetime of negotiating danger, inside and outside the home (Stanko 1990). Yet when women are asked about danger, their fears translate into concerns about the danger lurking in the physical environment. For instance, they typically name parking lots, public stairwells, and public transit as dangerous places in community safety audits collected by campaign groups or local crime prevention initiatives (Lawrence 1991).

What these studies show is that the acknowledgment of the potential of sexual violence—whether from known or unknown men—is a core component of *being female*. The *danger and risk* they manage through a wide range of everyday, mundane tactics, such as walking a particular route, wearing a particular pair of shoes, and so forth, is the potential violation of their sexual integrity. What women define as sexually threatening, moreover, is not confined to what is statutorily defined as rape. Sexual humiliation and degradation are clearly included in women's list of what to avoid. Moreover, women are expected to not only behave as if they are aware of these potential dangers but also to acknowledge the naturalness of these dangers arising from men's behavior and attitudes toward women.

David Garland recently suggested that

> for most people, crime is no longer an aberration or an unexpected, abnormal event. Instead, the threat of crime has become a routine part of modern consciousness, an everyday risk to be assessed and managed in much the same way that we deal with road traffic. (1996, 446)

What does this mean in terms of the way many women understand danger? What is, after all, women's "modern consciousness" about danger? The research on fear of crime strongly suggests that fear of physical harm is wider than actual experiences of such harm. Many women prepare themselves to avoid men's violence as an "impending disaster." Such preparation has become a routine, expected part of being a woman (Stanko 1997; see also Madriz 1997). Such normalization of women's anxiety about crime has evolved in criminology, influenced by the study of fear of crime and the hidden figure of unreported crime (Maguire 1994). This normalization has occurred despite radical feminist challenges; its acceptance is an acceptance of subordination. Second-class citizens should not expect to walk the streets unhindered. When anxiety about crime is treated as a valid concern by researchers, it is explained as the effect of direct or vicarious victimization or of wider sources of uncertainties and disadvantage (see Hale 1996 for a summary of the literature on fear of crime). I choose to treat it as an indicator of women's place in society. Thinking about danger allows us to think about women's place in the wider world.

Many existing meanings are linked to explanations about the nature of crime, fear, danger, blame, or responsible citizenry (Douglas 1992), but these are typically left out of contemporary criminological debates (Sparks 1992; Walklate 1997). Fear of crime—and especially women's fear—has great value in popular cultural portrayals of good and evil (Sparks 1993). So regardless of whether fear stems from *actual* crime or its risk, ignoring whether the danger is real or imagined, as Garland observes above, women are increasingly encouraged by the state to be literate about crime prevention as a way to combat both. To avoid the dangerous, lurking male menace, the other women are advised how to travel locally ("with petrol in our car") and afar, how to dress, how to walk, how to talk to a potential intimidator, how to appear assertive and in control of their lives (Gardner 1988; Stanko 1990). At the same time, women's precautionary strategies for minimizing men's violence are practices that display an awareness of the relationship of women to men—the dangerous "other." But awareness of their relational insecurity is not restricted to crime prevention advice; it is embedded in the routine consciousness about being respectable women in contemporary life. What is *at risk* for women in an encounter with any potentially violent man is a sullied self. And while risk is normalized (Walklate 1997), the dangerous *other*—the criminal—becomes more vilified.

As gender is the most significant predictor of fear of crime, though, and as fear of sexual violence is by far the greatest concern among the most fearful gender, it seems reasonable to state that fear of sexual violence accounts for a sizeable measure of all fear of crime. *Women, though, are not fearing crime; they are noting the potential for danger stemming from the behavior of men.* Gill Valentine (1992) characterizes women's fear as a spatial expression of patriarchy. Rachel Pain (1993) suggests that fear, for women, ought to be taken as more a pervading state of alertness than a momentary terror. As a consequence of this state of alert, women police themselves by restricting public activities; because of the anxiety about potential violence, they use more safety precautions than men do (Gardner 1995; Stanko 1996). The routines of precaution, though, become an invisible, *and* worrying, commentary about the unspeakable: It is largely men—who are supposed to be the protectors, the intimates, the sources of support—who are the source of danger.

Women, Danger, and Criminology

Research on risk and danger suggests that in general women position themselves as fearful and at risk to hazards more than men do (Irwin 1996). Safety, it seems, is an important feature of women's lives. I'm not implying that there is only one way women are fearful, but the strength of the general findings about gender and fear are consistent, regardless of whether women are asked about environmental hazards or crime. In terms of personal violence, women worry about what it means to be at risk to men's violence. Feminist research has explored the impact of men's violence in public space (see Gardner 1995 for the best example), with the descriptions of private violence often focusing on domestic or dating violence, heterosexual harassment in the workplace, or abuse from other known males. This does not dampen the anxiety of being at risk in public. Wider notions of the uncertainty of contemporary life (Beck 1992; Giddens 1990) lurk in the background of the feminist work on violence against women. Many contemporary discussions about risk link it directly with fear and anxiety (cf. Beck 1992; Giddens 1990) and notions of danger and peril (Ewald 1990), as do the feminist expositions on men's violence. "Risk society," suggests Erickson, "cannot escape the problem of insecurity" (1994, 168). Danger in the modern world is inevitable.

But we must link feminist claims about women's fear—that women's anxiety is an insecurity stemming from a fear of men (Stanko 1987; Pain 1993)—with a critique of how criminal women continue to be constructed as other than real women. Danger, for women trying to avoid men's violence, is made invisible by the process of placing women in charge of its avoidance at all times. By extension, we also recast criminal women as posing the same danger as criminal men, by making the criminal the visible agent in the disruption of democracy. The strength of characterizing women who avoid violence or who defend their children against danger—the good parent (who protects her children), the respectable nonprostitute, the defending homeowner, virtuous single woman—informs both the construction of the good victim and the vilification of the bad woman criminal. And what is the outcome in our debates about danger of failing to take on traditional assumptions about what constitutes a good woman? We overlook the usefulness of blame, both from within the individual and from the wider community (Douglas 1992). At present, self-policing acts to keep women in line; their failure often excludes women from the protection of the state. Any woman recognizes that *danger* is more than just about crime; it is linked with a risk of self and self-respect. Feminist research clearly shows that being a woman puts one at risk— whether a woman is in a position to be judged as dangerous by her criminality or to be exposed to danger for just being a woman.

For the past 20 years or so, public policy has attempted to address women's fear of crime, domestic violence, sexual assault, and sexual harassment to enhance women's safety. In many jurisdictions around the world, countless laws and innovative policies have addressed many identified deficiencies in the public provision of protection for women confronting violence in the home

and elsewhere (Dobash and Dobash 1992; Roberts and Mohr 1994). Such observations have specifically named the danger to women as linked to their second-class citizenship. But any changes meant to address danger to women have been connected to a wider "penal-welfare strategy linked into a broader politics of social change" and vision of social justice (Garland 1996, 26; Cohen 1996). What we find, however, is that when women bring the violence of men to the criminal justice system, they often meet insensitive treatment themselves. The resources for such insensitivity are drawn from finding ways to shame or blame victimized women (Lees 1996). In England and Wales, for instance, it was more difficult to convict a rapist in 1996 than it was in 1985 (Harris 1997). What research finds in explorations of sexual assault trials is that the traditional imagery about how proper women should act provides ample ammunition for defense attorneys seeking to acquit their defendants on trial for rape (see Mathoesian 1996 for his analysis of the Kennedy Smith trial). And, whatever we have learned about the criminality of women—that they are largely petty offenders and regularly come to police attention as drug misusers who may sell small quantities of drugs to others—has failed to divert female offenders away from the harshness of the criminal justice system. As noted earlier, convicted women are currently being sentenced to imprisonment in greater numbers than ever before.

Criminologists' fascination with violence continues to embrace an underlying anxiety about public danger (Sparks 1993). This violence of the public, not the private, occupies the forefront of criminological thinking. The claim to stem the tide of violence has been met with widespread imprisonment of women caught in this net of rounding up the *dangerous*. The transformation of official criminological debates about the dangers of crime and criminals sustains a feeling of impending risk. These debates, I believe, have superseded and appropriated the politics of the feminist message of feminist criminologies—commentaries on the need for a *gendered* social justice. In its place is the expectation that all good citizens will avoid crime individually and the belief that the solution to criminality is the confinement of the convicted. As such, women's fear of crime has become just another metaphor for societal decline, a normal response to a normal risk. Women's criminality is roundly condemned and rarely understood as conceptually linked to thinking about the expectations of women in society. Unaided by a lens that demonstrates its gendered viewpoint, criminology's use of the concept of danger overlooks what might promote greater safety for us all: the promotion of equality.

Discussion Questions

1. What is the societal understanding and perception of the real danger posed by women criminals?

2. What are the three characteristics of women's criminal activity?

3. How does ignoring the impact of gender on crime affect the process of law and punishment?

4. What is ironic about women's own perceptions of danger in private and public situations? What about crime and prevention strategies for these two situations?

References

Allen, J. 1988. *Sex and Secrets*. Sydney: Allen and Unwin.

Beck, U. 1992. *The Risk Society*. London: Sage.

Cameron, D. and Frazer, E. 1987. *The Lust to Kill: A Feminist Investigation of Sexual Murder*. New York: New York University Press.

Caputi, J. 1987. *The Age of Sex Crime*. Bowling Green, OH: Bowling Green State University Press.

Carlen, P. 1992. "Criminal Women and Criminal Justice: The Limits to, and Potential of, Feminist and Left Realist Perspectives." In R. Matthews and J. Young, eds., *Issues in Realist Criminology*, London: Sage.

Chesney-Lind, M. 1997. *The Female Offender: Girls, Women, and Crime*. Thousand Oaks, CA: Sage.

Clark, A. 1988. *Criminal Violence, Criminal Silence*. London: Pandora.

Cohen, S. 1996. "Crime and Politics: Spot the Difference." *British Journal of Sociology* 47:1–21.

Connell, R. 1987. *Gender and Power*. Stanford: Stanford University Press.

———. 1995. *Masculinities*. Cambridge: Polity.

Daly, K. 1995. *Gender, Crime and Punishment*. New Haven: Yale University Press.

Daly, M. and Wilson, M. 1988. *Homicide*. New York: Aldine du Gryuter.

Dobash, R. E. and Dobash, R. P. 1979. *Violence Against Wives*. New York: Free Press.

———. 1992. *Women, Violence and Social Change*. London: Routledge.

Douglas, M. 1992. *Risk and Blame*. London: Routledge.

Eaton, M. 1986. *Justice for Women*. Milton Keynes: Open University Press.

Erickson, R. 1994. "The Division of Expert Knowledge in Policing and Security" *British Journal of Sociology* 45:149–75.

Ewald, F. 1990. "Insurance and Risk." In G. Burchell, C. Gordon, and P. Miller, eds., *The Foucault Effect*. London: Harvester Wheatsheaf.

Feeley, M. and Simon, J. 1994. "Actuarial Justice: The Emerging New Criminal Law." In David Nelken, ed., *The Futures of Criminology*. London: Sage.

Gardner, C. B. 1988. "Access Information." *Social Problems* 35 (3):384–97.

———. 1995. *Passing By: Gender and Public Harassment*. Berkeley: University of California Press.

Garland, D. 1996. "The Limits of the Sovereign State: Strategies of Crime Control in Contemporary Society." *British Journal of Criminology* 36(4):445–71.

Giddens, A. 1990. *The Consequences of Modernity*. Cambridge: Polity.

Goodey, J. 1994. "Fear of Crime: What Can Children Tell Us?" *International Review of Victimology* 3:195–210.

Gordon, L. 1988. *Heroes of Their Own Lives*. London: Virago.

Gordon, M. and Riger, S. 1988. *The Female Fear*. New York: Free Press.

Hale, C. 1996. "Fear of Crime: A Review of the Literature." *International Review of Victimology* 4: 79–150.

Harris, J. 1997. *The Processing of Rape Cases by the Criminal Justice System*. Unpublished. London: Home Office.

Heidensohn, F. 1985. *Women and Crime*. London: Macmillan.

Hoff, L. A. 1990. *Battered Women as Survivors*. London: Routledge.

Irwin, A. 1996. "The Fascination of Fear." *The Times Higher Education Supplement* 31 May: I.

Johnson, H. and Sacco, V. 1995. "Researching Violence Against Women: Statistics Canada's National Survey." *Canadian Journal of Criminology* 37:281–304.

Klein, D. 1973. "The Etiology of Female Crime: A Review of the Literature." *Issues in Criminology* 8(3):3–30.

Koss, M. and Harvey, M. 1992. *The Rape Victim*. London: Sage.

Lawrence, M. 1991. "Improving Women's Urban Safety: The Centretown Experience," Ottawa, Canada: Centretown Citizens' Community Association.

Lees, S. 1996. *Carnal Knowledge*. London: Hamish Hamilton.

Madriz, E. 1997. *Nothing Bad Happens to Good Girls*. Berkeley: University of California Press.

Maguire, M. 1994. "Crime Statistics, Patterns And Trends." In M. Maguire, R. Morgan, and R. Reiner, eds., *The Oxford Handbook of Criminology*. Oxford: Oxford University Press.

Mathoesian, G. 1996. "Language, Law and Society: Policy Implications of the Kennedy Smith Rape Trial." *Law and Society Review* 29(4): 669–701.

Maxfield, M. 1984. *Fear of Crime in England and Wales*. London: Her Majesty's Stationery Office.

Mirrlees-Black, C., Mayhew, P., and Percy, A. 1996. *The 1996 British Crime Survey*. London: Her Majesty's Stationery Office.

Morris, A. 1987. *Women, Crime and Criminal Justice*. Oxford: Blackwell.

Newburn, T. and Stanko, E. (eds.) 1994. *Just Boys Doing Business: Men, Masculinity and Crime*. London: Routledge.

O'Malley, P. 1992. "Risk, Power and Crime Prevention." *Economy and Society* 21:252–75.

Pain, R. 1993. "Crime, Social Control and Spatial Constraint." Unpublished Ph.D. dissertation: University of Edinburgh.

Roberts, J. and Mohr, R. 1994. *Confronting Sexual Assault*. Toronto: University of Toronto Press.

Russell, D. 1982. *Rape in Marriage*. New York: Free Press.

——. 1984. *Sexual Exploitation*. Beverly Hills, CA: Sage.

Sasson, T. 1995. *Crime Talk*. New York: Aldine du Gryuter.

Skogan, W. and Maxfield, M. 1981. *Coping with Crime*. Beverly Hills, CA: Sage.

Sparks, R. 1992. "Reason and Unreason in Left Realism: Some Problems in the Constitution of the Fear of Crime." In R. Matthews and J. Young, eds., *Issues in Realist Criminology*. London: Sage.

——. 1993. *Television and the Drama of Crime*. Milton Keynes: Open University Press.

Stanko, E. A. 1987. "Typical Violence, Normal Precaution: Men, Women and Interpersonal Violence in England, Wales, Scotland and the USA." In J. Hanmer and M. Maynard, eds., *Women, Violence and Social Control*. London: Macmillan.

——. 1988. "Hidden Violence Against Women." In M. Maguire and J. Pointing, eds., *Victims: A New Deal?* Milton Keynes: Open University Press.

——. 1990. *Everyday Violence*. London: Pandora Press.

——. 1996. "Warnings to Women: Police Advice and Women's Safety in Britain." *Violence Against Women* 2:5–24.

——. 1997. "Safety Talk: Conceptualizing Women's Risk Assessment as a 'Technology of the Soul'." *Theoretical Criminology* 1(4):479–99.

Valentine, G. 1992. "Images of Danger: Women's Sources of Information About the Spatial Distribution of Male Violence." *Area* 24(1):22–9.

Walklate, S. 1997. "Risk and Criminal Victimization: A Modernist Dilemma?" *British Journal of Criminology* 37(1):35–46.

Warr, M. 1984. "Fear of Victimization: Why Are Women and the Elderly More Afraid?" *Social Science Quarterly* 65:681–702.

Worrall, A. 1990. *Offending Women*. London: Routledge. ✦

3
'Out of Sight, Out of Mind':[1] Girls in the Juvenile Justice System

Meda Chesney-Lind

Even though girls make up a quarter of the youth arrested in the United States, the popular conception of "delinquency" is so tied up in boys' delinquency that girl delinquents are virtually invisible. The silence about girls in trouble has meant that the serious problems bringing them into the system (including physical and sexual abuse) have also been ignored or trivialized. Also overlooked has been the longstanding sex bias that has haunted the juvenile justice system—a system that blames girls for their own problems and criminalizes their attempts to escape abusive homes. Current congressional moves to loosen restrictions on the jailing of runaways make it essential that we end the silence about girls in trouble.

Every year, girls account for one out of four arrests of young people in America (Federal Bureau of Investigation 1996). Despite this fact, the young women who find themselves in the juvenile justice system, either by formal arrest or referral,[2] are almost completely invisible. Our stereotype of the juvenile delinquent is so indisputably male that the general public, experts whose careers in criminology have been built studying "delinquency," practitioners working with delinquent youth, and policymakers who respond to public concerns about youth crime rarely consider girls and their problems. But girls do have problems, and, as this chapter will show, they enter a system that is,

at best, ill-equipped to handle them, and, at worst, ready to blame them for their own difficulty.

Girls' Trouble and 'Female Delinquency'

Although many people may not realize it, young people can be taken into custody for both criminal acts and a wide variety of what are often called "status offenses" (noncriminal offenses such as "running away from home," "being a minor in need of supervision," or being "incorrigible," "beyond control," or truant in need of "care and protection"). In fact, these offenses play a major, not minor, role in girls' delinquency.

Examining the types of offenses for which youth are actually arrested, it is clear that most are the less serious criminal acts and status offenses. About one-fifth (19 percent) of youth are arrested for a single offense (larceny theft), much of which, particularly for girls, is shoplifting (Shelden and Horvath 1986).While less serious offenses dominate both male and female delinquency, this is particularly the case with girls' delinquency. In 1995 well over half of girls' arrests were for either status offenses (27.5 percent) or larceny theft (23.8 percent); boys' arrests were far more dispersed (see Table 3.1).

Finally, despite the intention of the Juvenile Justice and Delinquency Prevention Act in 1974, which, among other things, encouraged jurisdictions to divert and deinstitutionalize youth charged with status offenses, arrests for these offenses have been climbing in recent years. Between 1986 and 1995, for example, girls' runaway arrests increased by 40.9 percent, and arrests of girls for curfew violations increased 93.7 percent (Federal Bureau of Investigation 1996).

For many years, statistics showing a large number of girls arrested for status offenses were taken to be representative of the different types of male and female delinquency. However, self-report studies of male and female delinquency (which ask school-age

Table 3.1

**Rank Order of Adolescent Male and Female
Arrests for Specific Offenses, 1985 and 1994**

Male				Female			
1986 Arrests	% of Total	1995 Arrests	% of Total	1986 Arrests	% of Total	1995 Arrests	% of Total
(1) Larceny-Theft	20.2	(1) Larceny-Theft	17.1	(1) Larceny-Theft	25.7	(1) Larceny-Theft	23.8
(2) Other Offenses	16.8	(2) Other Offenses	15.8	(2) Runaway	20.7	(2) Runaway	21.1
(3) Burglary	8.3	(3) Drug Abuse	8.3	(3) Other Offenses	16.1	(3) Other Offenses	13.2
(4) Liquor Laws	6.2	(4) Other Assaults	7.6	(4) Other Assaults	5.0	(4) Other Assaults	8.4
(5) Vandalism	6.1	(5) Vandalism	6.0	(5) Curfew & Loitering	4.6	(5) Curfew & Loitering	6.4
		(5) Burglary	6.0				

	1986	1995			1986	1995
Arrests for Serious Violent Offenses[a]	5.0	6.5		Arrests for Serious Violent Offenses[a]	2.2	3.2
Arrests for All Violent Offenses[b]	9.8	14.1		Arrests for All Violent Offenses[b]	7.1	11.6
Arrests for Status Offenses[c]	8.2	10.5		Arrests for Status Offenses[c]	25.3	27.5

Source: Compiled from Federal Bureau of Investigation (1996). *Crime in the United States–1995.* Washington, D.C.: U.S. Department of Justice, p. 213.

a. Arrests for murder and nonnegligent manslaughter, robbery, forcible rape, and aggravated assault.

b. Also includes arrests for other assaults.

c. Arrests for curfew and loitering law violation and runaway.

youth whether they have committed delinquent acts) do not reflect the dramatic differences in misbehavior found in official statistics. Specifically, it appears that girls charged with these noncriminal status offenses have been, and continue to be, significantly overrepresented in court populations (see Figueira-McDonough and Barton 1985; Teilman and Landry 1981). As an example, in a National Youth Survey, Canter (1982b) found no evidence of greater female involvement, compared to males, in any category of delinquent behavior. Indeed, in this sample, males were significantly more likely than females to report status offenses.

Numbers tell only part of the story. How do we explain these patterns and, in particular, the relative absence of serious property crimes and violent delinquency in girls, as compared to boys? To answer this question, we must turn to the theories that have long speculated on the causes of delinquent behavior in young people.

Even though existing delinquency theories were developed to explain the behavior of boys, some experts contend that these theories can be adapted to explain girls' behavior as well (Baskin and Sommers 1993; Canter 1982a; Figueria-McDonough and Selo 1980; Rowe, Vazsonyi, and Flannery 1995; Smith and Paternoster 1987). This chapter makes the case for a model of female delinquency that accounts for rather than ignores gender. Reviewing the available evidence on girls' lives and the relationships between girls' problems and their official delinquency, the model draws on the best of the insights from traditional delinquency theory while also incorporating contemporary research on gender, adolescence, and social control.

A feminist perspective on delinquency also requires a review of girls' experiences with the juvenile justice system—both past and present. The juvenile justice system, as this chapter will also demonstrate, should be understood as a major force in the social control of women, as it has historically served to reinforce the sexual piety of girls by holding them to a different standard of behavior than boys.

Most of traditional delinquency theory has emphasized the degree to which the delinquent is a young man growing up in economically marginalized communities (see Chesney-Lind and Shelden 1997 for a summary of these perspectives). Such a persistent focus on social class and such an absence of interest in gender in regards to delinquency is ironic. As Hirschi (1969) demonstrated, and as later studies would validate, a clear relationship between social class position and delinquency is problematic, while *it is* clear that gender has a dramatic and consistent effect on delinquency causation (Hagan, Gillis, and Simpson 1985).

Feminist criminologists have faulted all theoretical schools of delinquency for assuming that male delinquency, even in its most violent forms, is somehow a "normal" response to boys' situations. Yet girls who share the same social and cultural milieu as delinquent boys but who are less delinquent (or violent) are somehow abnormal or "over controlled" (Cain 1989). Essentially, law-abiding behavior on the part of at least some boys and men is taken as a sign of character, but women's avoidance of crime and violence is seen as an expression of weakness (Naffine 1987).

Certainly, none of the traditional theories address the life situations of girls on the economic and political margins, as the theorists were not looking at or talking to these girls. So what might be another way to approach the issue of gender and delinquency? First, it is necessary to recognize that girls grow up in a different world than boys (Block 1984; Orenstein 1994). Girls are aware very early in life that, while girls and boys have similar problems, girls "have it heaps worse" (Alder 1986).

Likewise, girls of color grow up in worlds very different from that of their white counterparts. Since racism and poverty are often fellow-travelers, these girls are forced by their color and often by poverty to deal early and often with problems of violence, drugs, and abuse. Their strategies for coping with these problems, often clever, strong, and daring, also tend to place them outside the conventional expectations of white girls (Campbell 1984; Orenstein 1994; Robinson 1990).

Criminalizing Girls' Survival: Abuse, Victimization, and Girls' Official Delinquency

Girls and their problems have long been ignored. When gender was considered in criminological theory, it was often as a "variable" in the testing of theories devised to explain boys' behavior and delinquency. As a result, few theorists have considered the possibility that some, if not many, of the girls arrested and referred to court have unique and different sets of problems when compared with the boys. Hints of these differences, though, abound.

As an example, it has long been understood that a major reason for the presence of many girls in the juvenile justice system was the fact that their parents insisted on their arrest. After all, who else would report a youth as having "run away" from home? In earlier decades, conflicts with parents were by far the most significant referral source; in Honolulu, 44 percent of the girls who appeared in court from 1929 to 1930 were referred by parents (Chesney-Lind 1971).

Recent national data, while slightly less explicit, also show that girls are more likely to be referred to court by sources other than law enforcement agencies. In 1991, only 15 percent of youth referred for delinquency offenses, but 58 percent of youth referred for status offenses, were referred to court by non–law-enforcement sources. The pattern among youth referred for status offenses, for which girls are overrepresented, is also clear: Well over half of the youth referred for running away from home (two-thirds of whom were girls) and 92 percent of the youth charged with ungovernability (over half of whom were girls) were referred by non–law-enforcement sources, compared to only 9 percent of youth charged with liquor offenses (72 percent male) (Butts et al. 1994; see also Pope and Feyerherm 1982).

The fact that parents are often committed to two standards of adolescent behavior is one explanation for such a disparity—and one that should not be discounted as a major source of tension even in modern families. Despite expectations to the contrary, gender-specific socialization patterns have not changed very much, and this is especially true for parents' relationships with their daughters (Ianni 1989; Katz 1979; Orenstein 1994; Thorne 1994). It appears that even parents who oppose sexism in general feel "uncomfortable tampering with existing traditions" and "do not want to risk their children becoming misfits" (Katz 1979, 24).

Thorne, in her ethnography of gender in grade school, found that girls were still using "cosmetics, discussions of boyfriends, dressing sexually, and other forms of exaggerated 'teen' femininity to challenge adult, and class and race-based authority in schools" (p. 156). She also found that "the double standard persists, and girls who are overly sexual run the risk of being labeled sluts" (p. 156).

Contemporary ethnographies of school life echo the validity of these perceptions. Orenstein's (1994) observations also point to the durability of the sexual double standard; at the schools she observed "sex 'ruins' girls; it enhanced boys" (p. 57). Parents, too, according to Thorne, have new reasons to enforce the time-honored sexual double standard. Perhaps correctly concerned about sexual harassment and rape, to say nothing of HIV/AIDS if their daughters are heterosexually active, "parents in gestures that mix protection with punishment, often tighten control of girls when they become adolescents, and sexuality becomes a terrain of struggle between generations" (Thorne 1994, 156). Finally, Thorne notes that as girls use sexuality as a proxy for independence, they sadly and ironically reinforce their status as sexual objects seeking male approval—ultimately ratifying their status as the subordinate sex.

Whatever the reason, parental attempts to adhere to and enforce the sexual double standard will continue to be a source of conflict between them and their daughters. Another important explanation for girls' problems with their parents that has received attention only in more recent years is the problem of physical and sexual abuse. It is increasingly clear that childhood sexual abuse is a particular problem for girls. Girls are much more likely to be the victims of such abuse than boys are. From a review of community studies, Finkelhor estimates that roughly 70 percent of the victims of sexual abuse are female (Finkelhor and Barron 1986). Girls' sexual abuse also tends to start earlier than boys (Finkelhor and Barron 1986), they are more likely than boys to be assaulted by a family member (often a stepfather) (DeJong, Hervada, and Emmett 1983; Russell 1986), and, as a consequence, their abuse tends to last longer than that of boys (DeJong, Hervada, and Emmett 1983). All of these factors are associated with more severe trauma—causing dramatic short- and long-term effects in victims (Adams-Tucker 1982). The effects noted by researchers in this area move from the well-known "fear, anxiety, depression, anger, and hostility, and inappropriate sexual behavior" (Browne and Finkelhor 1986, 69) to behaviors of greater familiarity to criminologists, including running away from home, difficulties in school, truancy, and early marriage (Browne and Finkelhor, 1986).

Recent research on the backgrounds of girls in the juvenile justice system clearly shows the role played by physical and sexual abuse in girls' delinquency. According to a study of girls in the California Youth Authority in 1996 (N = 181), 85 percent had experienced some form of abuse (physical, sexual, or emotional); 69.8 percent had suffered physical abuse, 45.7 percent had experienced sexual abuse, and 34.6 percent had experienced sexual assault (Owen and Bloom 1997, 12). Most of these girls were young women of color (about half were either Hispanic or African American, and another quarter were mixed or other minorities).

Similar findings about abuse histories among incarcerated girls were also found in an earlier national study conducted by the American Correctional Association (1990). It should be no surprise that the ACA study found that the vast majority of its sample had run away from home (80.7 percent), and of those, 39 percent had run ten or more times. Over half (53.8 percent) said they had attempted suicide, and when asked why, they said it was because they "felt no one cared" (American Correctional Association 1990, 55).

Detailed studies of youth entering the juvenile justice system in Florida have compared the "constellations of problems" presented by girls and boys entering detention (Dembo, Williams and Schmeidler 1993; Dembo et al. 1995). These researchers found that female youth were more likely than male youth to have abuse histories and con-

tact with the juvenile justice system for status offenses, while male youth had higher rates of involvement with various delinquent offenses. Further research on a larger cohort of youth (N = 2,104) admitted to an assessment center in Tampa concluded that "girls' home life, whereas boys' law-violating behavior, reflects their involvement in a delinquent lifestyle" (Dembo et al. 1995, 21).

This portrait suggests that many young women are running away from profound sexual victimization at home, and once on the streets they are forced further into crime in order to survive. The backgrounds of adult women in prison underscores the important links between women's childhood victimizations and their later criminal careers (Snell and Morton 1994). The interviews revealed that many of the women in this national sample (43 percent) were the victims of physical and/or sexual abuse.

Given this information, a feminist perspective on the causes of female delinquency seems appropriate. First, like young men, girls are frequently the recipients of violence. But unlike boys, girls' victimization and their response to that victimization is specifically shaped by their female status. Perhaps because of the gender and sexual scripts found in patriarchal families, girls are much more likely than boys to be the victim of family-related sexual abuse. Men, particularly men with traditional attitudes toward women, are likely to define their daughters or stepdaughters as their sexual property (Finkelhor 1982). In a society that idealizes inequality in male/female relationships and venerates youth in women, girls are easily defined as sexually attractive by older men (Bell 1984). In addition, girls' vulnerability to both physical and sexual abuse is heightened by norms that require them to stay at home where their victimizers have access to them.

Moreover, as we shall see later in this chapter, girls' victimizers (usually males) have the ability to invoke official agencies of social control in their efforts to keep young women at home and vulnerable. That is to say, abusers have traditionally been able to utilize the uncritical commitment of the juvenile justice system toward parental authority to force girls to obey them. Girls' complaints about abuse were, until recently, routinely ignored, or worse, they were blamed for their own victimization. For this reason, statutes that were originally placed in law to "protect" young people have, in the case of some girls' delinquency, criminalized their survival strategies. When girls run away from abusive homes, parents have been able to employ agencies to enforce their return. If they persist in their refusal to stay in that home, however intolerable, they are incarcerated.

These many young women are forced, by the very statutes designed to protect them, into the lives of escaped convicts. Unable to enroll in school or take a job to support themselves because they fear detection, young female runaways are forced into the streets, where they engage in panhandling, petty theft, and occasional prostitution in order to survive.

In addition, the fact that young girls (but not necessarily young boys) are defined as sexually desirable—and, in fact, more desirable than their older sisters because of the double standard of aging—means that their lives on the streets (and their survival strategies) take a unique form, once again shaped by patriarchal values. It is no accident that girls on the run from abusive homes, or on the streets because of profound poverty, get involved in criminal activities that exploit their sexual object status. American society has defined as desirable youthful, physically perfect women. This means that girls on the streets, who have little else of value to trade, are encouraged to utilize this "resource" (Campagna and Poffenberger 1988). It also means that the criminal subculture views them from this perspective (Miller 1986).

The model I've just outlined is clearly not the "entire" story on female delinquency, but it is a theory that starts with the assumption that experiences that differentiate male and female youth might illuminate perplexing

but persistent facts, such as the fact that more female than male status offenders find their way into the juvenile justice system. Obviously, theories that are sensitive to shared aspects of girls' and boys' lives should not be entirely neglected in an attempt to understand delinquency (see Chesney-Lind and Shelden 1997 for a discussion of how these theories might shed light on female delinquency). However, these theories were crafted without any thought to the ways in which gender shapes both boys' and girls' realities, and they need to be rethought with gender in mind.

Two additional comments seem important here. First, a recent attempt to salvage the theories crafted to explain boys' behavior argues essentially that the theories are correct; it is true that girls and boys are raised differently, but if girls were raised like boys and found themselves in the same situations as boys, they would be as delinquent as boys (Rowe, Vazsonyi, and Flannery 1995). This seems to be a step backward. Girls and boys inhabit a gendered universe and find themselves in systems (especially families and schools) that regulate their behavior in radically different ways that have significant consequences for their lives. We need to think about these differences and what they mean, not only for crime but, more broadly, in the life chances of girls and boys.

In the main, the socialization experiences of boys, especially of white privileged boys, prepare them for lives of power (Connell 1987). The experiences of girls, particularly during adolescence, are very different. Even for girls of privilege, dramatic and negative changes occur in their self-perception that are, in turn, reflected in lowered achievement (particularly in math and science) (American Association of University Women 1992; Orenstein 1994). Sexual abuse and harassment are just being understood as major, rather than minor, themes in the lives of all girls. The lives of girls of color show the additional burdens that these young women face as they attempt to contend with high levels of sexual and physical victimization in the home, as well as other forms of neighborhood violence and institutional neglect (Joe and Chesney-Lind 1995; Orenstein 1994).

Not surprisingly, work focusing on the lives of girls and women, particularly the data on the extent of girls' and women's victimization, has begun to occasion a "backlash," with some experts suggesting that the numbers are inflated and meaningless (Roiphe 1993; Wolf 1993). Others have argued that images of victimization construct girls and women as without agency (Baskin and Sommers 1993). Both these perspectives (arguably one from the right and another from the left) seek to shift the focus away from the unique experiences of women back to a more familiar and less threatening (intellectually and politically) terrain of the injuries of race and class. They also seek to rob from the starkest victims of the sex-gender system the ability to speak about their pain. To say that individuals have had a set of experiences (even very violent ones) is not to reduce them to being a mindless pawn of that personal history, but rather to fully illuminate the context within which they move and make their "choices."

Girls live, play, and go to school in the same neighborhoods as boys, but their lives are dramatically shaped by gender. A glance at the pattern of girls' arrests produces as many questions as answers for those theorizing about girls' defiance. Why is running away such a major part of girls' delinquency and such a relatively minor part of boys' misbehavior? Also interesting is the relative absence of the mainstays of boys' delinquency (such as burglary) and serious crimes of violence among both self-reported and official female delinquency. Conventional theories of delinquency are likely the best situated to explain the relative absence of girls from traditional boys' delinquency. In the main, these theories talk about how boys learn the skills and attitudes to commit delinquency and how they get the opportunity to engage in these behaviors.

Now that I have noted the major differences between girls' and boys' official delinquency and have offered a gender-based theory to account for these differences, let us turn to the juvenile justice system itself and place it in its social context of patriarchy.

The Family Court and the Female Delinquent: A Legacy of Sexism

Ironically, while the fathers of criminology had little interest in female delinquents during the early part of this century, the same could not be said for the founders of the juvenile justice system. Concerns about girls' immoral conduct were at the center, rather than the periphery, of the movement that established the juvenile court (Kunzel 1993; Odem 1995; Platt 1969). Most recently, juvenile justice reforms in the United States that indirectly benefited girls (particularly the efforts to deinstitutionalize status offenders) have been directly challenged by conservative congressional initiatives. Republican lawmakers in both the House and the Senate introduced bills that, while ostensibly refocusing national attention on youthful violence, also make it far easier to detain and institutionalize girls charged with running away from home while dramatically cutting back on state and federal oversight of juvenile institutionalization and eliminating the small amount of money set aside for girls' programs (Howard 1996; Youth Law Center 1997).

'The Best Place to Conquer Girls'[3]

The movement to establish separate institutions for youthful offenders was part of the larger Progressive movement, which, among other things, was keenly concerned about prostitution and other "social evils" (e.g., white slavery) (McDermott and Blackstone 1994; Platt 1969; Rafter 1990; Schlossman and Wallach 1978). A disturbing part of this history is the role played by upper-middle-class white women in the construction of "female delinquency" as a way to regulate the sexual activity of working-class girls. Just exactly how women, many of them highly educated, became involved in patrolling the boundaries of working-class girls' sexuality is a depressing but important story to tell, particularly since reformers' initial impetus was to regulate male, not female, sexuality by raising the age of consent (Odem 1995).

In the late nineteenth century, a new group of women reformers arose who saw girls and young women as possessing sexual agency that required careful policing, control, and direction. Inextricably linked to this new view of girlhood was the need for a professional state maternalism: "the state as near as possible to a real mother to the girl" (Odem 1995, 109). This governmental maternalism, in turn, created new opportunities for female social workers. In fact, the first woman police officer, Alice Stebbins Wells, was hired in 1910 specifically to do "protective work for women, children and the home" (Odem 1995, 111). It was assumed that women were inherently better suited to deal with women's problems, but ironically, to do "protective" work with "wayward" girls meant that Wells needed the power to arrest them.

Interest in monitoring and containing girls' sexuality extended well past the point of arrest. Odem's work carefully documents the extensive involvement of bright women professionals like Miriam Van Walters in the minute details of working-class girls' sexual experiences. In the process, Odem unmasks some of the mythology that has arisen about these first women social workers. Particularly haunting is Odem's work documenting the detailed, petty, and sometimes prurient questioning of young working-class women about their sexual experiences. Coercive pelvic exams of all girls brought into the system specifically to determine virginity were also routine, and the results of these exams (as well as medical tests for sexually transmitted diseases) were a feature of girls' but not boys' files. Finally, state maternalism resulted in extensive use of institutionalization as a response to girls', but not boys', sexuality.

It is thus no surprise that virtually all the girls who appeared in early family courts were charged with "immorality" or "waywardness" (Chesney-Lind 1971; Odem 1995; Schlossman and Wallach 1978; Shelden 1981). More to the point, the sanctions for such misbehavior were severe. For example, in Chicago (where the first family court was founded), half of the girl delinquents, but only a fifth of the boy delinquents, were sent to reformatories between 1899 and 1909. In Milwaukee, twice as many girls as boys were committed to training schools (Schlossman and Wallach 1978); in Memphis similar statistics were found (Shelden 1981).

The overt sexism of the juvenile justice system shifted during the next few decades (see Chesney-Lind and Shelden 1997), but the vague nature of status offenses meant that de facto bias against girls (and the use of these offenses to control girls' sexuality) continued to haunt the juvenile justice system of the sixties and seventies. Status offense categories, students of the court during this period noted, were essentially "buffer charges" for suspected sexual behavior when applied to girls (Vedder and Sommerville 1970).

Empirical studies of processing of girls' and boys' cases conducted between 1950 and the early 1970s clearly documented the impact of these sorts of judicial attitudes. That is, girls charged with status offenses were often more harshly treated than other juveniles charged with crimes (Chesney-Lind 1973; Cohn 1970; Datesman and Scarpitti 1977; Gibbons and Griswold 1957; Kratcoski 1974; Mann 1979; Pope and Feyerherm 1982; Schlossman and Wallach 1978; Shelden 1981).

Careful studies of the juvenile courts well into the second half of this century suggest that judges and other court workers participated rather directly in the judicial enforcement of the sexual double standard. The baldest evidence is found in the courts' early years, but there is also evidence that this pattern continues in many parts of the country.

Ironically, these abuses continued while the same decades ushered in a series of Supreme Court decisions sharply critical of the courts' handling of youthful offenders. However, the landmark decisions of that era focused on youth charged with crimes, so boys' and not girls' problems were the subject of judicial scrutiny (see Chesney-Lind and Shelden 1997).

The juvenile justice system's abuse of the status offense category was, however, severely tested, and in some locales eroded, during the 1970s when court critics around the world mounted a major push to "deinstitutionalize and divert" status offenders from formal court jurisdiction.

Deinstitutionalization and Judicial Paternalism: Challenges to the Double Standard of Juvenile Justice

Correctional reformers, concerned about abuse of the status offense category by juvenile courts, were instrumental in urging Congress to pass the Juvenile Delinquency and Prevention (JJDP) Act of 1974. This legislation required that states receiving federal delinquency prevention funds begin to divert and deinstitutionalize their status offenders. Despite erratic enforcement of this provision and considerable resistance from juvenile court judges, girls were the clear beneficiaries of the reform. Incarceration of young women in training schools and detention centers across the country has fallen dramatically in the decades since its passage, in distinct contrast to patterns found early in the century.

National statistics on girls' incarceration reflect both the official enthusiasm for the incarceration of girls during the early part of this century and the impact of the JJDP Act of 1974. Girls' share of the population of juvenile correctional facilities increased from 1880 (19 percent) to 1923 (28 percent). By 1950, girls had climbed to 34 percent of the total, and in 1960 they were still 27 percent

of those in correctional facilities. By 1980, this pattern appeared to have reversed, and girls again made up 19 percent of the correctional population (Cahalan 1986). In 1991, girls were 11 percent of juveniles held in public detention centers and training schools (Moone 1993a).

Despite its success in reducing the number of status offenders—and hence girls—in facilities, the reform effort faced broad resistance from the outset. In 1980, the National Council of Juvenile and Family Court Judges was able to narrow the definition of "status offender" in the amended act so that any child who had violated a "valid court order" would no longer be covered under the deinstitutionalization provisions (U.S. Statutes at Large 1981). This change effectively gutted the 1974 JJDP Act by permitting judges to reclassify a status offender who violated a court order as a "delinquent." This meant that a young woman who ran away from a court-ordered placement (a halfway house or foster home) could be relabeled a delinquent and locked up.

Judges have long used tactics like "violation of a valid court order" or contempt citations to "bootstrap" status offenders into categories that permit their detention. They thereby circumvent the deinstitutionalization component of the act (Costello and Worthington 1981).

These judicial maneuvers clearly disadvantage girls. For example, a Florida study (Bishop and Frazier 1992) reviewed 162,012 cases referred to juvenile justice intake units during 1985–1987. They found only a weak pattern of discrimination against female status offenders compared to the treatment of male status offenders. However, when they examined the impact of contempt citations, the patterns changed markedly. They found that female offenders referred for contempt were more likely to be petitioned to court than males referred for contempt. Moreover, the girls were far more likely to be sentenced to detention. Specifically, the typical female offender in their study had a probability of incarceration of 4.3 percent, which increased to 29.9 percent if she was held in contempt. Such a pattern was not observed among the males in the study. The authors conclude that "the traditional double standard is still operative. Clearly neither the cultural changes associated with the feminist movement nor the legal changes illustrated in the JJDP Act's mandate to deinstitutionalize status offenders have brought about equality under the law for young men and women" (Bishop and Frazier 1992, 1186).

During the early part of the 1990s, things seemed to be turning around for girls. Hearings held in 1992, in conjunction with the reauthorization of the Juvenile Justice and Delinquency Prevention Act, addressed for the first time the "provision of services to girls within the juvenile justice system" (U.S. House of Representatives 1992). At this hearing, both the double standard of juvenile justice and the paucity of services for girls were discussed. The chair of the hearing, Rep. Matthew Martinez, noted the high number of girls arrested for status offenses, the high percentage of girls in detention as a result of violation of court orders, and the failure of the system to address girls' needs. He ended with the question, "I wonder why, why are there no other alternatives than youth jail for her?" (U.S. House of Representatives 1992, 2).

As a result of this landmark hearing, the 1992 reauthorization of the act included specific provisions requiring plans from each state receiving federal funds to include "an analysis of gender-specific services for the prevention and treatment of juvenile delinquency, including the types of such services available and the need for such services for females and a plan for providing needed gender-specific services for the prevention and treatment of juvenile delinquency" (Public Law 102–586, November 1992). Additional funds were set aside as part of the JJDP Act's challenge grant program for states wishing to develop policies to prohibit gender bias in placement and treatment and to develop programs that assure girls equal access to services. As a result, 23 states embarked on such programs—by far the most popular of the ten possible challenge grant activity areas (Girls Incorporated 1996). Finally, the legislation moved to make the "bootstrapping" of status offenders more difficult (U.S. House of Representatives 1992).

Sadly, these changes, while extremely hopeful, were short-lived. Currently, Congress is undertaking a major overhaul of the Juvenile Justice and Delinquency Prevention Act, and virtually all of the initiatives being considered are ominous for girls. The bills introduced to date intend to refocus national attention on the "violent and repeat juvenile offender" (read "boys"), while also granting states "flexibility" in implementing the four core mandates of the JD Act. Key among these mandates, of course, is the deinstitutionalization of status offenders, though conservative lawmakers are also taking aim at efforts to separate youth from adults in correctional facilities, efforts to reduce minority overrepresentation in juvenile detention and training schools, and efforts to remove juveniles from adult jails (National Criminal Justice Association 1997).

Most ominous for girls are efforts to loosen restrictions on the detention of status offenders. Take the proposed Senate Bill 10, titled the "Violent and Repeat Juvenile Offender Act of 1997": It allows for the incarceration of runaways if a hearing determines "the behavior of the juvenile constitutes a clear and present danger to the juvenile's physical or emotional well-being" or when "secure detention is necessary for guarding the safety of the juvenile" or finally when "the detention is necessary . . . to obtain a suitable placement." Both House and Senate bills currently under consideration weaken the 1992 initiatives in the area of the detention of youth for violation of a valid court order. Even more worrisome, all the bills make it easier to hold youth in adult jails. This is particularly disturbing, since girls were commonly held in such situations in the past (as de facto detention centers in rural America). Sadly, abuse is not uncommon in such settings. In Ohio, for example, a 15-year-old girl was sexually abused by a deputy jailer after having been placed in an adult jail for a minor infraction (Ziedenberg and Schiraldi 1997). Because of the isolation and abuse in these settings, girls are also at great risk for suicide (see Chesney-Lind 1988).

These initiatives should not surprise any student of the courts' history, since they represent a return to the courts' backstopping the sexual double standard (and parental authority) at the expense of girls' freedom. Indeed, a careful review of the data on incarceration patterns (during deinstitutionalization) shows the resiliance of the courts' bias against girls as well as the special meaning of this situation for girls of color. Specifically, recent research suggests that the impact of deinstitutionalization has produced a racialized, two-track system of juvenile justice—one in which white girls are placed in mental hospitals and private facilities, while girls of color are detained and institutionalized.

Deinstitutionalization Under Siege

While DSO stressed the need to deinstitutionalize status offenders, we have seen the number of girls and boys arrested for these noncriminal offenses continue to increase. What has emerged out of this pressure is a complex and not necessarily equitable system. Notably, the last two decades have seen a distinct rise in the number of youth confined in "private" facilities, and this trend has special significance for girls, since there are many more girls in private facilities than in public facilities. In 1991, girls were 11 percent of those in public institutions but 29 percent of those held in private institutions (Moone 1993a, 1993b). Another way to look at this situation is to note that of girls held in facilities of any sort, over half (62 percent) are held in private facilities. The vast majority of girls (85 percent) held in private facilities are being held for "nondelinquent" offenses, including status offenses, dependency and neglect, and "voluntary" admis-

sions; for boys, only slightly over half (57.5 percent) are held for these reasons, with the rest being held for criminal offenses (Jamieson and Flanagan 1989). Ethnic differences are also apparent in the populations of these institutions; whites constituted about 40 percent of those held in public institutions in 1989, but 60 percent of those held in private facilities (Krisberg et al. 1991).

Finally, the numbers indicate that after a dramatic decline in the early 1970s, the number of girls held in public training schools and detention centers has declined little, while the number of girls in private facilities has soared. As an example, on one day in 1979 there were 6,067 girls in public facilities (mainly detention centers and training schools); in 1991, the figure was 6,328. Meanwhile, the number of girls held in private facilities increased 27 percent—from 8,176 in 1979 to 10,389 in 1991 (Krisberg et al. 1991; Moone 1993a, 1993b).

Some research indicates a reason for this pattern. Deinstitutionalization may have actually signaled the development of a two-track juvenile justice system—one track for girls of color and another for white girls. In a study of investigation reports from one area in Los Angeles, Jody Miller (1994) examined the impact of race and ethnicity on the processing of girls' cases during 1992–1993. She found that Latinas made up the largest proportion of the population (43 percent), followed by white girls (34 percent), and African-American girls (23 percent). Predictably, girls of color were more likely to be from low-income homes, but this was especially the case for African-American girls (53.2 percent were from AFDC families, compared to 23 percent of white girls and 21 percent of Hispanic girls). Most important, Miller found that white girls were significantly more likely to be recommended for a treatment rather than a "detention-oriented" placement than were African-American or Latina girls. In fact, 75 percent of the white girls were recommended for a treatment-oriented facility compared to 34.6 percent of the Latinas and only 20 percent of the African-American girls (Miller 1994).

Examining a portion of the probation officers' reports in detail, Miller found key differences in the ways that girls' behaviors were described, reflecting what she called "racialized gender expectations." In particular, African-American girls' behaviors were often framed as products of "inappropriate 'lifestyle' choices," while white girls' behaviors were described as resulting from low self-esteem, being easily influenced, and "abandonment" (Miller, 1994 p. 20). Latina girls, Miller found, received "dichotomized" treatment, with some receiving the more paternalistic care white girls received, while others received the more punitive treatment (particularly if they committed "masculine" offenses such as car theft).

Robinson (1990), in her in-depth study of girls in the social welfare (CHINS) and juvenile justice system (DYS) in Massachusetts, documents the racialized pattern of juvenile justice quite clearly. Her social welfare sample (N = 15) was 75 percent white/non-Hispanic and her juvenile justice system sample (N = 15) was black or Hispanic. Her interviews document the remarkable similarities of the girls' backgrounds and problems. As an example, 80 percent of the girls committed to DYS reported being sexually abused compared to 73 percent of the girls "receiving services as a child in need of supervision" (Robinson 1990, 311). The difference between these girls was in the offenses for which they were charged; all the girls receiving services were charged with traditional status offenses (chiefly running away and truancy), while the girls committed to DYS were charged with criminal offenses. Here, though, her interviews reveal clear evidence of bootstrapping. Take, for example, the 16-year-old girl who was committed to DYS for "unauthorized use of a motor vehicle." In this instance, Beverly, who is black, had "stolen" her mother's car for three hours to go shopping with a friend. Previous to this conviction, according to Robinson's interview, she had been a "CHINS" for "running away

from home repeatedly." Beverly told Robinson that her mother had been

> advised by the DYS social worker to press charges for unauthorized use of a motor vehicle so that Beverly could be sent to secure detention whenever she was caught on the run. (Robinson 1990, 202).

Other evidence of this pattern is reported by Bartollas (1993) in his study of youth confined in juvenile "institutional" placements in a Midwestern state. His research sampled female adolescents in both public and private facilities. The "state" sample (representing the girls in public facilities) was 61 percent black, while the private sample was 100 percent white. Little difference, however, was found in the offense patterns of the two groups of girls. Of the girls in the "state" sample, 70 percent had been "placed in a training school as a result of a status offense" (Bartollas 1993, 473). This state, like most, does not permit youth to be institutionalized for such offenses; however, Bartollas noted that "they can be placed on probation, which makes it possible for the juvenile judge to adjudicate them to a training school" (Bartollas 1993, 473). In the private sample, only 50 percent were confined for status offenses; the remainder were there for "minor stealing and shoplifting-related offenses" (Bartollas 1993, 473). Bartollas also noted that both of these samples of girls had far less extensive juvenile histories than did their male counterparts.

Programming for Girls

National data indicate that between 1989 and 1993, detentions for girls increased by 23 percent, compared to an 18 percent increase in boys' detentions (Poe-Yamagata and Butts 1996). San Francisco researchers examining their juvenile justice system concluded that girls would languish in detention centers waiting for placement, while boys were released or put in placement. As a result, 60 percent of the girls were detained for more than seven days, compared to only 6 percent of the boys (Shorter et al. 1996). These figures reflect a system that has failed to develop programs shaped by girls' unique situations, as well as to address the special problems girls have in a gendered society.

After decades of "deinstitutionalization efforts," girls remain, in the words of one researcher, "all but invisible in programs for youth and in the literature available to those who work with youth" (Davidson 1983, viii; see also Bergsmann 1989). As an example, a 1993 study by the San Francisco chapter of the National Organization for Women found that only 8.7 percent of the programs of major city organizations funding children and youth programs "specifically addressed the needs of girls" (Siegal 1995, 18). Not surprisingly, then, a 1995 study of youth participation in San Francisco after-school and summer sports programs found that only 26 percent of the participants were girls (Siegal 1995).

In addition, people who work in the juvenile justice system typically prefer working with girls but routinely stress the "difficulty" of working with them. Belknap and her colleagues in Ohio, in their study of youth workers, reported that "most of the professionals, unless they worked exclusively with girls, had a difficult time not talking solely about the male delinquents" (Belknap, Dunn, and Holsinger 1997, 28). Likewise, Alder (1997) has noted that "willful" girls produce problems for a system initially devised to handle boys; girls in these systems get constructed as "hysterical," "manipulative," "verbally aggressive," and "untrusting," while boys are "honest," "open," and "less complex." Clearly the juvenile justice system has its work cut out for it if it hopes to deal fairly with girls, to say nothing of creating programs and services tailored to girls' problems and needs.

What are the specific needs of young women in general and, in particular, those who come into contact with the juvenile justice system, either as victims or offenders? Davidson (1983) argues that "the most desperate need of many young women is to find the economic means of survival" (p. ix).

Other research has stressed homeless girls' urgent needs for housing, jobs, and medical services (Iwamoto, Kameoka, and Brasseur 1990).

The Minnesota Women's Fund noted that the most frequent risk factors for girls and boys differ and that for girls the list includes emotional stress, physical and sexual abuse, negative body image, disordered eating, suicide, and pregnancy. For boys, the list included alcohol use, polydrug use, accidental injury, and delinquency (cited in Adolescent Female Subcommittee 1994). While not all girls at risk will end up in the juvenile justice system, this gendered examination of youth problems sets a standard for evaluation of delinquency prevention and intervention programs.

Among other needs that girls' programs should address are dealing with the physical and sexual violence in their lives (from parents, boyfriends, pimps, and others), the risk of AIDS, pregnancy and motherhood, drug and alcohol dependency, and family problems; vocational and career counseling; managing stress; and developing a sense of efficacy and empowerment. Many of these needs are universal and should be part of programs for all youth (Schwartz and Orlando 1991). However, most of them are particularly important for young women.

Alder (1986, 1995) points out that serving girls effectively will require different and innovative strategies since "young men tend to be more noticeable and noticed than young women" (Alder 1995, 3). When girls go out, they tend to move in smaller groups. There are greater proscriptions against girls "hanging out"—and girls may be justly fearful of being on the streets at night. Finally, girls have many more domestic expectations than their male counterparts, which may keep them confined to their homes. Alder notes that this may be a particular issue for immigrant girls.

Programs must also be scrutinized to assure that they are culturally specific as well as gender specific. Increasing numbers of girls of color are drawn into the juvenile justice system (and bootstrapped into correctional settings), while their white counterparts are deinstitutionalized. Since it is clear that girls of color have different experiences of gender, as well as different experiences with the dominant institutions in the society (Amaro 1995; Amaro and Agular 1994; LaFromboise and Howard-Pitney 1995; Orenstein 1994), programs to divert and deinstitutionalize *must* be shaped by the unique developmental issues confronting minority girls, as well as built into the specific cultural resources available in ethnic communities.

The short-lived congressional focus on girls has unfortunately been followed by a major retreat from such initiatives. Not only that, Congress is apparently encouraging the recriminalization of status offenses, which suggests that without powerful local advocacy, the nation could once again see large numbers of girls incarcerated "for their own protection." A girl-centered response to this backlash, along with continued pressure on the juvenile justice system to do more to help girls, is essential. Much more, not less, work needs to be done to support the fundamental needs of girls on the margin.

Discussion Questions

1. What are status offenses, and why are they so important in female delinquency?

2. How did the juvenile justice system become involved in the enforcement of the sexual double standard?

3. What are the major risk factors for adolescent girls? How do these differ from boys' risks?

4. Why are current congressional initiatives that focus on youth violence bad news for girls?

Endnotes

1. This phrase is drawn from the title of the Center on Juvenile and Criminal Justice's

report on adolescent girls in San Francisco (Shorter et al. 1996).

2. Children, unlike adults, can be "referred" to the juvenile justice system by a variety of sources, including teachers, social workers, and even parents. In fact, these other sources are particularly significant in the case of girls' entry into the juvenile justice system.

3. This phrase was taken from an inmate file by Nicole Hahn Rafter (1990) in her review of the establishment of New York's Albion Reformatory. Rafter notes that between one-half and three-quarters of the young women admitted to the facility were incarcerated merely for having been sexually active.

References

Adams-Tucker, C. 1982. "Proximate Effects of Sexual Abuse in Childhood." *American Journal of Psychiatry* 193:1252–1256.

Adolescent Female Subcommittee. 1994. *Needs Assessment and Recommendations for Adolescent Females in Minnesota*. St. Paul: Minnesota Department of Corrections.

Alder, C. 1986. " 'Unemployed Women Have Got it Heaps Worse': Exploring the Implications of Female Youth Unemployment." *Australia and New Zealand Society of Criminology* 19:210–224.

——. 1995. *Delinquency Prevention With Young Women*. Paper presented at the Delinquency Prevention Conference, Terrigal, NSW, Australia.

——. 1997. *'Passionate and Willful' Girls: Confronting Practices*. Paper presented at the Annual Meeting of the Academy of Criminal Justice Sciences, Louisville, KY.

Amaro, H. 1995. "Love, Sex and Power: Considering Women's Realities in HIV Prevention." *American Psychologist* 50:437–447.

Amaro, H. and Agular, M. 1994. "Programma Mama: Mom's Project." *A Hispanic/Latino Family Approach to Substance Abuse Prevention*. Center for Substance Abuse Prevention, Mental Health Services Administration.

American Association of University Women (AAUW). 1992. *How Schools Shortchange Girls*. Washington, DC: Author.

American Correctional Association. 1990. *The Female Offender: What Does the Future Hold?* Washington, DC: St. Mary's Press.

Bartollas, C. 1993. "Little Girls Grown Up: The Perils of Institutionalization." In C. Culliver, ed., *Female Criminality: The State of the Art*. New York: Garland.

Baskin, D. and Sommers, I. 1993. "Females' Initiation Into Violent Street Crime." *Justice Quarterly* 10:559–581.

Bell, I. P. 1984. "The Double Standard Age." In J. Freeman, ed., *Women: A Feminist Perspective*. Palo Alto, CA: Mayfield.

Belknap, J., Dunn, M., and Holsinger, K. 1997. *Gender Specific Services Work Group: Report to the Governor*. Columbus, OH: Office of Criminal Justice Services.

Bergsmann, I. R. 1989, March. "The Forgotten Few: Juvenile Female Offenders." *Federal Probation*, pp. 73–78.

Bishop, D. and Frazier, C. 1992. "Gender Bias in the Juvenile Justice System: Implications of the JJDP Act." *Journal of Criminal Law and Criminology* 82:1162–1186.

Block, J. H. 1984. *Sex Role Identity and Ego Development*. San Francisco: Jossey-Bass.

Browne, A. and Finkelhor, D. 1986. "Impact of Child Sexual Abuse: A Review of Research." *Psychological Bulletin* 99:66–77.

Butts, J. A., Snyder, H. N., Finnegan, T. A., Aughenbaugh, A. L., Tierney, N. J., Sullivan, D. P., Poole, R. S., Sickmund, M. H., and Poe, E. C. 1994. *Juvenile Court Statistics 1991*. Pittsburgh: National Center for Juvenile Justice, Office of Juvenile Justice and Delinquency Prevention.

Cahalan, M. 1986. *Historical Corrections Statistics in the United States, 1850–1984*. Washington, DC: Bureau of Justice Statistics.

Cain, M. (ed.) 1989. *Growing Up Good: Policing the Behavior of Girls in Europe*. London: Sage.

Campagna, D. S. and Poffenberger, D. L. 1988. *The Sexual Trafficking in Children*. Dover: Auburn House.

Campbell, A. 1984. *The Girls in the Gang*. Oxford: Basil Blackwell.

Canter, R. 1982a. "Family Correlates of Male and Female Delinquency." *Criminology* 20:149–167.

———. 1982b. "Sex Differences in Self-report Delinquency." *Criminology* 20:373–393.

Chesney-Lind, M. 1971. *Female Juvenile Delinquency in Hawaii*. Unpublished master's thesis, University of Hawaii.

———. 1973. "Judicial Enforcement of the Female Sex Role." *Issues in Criminology* 8:51–71.

———. 1988. "Girls in Jail." *Crime and Delinquency* 34:150–168.

Chesney-Lind, M. and Shelden, R. G. 1997. *Girls, Delinquency and the Juvenile Justice System*. Belmont, CA: Wadsworth.

Cohn, Y. 1970. "Criteria for the Probation Officer's Recommendation to the Juvenile Court." In P. G. Garbedian and D. C. Gibbons, eds., *Becoming Delinquent*. Chicago: Aldine.

Connell, R. W. 1987. *Gender and Power*. Stanford, CA: Stanford University Press.

Costello, J. C. and Worthington, N. L. 1981. "Incarcerating Status Offenders: Attempts to Circumvent the Juvenile Justice and Delinquency Prevention Act." *Harvard Civil Rights-Civil Liberties Law Review* 16:41–81.

Datesman, S. and Scarpitti, F. 1977. "Unequal Protection for Males and Females in the Juvenile Court." In T. N. Ferdinand, ed., *Juvenile Delinquency: Little Brother Grows Up*. Newbury Park, CA: Sage.

Davidson, S. (ed.) 1982. *Justice for Young Women*. Tucson, AZ: New Directions for Young Women.

———. (ed.) 1983. *The Second Mile: Contemporary Approaches in Counseling Young Women*. Tucson, AZ: New Directions for Young Women.

DeJong, A. R., Hervada, A. R. and Emmett, G. A. 1983. "Epidemiologic Variations in Childhood Sexual Abuse." *Child Abuse and Neglect* 7:155–162.

Dembo, R., Sue, S. C., Borden, P., and Manning, D. 1995. *Gender Differences in Service Needs Among Youths Entering a Juvenile Assessment Center: A Replication Study*. Paper presented at the Annual Meeting of the Society for the Study of Social Problems. Washington, DC.

Dembo, R., Williams, L. and Schmeidler, J. 1993. "Gender Differences in Mental Health Service

Needs Among Juveniles Entering a Juvenile Detention Center." *Journal of Prison and Jail Health* 12:73–101.

Federal Bureau of Investigation. 1996. *Crime in the United States, 1995*. Washington, DC: U.S. Department of Justice.

Figueria-McDonough, J. and Barton, W. H. 1985. "Attachments, Gender and Delinquency." *Deviant Behavior* 6:119–144.

Figueria-McDonough, J. and Selo, E. 1980. "A Reformulation of the 'Equal Opportunity' Explanation of Female Delinquency." *Crime and Delinquency* 26:333–343.

Finkelhor, D. 1982. "Sexual Abuse: A Sociological Perspective." *Child Abuse and Neglect* 6:95–102.

Finkelhor, D. and Barron, L. 1986. "Risk Factors for Child Sexual Abuse." *Journal of Interpersonal Violence* 1:43–71.

Gibbons, D. and Griswold, M. J. 1957. "Sex Difference Among Juvenile Court Referrals." *Sociology and Social Research* 42:106–110.

Girls Incorporated. 1996. *Prevention and Parity: Girls in Juvenile Justice*. Indianapolis, IN: Author.

Hagan, J., Gillis, A. R., and Simpson, J. 1985. "The Class Structure of Gender and Delinquency: Toward a Power-Control Theory of Common Delinquent Behavior." *American Journal of Sociology* 90:1151–1178.

Hirschi, T. 1969. *Causes of Delinquency*. Berkeley: University of California Press.

Howard, B. 1996, July/August. "Congress Debating Juvenile Justice Mandates: To Stay or Go?" *Youth Today*, p. 22.

Ianni, F. A. J. 1989. *The Search for Structure: A Report on American Youth Today*. New York: Free Press.

Iwamoto, J. J., Kameoka, K., and Brasseur, Y. C. 1990. *Waikiki Homeless Youth Project: A Report*. Honolulu: Catholic Services to Families.

Jamieson, K. M. and Flanagan, T. (eds.) 1989. *Sourcebook of Criminal Justice Statistics, 1988*. Washington, DC: Bureau of Justice Statistics.

Joe, K. and Chesney-Lind, M. 1995. " 'Just Every Mother's Angel': An Analysis of Gender and Ethnic Variation in Youth Gang Membership." *Gender and Society* 9:408–430.

Katz, P. A. 1979. "The Development of Female Identity." In C. B. Kopp, ed., *Becoming Female*. New York: Plenum.

Kratcoski, P. C. 1974. "Delinquent Boys and Girls." *Child Welfare* 5:16–21.

Krisberg, B., DeComo, R., Herrara, N. C., Steketee, M., and Roberts, S. 1991. *Juveniles Taken Into Custody: Fiscal year 1990 report*. San Francisco: National Council on Crime and Delinquency.

Kunzel, R. 1993. *Fallen Women and Problem Girls: Unmarried Mothers and the Professionalization of Social Work, 1890–1945*. New Haven: Yale University Press.

LaFromboise, T. D. and Howard-Pitney, B. 1995. "Suicidal Behavior in American Indian Female Adolescents." In S. Canetto and D. Lester, eds., *Women and Suicidal Behavior*. New York: Springer.

Mann, C. 1979. "The Differential Treatment Between Runaway Boys and Girls in Court." *Juvenile and Family Court Journal* 30:37–48.

McDermott, M. J. and Blackstone, S. J. 1994. *White Slavery Plays of the 1910s: Fear of Victimization and the Social Control of Sexuality*. Paper presented at the Annual Meeting of the American Society of Criminology, Miami, FL.

Miller, E. 1986. *Street Woman*. Philadelphia: Temple University Press.

Miller, J. 1994. "Race, Gender, and Juvenile Justice: An Examination of Disposition Decision-making for Delinquent Girls." In M. D. Schwartz and D. Milovanovic, eds., *The Intersection of Race, Gender and Class in Criminology*. New York: Garland.

Moone, J. 1993a. *Children in Custody: Public Facilities*. Washington, DC: Office of Juvenile Justice and Delinquency Prevention.

——. 1993b. *Children in Custody: Private Facilities*. Washington, DC: Office of Juvenile Justice and Delinquency Prevention.

Naffine, N. 1987. *Female Crime: The Construction of Women in Criminology*. Sydney, Australia: Allen and Unwin.

National Criminal Justice Association. 1997, April. Congressional Roundup. *Justice Bulletin*, pp. 1–3.

Odem, M. E. 1995. *Delinquent Daughters*. Chapel Hill: University of North Carolina Press.

Odem, M. E. and Schlossman, S. 1991. "Guardians of Virtue: The Juvenile Court and Female Delinquency in Early 20th Century Los Angeles." *Crime and Delinquency* 37:186–203.

Orenstein, P. 1994. *Schoolgirls*. New York: Doubleday.

Owen, B. and Bloom, B. 1997. *Profiling the Needs of Young Female Offenders: Final Report to Executive Staff of the California Youth Authority*. National Institute of Justice, Grant 95-IJ-CX-0098.

Platt, A. M. 1969. *The Childsavers*. Chicago: University of Chicago Press.

Poe-Yamagata, E. and Butts, J. A. 1996. *Female Offenders in the Juvenile Justice System*. Pittsburgh: National Center for Juvenile Justice.

Pope, C. and Feyerherm, W. H. 1982. "Gender Bias in Juvenile Court Dispositions." *Social Service Research* 6:1–17.

Rafter, N. H. 1990. *Partial Justice*. New Brunswick, NJ: Transaction.

Robinson, R. 1990. *Violations of Girlhood: A Qualitative Study of Female Delinquents and Children in Need of Services in Massachusetts*. Unpublished Ph.D. dissertation, Brandeis University.

Roiphe, K. 1993. *The Morning After*. Boston: Little, Brown.

Rowe, D. C., Vazsonyi, A. T., and Flannery, D. J. 1995. "Sex Differences in Crime: Do Means and Within-Sex Variation Have Similar Causes?" *Journal of Research in Crime and Delinquency* 31:84–100.

Russell, D. 1986. *The Secret Trauma: Incest in the Lives of Girls and Women*. New York: Basic Books.

Schlossman, S. and Wallach, S. 1978. "The Crime of Precocious Sexuality: Female Juvenile Delinquency in the Progressive Era." *Harvard Educational Review* 48:65–94.

Schwartz, I. M. and Orlando, F. 1991. *Programming for Young Women in the Juvenile Justice System*. Ann Arbor: Center for the Study of Youth Policy, University of Michigan.

Shelden, R. 1981. "Sex Discrimination in the Juvenile Justice System: Memphis, Tennessee, 1900–1971." In M. Q. Warren, ed., *Comparing Male and Female Offenders*. Beverly Hills, CA: Sage.

Shelden, R. and Horvath, J. 1986. *Processing Offenders in a Juvenile Court: A Comparison of Male and Female Offenders*. Paper presented at the Annual Meeting of the Western Society of Criminology, Newport Beach, CA.

Shorter, A. D., Schaffner, L., Shick, S., and Frappier, N. S. 1996. *Out of Sight, Out of Mind: The Plight of Girls in the San Francisco Juvenile Justice System*. San Francisco: Center for Juvenile and Criminal Justice.

Siegal, N. 1995, October 4. "Where the Girls Are." *San Francisco Bay Guardian*, pp. 19–20.

Smith, D. and Paternoster, R. 1987. "The Gender Gap in Theories of Deviance: Issues and Evidence." *Journal of Research in Crime and Delinquency* 24:140–172.

Snell, T. L. and Morton, D. C. 1994. *Women in Prison*. Washington, DC: Bureau of Justice Statistics.

Teilman, K. and Landry, P. 1981. "Gender Bias in Juvenile Justice." *Journal of Research in Crime and Delinquency* 18:47–80.

Thorne, B. 1994. *Gender Play: Girls and Boys in School*. New Brunswick, NJ: Rutgers University Press.

U.S. House of Representatives. 1992. *Hearings on the Juvenile Justice and Delinquency Prevention Act of 1974*. Washington, DC: U.S. Government Printing Office.

U.S. Statutes at Large, 96th Congress, 2d sess. 1981. *Public Law 96–509—December, 1981*. Washington, DC: U.S. Government Printing Office.

Vedder, C. B. and Sommerville, D. B. 1970. *The Delinquent Girl*. Springfield, IL: Charles C. Thomas.

Wolf, N. 1993. *Fire With Fire*. New York: Random House.

Youth Law Center 1997, June. *Pending Federal Legislation: The Impact on State Law*. San Francisco: Author.

Ziedenberg, J. and Schiraldi, V. 1997. *The Risks Juveniles Face When They Are Incarcerated With Adults*. Washington, DC: Center for Juvenile and Criminal Justice. ✦

4

Girls and Gangs

Rodney K. Brunson
and Jody Miller

This chapter reveals the prevalence of girls' involvement in gangs and gang activity throughout the one-in-five major U.S. cities that report the existence of gangs. After describing the economic and social factors that contribute to the increasing number of gangs across the country, the authors explain girls' motivations for becoming gang members, describe activities and expectations that pertain particularly to girl members, and examine girls' delinquencies in contrast to boys' and to the behavior of nongang members of the same and opposite sex. The chapter also analyzes the many double standards that exist for girls in gangs in terms of sexual behavior, gender-based roles, and relationships between female and male members of gangs.

The 1980s and 1990s witnessed monumental national growth in gangs and a renewed academic interest in the study of gangs. Female gang involvement, which until recently was typically either stereotyped or ignored, has also garnered new interest among researchers, thanks in part to the work of feminist scholars, who have struggled to bring the study of women's lives more fully into the field of criminology. One consequence of this renewed interest in gangs, and girls' involvement in particular, has been improved information about the topic, including answers to a number of important questions: (1) Why do girls join gangs? (2) What are girls' experiences within gangs? and, (3) What are the consequences of girls' participation in gangs? In this chapter, we address each of these issues in two ways: first, by reviewing what we know from recent research on girls' gang involvement and second, by providing evidence from our own research on the topic.[1] We will begin by providing an overview of the growth and nature of gangs in the last decade.

Recent Data on Gangs in the 1990s

One reason behind the renewed scholarly interest in gangs is the proliferation of gangs across the United States in the last decade into a "growing number of large and small cities, suburban areas, and even some small towns and rural areas" (Klein 1995; Maxson, Woods, and Klein 1995; Spergel and Curry 1993, 359). A tremendous increase has occurred in the number of gangs, gang members, and communities with gangs since the mid-1980s. According to Malcolm Klein (1995), who has been studying gangs since the 1960s, more than 1,000 communities across the United States now report the existence of gangs—most of them with new or "emergent" gang problems.

Although some media and other accounts suggest that the growth in gangs has resulted from the organized migration of groups across cities, most evidence refutes this notion. Instead, the proliferation of gangs appears to be the result of the independent development of gangs in a number of sites, seemingly simultaneously (see Hagedorn 1988; Huff 1989; Klein 1995). To account for these changes, many criminologists have focused on compelling evidence that much—though not all—of the new growth in gangs has been spurred by the deterioration in living conditions for many Americans caused by structural changes brought about by deindustrialization (see Hagedorn 1988, 1991; Klein 1995; Moore 1988; Padilla 1992). In addition, some scholars have begun to pay attention to a second contributing factor—the diffusion of gang culture through popular media attention to gangs and the commercialization of gang style (see Decker and Van Winkle 1996; Klein 1995; Miller 1995).

Structural changes brought about by de-industrialization have resulted in the growth of what scholars refer to as an urban "under-class"—disproportionately African-American and Latino individuals living in conditions of entrenched poverty in inner-city communities. These communities are characterized by intense racial and economic segregation and isolation, an outmigration of middle-class families, and a precipitous decline in social services for those left behind (see Moore and Pinderhughes 1993; Sampson and Wilson, 1995; Wilson, 1987, 1996). The lack of alternatives resulting from these conditions is believed to have contributed to the growth of gangs in many cities. Recently, it also has meant that youthful gang members—given less opportunity for maturing out of gangs and into the formal economy—are more likely to continue their gang and criminal involvement into adulthood (Hagedorn 1988, 1994; Klein 1995; Moore 1991). As Jackson (1991) summarizes,

> higher crime rates and more youth gangs are among the unintended consequences of the nation's pattern of postindustrial development. (p. 379)

As noted above, another factor worth considering is the cultural diffusion of information about gangs and of gang style. Music, films, the news media's attention to gangs, and the resulting popularity of various aspects of gang culture such as clothing, hand signs, and tattoos all add to youthful identification with gang culture (Klein, Maxson, and Miller, 1995). Cultural diffusion may help explain the simultaneous growth of gangs in so many communities across the United States, contributing to the formation of what Spergel and Curry (1993) describe as "copycat gangs." Groups of youths who otherwise might be involved in minor delinquent activities adopt gang names for themselves; when they do, they may be recognized and responded to as such by others in their community and by institutions with social

control capacities. A number of scholars have suggested that group processes operate in gangs such that negative sanctions from external sources may strengthen the groups' cohesiveness; thus, responses to youths who begin to adopt gang names may exacerbate the extent of gang activity in a given community (see Klein 1993; Klein and Crawford 1967; Short and Strodtbeck 1965).

An emphasis on gangs as principally a male phenomenon has been a longstanding tradition in the academic study of gangs (for example, see Cloward and Ohlin 1960; Cohen 1955; Hagedorn 1988; Jankowski 1991; Short and Strodtbeck 1965; Vigil, 1988). In fact, until recently many gang scholars actually gained their information about female participation in gangs from male gang members rather than from the young women themselves (for a discussion, see Campbell 1984, 1990a, 1990b).

Consequently, most traditional gang research emphasized the auxiliary and peripheral nature of girls' gang involvement and often resulted in a near exclusive emphasis on their sexuality and sexual activities with male gang members. Young women were often depicted as particularly physically unattractive, and their activities were described in narrow terms: as weapons carriers, decoys or spies for infiltrating rival gangs, sexual outlets for male gang members, instigators or provokers of conflict between male gangs, and cat fighters—fighting one another for the attention of male gang members. These notions of girls' participation in gangs were a reflection of male gang members' views of girls, as well as the frameworks brought to bear on the topic by male researchers (see Campbell 1990a).

Fortunately, times have changed, and feminist scholars have made strides toward improving our knowledge of female gang involvement—*from young women's points of view*. In fact, recent evidence suggests that young women are more gang involved and that their participation and experiences in gangs are much more varied than was previously believed. While data from official sources tend to underestimate the extent of girls' gang membership (Curry, Ball, and Fox 1994), a number of recent studies with juvenile populations estimate that young women make up 20 to 46 percent of gang members and that in some urban areas upwards of one-fifth of girls report having gang affiliations (Bjerregaard and Smith 1993; Esbensen and Huizinga 1993; Esbensen and Winfree, forthcoming; Winfree et al. 1992).

Now that we've provided a broad context within which to view young women's gang participation, let us return to the questions we raised in our introduction, beginning with the question of why girls join gangs.

Why Do Girls Join Gangs?

Earlier gang research tended to trivialize or ignore female participation; that situation is changing. Despite a relative paucity of academic research on girls and gangs, there is nonetheless a growing body of knowledge—including both qualitative and quantitative studies—that provides some insight into the causes of girls' involvement in gangs. Here we will review some of the background factors scholars have found to be associated with girls' gang participation, and we will also discuss the functions and meanings of gang involvement for girls.

Understanding the life contexts of girls in gangs provides insight into those factors shaping their decisions to join. These contexts include structural conditions such as poverty, neighborhood crime, racism, and limited opportunities, as well as such things as family problems, gang-involved family members, and peer contexts that provide incentives to join gangs.

Researchers suggest that gangs are an important element of the social support systems of their members (Soriano 1993; Vigil and Long 1990), and likely meet specific needs for young women (Campbell 1990a; Joe and Chesney-Lind 1995). For instance, many scholars have pointed to the gang as a means for inner-city youths to adapt to oppressive living conditions imposed by their environments. Young women living in urban "underclass" communities face a number of problems, including limited educational and occupational opportunities, subordination to men, and childcare responsibilities, in addition to the powerlessness of underclass membership shared with males in their communities (Campbell 1990a). According to Joe and Chesney-Lind (1995), "the gang assists young women and men in coping with their lives in chaotic, violent, and economically marginalized communities" (p. 411). Specifically, because of the dangers they face in their communities, the gang may assist young women in protecting themselves—by "provid[ing] opportunities to learn such traditional male skills as fighting skills and taking care of themselves on the streets" (Fishman 1988, 15).

Not surprisingly, the characteristics of the neighborhoods we drew our sample from were quite dismal and very much in keeping with the image of urban poverty described above. In both Columbus and St. Louis, the vast majority of girls lived in neighborhoods with higher rates of poverty and lower median incomes than the rest of the city; moreover, they lived in racially segregated neighborhoods that were predominantly African American. These neighborhoods tend to have high rates of crime, and a majority of the girls we interviewed joined gangs in large part because they were exposed to these groups in their neighborhoods. Cookie, a young woman from our study, described how she became involved:

> Well, I used to be walking to school, back and forth to school and I would see them . . . and after a while I just [started] hanging around smoking weed and just kicking it with them. Later on, I joined the gang.

Although this assessment appears to be accurate, it nevertheless remains only a partial answer to the question of why girls join gangs. Most research shows that fewer than one-quarter of youths living in high-risk neighborhoods claim gang membership (Bjerregaard and Smith 1993; Winfree et al. 1992), and researchers have not found differences in perceived limited opportunities between gang and nongang youths in these communities (Esbensen, Huizinga, and Weiher 1993). Thus, we need to look at what other factors might lead some girls into gang involvement, even while others within the same impoverished communities exercise other options. One factor that has received quite a bit of attention is the family.

The family has long been considered crucial for understanding delinquency and gang behavior among girls (Canter 1982; Cernkovich and Giordano 1987; Moore 1991; Smith and Paternoster 1987). Problems such as weak supervision, lack of attachment to parents, the gang involvement of other family members, family violence, and drug and alcohol abuse by family members have all been suggested as contributors to the likelihood that girls will join gangs. Joe and Chesney-Lind (1995) observe that the young women they spoke with sometimes had parents who worked long hours or parents who were unemployed or underemployed—circumstances they suggest affected the girls' supervision and the quality of their family relationships. In fact, Moore (1991) documents myriad factors within families that may contribute to the likelihood of gang involvement, including having alcoholics or drug addicts in the family, witnessing the arrest of family members, having a family member who is chronically ill, and experiencing a death in the family during childhood. Her conclusion is that gang members, particularly girls, come from families that are troubled.

Two family situations in particular are strongly associated with girls' gang involvement: the gang involvement of other family members, and family violence. Moore (1991) reports that while boys are more likely to join gangs as a result of growing up around gangs, girls are more likely to join because of a relative's or close friend's association with the gang. We found evidence of this situation in our study as well. Three-quarters of the gang members we spoke with had family members—brothers, sisters, cousins, aunts or uncles, or parents—in gangs. Moreover, while 44 percent of the gang members we interviewed had siblings or parents in gangs, only 17 percent of the nongang girls we interviewed did. Many of the young women we interviewed described these familial relationships as important factors in their decisions to join. For instance, Veronica joined her gang to follow in her older brothers' footsteps. She explained, "[the gang] was right there in my neighborhood . . . then I seen that my brothers, 'cause I seen my brothers get put in. So then I said I wanna be put in." And Lisa said she "claimed [her gang] because that's what my brother was so I wanted to be like that too."

Research also suggests that young women in gangs have disproportionate histories of victimization prior to gang involvement, particularly in the context of the family. In Joe and Chesney-Lind's (1995) study, 55 percent of the male gang members and 75 percent of the female gang members who were asked reported physical abuse in their families; moreover, 62 percent of the girls reported sexual abuse. Campbell (1984) also reports anecdotal evidence of family violence and sexual abuse among the young women in her study of female gang members. Moore's (1991) comparison of male and female gang members' histories of family violence provides the most detailed account. She concludes that female gang members recount more cases of childhood abuse and neglect than males and more frequently come from homes where wife abuse and sexual assault are present.

Our findings, which compare gang and nongang girls, provide additional evidence of this relationship between family violence, other victimization, and gang involvement. For instance, 44 percent of the gang members we spoke with reported having been abused by family members, compared to 22 percent of the nongang girls; 52 percent of gang members, versus 28 percent of nongang members, had seen adults in their home hit each other. Moreover, more than half of the gang members we spoke with had been sexually assaulted, compared to 22 percent of the nongang girls.

Erica's story serves as an excellent illustration of the impact that family violence and sexual abuse can have on young girls and how, given particular circumstances, these experiences can result in gang involvement. Erica was 17 when we spoke and had joined her gang when she was 15. She had lived with her father and stepmother throughout most of her childhood, until her father raped her at the age of 11 and she was removed from the home. Since that time, she has been shuffled back and forth between foster homes, group homes, and residential facilities. She has had little contact with her family since she was 11, because family members turned their backs on her.

Although she says her stepmother was the primary person who raised her as a child, their relationship was severely damaged by the rape. Erica explains, "She doesn't, she doesn't believe it. I mean, even after he pleaded guilty she still doesn't believe it." Erica's childhood up to that point had been filled with violence as well. Her father was physically abusive toward her biological mother. Both her father and stepmother have spent time in jail, and she witnessed regular alcohol and drug use in the home as she was growing up. As a result, she was a physically aggressive child. She says, "In elementary school before I even knew anything about gangs, I'd just get in a lot of fights." Her initial contact with gangs came when she was 14 and living in a foster home. During her stay there, she met a group of kids with whom she began spending time. She explains her relationship to them:

I didn't know 'em, but I just started talkin' to 'em. And, they always wore them blue rags and black rags and all that. And, I asked them, I said, 'Well you part of a gang?' And they tell me what they're part of. So it was like, everywhere I went, I was with them. I was never by myself. . . . If they did anything, I was with them. And um, we went down to some club one night and it was like a whole bunch of 'em got together and um, I asked to join. I wanted to join.

Erica says she joined the gang "just to be in something," and so it could be "like a family to me since I don't really have one of my own." Being in the gang allowed her to develop meaningful relationships. She explains, "People trust me and I trust them. It's like that bond that we have that some of us don't have outside of that. Or didn't have at all. That we have inside of that gang."

As Erica's experiences indicate,

> The gang can serve as a surrogate extended family for adolescents who do not see their own families as meeting their needs for belonging, nurturance, and acceptance. (Huff 1993, 6; Brown 1978; Campbell 1990a; Joe and Chesney-Lind 1995; but see also Decker and Van Winkle, 1996).

Other gang members offer support, solidarity, and a network of friends for those girls whose parents are unable to provide stable family relations; moreover, girls' friendships within the gang provide an outlet for members to deal with family problems and cope with abuse and other life problems (Joe and Chesney-Lind 1995).

There is also strong evidence that peer influences are important for understanding gang participation among females, as well as males (Brown 1978; Bowker and Klein 1983; Campbell 1990a, 1990b; Giordano 1978; Morash 1983). We know from much research that youths who participate in gangs often extol the importance of the gang in their lives (Moore, 1991). Short and Strodtbeck (1965) argue that the group meets self-esteem needs. The rewards provided by the gang—status, companionship, excitement, protection, and belonging—facilitate the building of esteem. Participation in the gang results from group dynamics that encourage member involvement through the provision of self-esteem and identity. Moreover, gang activities provide these youths with a way to alleviate the boredom of their daily lives, given the limited options for recreation and entertainment found in impoverished communities. Quicker (1983) summarizes, "To be in a gang is to be part of something. It means having a place to go, friends to talk with, and parties to attend. It means recognition and respected status"(p. 80).

The girls in our study reported similar experiences. For example, Nikkie said she joined in order to fit in with her peers in the neighborhood. She noted, "If you ain't in it you just be . . . you just be feelin' left out. You be like, oh, they all in a gang and I'm just sittin' here." As a result, she said, "I was like, 'I wanna get in it.' And I got in it." Jennifer joined her gang after her best friend joined. She explained, "She'd talk about all the, how it's real, it's just real cool to be in and everything like that." Many of the girls we spoke with felt that gang members were among the more popular and recognized youths in school and around the neighborhood, which shaped their motivations to join.

This section has described what we know about why girls join gangs. But even though they join gangs to meet particular needs, the gang may not necessarily live up to their expectations. To examine this issue, we need to turn to what we know about the nature of gangs and about the consequences of gang involvement for the young women involved. We need to ask: What are gangs like? How do gang members spend their time? What are girls' roles within their gangs?

'Life in the Gang':[2] What Is It Like for Girls?

One reason gangs have received so much attention among criminologists is that young people who are in gangs—male and female—are substantially more involved in delinquency than their nongang counterparts. Research comparing gang and nongang youths has consistently found that serious criminal involvement is a feature that distinguishes gangs from other groups of youths (Esbensen et al. 1993; Esbensen and Huizinga 1993; Fagan 1989, 1990; Klein 1995; Thornberry et al. 1993; Winfree et al. 1992), and this pattern holds for both female and male gang members (Bjerregaard and Smith 1993; Esbensen and Winfree, forthcoming; Thornberry et al. 1993). The enhancement effect of gang membership is most noticeable for serious delinquency and marijuana use (Thornberry et al. 1993). Bjerregaard and Smith (1993) summarize,

> Our study suggests that for females [as well as males], gangs are consistently associated with a greater prevalence and with higher rates of delinquency and substance abuse. Furthermore, the results suggest that for both sexes, gang membership has an approximately equal impact on a variety of measures of delinquent behavior. (p. 346)

Perhaps what's most significant about this research is the evidence that female gang members are not only more delinquent than their female nongang counterparts but also more delinquent than their *male* nongang counterparts. For instance, Fagan reports that "prevalence rates for female gang members exceeded the rates for nongang males" for all the categories of delinquency he measured (see also Esbensen and Winfree, forthcoming). He summarizes his findings in relation to girls:

> More than 40 percent of the female gang members were classified in the least serious category, a substantial difference from their male counterparts [15.5 percent]. Among female gang members, there was a bimodal distribution, with nearly as many multiple index offenders as petty delinquents. Evidently, female gang members avoid more serious delinquent involvement than their male counterparts. *Yet their extensive involvement in serious delinquent behaviors well exceeds that of nongang males or females.* (Fagan 1990, 201, our emphasis)

In research in Columbus and St. Louis, we also found differences in the extent of girls' criminal offending—specifically that gang members were more likely to be involved in serious delinquency. For instance, 67 percent of girl gang members, compared to 30 percent of nongang girls, reported that they had attacked someone with a weapon or with the idea of seriously hurting or killing them; 74 percent of the girl gang members had carried a hidden weapon, compared to 19 percent of the nongang girls; and 63 percent of the girl gang members—versus only 5 percent of the nongang girls—had engaged in crack cocaine sales.[3]

Keep in mind that our comparison group of nongang girls were *still* girls who were "at-risk," many of whom had arrest records or were interviewed in detention or other facilities. It's clear, then, that one aspect of girls' gang involvement is their participation in delinquency. In fact, many young women talk about delinquency as a source of fun and excitement as well as a means of making money and dealing with rival gangs. For instance, Tanya says,

> Once you a gang member, you try to get everybody you know in. You be like, 'Girl, you can do this and this and you can make all this money,' and they be like, 'For real? I can have all that, all I got to do is be in the gang?'

At the same time, there is also evidence of gender differences within gangs with regard to criminal involvement. For instance, Bowker, Gross, and Klein (1980) suggest the existence of "the structural exclusion of young women from male delinquent activities" within gangs (p. 516). Their (male) respondents suggested that not only were girls excluded from the planning of delinquent acts, but when girls inadvertently showed up at the location of a planned incident, it was frequently postponed or terminated. Likewise, Fagan (1990) reported greater gender differences in delinquency between gang members than between nongang youth. Male gang members were significantly more involved in the most serious forms of delinquency, although gender differences were not significant for alcohol use, drug sales, extortion, and property damage.

It is likely that girls' participation in delinquency, and especially the extent that male gang members exclude them from activities, is shaped by the gender composition of their gangs. For instance, Lauderback and his colleagues (1992) describe an autonomous female gang in San Francisco—the Potrero Hill Posse—whom they describe as "doin' it for themselves." The Potrero Hill Posse is heavily involved in drug sales, and the behavior and activities of the young women in this gang are very much in line with those typically attributed to male gang members. There is no "structural exclusion" of these young women from certain gang crimes, because they don't have any male members to behave in such a way. In fact, Lauderback et al. (1992) suggest that the Potrero Hill Posse actually came about because these young women were dissatisfied with a "less than equitable . . . distribution of the labor and wealth" (p. 62) that had been part and parcel of their previous involvement selling drugs with males. Nonetheless, most research has shown that all-female gangs account for a small percentage of girls' gang involvement. For example, from interviews with female gang members in three cities, Curry (1997) found that only 6.4 percent described being in independent female gangs, while 57.3 percent described their gangs as mixed-gender, and another 36.4 percent said they were in female auxiliaries of male gangs.

In our research, nearly all of the young women we interviewed were in mixed-gender gangs that were primarily male, and this structure clearly shaped the nature of girls' participation in delinquency. The young women consistently reported little difference in their perceptions of gender-specific roles. Neither did they report any extreme variations in the criminal activities of male and female members of their gangs. However, when pressed, a number of them conceded that their involvement in more serious criminal endeavors was often more limited than young men's. For instance, Erica offers the following explanation:

It's mostly the guys that does all the selling and the, uh, buying. And um, with us, as far as females when it goes to selling, we're always supposed to have a male with us. Always. Or, at least two or three males with us all the time. That way, we can't [get] robbed or anything. Or, if somethin' was to go down, we would always have somebody there with us, instead of by ourselves.

Data from the St. Louis Homicide Project (Decker et al. 1991) also offer support that female gang members are not nearly as involved in the most serious forms of gang violence as male gang members. From 1990 to 1995, there were 207 gang homicides within the study area of this project. Only 17 of these (8 percent) involved female victims, and in only one case was one of the suspects a female (see Brunson 1997). In fact, the homicide involving the female suspect reportedly occurred as she attempted to protect her children from gang members. She was not involved in a gang, but both of her children were being threatened and harassed by local gang members, and she shot the victim after he assaulted her son.[4] When it comes to serious crime, then, male gang members are clearly more involved than their female counterparts. Nonetheless, all of this evidence does suggest that young women in gangs are more involved in serious criminal activities than nongang youths— male or female.

Although one reason there is so much concern about gangs is their criminal involvement, it's important to recognize that not all of gang members' activities are delinquent. In fact, gang members spend much of their time involved in the same activities as other adolescents—hanging out, talking and laughing, playing games, listening to music, or watching television. Gang members are more likely to drink and use marijuana than other youths are, but even these activities re-main well within the purview of nongang adolescent activities. For instance, we asked the girls in our study to describe a typical day with their gang friends, and their responses were nearly uniform. Brandi said,

A typical day would be sittin' back at the park or somethin' like that or one of our friends' houses, or a gang member's house, gettin' drunk, gettin' high, and, you know, watchin' TV, listenin' to the radio.

Likewise, Cookie said,

Get up, get dressed, hit the hood, see what they have on the weed, get some weed, sit around and get high, go to one of the homies' house and just chill, play dominos, play music and stuff like that. Then more homies could come and that's more weed and drink and that [is] a typical day for real, we just sit around and just chill . . . nothing happening.

All of this makes sense, given our discussion in the previous section about why youths, including girls, join gangs. They believe the gang will provide a sense of belonging and support, status and identity, along with recreation and excitement. For some, delinquency is part of the allure, but evidence suggests that some gang members— particularly young women—are somewhat ambivalent about their criminal involvement, even though they report finding it fun or exciting at times. On the one hand, it brings them status and recognition within the group; on the other hand, it can get them into trouble with the law, can put them at risk for being victimized by rival gang members or others on the streets, and may go against their image of themselves. Erica articulated this ambivalence:

In some ways [being in the gang] makes me feel like a person, like actually somebody. But, in other ways, it's like, I don't know. It's, it just doesn't feel right. I mean, 'cause sometimes I sit back and I think that there are other things that I could be doing to get that respect or that attention without bein' in a gang.

It's just not the right picture of my life would be to be part of a gang. . . . I gotta be more aggressive than I have to be with my friends. 'Cause I mean, if I really wanted to I could be a nice person. But around them, I, sometimes I just don't act like that. I act like I'm some real mean bully-type person.

For girls in particular, many aspects of gang involvement—including delinquency—go against dominant notions of appropriate femininity. This shapes girls' experience within and outside of their gangs, often locking them into what Swart (1991) describes as a series of double binds. This point brings us to the last section of our chapter—the consequences of gang involvement for girls, while they're active in gangs and in the long run. Though young people often turn to gangs as a means of meeting a variety of needs within their lives, it is often the case that their gang affiliation does as much or more harm than good—increasing their likelihood of victimization, and decreasing their opportunities and life chances.

The Consequences of Girls' Gang Involvement

As we noted above, girls' gang participation can be viewed as transgressing social norms concerning appropriate "feminine" behavior. In addition, we suggested that within gangs with both male and female members, young women are sometimes excluded from those activities—such as serious crime—that confer status within the gang. Consequently, girls in gangs often face a series of "double binds," in which various courses of action subject them to different penalties or disadvantages. Moreover, there is some evidence of long-term detrimental consequences for gang-involved young women (Moore 1991; Moore and Hagedorn 1996).

Research has shown that girls in gangs face social sanctions, both within and outside the gang, for not behaving in gender-appropriate ways. For instance, Swart (1991) suggests that girls' experiences in gangs are complicated by the contradictions they face as they balance deviant and gender norm expectations. On the one hand, he argues, "The female gang member's behavior must be 'deviant' to those outside of the gang in order to ensure her place within the gang itself" (p. 45). On the other hand, if her behavior is too deviant, a girl risks the danger of offending other gang members who maintain certain attitudes about appropriate female conduct when it comes to issues of sexual activity, drug use, violence, and motherhood. Swart explains further:

> As part of a delinquent subculture, there are expectations of female gang members that are in normative conflict with the larger society; while at the same time gender-typed behavior that is synonymous with that in society as a whole is required. The result is that female gang members must operate within competing and often contradictory normative contexts, in order to find a level of behavior which is 'acceptably deviant' to the other gang members. (p. 46)

These findings are further complicated by evidence suggesting that young women's gang involvement provides a means of resisting limitations placed on them by narrow social definitions of femininity, which they recognize as limiting their options in an environment in which they are already quite restricted. Campbell (1987), for instance, found that

> gang girls see themselves as different from their [female] peers. Their association with the gang is a public proclamation of their rejection of the lifestyle which the community expects from them. (pp. 463–464; see also Harris 1988).

Likewise, Taylor's (1993) study of female gang members in Detroit found them to be highly critical of the entrenched misogyny on the streets and the difficulties females often face interacting in these environments.

Regardless of girls' awareness of gender inequality, it remains an inescapable element of their experiences within gangs and brings with it particular sorts of consequences. For instance, a clear sexual double standard operates within gangs, as in American society as a whole (Campbell 1990a; Fishman 1988; Horowitz 1983; Moore 1991; Swart 1991). In Moore's 1991 study, for example, many of the male gang members admitted that female members were "treated like a piece of ass" (p. 52). Girls' dating options were narrowed as well. Being a Chola and having the look of a Chola was stigmatizing for girls, making them less attractive to boys outside the gang. On the other hand, male gang members frequently had girlfriends outside the gang who were "square," and these "respectable" girls were looked to by the boys as their future (Moore 1991; see also Fishman 1988).

Moreover, research suggests that rather than challenging this sexual double standard, young women often reinforce it in their interactions with one another. Several studies reveal that gang girls create hierarchies among themselves, sanctioning other girls, for being too "square" or for being too promiscuous. Typically, the sexual double standard is reinforced by girls as sanctions against those they perceive as too sexually active. Girls have not been found to gain status among their peers for sexual promiscuity (Campbell 1990a; Horowitz 1983; Swart 1991); rather, they are expected to engage in serial monogamy. Campbell (1987) explains that girls

> not only reject sexual activity outside the context of a steady relationship but even reject friendships with 'loose' girls whose reputations might contaminate them by association. (p. 452)

On the whole, then, the sexual double standard, enforced by both males and females, tends to disadvantage girls in their relationships with boys but also interferes with the strength of their own friendship groups. Campbell summarizes,

> The necessity of being attached to a male in order to have sexual relations, combined with a reluctance to challenge the boy directly over his infidelity, had a very divisive effect upon the girls' relationships with one another. (p. 462)

Our research suggests additional problems caused by gender inequality within gangs, specifically in relation to victimization risk. On the whole, gang participation is likely to involve high risks of victimization. We know, for instance, that delinquent lifestyles in general are associated with increased victimization risk (Lauritsen, Sampson, and Laub 1991). As we have highlighted, gangs are social groups organized around delinquency (see Klein 1995), and participation in gangs escalates youths' involvement in crime, including violent crime. Moreover, research on gang violence indicates that the primary targets of this violence are other gang members (Block and Block 1993; Decker 1996; Klein and Maxson 1989; Sanders 1993). Gang members, then, are likely to be at greater victimization risk than youths not involved in gangs.

Our research suggests that gang girls' victimization risk is also explicitly shaped by gender. Status hierarchies in the mixed-gender gangs we examined were male-dominated. Leadership was almost exclusively male, male members outnumbered female members, and status in the gang was related to characteristically masculine traits—being tough, willing to "do dirt" (e.g., commit crime, engage in violence) for the gang. Though young women could behave in these ways—and many did—it wasn't as necessary for them as it was for young men. Consequently, in some contexts—particularly with regard to rival gangs—girls' lack of involvement in delinquency provided them with greater protection from victimization than male members, because they were less likely to engage in those activities that would increase their exposure to violence. For instance, Lisa, a gang member in our study, noted, "Girls don't face as much violence as [guys]."

On the other hand, because some girls were excluded or excluded themselves from activities that confer status to gang members—such as drive-by's and drug sales—they were often viewed as lesser members within their gangs. Chantell reported her frustration that male gang members often "think that you're more of a punk" when you're a female. This devaluation of young women can lead to girls' mistreatment and victimization, especially by members of their own gang, because they aren't seen as deserving of the same respect. For instance, describing one girl in her gang who was routinely mistreated by the male members, Monica said, "Oh my God, they dog Andrea so bad." Andrea was ordered around and physically assaulted by the members of her gang, but Monica blamed her for it: "I put that on her. They ain't gotta do her like that, but she don't gotta let them do her like that either." Monica and the other gang members viewed Andrea as weak because she didn't stand up to the males in her gang; thus they saw her mistreatment as deserved.

These problems for girls were further exacerbated by the sexual double standard—specifically by the practice of "sexing in" as a form of initiation. Female but not male members could be initiated into the gang by having sexual intercourse with multiple male members. The girls who were initiated in this way were subsequently viewed as sexually available and promiscuous and were mistreated by other members. As Keisha described,

> If you get sexed in, you have no respect . . . when they say you give 'em the pussy you gotta give it to 'em. If you don't, you gonna get your ass beat.

Furthermore, the stigma often extended to female members in general, regardless of whether they were sexed in, creating a sexual devaluation with which all of the girls had to contend. Our findings thus suggest that increased risk of victimization is one consequence of gang involvement for young women.

Thus far we have specifically discussed the impact of gang involvement for girls while they are in their gangs. But what about after they leave? Few studies offer evidence of the long-term consequences of gang involvement for girls (see Moore 1991; Moore and Hagedorn 1996). However, the available evidence suggests that young women in gangs are at greater risk than others for a number of problems into and within their adult lives. Whereas many opportunities for legitimate success are gravely limited for young women living in impoverished communities, the negative consequences associated with gang membership can prove crippling—gang membership exacerbates already troubled lives. Moore and Hagedorn note that while many young women turn to gangs as a means of dealing with multiple life problems, "For most women, being in a gang does have a real impact on later life" (p. 215).

Moore's (1991) research on Chicano/a gang members in Los Angeles found that ex-gang members could be divided into three categories: tecatos, cholos, and squares. She reports that approximately a quarter of the males in her study, and "a much smaller proportion of the female sample" (p. 125) were tecatos—heroin addicts involved in street life; about a third of the men but more of the women were cholos—persisting in gang and criminal involvement into adulthood. Women and men in this category typically had not held down regular jobs and had unstable marriage patterns, often characterized by early marriage and childbearing, followed by early divorce. Finally, she reports that while around 40 percent of the males in her sample went on to lead conventional lives ("squares"), this was the case for fewer of the women.[5]

While Moore's Los Angeles research was about individuals who had been in gangs in the 1950s and 1970s, her more recent work with Hagedorn (1996) followed contemporary African-American and Latino/a gang members in Milwaukee, Wisconsin. They report that substantially fewer of these women continued their gang involvement into adulthood, concluding that "for women—but not for men—the gang was almost completely an adolescent experience" (p. 209). Latinas were more likely to be involved in drug sales and use into adulthood, compared with African-American women. Moore and Hagedorn (1996) conclude that

> For Latinas in both cities, gang membership tended to have a significant influence on their later lives, but for African American women in Milwaukee, the gang tended to be an episode. There is much less sense in Milwaukee that gang girls of any ethnicity were as heavily labeled in their communities as were Chicana gang girls in Los Angeles. (p. 210)

It seems reasonable to suggest that the earlier a girl exits the gang, the greater her chances for a better life. Some evidence suggests that childbearing, and the childrearing responsibilities that come along with it, often facilitate young women's maturation out of gangs. According to Moore and Hagedorn (1996):

> No matter what the cultural context, and no matter what the economic opportunity structure, there seems to be one constant in the later life of women in gangs. Most of them have children, and children have more effect on women's lives than on men's. (p. 211)

In our study, we found that giving birth was often (though not always) very effective in curtailing girls' gang involvement. Only a small proportion of the girls we interviewed had children (15 percent), and others explained that young women typically reduced the time they spent with their gang when they became pregnant.

Though having children may expedite girls' leaving their gangs, doing so does not necessarily increase their chances for successful lives. This is partly because stable marriages and jobs are less available in the current socioeconomic climate than they were in the past. Urban communities where many gangs are located have dwindling numbers of males in the marriage pool; skyrocketing rates of incarceration and lethal violence have greatly contributed to this shortage (Moore and Hagedorn 1996). Moreover, considering the high unemployment rates in most gang neighborhoods, many young men have few conventional opportunities and, as we noted earlier, are therefore increasingly likely to continue their gang and criminal involvement into adulthood. Thus, the bleak futures that await the men in their communities often makes marriage no longer a desirable component of gang-involved women's lives (Moore and Hagedorn 1996). The attacks on many social programs have also negatively affected young women's lives after gang membership. Moore and Hagedorn (1996) make the following observation:

> Ironically, the most important influence on gang women's future may be the dismantling of the nation's welfare system in the 1990s. This system has supported women with children who want to stay out of the drug marketing system and in addition has provided a significant amount of cash to their communities. Its disappearance will deepen poverty and make the fate of gang women ever more problematic. (p. 217)

Conclusion

This chapter has addressed a number of issues concerning young women's involvement in gangs—why they become involved, what their experiences in gangs are like, and the consequences of gang involvement. As we have shown, young people join gangs in response to myriad problems in their lives—impoverished neighborhoods and the resulting social and economic consequences, troubled family lives, abuse, and the desire to belong. However, gang involvement tends to exacerbate rather than improve their problems. Unfortunately, responses to gangs and gang members are primarily punitive, disregarding the social, economic, and personal contexts that cause youth crime and gang participation.

We have not directly addressed policy considerations in this chapter; however, given the information we have provided about the causes and consequences of gang involvement for young women, we believe the issue of how to respond to gangs and gang members is an important one. The current punitive orientation toward gang members means that gang-involved youths are not seen as in need of assistance and protection, and this punishment—coupled with the problems they face in their daily lives—has further detrimental effects. Given the findings we've detailed here, it makes sense that the best course of action with regard to young women's gang involvement should include policies that consider the social, economic, and personal contexts that influence gang participation and gang crime. Initiatives that actually consider the best interest of youths, rather than those reflecting a political climate, are desperately needed in order to rationally respond to gangs and young women's involvement in them.

Discussion Questions

1. What factors are particular to a girl's decision to join a gang?

2. How does gender affect girls' participation in gangs and how they are perceived and treated by male and female members?

3. How are sexual norms for girls in gangs different from those for nongang females?

Endnotes

1. We have just completed a comprehensive study of girls in gangs in two Midwestern cities—St. Louis, Missouri, and Columbus, Ohio. Our sites were chosen because they are representative of new or "emergent" gang cities, rather than traditional gang cities like Los Angeles or Chicago. We completed survey interviews with 94 girls in these two cities, including 48 gang members. We also conducted in-depth qualitative interviews with the gang members. The vast majority of girls in our study were African American, though five of the gang girls in Columbus were white. We had two goals. First, comparing gang girls with nongang girls allowed us to explore what factors help account for why some girls join gangs while others from the same neighborhoods and communities do not. Second, through the in-depth interviews, our goal was to understand the nature and meanings of gang participation for the young women involved. In this chapter, we draw from both sets of findings.

2. This phrase was borrowed from Decker and Van Winkle (1996).

3. These last figures—carrying a hidden weapon and crack sales—are based only on the St. Louis data.

4. In fact, police records indicate that the fatal injury was not inflicted by the female suspect, but rather by an unidentified male who had accompanied her.

5. This finding is partly an artifact of the underrepresentation of "square" women in Moore's (1991) sample. She notes, "Some such women refused the interview because their husbands would not allow them to discuss their 'deviant' adolescence; others refused because they were afraid that they would be questioned about what they now define as 'deviance'—particularly about sexual activity" (p. 130). Moore concludes, "These views offer a poignant confirmation of the stigma attached to women's gang membership" (p. 130).

References

Bjerregaard, B. and Smith, C. 1993. "Gender Differences in Gang Participation, Delinquency, and Substance Use." *Journal of Quantitative Criminology* 4:329–355.

Block, C. R. and Block, R. 1993. "Street Gang Crime in Chicago." *Research in Brief*. Washington, DC: National Institute of Justice.

Bowker, L. H., Gross, H. S., and Klein, M. W. 1980. "Female Participation in Delinquent Gang Activities." *Adolescence* 15(59):509–519.

Bowker, L. H. and Klein, M. W. 1983. "The Etiology of Female Juvenile Delinquency and Gang Membership: A Test of Psychological and Social Structural Explanations." *Adolescence* 18(72):739–51.

Brown, W. K. 1978. "Black Female Gangs in Philadelphia." *International Journal of Offender Therapy and Comparative Criminology*. 21:221–28.

Brunson, R. K. 1997. "Pumping Up the Set: Comparing Male and Female Perceptions of Female Gang Involvement." Paper presented at the Annual Meeting of the American Society of Criminology, San Diego CA.

Campbell, A. 1984. *The Girls in the Gang*. New York: Basil Blackwell.

——. 1987. "Self Definition By Rejection: The Case of Gang Girls." *Social Problems* 34(5): 451–466.

——. 1990a. "Female Participation in Gangs." In C. R. Huff, ed., *Gangs in America*. Newbury Park, CA: Sage.

——. 1990b. "On the Invisibility of the Female Delinquent Peer Group." *Women and Criminal Justice* 2:41–62.

Canter, R. J. 1982. "Family Correlates of Male and Female Delinquency." *Criminology* 20:149–167.

Cernkovich, S. A. and Giordano, P. C. 1987. "Family Relationships and Delinquency." *Criminology* 25:295–319.

Cloward, R. and Ohlin, L. 1960. *Delinquency and Opportunity*. Glencoe, IL: Free Press.

Cohen, A. 1955. *Delinquent Boys*. Glencoe, IL: Free Press.

Curry, G. D. 1997. "Selected Statistics on Female Gang Involvement." Paper presented at the Fifth Joint National Conference on Gangs, Schools, and Communities.

Curry, G. D., Ball, R. A., and Fox, R. J. 1994. "Gang Crime and Law Enforcement Recordkeeping." *Research in Brief*. Washington, DC: National Institute of Justice.

Decker, S. H. 1996. "Collective and Normative Features of Gang Violence." *Justice Quarterly* 13(2):243–264.

Decker, S., Kohfeld, C., Rosenfeld, R., and Sprague, J. 1991. *St. Louis Homicide Project: Local Responses to a National Problem*. St. Louis: University of Missouri-St. Louis.

Decker, S. H. and Van Winkle, B. 1996. *Life in the Gang*. Cambridge: Cambridge University Press.

Esbensen, F. and Huizinga, D. 1993. "Gangs, Drugs, and Delinquency in a Survey of Urban Youth." *Criminology* 31:565–589.

Esbensen, F., Huizinga, D., and Weiher, A. W. 1993. "Gang and Non-Gang Youth: Differences in Explanatory Factors." *Journal of Contemporary Criminal Justice* 9:94–116.

Esbensen, F. and Winfree, L. T. Forthcoming. "Race and Gender Differences Between Gang and Non-Gang Youth: Results from a Multi-Site Survey." *Justice Quarterly*

Fagan, J. 1989. "The Social Organization of Drug Use and Drug Dealing Among Urban Gangs." *Criminology* 27(4):633–667.

——. 1990. "Social Processes of Delinquency and Drug Use Among Urban Gangs." In C. R. Huff, ed., *Gangs in America*. Newbury Park: Sage.

Fishman, L. 1988. "The Vice Queens: An Ethnographic Study of Black Female Gang Behavior." Paper presented at the Annual Meeting of the American Society of Criminology, Chicago, IL.

Giordano, P. C. 1978. "Girls, Guys and Gangs: The Changing Social Context of Female Delinquency." *Journal of Criminal Law and Criminology* 69(1):126–132.

Hagedorn, J. M. 1988. *People and Folks: Gangs, Crime and the Underclass in a Rustbelt City*. Chicago: Lake View Press.

——. 1991. "Gangs, Neighborhoods and Public Policy." *Social Problems* 38:529–542.

——. 1994. "Homeboys, Dope Fiends, Legits and New Jacks." *Criminology* 32:197–219.

Harris, M. G. 1988. *Cholas: Latino Girls and Gangs*. New York: AMS.

Horowitz, R. 1983. *Honor and the American Dream: Culture and Identity in a Chicano Community*. New Brunswick, NJ: Rutgers University Press.

Huff, C. R. 1989. "Youth Gangs and Public Policy." *Crime and Delinquency* 35:524–537.

———. 1993. "Gangs in the United States." In Arnold P. Goldstein and C. Ronald Huff, eds., *The Gang Intervention Handbook*. Champaign, IL: Research Press.

Jackson, P. I. 1991. "Crime, Youth Gangs and Urban Transition: The Social Dislocations of Postindustrial Economic Development." *Justice Quarterly* 8:379–396.

Jankowski, M. S. 1991. *Islands in the Streets: Gangs and American Urban Society*. Berkeley: University of California Press.

Joe, K. A. and Chesney-Lind, M. 1995. " 'Just Every Mother's Angel': An Analysis of Gender and Ethnic Variations in Youth Gang Membership." *Gender and Society* 9:408–430.

Klein, M. W. 1993. "Attempting Gang Control by Suppression: The Misuse of Deterrence Principles." In *Studies on Crime and Crime Prevention*. Stockholm, Sweden: Scandinavian University Press.

———. 1995. *The American Street Gang: Its Nature, Prevalence and Control*. New York: Oxford University Press.

Klein, M. W. and Crawford, L. Y. 1967. "Groups, Gangs and Cohesiveness." *Journal of Research in Crime and Delinquency* 4:63–75.

Klein, M. W. and Maxson, C. L. 1989. "Street Gang Violence." In N. Weiner and M. Wolfgang, eds., *Violent Crime, Violent Criminals*. Newbury Park, CA: Sage.

Klein, M. W., Maxson, C. L., and Miller, J. 1995. "Introduction to Section II." In M. W. Klein, C. L. Maxson, and J. Miller, eds., *The Modern Gang Reader*. Los Angeles: Roxbury Publishing Company.

Lauderback, D., Hansen, J., and Waldorf, D. 1992. " 'Sisters Are Doin' It For Themselves': A Black Female Gang in San Francisco." *The Gang Journal* 1(1):57–70.

Lauritsen, J. L., Sampson, R. J., and Laub, J. H. 1991. "The Link Between Offending and Victimization Among Adolescents." *Criminology* 29(2):265–292.

Maxson, C. L., Woods, K., and Klein, M. W. 1995. "Street Gang Migration in the United States." Final Report to the National Institute of Justice, Washington, DC.

Miller, J. 1995. "Struggles Over the Symbolic: Gang Style and the Meanings of Social Control." In J. Ferrell and C. Sanders, eds., *Toward a Cultural Criminology*. Boston: Northeastern University Press.

Moore, J. 1988. "Gangs and the Underclass: A Comparative Perspective." In J. M. Hagedorn, ed., *People and Folks: Gangs, Crime and The Underclass in a Rustbelt City*. Chicago: Lake View Press.

———. 1991. *Going Down to the Barrio: Homeboys and Homegirls in Change*. Philadelphia: Temple University Press.

Moore, J. W. and Hagedorn, J. M. 1996. "What Happens to Girls in the Gang?" In C. R. Huff, ed., *Gangs in America*, 2nd ed. Thousand Oaks, CA: Sage Publications.

Moore, J. and Pinderhughes, R. 1993. *In the Barrios: Latinos and the Underclass Debate*. New York: Russell Sage Foundation.

Morash, M. 1983. "Gangs, Groups and Delinquency." *British Journal of Criminology* 23: 309–331.

Padilla, F. M. 1992. *The Gang as an American Enterprise*. New Brunswick, NJ: Rutgers University Press.

Quicker, J. C. 1983. *Homegirls: Characterizing Chicana Gangs*. San Pedro, CA: International University Press.

Sampson, R. J. and Wilson, W. J. 1995. "Toward a Theory of Race, Crime and Urban Inequality." In J. Hagan and R. D. Peterson, eds., *Crime and Inequality*. Stanford: Stanford University Press.

Sanders, W. 1993. *Drive-Bys and Gang Bangs: Gangs and Grounded Culture*. Chicago: Aldine.

Short, J. F. and Strodtbeck, F. L. 1965. *Group Process and Gang Delinquency*. Chicago: University of Chicago Press.

Smith, D. A. and Paternoster, R. 1987. "The Gender Gap in Theories of Deviance: Issues and Evidence." *Journal of Research in Crime and Delinquency* 24:140–172.

Soriano, F. I. 1993. "Cultural Sensitivity and Gang Intervention." In A. P. Goldstein and C. R. Huff, eds., *The Gang Intervention Handbook*. Champaign, IL: Research Press.

Spergel, I. A. and Curry, G. D. 1993. "The National Youth Gang Survey: A Research and Developmental Process." In A. P. Goldstein and C. R. Huff, eds., *The Gang Intervention Handbook*. Champaign, IL: Research Press.

Swart, W. J. 1991. "Female Gang Delinquency: A Search for 'Acceptably Deviant Behavior.'" *Mid-American Review of Sociology* 15(1):43–52.

Taylor, C. 1993. *Girls, Gangs, Women and Drugs*. East Lansing: Michigan State University Press.

Thornberry, T. P., Krohn, M. D., Lizotte, A. J., and Chard-Wierschem, D. 1993. "The Role of Juvenile Gangs in Facilitating Delinquent Behavior." *Journal of Research in Crime and Delinquency* 30(1):75–85.

Vigil, J. D. 1988. *Barrio Gangs: Street Life and Identity in Southern California*. Austin: University of Texas Press.

Vigil, J. D. and Long, J. M. 1990. "Emic and Etic Perspectives on Gang Culture: The Chicano Case." In C. Ronald Huff, ed., *Gangs in America*. Newbury Park, CA: Sage.

Wilson, W. J. 1987. *The Truly Disadvantaged: The Inner City, the Underclass, and Public Policy*. Chicago: University of Chicago Press.

———. 1996. *When Work Disappears: The World of the New Urban Poor*. New York: Alfred A. Knopf.

Winfree, L. T. Jr., Fuller, K., Vigil, T., and Mays, G. L. 1992. "The Definition and Measurement of 'Gang Status': Policy Implications for Juvenile Justice." *Juvenile and Family Court Journal*, pp. 29–37. ✦

5

Gender Troubles: The Entanglement of Agency, Violence, and Law in the Lives of Women in Prostitution

Lisa Sanchez

Across cultural and historical divides, women in prostitution remain among the most marginalized of all women. Operating in the shadows of the law and social life, they are both active participants in illicit sexual activities and frequent victims of physical and sexual assault. Yet the complex entanglement of agency and victimization in the everyday lives of women in prostitution remains widely unacknowledged in law and culture. In recent years, feminist scholars have begun to examine these mutually exclusive legal categories of victimization and offending. Moreover, they have proposed that a more contextualized and gender-specific theory of women's crime and punishment must start from the position of those women who are most marginalized in society. It is within the spirit of recent feminist studies that contest these forms of marginalization and seek to complicate rather than reinforce the dichotomy between victimization and offending that this chapter resides.

Female Lawbreakers: Victims or Agents?

In *Sisters in Crime* (1975), Freda Adler proposed that a "new female criminal" had emerged as a result of the advancement of gender equality sparked by the second-wave women's movement. Feminist criminologists have since added layers of complexity to this thesis, some contesting its assumptions entirely and others noting that most women who become involved in illicit activities have yet to reap the benefits of "women's liberation" (Chesney-Lind 1997; Gora 1982; Steffensmeier 1980). Nevertheless, the book stood as a beacon, calling criminologists to take notice that crime and punishment are not the exclusive domain of the masculine gender.

Although many criminologists and urban sociologists continue to presume an abstract (gender neutral) or explicitly male subject as a focal point for the study of crime and urban conflict, feminist criminologists have maintained an interest in building a deeper understanding of the experiences and legal treatment of those women who break the law. A number of recent studies in criminological and sociolegal theory have shown that gender and sexuality function as an interpretive frame that shapes the legal process and gives meaning to particular acts in violation of the law (Daly and Chesney-Lind 1988; Messerschmidt 1993). In addition, some of the earlier studies on rape and battering, prostitution, drug use, and gang activities, for example, separated women's victimization experiences from practices of resistance and active participation in illegal activities. More recently, however, feminist criminologists and sociolegal scholars have begun to view agency and victimization as more closely interwoven (Chesney-Lind 1997; Crenshaw 1994; Daly 1994; Fineman and Mykitiuk 1994; Maher and Curtis 1991; Mahoney 1994; Miller 1993; Musheno 1995; Sanchez 1997).

My analysis of the intersection of agency and victimization in the lives of five women involved in prostitution is drawn from a broader ethnographic study conducted with prostitutes, their customers, and police officers in one American city over a five-year period. To protect the identities of those who participated in the study, I have altered their names and use the pseudonym "Evergreen" to refer to this city. The cultural meanings assigned to prostitution practices and the identities imposed upon the women who practice prostitution are constructed chiefly through legal categories and practices that forge sharp boundaries between victims and offenders. Yet the findings of this study suggest that prostitution is a social practice characterized by both active participation in illicit sexual exchanges and routine subjection to violence.

The next section maps the roots of sexual regulation in the legal institutionalization of separate-spheres ideology and in the history of American sex law. This section discusses how the prostitute identity is shaped in the legal process and is used in the enforcement of prostitution and prostitution procurement or solicitation laws. The third section explores the everyday life narratives of women involved in prostitution, focusing on the relationship between active participation in prostitution and victimization experiences. The fourth section contrasts the regulatory practices of local police officers with participants' knowledge of practice. The chapter concludes by considering how subjection to multiple forms of legal and sexual discipline and exploitation illustrated in the everyday life narratives of the participants of this study might inform a more complex and contextualized conceptual framework for understanding female crime and punishment.

'Women's Place': Sex and Gender Regulation in Historical Perspective

Historically, the exclusion of women from participation in civil and political life and the containment of women in the domestic arena served to preserve traditional gender hierarchies and maintain the conventional family structure. In modern Western societies, legal strategies of exclusion and containment have been achieved primarily through sex law and through the incorporation of the overarching principles of separate-spheres doctrine into the structure of American law. Importantly, sex law and separate-spheres doctrine are spatial forms of gender regulation that attempt to confine women to the private sphere and limit their mobility in public places. Such laws thus articulate "women's place" both in the social order and the geographic landscape.

Rooted in the philosophy of social contract,[1] the ideology of separate spheres developed during the transition from feudalism to capitalism (Pateman 1988). This historical transition, which Carol Pateman has referred to as a transition to "fraternal capitalism," was characterized by a more inclusive, if still limited, distribution of political and economic power from the patriarchs of the feudal system to a broader array of privileged, propertied men (Collier, Maurer, and Suarez-Naváz 1995; MacPherson 1962; Pateman 1988). Internal to the logic of fraternal capitalism, seventeenth and eighteenth century political thinkers separated civil society into public (political and economic) and private (domestic) spheres, but they gave order and attention primarily to the public sphere, and only propertied white men moved freely between the two spheres.

Under the new social order of fraternal capitalism, the "inalienable rights" of citizenship, fundamentally conceived as the right to liberty and equality, were vested only in those men who counted as legitimate, rights-bearing citizens (Pateman 1988; Williams 1991). All others were denied the rights of citizenship and were treated as property themselves[2] or held under the protection and guardianship of these enfranchised men (Hartog 1993; Tushnet 1981; Williams 1991). For example, under the common law doctrine of coverture, married women's civil legal personhood was subsumed under that of her husband (Hartog 1993). Almost without exception, women were precluded from owning property, voting, and publicly participating in politics, and they were commonly prevented from representing themselves in court until the twentieth century.

Vivid illustrations of the legitimation of gender violence under the rule of law are abundant in the annals of American legal history. For instance, within the common law, it was legal for men to beat their wives under certain circumstances. Though wife battery is no longer legally sanctioned or widely tolerated, we have yet to see it completely eliminated from social life. The marital rape exclusion, which protects husbands accused of raping their wives from prosecution in criminal court, provides us with an example of gender subordination that has proven to be even more historically recalcitrant. It was not until the late 1970s that individual states began to remove the marital rape exclusion from the statutes of criminal law, and by 1985 only ten states had completely eliminated the marital rape exemption (Estrich 1987). Although most states have now altered rape laws, a handful have yet to effect reforms of the rape law statutes.

The common law practice of coverture, along with the legitimation of wife battery and marital rape, illustrate the pervasive effects of separate-spheres ideology and the embeddedness of gender subordination in legal and social life. It is not insignificant that many of the key historical examples of legally sanctioned gender subordination take shape around the marital relationship. The primary objective of these laws and the guiding principle in their historical development was to legitimate the conventional structure of kinship and to prohibit alternative family configurations and expressions of sexuality. By confining sex and reproduction to a marital, heterosexual family unit, which could then be separated both discursively and geographically from the other dimensions of social life into a realm of "privacy,"

masculine control could be simultaneously maintained in the domestic sphere and in the public domain of law, politics, and economics.

In spite of the traditional directives of coverture and other legally sanctioned forms of gender confinement, some women could not or would not take a place within the logic and practice of bourgeois domesticity. For example, African-American women in the United States have moved historically from subjection under slavery to primarily devalued positions in the labor force (Hooks, 1981; Williams 1991), and immigrant women have been exploited in underground and informal labor markets without ever enjoying the benefits of citizenship. Similarly, poor and working-class white women were ambiguously positioned in public and private life. Because of their geographic and socioeconomic location, they moved more frequently through visible public spaces. They were considered unfit to take the "privately subordinate" but "protected" position that middle- and upper-class white women occupied in the conventional family structure, and they suffered greater social and economic marginalization. Taken together, the containment and subordination of some women in the private sphere and the sexual exploitation and regulation of other women in the public sphere unfold as a dual-sided disciplinary strategy that establishes "woman's place" in the social order by defining her social position and regulating the spaces in which she can conduct the daily activities of production, reproduction, leisure, and consumption. Though these sociolegal practices have changed over time, the legacy of gender hierarchy remains deeply embedded within the tacit knowledge and collective conscience of American culture, and it continues to be reinforced through the legitimating practices of modern law.

It is in the domain of sex law, and particularly in the enforcement of laws prohibiting prostitution and prostitution procurement, that gender inequality and immobilization most flourishes. Western prostitution developed as a distinct form of commercial sex in the United States and Western Europe during the eighteenth and nineteenth centuries alongside the rise of industrial capitalism (Pateman 1988; Rosen 1982; Walkowitz 1980). During this period, the movement of travelers, immigrant men, and businessmen into the cities was accompanied by a demand for sexually marketable female bodies that many people had begun to view as commodifiable objects within the logic of the capitalist cash economy (Gilfoyle 1992, Radin 1996). In the United States, prostitution was not a distinct criminal offense until the late nineteenth century Progressive era (Lucas 1995; Rosen 1982). However, prostitutes were subject to arrest through vagrancy laws and laws prohibiting nightwalking, public indecency, and disorderly conduct (Hobson 1987; Pateman 1988).

As feminist scholars have noted, the constitution of prostitution as an independent criminal offense was linked to fears and anxieties aroused by nineteenth-century moral crusaders concerned about expressions of sexuality that defied the boundaries of marital, heterosexual monogamy (Rubin 1984; Walkowitz 1980). It was during this era that much of the sex law currently on the books, including the first federal anti-obscenity law and the Mann Act (which intended to curtail "white slavery"), was developed (Rubin 1984). Ostensibly, these nineteenth-century sex laws were directed at forms of sexual conduct that were perceived as immoral. Because laws prohibiting prostitution tended to be disproportionately enforced against women, often without any direct evidence of sexual conduct, these laws can more accurately be seen as criminalizing women's *status* as prostitutes and their occupation of visible public spaces. These laws manage outward expressions of feminine sexuality and sexualization by outlawing visible signs of its manifestation in the public sphere and in visible spaces of sexual commerce.

But outlawing publicly visible signs of commercialized sexual activity did not extinguish (nor did it intend to extinguish) prostitution

as a social practice. Although the provision of "sex services" was considered deviant and immoral, the demand for sexual variation was considered a "natural" and "inevitable" aspect of male sexual desire (Gilfoyle 1992; Hobson 1987; Perry and Sanchez 1997). Any engagement in a serious campaign to abolish prostitution would restrict and punish quite a number of privileged men and business travelers who used brothels and street prostitutes in their destination cities. Thus, rather than eliminate prostitution entirely, nineteenth- and early twentieth-century legal codes delegitimated prostitution and prostitutes symbolically and pushed commercial sex practices and women suspected of prostitution into spaces of privacy or secrecy.

The Legal Construction of the Prostitute Identity and the Spatial Regulation of the Prostitute Body

The history of sex and gender regulation exposes the law as more than a set of objective rules and practices. Rather, sex law and separate-spheres doctrine function as a form of spatial regulation and a representational device in which women are preconceived as sexual by nature. Spatial strategies of exclusion and containment strive to "cover" feminine sexuality and to protect women against sexual exploitation, not by regulating men's conduct but by removing women from public view. Because the sex of prostitution cannot be conducted in plain view, women available for paid sexual exchanges have to be identifiable for the providers and consumers of sex services to converge in space and time. Likewise, for police officers to enforce prostitution laws without the benefit of catching participants in the act, some women have to be identified as prostitutes. Because customers are understood as more elusive and are usually arrested for prostitution *procurement* during special sting operations in which undercover police officers pose as prostitutes, no comparable process of identity inscription is undertaken for customers.

Modern law categorizes women in prostitution—"prostitutes"—by their sexual conduct and makes their involvement in prostitution the central component of their identity. In constructing the prostitute identity and imposing that identity upon some women, the law simultaneously limits women's citizenship rights and withdraws its protection. Prostitutes are "out of place" in two senses of the word. First, as "known prostitutes," they have no legitimate place in the law. Second, the law displaces these women spatially. This displacement takes form not just through the criminalization of specific acts of prostitution, but through laws that criminalize conduct prior to any actual sexual interactions (e.g., solicitation, procurement, and loitering).

What is the relationship between the law and violence, and how does the law construct a relationship between agency and victimization with regard to women's involvement in illicit sex practices? Historically, the law has acknowledged gender violence when third-party witnesses are present and marks on the body are produced (Merry 1995). Although a more complex discourse regarding justifications, gender roles, and intimate relations is entertained in contemporary legal practice, the law continues to focus on the visibility of violence in determining whether and how it will regulate violence. In making these determinations, the law constructs a boundary between legitimate and illegitimate violence (Merry 1995; Sanchez 1997). Similarly, the law constructs some forms of violence as "public" or within its purview and others as "private" (Fineman and Mykitiuk 1994; Thomas 1995). Historically, women have suffered first as victims of violence within spaces constructed as the private sphere, and second as victims of the law's privatization of the violence they experience (Fineman and Mykitiuk 1994; Schneider 1994). For women involved in illegal sexual activities, the consequences are even more serious. Although both these

women and their customers break the law, it is the women who are construed as the sexual outlaws. Women's abusers, on the other hand, are treated as "private enforcers of public morality" (Danielson and Engle 1995, 274).

The state's focus on regulating sexual conduct often blinds it to the victimization of women in prostitution. Implicit in the concept of the "victim" is the notion of innocence (Bumiller 1990; Frohmann 1997). To be a victim, one must be innocent, but to engage in prostitution is to be construed as being an active agent in a criminal offense. In a practical sense, legal authorities claim that they cannot protect women in prostitution from violence and instead ignore, disbelieve, or interpret women's claims of victimization as a failure to collect payment on an "illegal contract" (Frohmann 1997; Kandel 1992). In effect, once a woman is a "known prostitute," she loses the most fundamental aspect of citizenship—ownership of her own body.

The Entanglement of Agency and Victimization in the Everyday Lives of Women in Prostitution

This section explores the relationship between agency and victimization among women involved in prostitution through an interpretation of the everyday life narratives of five women in "Evergreen." Although the sample of participants is limited, the ethnographic method I use places participants' stories within the dynamics of the geographic and social contexts in which their activities take place. As such, it paints a more complex picture of everyday life experiences and provides a more solid interpretational framework for reconceptualizing women's lawbreaking experiences.

All five of the women whose testimonies I will discuss were involved in street prostitution. They ranged in age from 18 to 34 at the time of these interviews. With the exception of one woman, who began prostitution in her mid-20s, all turned their first "date"[3] while they were still teenagers. One of them was initially compelled into prostitution by a boyfriend, who she eventually identified as a pimp. Another began working for an escort service but later turned to street prostitution. The most consistent factors influencing these women's initial involvement in prostitution include age, socioeconomic position, strained interpersonal and family relationships, drug use, exposure to the sex trade via informal social networks and geographic location, and basic needs, such as housing, food, and clothing. Only one of the women in this study had stable housing at the time of her initial involvement in prostitution, one stayed with her grandparents on occasion, and the remaining three frequented motels and "flop houses," searching daily for a place to stay. The unemployment rate in Evergreen is 16 percent for young women age 16 to 20, as compared to 7 percent on the average for all Evergreen residents who can be counted by the Census Bureau. Each of these women had struggled to support herself for an extended period of time, and some had worked jobs in the mainstream economy, but these "straight jobs" did not pay well enough for the women to support themselves on that income alone.

Drug use was also a significant factor shaping women's involvement in prostitution. Three of these young women were addicted to heroin and sometimes used cocaine and methamphetamine as well. One other participant used cocaine on occasion and one was drug-free. Each of these women used alcohol, though none of them appeared or claimed to be addicted to alcohol. For some of these women, drug use came at a significant financial and personal cost, drawing much of their time, energy, and money into supporting their drug habit, procuring and using drugs, and recovering from their drug use. For these women, however, drug use and prostitution did not take shape as a simple cause-and-effect relationship. Only one of these women claimed that she began prostitution to support her drug habit. Others began using drugs to cope with the

risks and insults of prostitution, and others stayed away from drugs completely or kept their drug use to a minimum. However, all women claimed that using drugs or finding some other way to alter their consciousness, at least temporarily, made the experience of prostitution more manageable.

A remarkable illustration of the contradictions between women's agency and their victimization was expressed in one of the first interviews I conducted in the field. "Cory's" road to involvement in prostitution began at age 14, when she left home. Describing a physically and sexually abusive relationship with her stepfather, Cory said, "I was just old enough that I had some options. Just old enough to go out and make a choice." Shortly thereafter, Cory met and moved in with "Mike," whom she described as a "speed cook."[4] With Mike's "help," Cory became addicted to speed and later began using heroin to help her come down from her speed high (regular users of speed report staying awake for one to two weeks at a time).

At age 17, addicted to speed and heroin, Cory began walking the streets of Evergreen after her boyfriend kicked her out of the house. As she put it,

> I first got involved in prostitution by myself. I couldn't take care of the habit I had anymore . . . but I didn't know how much they charged or where to go. So . . . I went down to this one area and just walked and walked before I got brave enough to realize who was stopping and who wasn't stopping.

She explained that even though she got "screwed over" a lot at first, she always met a few people who were "concerned" for her: "They were mostly the guys I dated, told me how to do it."

Cory's explanation that she got involved in prostitution both by herself *and* with the assistance of the guys she met who "told [her] how to do it" highlights the copresent quality of these paid sexual exchanges. *Copresent* interactions refer to face-to-face or bodily interactions in which two or more people interact in the same physical space and time.

The copresent interactions of prostitution differ from constructions of such activities as *rational actions* or *individual choices* because the presence of two active bodies requires negotiation of the desires and intentions of each interacting party and because power differentials between the two interacting parties influence outcomes in a way that favors the more powerful party (see, for example, Boden and Molotch 1994; Giddens 1979; Goffman 1969; and Sanchez 1997, 1999). While Cory did not and could not have engaged in prostitution in social isolation, she refrained from characterizing her involvement as a form of forced sexual abuse or "sexual slavery,"[5] stating that she "did what [she] had to do."

> Cory: You just kinda keep going and make yourself do it because when you got 50 dollars in your hand, all of the sudden, now you know tomorrow you're not gonna be sick [from heroin withdrawal]. So, it makes it pretty easy to go back out. Until you get hurt. Then the first time you get hurt, you get scared when you go back out.
>
> LS.: Have you been hurt before?
>
> Cory: Yeah. Raped, getting beat up and stuff.
>
> LS.: How often would you say that happened?
>
> Cory: Probably a hundred times. The hurt just kinda goes along with it. Getting stranded, having your clothes stolen, having your money stolen, robbed at gunpoint, whatever, all of that. Just hurt.

In Cory's experience, agency and victimization are inseparably linked. Agency surfaces in her narrative as an expression of "practical consciousness." By practical consciousness I mean talk that focuses on "making do" or "doing what has to be done" (de Certeau 1984; Garfinkel 1967; Giddens 1979). The language of practical consciousness is a way of expressing what one does under conditions she would not otherwise "choose," while violence is represented as that part of experience that is unexpected and out of her locus of control. Having become involved in prostitution, Cory's everyday practices involved not only active and copresent participation in illicit sexual activities but also an understanding of how to resist violence. But it is important to remember that basic necessities and physical addictions motivated Cory's participation in prostitution. She understood her activities not as a "free choice" but as a way to get by or make do. This does not mean, however, that she voluntarily consented to everything that happened, as many customers, police officers, and community members assume.

Cory's description of an assault and attempted rape shows how the spatial context of prostitution as framed by conditions of illegality and gender inequality can benefit customers. As Cory explained, a man picked her up in his car and wanted to have sex with her, but she refused because, in her words, "the guy was sketchy." When she asked the man to drop her off where he had picked her up, he pulled a knife on her and attempted to rape her:

> He had the knife right up against my neck. The guy got pissed off at me because I wouldn't shut the fuck up, you know, which was probably stupid, but I was just pushin' as hard as I could push, and I just wanted to get out of there. He was goin' 'No, no, no, give it up, give it up,' and I was saying, 'Get away from me' . . . and I had like maybe a dozen little poke holes that I wasn't aware of at that time, but I could feel it. Finally he just got so pissed off that I grabbed the door handle, and he shoved me out on the ground. I was just thinking I wanted to get out of there as fast as I could. I just wanted to get out alive.

Cory's narrative punctuates the felt experience and volatility of these embodied interactions. Her expressed knowledge of how to resist these sorts of attacks further highlights the role of space and the element of time in these interactions:

> You gotta watch 'em close, and if they move or anything or they turn around and face you in the car, you gotta watch out. You

know, if they got one hand on the wheel, if they slow down and look at you like this, that's not good—I'm like back against the door handle . . . and you never wanta close your eyes when you're with 'em, never, never, never, because it's just that fast and they've got a knife out and you don't really have too many options too quick.

As Cory put it, "Out here you got a 50-50 chance every time you get in a car. Now you know what *time* that is."

Close attention to the microeffects of practice reveal these paid sexual interactions not as arm's-length contractual arrangements or as forced sexual slavery but as dynamic, copresent, and embodied interactions that are structured by gender inequality and marked with conflict. Cory's narrative emphasizes these points: The potential for violence was always linked to her efforts to "do what [she] had to do."

Similar contradictions between agency and violence emerged in the stories of two teenage girls, "Helen" and "Mary," who had each participated in street prostitution and heroin use for over a year at the time of these interviews. At ages 17 and 18, Helen and Mary had met each other in a psychiatric inpatient clinic and had subsequently run away together both from the clinic and from their families. In one conversation, Helen and Mary began to discuss their vulnerability to violence within their life context. The two girls agreed that Helen was "picked on" more often than Mary because Mary "tells it like it is":

Mary: I tell 'em if I don't want to do something. I tell them.

Helen: Yeah, I tell them too. But you're more assertive than me.

Mary: I'm very, you know, like they push your head down when you start a blowjob or something, I say, 'No.' I can't handle it—being forced or manhandled.

It was clearly important for Helen and Mary to represent themselves as the authors of their own life experience. But the fact that

their actions formed in relation to being "manhandled" or forced to perform sexual acts in ways that they did not expect highlights the centrality of violence and coercion in shaping the girls' understandings of what it means to participate actively in prostitution. A conversation between the girls about a situation in which Mary was raped illustrates the degree to which routine subjection to violence shaped daily life and contributed to the girls' desensitization to their own victimization.

Mary: There was this one time I was raped. It's been quite a while actually.

Helen: Yeah, but he didn't really, I mean he just barely got in you.

Mary: Helen woke up and helped me out. I was sleeping.

Helen: Then she woke up and he was in her. Then we just left. He crashed, passed out, and we stole twenty bucks from him. We just did it 'cuz of what he did. We didn't really need the money.

Mary: Well, he deserved it.

Helen: In a way he paid for it too.

L. S.: Was he one of your dates or just some guy you were hanging out with?

Mary: No, he was just drunk . . . or he was . . .

Helen: No, he was not. I thought he was a date.

Helen and Mary debated over whether this man had been a "date" or just some guy who "wanted to party." Then Helen decided that he was "just drunk." Turning her attention to Mary, Helen said, "He picked us up and took us to a Holiday Inn. He seemed nice, too. Then he just turned on you. He wasn't being violent. He was just really horny and he took advantage of you." Casually, Mary replied, "He ordered some pizza."

What is most striking about Helen and Mary's matter-of-fact representation of these events is that in the space of a few hours, a number of extraordinary events (represented as ordinary) had taken place. The girls had been picked up by an older man with the means to rent a hotel room, and they had "partied" with this man and fallen asleep, at which time Mary was raped. They then stole $20 and left the room only to return to the city streets in the middle of the night. Yet there was some confusion between the girls about their role in these exchanges and about whether Mary had "really" been raped. But the girls' concurrence that stealing $20 from this man was justified indicates that they had a sense that this man had mistreated them, and both of them took comfort in what *they did* to rectify the situation. Although the men that Helen and Mary dated probably perceived their sexual involvement with these two young girls as an expression of sexual desire, the girls experienced these interactions as violent and coercive. In spite of their mutually undisputed understanding of their overall role as active agents in prostitution, they described their activities as, in a word, "survival."

The kinds of experiences Helen and Mary described were not uncommon among the women who participated in this study: for every negotiation that went smoothly, the possibility that the next one would end in violence or conflict was great. The examples of active participation in prostitution represented here cannot be interpreted as freely chosen "sex work," nor can they be interpreted as the blanket enforcement of sexual slavery. Rather, these young women's articulation of their experiences suggests that acts of prostitution take shape as practically oriented sexual interactions and as tactics of resistance within the violent and unpredictable spaces of the Evergreen sex trade.

Some of the young women were initially compelled into prostitution by a pimp. At age 12, "Meagan" was "hanging out downtown" when she met a guy who later became her boyfriend: "Here was this older guy telling me he loved me, and that made me feel secure. I finally realized he was a pimp after about one month. People told me." Meagan then went on to detail how her "boyfriend"

eventually convinced her to start turning dates:

> Meagan: [Darryl] needed some money and asked if I would work, and I said no. Finally I said I'd try once, so his brother's girlfriend took me out. I didn't know how much to charge, so I came back with too little money, and he beat me up severely.
>
> LS.: How much did you get?
>
> Meagan: Ninety dollars. I didn't want to leave him and the security I had. But he changed. He became highly controlling. I couldn't talk to anyone . . . The beatings still occurred; he would get mad for no reason. I had to go in the hospital twice. I was 14 by that time.

Meagan's discussion of a rape that she was subjected to underlines some of the same kinds of conflicts that surfaced in the other girls' lives. Describing two different occasions in which she was raped, Meagan stated that the first man was "nice" and "didn't intend to hurt [her]," but she described the second experience as a "violent rape":

> This other man who raped me, he raped me violently. He had a gun, and then afterwards he told me he was sorry. 'I'm so sorry.' He dropped me off and I went to the hospital and I was all beat up.

Unlike what Cory described, Meagan thought she would be better off just to "get it over with." She did, however, attempt to deal with the situation after the fact by reporting it to the police. But, according to Meagan, the police officer told her that it was her own fault and refused to take a report. Having had her claim ignored, Meagan turned to extralegal channels to deal with the problem:

> The tables got turned around on him though at the end, because I did get his license plate number [even though] no one [referring to the police] listened to me. I had a guy [customer] that worked at the DMV and I had this man's license plate number and I found out where he was at and so a bunch of people, you know, beat him up. That made me feel better.

The legal construction of women in prostitution as "offenders" who are unrapable by virtue of their involvement in prostitution had serious consequences for Meagan. Paralleling the testimonies of the other women who participated in this study, Meagan emphasized what she did to handle the situation. She foregrounded what was within her control, while the violent and coercive context of prostitution and the legal practices that facilitated her abuse remained in the background, framing her every action.

As a final illustration of the entanglement of agency and violence in these women's everyday lives, I turn to a story provided by "Amanda," who was the oldest, most experienced, and probably least marginalized individual who participated in this study. Amanda was working as a secretary when the owner of an escort service asked whether she would be interested in taking some clients. Amanda expressed her opinion of prostitution using a language of sexual liberation and free choice: "If two consenting people want to do that and it's comfortable for both of them, so be it." However, as our conversation progressed, Amanda's articulation of her own reasons for becoming involved in prostitution unfolded as deeply rooted in violence:

> When I was raped at gunpoint, this was a way for me to get men to give me their money for me having the control. [So you thought of it that way?] That's right, revenge. It's like, you want it, you pay for it, I'll tell you when, I'll tell you how, I'll tell you why.

For Amanda, active participation in prostitution was a kind of payback or "revenge" against men who had previously abused her.

The practices described in the foregoing narrative analysis involve bodily contact and cannot be reduced to a single moment of choice. They are better understood as a series of copresent, embodied interactions negotiated and renegotiated for the duration of each interaction. Although women frequently use a language of choice to describe

their actions, their narratives are shaped by their social and economic situation, by the context of practice, by legal/regulatory practices, and by the desires and demands of their customers. Although the women in this study each represented themselves as active participants in prostitution, they do not "choose" many of the interactions that took place, nor do they "choose" the conditions under which the actions occurred. Under these conditions, the women who participated in this study at best negotiated an interaction that satisfied their instrumental needs and the emotional and physical desires of their customers. Often, however, agency in these interactions played out as active resistance and survival tactics.

Policing Identities, Policing Space

In this section I look at the legal construction and imposition of the prostitute identity and question the separation of agency and violence into mutually exclusive categories by analyzing the everyday practices of Evergreen police officers. The Evergreen Metropolitan Police Bureau distributes specific prostitution enforcement duties to patrol, prostitution detail, and vice. Each neighborhood is patrolled by a different precinct within the bureau, and individual precincts occasionally conduct "prostitution missions" in their area. Prostitution detail officers and street patrol officers in each precinct handle the day-to-day enforcement of prostitution and prostitution procurement, and the vice division investigates cases of promoting and compelling prostitution. Detail and patrol officers can arrest women for prostitution procurement if the women have taken significant action toward procuring prostitution, meaning they have been spotted flagging down cars, hitchhiking, lingering at phone booths and street corners, or walking the street alone in a "high vice" area. If a woman makes an explicit offer to exchange sex acts for money, she can be charged with prostitution (city ordinance, police interview, 4/97).

I have intentionally chosen to use the feminine subject to describe the target of police officers' enforcement practices. In my conversations and ride-alongs with police officers, many described their enforcement of the law prohibiting *prostitution procurement* in explicitly gendered terms, but they did not seem to understand their practices as unfair and even unlawful gender discrimination. In everyday conversation, police officers rationalized their enforcement practices, claiming that "women *walking* the street" were more visible and more likely to be the subject of a "citizen complaint" (field conversations, 3/97, 8/97). One officer even stated that "prostitution procurement applies just to the girls, whereas the guy gets a prostitution charge" (police interview, 3/97). Though the procurement ordinance is worded in gender neutral terms, most officers refrain from enforcing the law against male customers because men's solicitation practices—*driving* up and down the same street in a privately owned car—are seen as more elusive than women's solicitation practices.

The officers viewed these unevenly gendered enforcement practices as innocuous because, after all, the men get a prostitution charge. But procurement is the more frequently used charge, since prostitution is presumably harder to prove. By police officers' own accounts of their practices, procurement is thought to be an easy charge but only if the subject of the charge is a woman. In addition to treating women's habits of conduct as disproportionately actionable, officers often rely on a woman's prior record of prostitution as testimony to her guilt in the event that she attempts to contest the charge in court. The Evergreen Police Bureau claims gender neutrality in the enforcement of prostitution laws and supports its claim by publicizing arrest statistics gathered in *prostitution missions*, which target female solicitors and male buyers primarily. However, the majority of prostitution arrests come from the *day-to-day enforcement* of prostitution procurement. The same women are often arrested repeatedly for violating the prostitution procurement law, while a vastly larger number of individual men who engage in prostitution never get arrested. Predictably, the bureau rarely publishes statistics on daily arrests for prostitution procurement in the local news media.

From these enforcement practices, we can locate the construction of "suspicious activities" at the intersection of discourses of gender, sexuality, public space, and socioeconomic status. While male customers *driving* the boulevards are arguably just as "visible" as women *walking* the streets, police officers implicitly locate men's activities within the normal range of masculine conduct; such practices are perceived as natural expressions of masculinity and sexual desire. As one officer stated, "It's a quick, easy deal [for men who have a] high sex drive." Continuing, he explained that these men often have "personal problems and dysfunctional sexual relationships with their wives; 85 percent want blowjobs and their wife won't do it." Male customers are further privileged by the mobility and privacy that property ownership—in this case, ownership of a car—signifies. While the officers believe they have to catch a man "in the act" or have tight evidence of an explicit offer to enforce the law, their practices more realistically reflect the power differential between these marginalized women and male customers, who have the status and resources to contest questionable police practices.

The language police officers use to describe their enforcement practices makes explicit their unself-consciously gendered construction of prostitution. Male customers are viewed as nameless, faceless bodies while the bodies of the women are inscribed with the prostitute identity. This is not just a matter of semantics. Police practices operate quite concretely as surveillance and recordkeeping practices directed specifically at the women. For example, prostitution detail officers keep a book with them during their patrol that contains the names, addresses, telephone numbers, birth dates, and partial information on the criminal record of women with prior prostitution convictions. During a ride-along, a detail officer proudly claimed that he was the best person for the job because he was the "most knowledgeable" officer on the force—he had a "great memory for names, faces, and birth dates" (field conversation, 8/97). When asked whether he used the same techniques to monitor male customers, the officer said he didn't keep records on the customers because "to do Johns, you have to have decoys." In other words, customers can only be arrested during prostitution missions. Continuing, the officer added, "If I stop a man just because he has a prostitute in his car, he would deny it and say that he was only giving the girl a ride" (8/97). By contrast, the officer claimed that the woman could not deny it: "Even if they deny it, they know I know what they're doing."

Additionally, the precincts and the vice division keep a book of mug shots of women who have been convicted of procurement or prostitution within the previous few years. Although the police encourage citizens to take photographs of men thought to be engaging in prostitution, these photographic records are not maintained on file in the bureau. Rather, the act of taking a man's photograph is thought to deter him from further involvement in prostitution (police interviews, 3/97, 8/97, neighborhood association meeting, 8/97). Presumably, male customers are not considered a threat to the community but rather are seen as behaving in mischievous but predictably understandable masculine ways. Mirroring the unevenly gendered enforcement of late-nineteenth-century statutes prohibiting vagrancy, nightwalking, and disorderly conduct, the contemporary enforcement of legal prohibitions against prostitution is designed to regulate the activities of prostitutes and would-be prostitutes. In essence, these laws are like *status offenses*, making it illegal to be *identified* as a prostitute and to occupy visible public spaces. They are effective visibility-management tools that make nomads out of women in prostitution by requiring them to "keep moving."

Perhaps even more troubling are the discrepancies engendered in the process of taking rape and assault reports. Evergreen police officers sometimes file reports of rape and assault against women who are actively engaged in prostitution when the initial call comes from a hospital or social service agency, or when the crime can be linked to pimping or organized crime (police interviews, 8/97). However, by the officers' own admissions and women's testimonies, the police are far less likely to take a report when the complaint comes directly from the victim. As one woman explained,

> I flagged [an officer] down after I had been raped, and he didn't even give me the time of day. He said, 'It's your fault you're out here. I've got other things to do than worry about that.' I think it's wrong. It's a crime that was committed, and every crime should be looked at the same—just because he was an *honorable* citizen doesn't give him the right to hurt me.

Negative experiences of this sort compound women's problems and make them more reluctant to report physical and sexual assault to the police. The men who pick them up are aware of that fact and frequently take advantage of it. One male customer summarized the situation this way:

> I feel sorry for [these girls] because I have so much and I see that they have nothing. I mean they carry their clothes in a paper sack, and many times they even lose those. One of the girls I know got raped and then thrown out into the road without her clothes, and the only reason [these guys] can get away with it is because no workin' girl is gonna call the cops. So they're preying upon them is what they're doing.

Conclusion

This chapter has focused on the entanglement of agency and victimization in women's illicit lives and livelihoods, and it has critiqued the artificial separation of these two interrelated dimensions of experience into mutually exclusive domains through the imposition of legal identity categories and spatial forms of sex and gender regulation. Legal discourses on prostitution, like those illustrated in field interviews with police officers, oversimplify women's agency and misunderstand the negotiated quality of paid sexual exchanges. My analysis of women's testimonies illustrates that the necessary preconditions for making choices—knowledge, alternatives, power, and safe space— are absent in women's sphere of activity. First, women's material needs act in concert with the demands of customers to draw women into the sex trade and shape their ongoing participation. Second, women's initial involvement and daily practices are not individual, but copresent, embodied interactions. Finally, violence is used routinely as a definitive trump card on women's agency, drawing their energy into avoiding and resisting victimization.

Understanding the copresent quality of sex trade participation sheds light on the conflicted narratives of these women, particularly the tension between their agency and their victimization. While it is clear that women consent to, and in fact initiate, many of their activities, they also face unsolicited pressures and violations on a regular basis. Irrespective of the fact that women acknowledge the routine violence and marginalization in their lives, none of these women represented themselves as passive victims. They are active participants in the process of negotiating sexual interactions and resisting physical and sexual abuse. The fact that women's activities can neither be interpreted as those of a free agent—or as those of a helpless victim is testimony not to women's confusion, but to contradictions that are structured into the practice of prostitution.

The details of these negotiated interactions constitute a particular microstructure of practice whose continuities have to do with power relations and whose disjunctures have to do with the multiple positionings of those involved and the various tactics women use to cope with their situation. Domination of women's personal (bodily) space and the physical space in which prostitution takes place is one of the primary strategies of power used by customers and perpetrators. Importantly, this kind of spatial territoriality is also used by police officers who target women in their enforcement practices. Together, these spatial strategies of sexual regulation reproduce a long history of gender confinement and exclusion that is deeply rooted in American law. A woman can only respond to this kind of power by engaging in tactics of resistance and moving into spaces of secrecy. Paradoxically, the very tactics that women use to resist violence and police surveillance increase their chances of being victimized.

Can a more just strategy be conceived to regulate prostitution? The problem presented by the displaced woman of prostitution is that she faces multiple forms of oppression. She is not simply an offender to be punished or a victim to be recovered. She has no place in the community and no voice in law, politics, or society. To be sure, more just legal practices must recognize the multiple displacements and oppressions she faces. Opening space for women to speak in the public forum provides a good first step toward empowering women in prostitution. A second role for advocates is to provide these women with the tools for subverting the law's power to construct their identity and to limit their access to fundamental legal rights. The criminal justice system has been complicit with the sexual exploitation of these young women, while treating customers with relative impunity. Prostitution laws that criminalize women's status and speech should be challenged on the basis of their constitutionality, and law enforcement practices that facilitate exploitation and abuse should be challenged on the basis of their legitimacy.

Supporting these women's right to bodily integrity does not equate to legitimating broad-scale sexual commodification in legal and deregulated commercial sex markets. Other research has shown that women operating in loosely regulated, ostensibly legal, sex businesses, such as exotic dancing and escort services, are also subject to exploitation and are not necessarily any less victimized (Sanchez 1997). As part of the process of capital accumulation and market specialization, "open markets" of commercial sex lead to accelerated processes of commodification and sexual exploitation (Sanchez 1997). Under favorable market conditions, the number of sex clubs also tends to increase rapidly, necessitating an increased supply of expendable and marginalized workers (Sanchez 1997). Perhaps a preferable alternative strategy would be to decriminalize or remove the penalties for those who engage in prostitution. Reducing enforcement efforts against women in prostitution would free up resources that could be used to enforce laws prohibiting third-party profiteers from promoting and compelling prostitution. Given these women's stories, some of the men who are considered "customers" are in violation of the laws prohibiting promotion and compelling and would also be subject to arrest. At the same time, police departments and other regulatory agencies need to concentrate on limiting the expansion of legal sex businesses and on controlling the exploitation and abuse of women working in legal sex businesses by regulating employer, *not employee*, practices.

Ideally, these strategies stand to benefit women, but an overly narrow focus on the big legal questions of prohibition, legalization, and decriminalization leaves as unacknowledged, unrepresented, and effectively sacrificed the many women who continue to engage in prostitution under conditions of illegality. As we continue to debate and wait for the big legal question to be resolved, laws prohibiting serious violent crimes are already in place. Knife-point rape, kidnapping, and assault to the point of medical emergency would not be so readily tolerated under any other circumstances, save perhaps the position of prisoners and undocumented workers. When the victim is a "known prostitute," people all too often shrug their shoulders and feel safe in the knowledge that her victimization can be explained by her failure to obey the code of proper feminine sexuality. Thus, perhaps even more immediately, a campaign is needed to pressure law enforcement to engage in more serious efforts to enforce existing laws prohibiting crimes of sexual violence, *even when the victim is a "prostitute" and even when the violence occurs during an act of prostitution.*

Perhaps the hardest question is how to effect movement in the political economy so that women would have more humane and lucrative opportunities to support themselves. Given the continued history of gender and economic subordination, it is unclear what it would take for young, working-class women to participate more fully in the mainstream economy. Economic change has come slowly for older, middle-class women, but young women are already in a position of limited economic citizenship. While it is expected that all girls will be protected and financially supported by their families at least until the age of majority, many poor and working-class girls, like the ones who participated in this study, do not enjoy such reasonable benefits.

In this chapter, I attempted an alternative representation of women's experiences by paying attention to the relationship between agency and violence in the everyday lives of a small group of women. My interpretation should be considered contingent and locally specific, but it may provide a theoretical framework for developing a more contextualized and participatory knowledge of sex trade practices. Identifying sites of resistance to sexual exploitation and discriminatory legal practices can provide a small ray of hope in a generally dark domain. Thus, as researchers and advocates, we can whittle away at small pieces of the larger techniques of power operating in commercial sex markets and their regulatory bodies.

I end this chapter by highlighting women's voices. To quote Amanda:

> There's a really big price to be paid [for some of these offers]. There's a certain level of confidentiality that's necessary, and in those circles, all they do is pass you around. . . . Obviously, the price to be paid is that you have no freedom. . . . and they pay you big bucks because you're being paid for your silence.

By far, our most important role is to listen to what this silence tells us.

Discussion Questions

1. What is "fraternal capitalism"? How does it differ from "patriarchy," which is a term more commonly used in feminist theory?

2. Discuss the ideology of separate spheres. Give some examples of how this ideology has been incorporated into American legal and cultural practices.

3. What is the difference between criminal *status* and illegal *conduct*, and how are these dimensions of the criminal law constructed and enforced with regard to prostitution?

4. What are some of the potential strategies discussed for developing more just legal treatment of women in prostitution? Do you agree or disagree with the author's approach? Can you think of other strategies that were not mentioned?

Endnotes

1. The social contract was a political philosophy and informal social pact that effected a transfer of ownership of land and property from the patriarchs of the feudal system to the rising bourgeois class of merchants and other privileged men (MacPherson 1962; see also Locke 1689 for original writings developing the political philosophy of social contract).

2. The law of chattel slavery, for example, treated black men and women as "objects or property" who were denied the rights of citizenship and civil personhood (Tushnet 1981; Williams 1991).

3. The women in this study use the term "dating" to refer to exchanges of sex acts for money, which is more commonly known as prostitution.

4. A "speed cook" is someone who prepares methamphetamine, also known as speed, crank, or crystal meth, for sale.

5. See, for example, Kathleen Barry's (1979) discussion of prostitution as female sexual slavery. While her book, *Female Sexual Slavery*, represents a groundbreaking study of sexual trafficking and abuse, many of the women involved in prostitution, particularly those operating in Western democratic countries and those operating in their own neighborhoods without a pimp or other third-party profiteer, have rejected the characterization of their activities as a form of sexual slavery.

References

Adler, F. 1975. *Sisters in Crime*. New York: McGraw-Hill.

Barry, K. 1979. *Female Sexual Slavery*. New York: Basic Books.

Boden, D. and Molotch, H. L. 1994. "The Compulsion of Proximity." In Roger Friedland and Dierdre Boden, eds., *NowHere: Space, Time and Modernity*, Berkeley: University of California Press.

Bumiller, K. 1990. "Fallen Angels: The Representation of Violence Against Women in Legal Culture." *International Journal of the Sociology of Law* 32:125–42.

Chesney-Lind, M. 1997. *The Female Offender: Girls, Woman, and Crime*. Thousand Oaks, CA: Sage.

Collier, J. F., Maurer, B., and Suarez-Naváz, L. 1995. "Sanctioned Identities: Legal Constructions of Modern Personhood." *Identities* 2 (1–2):1–27.

Crenshaw, K. 1994. "Mapping the Margins: Intersectionality, Identity Politics, and Violence Against Women of Color." In Martha Albertson Fineman and Roxanne Mykitiuk, eds., *The Public Nature of Private Violence*. New York: Routledge.

Daly, K. 1994. *Gender, Crime and Punishment*. New Haven: Yale University Press.

Daly, K. and Chesney-Lind, M. 1988. "Feminism and Criminology." *Justice Quarterly* 5:497–538.

Danielson, D. and Engle, K. (eds.) 1995. *After Identity: A Reader in Law and Culture*. New York: Routledge.

de Certeau, M. 1984. *The Practice of Everyday Life*. Los Angeles: University of California Press.

Estrich, S. 1987. *Real Rape*. Cambridge: Harvard University Press.

Fineman, M. A. and Mykitiuk, R. (eds.) 1994. *The Public Nature of Private Violence*. New York: Routledge.

Frohmann, L. 1997. "Convictability and Discordant Locales: Reproducing Race, Class, and Gender Ideologies in Prosecutorial Decision-Making". *Law and Society Review* 31:533–55.

Garfinkel, H. 1967. *Studies in Ethnomethodology*. Englewood Cliffs, NJ: Prentice Hall.

Giddens, A. 1979. *Central Problems in Social Theory: Action, Structure, and Contradictions in Social Analysis*. Berkeley: University of California Press.

Gilfoyle, T. J. 1992. *City of Eros: New York City, Prostitution and the Commercialization of Sex, 1820–1920*. New York: Norton.

Goffman, E. 1969. *Strategic Interaction*. Philadelphia: University of Pennsylvania Press.

Gora, J. 1982. *The New Female Criminal: Empirical Reality or Social Myth*. New York: Praeger.

Hartog, H. 1993. "Abigail Bailey's Coverture: Law in a Married Woman's Consciousness." In Sarat and Kearns, eds., *Law in Everyday Life*. Ann Arbor: The University of Michigan Press.

Hobson, B. M. 1987. *Uneasy Virtue: The Politics of Prostitution in the American Reform Tradition*. New York: Basic Books.

hooks, b. 1981. *Ain't I a Woman: Black Women and Feminism*. Boston: South End Press.

Kandel, M. 1992. "Whores in Court: Judicial Processing of Prostitutes in the Boston Municipal Court in 1990." *Yale Journal of Law and Feminism* 4:329–52.

Locke, J. 1689. *Second Treatise of Government*. (C.B. MacPherson, trans.) Indianapolis: Hackett Publishing Company, 1980.

Lucas, A. M. 1995. "Race, Class, Gender and Deviancy: The Criminalization of Prostitution." *Berkeley Women's Law Journal* 10:47–60.

MacPherson, C. B. 1962. *The Political Theory of Possessive Individualism: Hobbes to Locke*. Oxford: Oxford University Press.

Maher, L. and Curtis, R. 1991. "Women on the Edge of Crime: Crack Cocaine and the Changing Contexts of Street-level Sex Work in New York City." *Crime, Law, and Social Change* 18: 221–58.

Mahoney, M. R. 1994. "Victimization or Oppression? Women's Lives, Violence, and Agency." In Martha Albertson Fineman and Roxanne Mykitiuk, eds., *The Public Nature of Private Violence*. New York: Routledge.

Merry, S. E. 1995. "Narrating Domestic Violence: Producing the 'Truth' of Violence in 19th- and 20th-Century Hawaiian Courts." *Law and Social Inquiry* 19:967–93.

Messerschmidt, J. W. 1993. *Masculinities and Crime: Critique and Reconceptualization of Theory*. Lanham, MD: Rowman and Littlefield.

Miller, J. 1993. "Your Life Is on the Line Every Time You're on the Streets." *Humanity and Society* 17(4):422–442.

Musheno, M. 1995. "Legal Consciousness on the Margins of Society: Struggles Against Stigmatization in the AIDS Crisis." *Identities* 2(1–2): 101–122.

Pateman, C. 1988. *The Sexual Contract*. Stanford: Stanford University Press.

Perry, R. and Sanchez, L. 1997. "Transactions in the Flesh: Toward an Ethnography of Embodied Sexual Reason." *Studies in Law, Politics and Society* 18:29–76.

Radin, M. J. 1996. *Contested Commodities*. Cambridge, MA: Harvard University Press.

Rosen, R. 1982. *The Lost Sisterhood: Prostitution in America, 1900–1918*. Baltimore: Johns Hopkins University Press.

Rubin, G. 1984. "Thinking Sex: Notes for a Radical Theory of the Politics of Sexuality." In Carol Vance, ed., *Pleasure and Danger*. New York: Basic Books.

Sanchez, L. E. 1997. "Boundaries of Legitimacy: Sex, Violence, Citizenship, and Community in a Local Sexual Economy." *Law and Social Inquiry* 22(3):543–580.

——. 1999. "Sex, Law and the Paradox of Agency in the Everyday Lives of Women in the 'Evergreen' Sex Trade." In Stuart Henry and Dragan Milovanovic, eds., *Constitutive Criminology at Work: Agency and Resistance in the Constitution of Crime and Punishment*. New York: SUNY Press.

Schneider, E. M. 1994. "The Violence of Privacy." In Martha Albertson Fineman and Roxanne Mykitiuk, eds., *The Public Nature of Private Violence*. New York: Routledge.

Steffensmeier, D. J. 1980. "Sex Differences in Patterns of Adult Crime, 1965–1977." *Social Forces* 58:1080–1108.

Thomas, K. 1995. "Beyond the Privacy Principle." In Dan Danielson and Karen Engle, eds., *After Identity: A Reader in Law and Culture*. New York: Routledge.

Tushnet, M. 1981. *The American Law of Slavery: 1810–1860, Considerations of Humanity and Interest*. Princeton, NJ: Princeton University Press.

Walkowitz, J. R. 1980. *Prostitution and Victorian Society: Women, Class, and the State*. New York: Cambridge University Press.

Williams, P. 1991. *The Alchemy of Race and Rights: Diary of a Law Professor*. Cambridge: Harvard University Press. ✦

6

Gender and Violence

Candace Kruttschnitt

This chapter offers a broad overview of the correlation between acts of violence and gender, including the causes of violence, the relationship between social and economic inequity and crime, and the dynamic between victimization and offending. The author examines national and international crime rates, the particular context of crime, including age, race, and social circumstances, and several theories of crime. In addition, she reviews the historical relationship between gender and crime, as well as more recent trends in the gender and crime area, particularly drug use.

Although many scholars acknowledge the sizable gender gap in criminal violence, relatively little advancement has been made in our understanding of this phenomenon. This chapter argues that much can be gained by looking at gender and violence in broader historical and social perspectives. Incorporating these perspectives, the chapter examines both aggregate- and individual-level data on gender and violence and compares the violent activities of women and men. It considers several levels of explanation for the gender-violence relationship, contrasting those that attempt to explain the persistent lower rate of female violence relative to male violence with those that address shifts in gender and violence over time and place.

Empirical Evidence on Gender and Violence

A wide range of data permit scholars to assess gender differences in violent crime. The most well-known data for addressing this issue in the United States come from the Uniform Crime Reports (UCR) and the National Crime Victimization Surveys (NCVS). It is beyond the scope of this essay to review the strengths and limitations of these data, as well as other subnational (e.g., surveys of violence in the home, records maintained by police departments and hospitals) and international databases.[1] Instead, recognizing the limitations of existing measurement systems, this chapter assumes that such data can be used to assess basic patterns and trends in the violent crimes committed by men and women. Given the attention devoted to UCR data in research on gender and crime, I begin with a brief review of these data drawn only from previously published works. I then reference cross-national and historical data to determine the generalizability of current U.S. patterns and the social processes that may aggravate or mitigate gender differences in violence.

Macro-Level Data on the Gender Distribution of Violence

Over the decades from 1960 to 1990, UCR data indicate considerable variability in the rates of violent crime in this country. Although media projections have reinforced a view of ever-increasing violence in American society, as well as more violence among women, the data do not reflect this pattern. Violence rose in the 1960s and 1970s, peaked in 1980, and then declined in the early 1980s; it began to rise again after 1985 and continued to increase through the first part of the 1990s (Roth 1994). Yet, underlying these swings is a relatively constant rate of violent female offending. The female rates of homicide remained constant at 2 percent over the three decades; while there were some notable increases in women's rates of aggravated and simple assaults, even these increases were relatively small by comparison to the increases in male rates in these same offense categories. As a result, the absolute gender gap in violent crime (male rate minus female rate) continued to widen (see Kruttschnitt 1994; Steffensmeier and Allan 1996). Data from the NCVS, which elicits information from crime victims about the characteristics of offenders, also suggest that female participation in crimes of violence is low (e.g., about 7 percent of robberies, 12 percent of aggravated assaults and 15 percent of simple assaults) and remained stable since the mid-1970s (Steffensmeier and Allan 1996).

Despite the obvious importance of determining whether these gendered patterns of violence appear in other societies, relatively little comparative research on women's involvement in violent crime has been undertaken. In part, this is because of the difficulty of obtaining valid and reliable cross-national data, but it is also a result of the predominance of the gender equality hypothesis (Adler 1975; Simon 1975) and the resulting scholarly focus on female arrest rates for property offending over the past few decades.

Cross-national data. Aggregate cross-national research on gender differences in offending is primarily based on analyses of INTERPOL data, covering various years between 1950 and 1980, and anywhere from 14 to 69 nations at widely differing stages of development (see Kruttschnitt 1995). Because homicide is used as the indicator of violent crime in all studies that rely on INTERPOL data, our knowledge of women's participation in other crimes of violence in other societies is severely limited.[2] Nevertheless, several interesting patterns can be gleaned from these analyses. First, consistent with data from the United States, the female contribution to the homicide rate is uniformly below the male rate in all nations and has remained relatively stable over the past 20 years. In fact, in most countries there has been a slight decline in the female percentage of arrests for homicide (see e.g., Messner 1985; Simon and Baxter 1989). Second, despite women's relatively small and stable contribution to national homicide rates, their arrest rates for homicide do vary substantially across nations. For example, during the early 1970s, the female arrest rate for homicide was four times greater in the United States than in Australia and twice as great in the Bahamas as in the United States (Messner 1985). Cross-cultural analyses of specific types of homicide (e.g., spousal, infanticide), as well as homicide victimization, also reveal substantial national variations in women's risks of encountering violence (Daly and Wilson 1988; Gartner 1990). The important question then arises as to why such variation occurs across societies.

Numerous studies find strong associations within nations between female and male homicide rates, and between overall arrest rates and female arrest rates, suggesting that the same social conditions affect crime rates irrespective of gender (see, for example, Messner 1985; Simon and Baxter 1989; Steffensmeier, Allan and Streifel 1989). This may explain why scholars have been generally unsuccessful in their attempts to identify significant covariates of the proportionate female murder rates (Kruttschnitt 1995), as well as the substantial similarity found between the predictors of male and female victimization rates in developed nations (Gartner 1990).

If attempts to derive gender-specific explanations for cross-national variations in violence are limited, it would seem important to direct our attention to the most consistent predictor of homicide rates, irrespective of gender, across nations and over time. In cross-sectional analyses of homicide, income inequality is consistently and positively associated with homicide rates. In time-series analyses designed to highlight the effects of social change, it has been found that economic inequality, disrupted family structures, and cultural support for violence are positively related to homicide rates in developed nations (Gartner 1995).

Women's crime in historical perspective.
Another way of determining how social
structures and social processes influence
men's and women's involvement in criminal
violence is to step back from this century to
see how social life may have shaped the relationship between gender and crime in earlier
times. In reviewing historical data, it is important to remember that the usual problems of reliability and validity of crime statistics (e.g., reporting systems relying on the
judgments about criminal acts made by offenders, victims, and officials) are compounded. Prior to the nineteenth century,
there were no police forces and no official records of persons charged with crimes (Lane
1980). Therefore, most of the information
we have on crime during these earlier periods comes from analyses of court records for
specific years in selected jurisdictions, counties, or cities (see Gurr 1981 for a more complete explication of this issue). Further,
despite the growing number of excellent historical accounts of crime and justice in Europe and elsewhere, systematic attention to
the relationship between gender and violent
crime is more limited.

Historians who have examined the long-
term trends in interpersonal violence, most
notably in England but also in other countries, have found a general decline or "civilizing process" over the past two to three centuries (Elias 1978; Garland 1990; Gatrell,
1980; Gurr 1981, 1989). This decline appears
to have affected women as much as men,
and crimes of violence as much as property
crimes (Beattie 1986; Boritch and Hagan
1990; Emsley 1996; Feeley and Little 1991).
This finding suggests that the social conditions influencing the control of violence affected all individuals irrespective of their
gender, and it contradicts the popular notion
that the criminalization of men and women
represents distinctive processes that require
unique explanations. Nevertheless, underlying these broad similarities in the declining rates of male and female violence is the
fact that the number of women adjudicated
for felonious offenses before this century

may have been three times as high as it is
today (Feeley and Little 1991; Hull 1987;
Zedner 1991). The question then arises as to
what social processes were responsible for
women's movement to the periphery of violent crime in the twentieth century. Several
explanations have been offered. Among
these, the most common is the increasing
subjugation of women to informal social
controls.

Feeley and Little (1991), examining criminal cases in London for the period 1687–
1912, systematically ruled out a number of
alternative explanations for what they call
the "vanishing" female criminal. These include, for example, selective reporting, shifting jurisdictions, short-lived enforcement
policies, the effects of war, and demographic
shifts. They concluded that, with the rise of
industrialism, women's social roles changed
dramatically. Women's work outside the
home rapidly declined over the course of the
nineteenth century, and the patriarchal control of women within the household intensi-
fied. Further support for this interpretation
can be found in analyses of urban and rural
crime. Despite the move to colonize women
in the home, urban areas always provided
women with less restricted environments,
and it appears that women committed not
only more crimes but also a wider range of
offenses in urban than rural areas (Beattie
1975; Hanawalt 1979; Rude 1985; Shoemaker 1991).

Overlaying these shifting social roles were
shifts in the legal and judicial system. Although the precise legal status of women
during the eighteenth and nineteenth centuries is subject to some debate, the acceptabil-
ity of women in the formal criminal process
was declining. It was during this period that
the crime of infanticide required formal
prosecution for the first time, and evidence
suggests that juries were increasingly reluctant to find women guilty of this offense.[3] It
was also during this period that Sir William
Blackstone declared that married women
had no separate legal identity from their husbands. This status not only affected their le-

gal culpability but also their legal avenues for redressing spousal violence (Emsley 1996). Zedner's (1991) analysis of nineteenth-century court records in England and Wales suggests that women were further removed from legal sanctions by the trend to medicalize their illegal behavior. She argues that during this period, serious female offenders were no longer seen as "depraved" but instead "feeble-minded."

This trend to remove women from formal legal sanctioning, subjecting them instead to informal systems, expanded in the twentieth century. In Toronto, both a private arm of the police department designed to deal with domestic assaults and a private court for female offenders were established to divert all but the most hardcore female offenders from formal legal processing (Boritch and Hagan 1990). In the United States, there is evidence that the police increasingly targeted those women who were subject to the least informal social control, as indicated by their age and single and minority statuses (Giordano, Kerbel, and Dudley 1981; see also Kruttschnitt 1985).

Scholars of female crime have been preoccupied with the relatively recent trends in official data from the United States. Yet both historical and cross-national data suggest that this preoccupation may be misplaced. The enormous social and economic changes that occurred in Europe and America over the past two centuries reduced violent offending for both men and women. It is generally felt that industrialization and urbanization encouraged more constraint and cooperation first among the upper and middle classes and then gradually in the lower classes. The prohibitions against violence were also reinforced by changes in the legal system (the introduction of police, the significant expansion of prosecution, the introduction of more "civilized" forms of punishment) and other informal systems of social control such as mandatory schooling (Gurr 1981, 1989; Lane 1980). Women were particularly affected by changes in household

economies and the growing concerns with morality as the Victorian ideology about women's social roles became firmly entrenched. It seems likely, then, that these developing systems of social control had a more substantial impact on women's, than men's, declining involvement in crimes of violence.

While this historical and cross-national focus allows us to assess the significance of social processes in shaping aggregate patterns of violence among both males and females, it ignores the particular individuals and the particular contexts in which violence occurs.

Micro-Level Data on Gender and Violence

The focus in this section is on how individual-level factors, such as age, race, and situational context, are related to the likelihood that women and men will be involved in crimes of violence. Are these patterns consistent across different data sources, times, and places, and can they inform our understanding of the aggregate-level data on gender and violence?

The demographics of violence. Violent crime in the United States has traditionally been concentrated with respect to age and gender. More than two-thirds of those arrested are age 30 or younger, irrespective of gender (Kruttschnitt 1994; Sampson and Lauritsen 1994). UCR data indicate that, for both males and females, the peak ages for robbery and assault are highest from the mid-teens to the late twenties. For murder, however, male and female involvement is distributed slightly differently over the life course. Female involvement peaks later, in the twenties, and continues at a relatively stable, albeit low, rate through the thirties; the comparable male rate drops off in the thirties. A frequent explanation for this gender difference is the greater likelihood of women being involved in familial homicides

(Daly and Wilson 1988; Maxfield 1989; Wolfgang 1958). The general stability of these patterns over the past 30 years has led some scholars to claim that this age-crime relationship is invariant over time and place (Gottfredson and Hirschi 1990). Yet recent data from the United States, Europe, and Australia indicate some increase in the proportion of females under the age of 18 arrested for violent crimes (Cook and Laub, forthcoming; Heidensohn 1991; Kruttschnitt 1995).

Violent crime in the United States has also been concentrated with respect to race. Among both males and females, blacks and other minorities are overrepresented in comparison to their representation in the population. Unfortunately, relationships among race, gender, and violence have not been well explicated. Some argue that this is a result of the politically sensitive nature of the issue (Simpson 1989); others point to the failure of the UCR to provide gender-race breakdowns in national-level data on violent crime. Nevertheless, most of what is known about the interaction between gender, race, and crime comes from homicide studies conducted in specific cities at various periods of time. These studies uniformly suggest that race may be a better predictor of violent crime than gender: Black women are more frequently involved in acts of lethal violence than white women and the homicide rates for black females are closer to those for white males than for white females (Kruttschnitt 1994). These findings have been replicated in other, albeit limited, studies of violent crime arrest rates in selected cities and states (Sommers and Baskin 1992; Steffensmeier and Allan 1988), in reports of violent crime victimizations perpetrated by juveniles (Laub and McDermott 1985) and in self-report data on assault (Ageton 1983; Hill and Crawford 1990).

One way of putting these findings into perspective is to examine how the interaction of gender and race influences crime in other cultures. Although scholars outside of the United States have generally paid far less attention to the racial distribution of offending, what is known suggests that the high rates of homicide among black females in this country may have little to do with their race. Black women living in both predominantly black countries, like Nigeria, and predominantly white countries, like Canada, do not have unusually high rates of violent crime. Additionally, analyses of the sex ratio of killing for blacks (homicides perpetrated by women per 100 by men) reveal that these ratios are unusually high only for spousal homicides and only for blacks in the United States (Kruttschnitt 1995). It seems likely, then, that black women's elevated risk of involvement in homicides is directly related to their and their partners' unique, and relatively disadvantageous, position in the U.S. economy and culture. This might also explain why meta-analyses of the correlations reported in U.S. studies examining sex, race, and violent crime reveal that the presence of statistical controls (for social status, family structure, and community characteristics) reduced the effect of race on violence but had no effect on the magnitude of the sex-violence relationship (Bridges and Weis 1989).

The context of violent offending. An equally important aspect of micro-level data on violent offending is the specific situations in which it occurs, which can help to shed light on the sources of violence. These include "those factors, outside the individual, that influence the initiation, unfolding, or outcome of the violent event" (Sampson and Lauritsen 1994, 30). The best source of uncovering these factors as they pertain to *both* women and men is homicide studies. The homicide research completed over the past 30 years is quite extensive. This review excludes anecdotal studies (i.e., media accounts and offender biographies) and clinical or case studies (which include much of the research on battered women who kill their abusers), and instead focuses on larger studies from which generalizations about victim-offender relationships and circumstances of the offense can be derived. Additionally, as allowed by the available research, efforts are made to determine whether gender moderates the context of other serious violent crimes in similar ways.

Several characteristics define violent encounters in modern state societies, irrespective of gender. These encounters are confined primarily to the poor and the unemployed and those with a history of deviance; they appear to be primarily intraracial (with the exception of felony homicides) and geographically bounded in areas of high poverty; and they are frequently associated with, but not necessarily causally related to, alcohol and drug use (Block and Christakos 1995; Cooney 1997; Daly and Wilson 1988; Mann 1996; Sampson and Lauritsen 1994; Sommers and Baskin 1992). Despite these similarities, some features of violent encounters appear to be conditioned by the gender of their participants.

Although most homicides involve people who know each other, women are far more likely to target family members than men. Findings from the United States, Canada, and England and Wales all indicate that less than half of women's lethal acts occur outside of the family, whereas over two-thirds of men's violence is directed toward nonfamily members (Mann 1996; Wilson and Daly 1992). This gender difference in targets reveals much about the motivations underlying different forms of violence. Men are more likely to kill strangers in the course of committing felony homicides and to kill acquaintances as a result of altercations over status competition and "face-saving" (Daly and Wilson 1988; Polk 1994; Wolfgang 1958). Although women's involvement in these activities is relatively rare, when they do occur the outcomes appear to be the same. Female robbers target strangers, and nondomestic assaults involving females reportedly occur as a result of an attempt at vindication or to restore personal integrity (Campbell 1984; Sommers and Baskin 1993).

Within the confines of family relationships, there is considerable variability across time and place in the probability that a spouse or child will be killed by a female offender. In fact, the killing of intimate partners by women is the one area where women approach gender equality with men in the United States. As previously noted, however, evidence suggests that this effect is race-specific and confined to African-American females (Block and Christakos 1995; Mann 1996). In other countries, the sex ratio of spousal killings is quite skewed. Women may even be more likely to target their children than their spouses, as is the case in England and Wales, or to change their targets from children to spouses over time, as is the case in Australia (Wallace 1986; Wilson and Daly 1992).

To examine these shifts in the targets of lethal female intimate violence over time, a few scholars have looked to women's legal relationships to their intimates, particularly as they are codified in divorce and abortion laws (Gillis 1996; Kruttschnitt 1995), but also as they pertain to domestic violence services (Dugan, Nagin, and Rosenfeld 1996). These studies suggest that the quality of legal resources may be an important correlate of explaining female violence against intimates. Where these resources are unavailable or do not function properly, women may resort to lethal actions to address their perceived wrongs (see Black 1983; Gauthier and Bankston 1997).

Two other factors commonly noted as important correlates of the situational context of violence are the presence of co-offenders and weapon use. It is frequently assumed that women are led into crime by men or engage in it on their behalf (Brownstein et al. 1995; Steffensmeier and Allan 1996). It is also thought that the availability of weapons increases the likelihood that assaults will result in lethal outcomes (Block and Christakos 1995). Both of these assertions should be qualified on the basis of the offender's gender and the crime setting. Women appear to be more likely to commit robberies with a partner, but not necessarily a man, and to act alone in the commission of an assault or homicide (Kruttschnitt 1994; Mann 1996; Sommers and Baskin 1993). The latter finding probably reflects the fact that most such crimes unfold in domestic settings and involve the use of guns and knives. However, lethality in these settings is not simply a function of the availability of these weapons. Men, but not women, are frequently reported to have beaten their partners to death (Block and Christakos 1995; Mann 1996; Wolfgang 1958).

Although much has yet to be uncovered about the situational correlates of both men's and women's violent offending, the research gaps are particularly notable in the case of female offenders. For example, there is mounting evidence that offending and victimization are strongly correlated; offenders and victims share similar demographic profiles and lifestyles, and, controlling for sex, violent offending increases victimization risk just as victimization increases the risk of offense involvement (Sampson and Lauritsen 1994). Whether gender conditions the relationship between victimization and offending, however, remains unclear. Some scholars suggest that prior victimization is less likely to produce subsequent offending in females than in males (Lauritsen 1997; Widom 1989). Others point to the importance of the types of lifestyles linked to victimization and the fact that women are less likely to lead such lifestyles (Miethe and Meier 1994), hence lowering their probability of offending (cf. Sommers and Baskin 1993). A related issue is the lack of information on nonviolent events. Violent crime data are incident-based and accordingly produce no information on situations that involve comparable characteristics but that result in nonviolent outcomes (Sampson and Lauritsen 1994). Are there important gender differences in responses to potentially violent contexts that would help explain women's aggregate lower arrest rates for violent offending?

To summarize, current research provides only the most rudimentary understanding of the situational factors that may influence violent offending. Without information on women's involvement in a wider range of violent crimes (e.g., Baskin and Sommers 1993) in various times and cultural contexts, we can only guess about the processes that are actually responsible for the longstanding relationship between gender and violence. Despite these limitations, scholars have tried to explain this relationship on varying analytical levels.

Explanations for the Gender-Violence Relationship

Perhaps the one fact that has had the most substantial impact on the character of the explanations for the gender-violence relationship is that women's rates of violent offending remain lower than men's in virtually all times and places. Add to this fact the frequently noted relational character of women's violence, and the result has been a scholarly focus on biological and related psychological explanations for the observed gender difference. The influential reviews of Maccoby and Jacklin (1974, 1980) of cross-cultural studies of aggression, studies of sub-human primates, experimental manipulation of sex hormones, and studies of "presocialized" children lead many developmental psychologists to one conclusion: Males may be biologically predisposed toward aggressive behavior. Despite counter-arguments that point to the inconsistencies in the experimental animal research, in the cross-cultural data (Tieger 1980; White 1983), and, more generally, in the literature on biology and aggression (Archer 1991; Hyde 1986), the influence of this perspective has been formidable. It can be found in the work of prominent sociologists (e.g., Gottfredson and Hirschi 1990; Gove 1985) and policymakers (Wilson and Herrnstein 1985). Clearly, then, for some the "ubiquity of gender differences has been enough to support or prove biological causation"; for others it is the exceptions in the research literature that provide the needed ammunition to invalidate the arguments of biological causation (Hood 1996, 309–310). It may be impossible at this time to sort out the complex relationships between sex and gender, or nature and nurture. Nevertheless, few would disagree that gender is imposed on sex by culturally and historically determined patterns of socialization and that its influence on individual behavior is profound. Thus, explanations for the gender-violence relationship that are based on the influence of social roles and opportunities within and across varying social contexts should be particularly relevant.

Socialization for Aggression

Scientists who advocate nurture over nature point to gender differences in the learning of and socialization for aggression. From this perspective, gender differences in violence are seen as directly related to differential reinforcement for aggressive acts among boys and girls. Boys are more likely than girls to have their aggressive acts condoned or reinforced, and girls are more likely than boys to have their acts of aggression ignored or extinguished. However, the empirical evidence on which this model rests is, at best, equivocal. Lytton and Romney (1991) conducted a meta-analysis of 172 studies of parental socialization of boys and girls in an attempt to determine in which, if any, areas of socialization mothers and fathers treat sons and daughters differently and the extent of the differences they make. This analysis, which included "discouragement of aggression" as a socialization area, revealed relatively few sex-distinctive parental socialization pressures that would explain the gender-violence relationship. In North American studies, the only socialization area that produced a significant effect for both parents was the encouragement of sex-typed activities, but even these effects were fairly mod-

est. In studies conducted in other Western countries, physical punishment appeared to be applied significantly more to boys than girls, but this finding is based on a relatively small number of studies (n = 5).

The lack of a strong effect of parental socialization on sex-stereotypic behavior is particularly important given the dominant place of gender roles in explanations for female crime and delinquency. Parental attachments have been a central focus in social control theory (Hirschi 1969), especially in its application to delinquent development in girls. More recently, the focus on gender role socialization shifted to an examination of the effects of the adoption of nontraditional gender roles on female offending. This occurred first with the popularization of the liberation thesis in the 1970s (Adler 1975) and second with the development of power-control theory in the 1980s (Hagan, Simpson, and Gillis 1987). Tests of these theories have, however, failed to produce any systematic body of empirical evidence that would support either the proposition that sex-stereotypic gender roles/attitudes reduce female offending or, conversely, the idea that proscribing nontraditional gender roles increases female crime or aggression (Kruttschnitt 1994, 1996; Steffensmeier and Allan 1996). Although research linking gender roles and crime, and especially violent crime, has not been very informative, the key to understanding the influence of gender roles and violence may lie in the specific social situations and contexts in which gender roles are actualized. This might explain, for example, why aggression among both boys and girls can be either tempered or aggravated by experimental stimuli and why the effects of the adoption of nontraditional gender roles on violence by and against women appears to be conditioned by women's social status (Bettencourt and Miller 1996; Kruttschnitt 1994, 1995; Wilson and Daly 1992).

Despite the fact that much violence takes place among youth, the specific influence of peers on the development of aggression has received less attention in the scholarly literature than the influence of family has. Nevertheless, recent empirical studies of gangs, which include a systematic analysis of the nature and extent of criminality by both male and female gang members, provide important clues to the socializing influence of peers. Gang affiliations serve to amplify the delinquent and aggressive behaviors of both males and females. However, while the delinquency of female gang members exceeds that of male nongang members, it is still lower than that of male gang members. Gender differences in peer associations and the ways in which girls' peer groups serve to explicitly limit outward expression of aggression in girls—in favor of ostracism, social exclusion, or what Hood (1996) calls "social sabotage"—may also, then, contribute to the noted gender gap in violence (see also Brunson and Miller, this volume; Kruttschnitt 1996).

Situational Explanations for Violence

Although there can be little question that most criminological research on violent offending focuses on the early socialization of offenders, attention has been directed to the specific situations in which violence occurs: the targets of, and the opportunities for, crime. Perhaps the best-known situational explanation for crime is routine activity/lifestyle theory.[4] This theory argues that the convergence of potential victims and offenders in the absence of suitable guardians will lead to a greater risk of crime, independent of individual motivations (Cohen and Felson 1979). Research on routine activity and lifestyle theories as they pertain to victimization risk is now fairly well established, even providing some indication of the factors that increase women's risks of violent crime victimization over time and within different cultural contexts (Kruttschnitt 1995). The implications of this approach for offending have, however, developed much more slowly, especially as they pertain to gender and violent offending. One reason for this scholarly

omission may be the predominantly relational nature of women's violent crime. Some scholars argue that focusing on the causal significance of the key concepts of routine activity theory (e.g., victim proximity, exposure to dangerous physical environments) makes little sense when the offenses involve offenders and victims who are well known to each other. It is assumed that such crimes are motivated by specific grievances that can be resolved any place, any time (Miethe and Meier 1994). There is some empirical evidence pertaining to femicide that supports this claim (Gartner and McCarthy 1991), but other data, which focus on victimization and household composition, might call it into question (Maxfield 1987). Until scholars explicitly address the applicability of routine activity/lifestyle theory to domestic violence, its ability to account for a large proportion of violent female offending will remain unknown.[5]

It is also difficult to determine whether this perspective provides an adequate explanation for the gender gap in nonintimate acts of violence (e.g., robberies, stranger assaults) because of the systematic inattention to females in these offense categories. The recent focus on the relationship between violent crime and the illicit drug industry has, however, provided some relevant data and hypotheses. Traditionally, scholars speculated that, because of the greater guardianship and supervision of females (Riley 1987; Riley and Shaw 1985), women would be less likely than men to be in the locations and situations that are conducive to nonintimate violent offending. More recently, however, it has been argued that shifts in the contemporary drug economy have placed more women on the streets in situations conducive to this type of violent crime (Fagan 1994; Inciardi and Pottieger 1994).[6] Despite the uncertainty as to whether there are, in fact, more women dealing drugs today than in the past, ethnographic studies of women who have committed violent crimes in the context of the drug market suggest perhaps more gender similarities than differences in the nature of their illicit activities. Women are reported to be opportunistic in targeting their victims and choosing the location of their offenses and rationale in protecting their economic interests (Brownstein, et al. 1995; Sommers and Baskin 1993).

Drug dealing and violent crimes are behaviors, and often lifestyles, that are situated in neighborhoods and communities. Although the broader research on routine activity theory suggests that disorganized and crime-ridden neighborhoods exert independent effects on the risk for victimization and offending (Sampson and Lauritsen 1994), we have much to learn about how this process occurs, and especially as to whether it differs for men and women. What are the neighborhood contexts and individual interactions within these contexts that seem to aggravate violent male offending and mitigate violent female offending (e.g., peer group involvement, single-parent households)? How are they influenced by the surrounding community characteristics, and do they shift over time?

Structural Explanations for Violence

The theoretical focus of structural or macro-level research on violent crime has centered primarily on the potentially criminogenic effects of economic inequality, cultural attitudes toward violence, and weakened social controls. Each of these factors has been used to explain variations in violent crime rates across cities, standard metropolitan statistical areas, and nations. However, attention to gender differences in the violent crime rates within any of these macro-units of analysis is virtually nonexistent. The only exception is a handful of studies that attempt to predict either national or international gender variation in homicide victimization (see Bailey and Peterson 1995; Kruttschnitt 1995). At this point, then, we can only speculate as to the relevance of these perspectives for understanding some of the shifts observed in the gender gap in violent crime over time and place.

Economic Inequality

"According to perspectives as diverse as evolutionary psychology, Marxism and anomie theory, economic stress resulting from inadequate or unequal distribution of resources is a major contributor to high rates of interpersonal violence" (Gartner 1990, 95). The crucial question in addressing the value of these different perspectives for gender differences in violent offending may depend on whether we focus on the *inadequate* or the *unequal* distribution of resources. Daly and Wilson (1988) argue that the absolute rate of inequality increases family homicide, the type of violence in which we are most likely to see women and hence most likely to observe shifts in the gender gap in violent crime. It is also the area in which we are most likely to see significant racial variations, especially in societies like the United States that have higher rates of economic and social stratification. It could be argued, then, that the particularly high rates of spousal homicide among black women in the United States are simply a function of the lowered economic value of black males in the United States. Black males escalating their violence toward their intimates, as a result of their own economic frustrations, may be more likely to encounter retaliation. However, we know that in other economically marginal cultures in the United States (e.g., Hispanics), as well as economically stratified countries, the gender gap in homicide is more pronounced (Wilson and Daly 1992). This suggests that we must also take account of the ways in which other social factors contribute to aggregate violent crime rates.

Cultural Norms

The macro-research on violent crime rates has directed attention to both the subculture of violence theory (Wolfgang and Ferracuti 1967) and modeling (Straus 1983).

In both cases it is assumed that underlying values proscribe or inhibit violent behavior. However, scholars who have focused specifically on gender also draw attention to the norms that regulate women's behavior in specific cultures. Cross-cultural research indicates, for example, that in certain societies women have stronger matrilineal linkages than in others, and in some societies males dominate all aspects of family life, including restricting the female's access to divorce (Kruttschnitt 1995; Wilson and Daly 1988). Thus, norms concerning the proper roles for women and the access they have to resources for escaping violence are also quite relevant to our understanding of the variations in the gender gap in violence over time and place. These factors have, in fact, been used to explain the lesser likelihood of Hispanic, as opposed to African-American, women's violence toward their spouses (Gauthier and Bankston 1997), as well as the decreased gender gap in victimization in societies where women have a relatively greater involvement in nontraditional social roles (Gartner, Baker, and Pampel 1990).

Social Control

In aggregate studies of homicide, it is assumed that a high rate of family dissolution weakens both formal and informal social controls, which in turn increases propensity toward violence. Research shows that this situation applies to both family and non-family homicides (Williams and Flewelling 1988). Relatedly, scholars have also drawn attention to the proportional representation of female-headed households in communities, showing its import in mediating the effects of unemployment on the rates of homicide and robbery among both blacks and whites (Sampson 1987; see also Phillips 1997). Based on both historical and cross-cultural analysis (Gillis 1996; Kruttschnitt 1995), we might expect that marital dissolution would reduce intimate female violence, as it provides women with an avenue of escape from unsatisfactory marriages. How-

ever, it is also well known that some of the most severe violence between intimates occurs once couples have separated (Fagan and Browne 1994). Perhaps it is under these circumstances, or when women have no economically vested interest in marital union (Wilson and Daly 1992), that their tolerance for abuse ceases and they resort to marital violence. Certainly, our understanding of these relationships will require more fine-tuned analyses that can disentangle the potential reciprocal effects between intimate violence and marital separation.

Conclusion

A number of implications can be drawn from this review. Here, I draw attention only to what may be considered the most important: We have achieved relatively little understanding of the gender-violent crime relationship. Although it is commonly assumed that this situation is due to the general lack of interest in female offending, I do not believe this to be true. Since the 1970s we have witnessed a tremendous growth in the research on women and crime. The problem, however, is that this growth has been largely unscientific. There has been little effort to consciously build a body of scholarship that would systematically address and build upon prior research pertaining to both men's and women's violence. Sociologists in the United States have been preoccupied with the effects of the women's movement on female criminality, despite the empirical and theoretical demise of this perspective (Kruttschnitt 1996). In so doing, they have also consistently ignored the historical and, albeit limited, cross-national work that should be critical to developing general propositions about the causes and conditions under which men and women engage in acts of criminal violence. We would all be well served by remembering that social factors not only contribute to the causes of crime but also structure our ability to understand it.

Discussion Questions

1. What are the predominant patterns that appear in the empirical research on gender and violence? How have these patterns changed over time?

2. What relevance do cross-cultural or cross-national data have for our understanding of the relationship between gender and violent crime?

3. How can historical and cross-cultural data on gender and violence be used to inform theory?

Endnotes

1. For an excellent overview of the difficulties of measuring violent crime, including those inherent in both UCR and NCVS data, see chapter 2 of the National Research Council's report on *Understanding and Preventing Violence* (Reiss and Roth 1993). For a comparable critique of international databases on violent crime, see Gartner (1995).

2. Cross-national homicide data from official sources are generally considered to be more reliable than other crime data for many analytic purposes, but they also have their limits (see Archer and Gartner 1984).

3. Until 1803, the crime of infanticide was tried under the Act of 1624, which confined the offense to unmarried women. Women charged with infanticide under this act had to prove that their child had been born dead. No doubt this was an attempt to control the behavior of lower-class women who may have had more tolerant views of premarital sex than the propertied classes and thus had higher illegitimacy rates (Stone 1977). The Act of 1803 made infanticide equivalent to any other murder, with the prosecution required to prove the offense (Emsley 1996).

4. Although routine activity and lifestyle theories are frequently combined, they do have different origins. Routine activity theory was initially developed to account for changes in crime rates over time. Lifestyle theory, in contrast, seeks to account for distribution of victimization risks across various social groups (Miethe and Meier 1994).

5. For example, victim proximity might be measured by marital status, and measures of lifestyle should include some of the noted correlates of domestic violence (e.g., prior victimization, frequency of alcohol use).

6. This is not to say that women's positions, or occupations, in the drug economy have substantially changed. Most evidence indicates that women's ability to participate as higher-level drug distributors is as limited today as it was in the past (Maher and Daly 1996; Steffensmeier and Allan 1996).

References

Adler, F. 1975. *Sisters in Crime*. New York: McGraw-Hill.

Ageton, S. 1983. "The Dynamics of Female Delinquency, 1976–1980." *Criminology* 21:555–584.

Archer, D. and Gartner, R. 1984. *Violence and Crime in Cross-National Perspective*. New Haven: Yale University Press.

Archer, J. 1991. "The Influence of Testosterone on Human Aggression." *British Journal of Psychology* 82:1–28.

Bailey, W. C. and Peterson, R. D. 1995. "Gender Inequality and Violence Against Women. The Case of Murder." In J. Hagan, ed., *Crime and Inequality*. Stanford, CA: Stanford University Press.

Baskin, D. and Sommers, I. 1993. "Females' Initiation into Violent Street Crime." *Justice Quarterly* 10:559–583.

Beattie, J. M. 1975. "The Criminality of Women in Eighteenth Century England." *Journal of Social History* 8:80–116.

———. 1986. *Crime and the Courts in England, 1660–1800*. Princeton NJ: Princeton University Press.

Bettencourt, B. A. and Miller, N. 1996. "Gender Differences in Aggression as a Function of Provocation: A Meta-Analysis." *Psychological Bulletin* 119:422–447.

Black, D. 1983. "Crime as Social Control." *American Sociological Review* 48:34–45.

Block, C. R. and Christakos, A. 1995. "Intimate Partner Homicide in Chicago Over 29 Years." *Crime and Delinquency* 41:496–526.

Boritch, H. and Hagan, J. 1990. "A Century of Crime in Toronto: Gender, Class, and Pattern of Social Control, 1859–1955." *Criminology* 28: 567–599.

Bridges, G. S. and Weis, J. G. 1989. "Measuring Violent Behavior." In Neil A. Weiner and Marvin E. Wolfgang, eds., *Violent Crime, Violent Criminals*. Newbury Park, CA: Sage.

Brownstein, H. H., Spunt, B. J., Crimmins, S. M., and Langley, S. C. 1995. "Women Who Kill in Drug Market Situations." *Justice Quarterly* 12: 473–498.

Campbell, A. 1984. *Girls in the Gang*. Oxford: Basil Blackwell.

Cohen, L. and Felson, M. 1979. "Social Change and Crime Rate Trends: A Routine Activity Approach." *American Sociological Review* 44:588–607.

Cook, P. J. and Laub, J. H. (forthcoming). "The Unprecedented Epidemic in Youth Violence." In Mark H. Moore and Michael Tonry, eds., *Crime and Justice. Annual Review of Research*. Chicago: University of Chicago Press.

Cooney, M. 1997. "The Decline of Elite Homicide." *Criminology* 35:381–407.

Daly, M. and Wilson, M. 1988. *Homicide*. New York: Aldine De Gruyter.

Dugan, L., Nagin, D., and Rosenfeld, R. 1996. *Explaining the Decline in Intimate Partner Homicide: The Effects of Changing Domesticity, Women's Status, and Domestic Violence Resources*. Paper presented at the Annual Meeting of the American Society of Criminology, Chicago, IL.

Elias, N. 1978 [1939]. *The Civilizing Process: The History of Manners*. New York: Pantheon.

Emsley, C. 1996. *Crime and Society in England, 1750–1900*. 2nd ed. London: Longman.

Fagan, J. 1994. "Women and Drugs Revisited: Female Participation in the Cocaine Economy." *Journal of Drug Issues* 24:179–225.

Fagan, J. and Browne, A. 1994. "Violence Between Spouses and Intimates: Physical Aggression Between Women and Men in Intimate Relationships." In A. J. Reiss, Jr. and J. A. Roth, eds., *Understanding and Preventing Violence*, Vol. 3. *Social Influences*. Washington, DC: National Academy Press.

Feeley, M. M. and Little, D. L. 1991. "The Vanishing Female: The Decline of Women in the Criminal Process, 1687–1912." *Law and Society Review* 25:719– 757.

Garland, D. 1990. *Punishment and Modern Society*. Chicago: University of Chicago Press.

Gartner, R. 1990. "The Victims of Homicide: A Temporal and Cross-National Comparison." *American Sociological Review* 55:92–106.

——. 1995. "Methodological Issues in Cross-Cultural Large-Survey Research on Violence." In R. B. Ruback and N. A. Weiner, eds., *Interpersonal Violent Behaviors. Social and Cultural Aspects*. New York: Springer Publishing.

Gartner, R., Baker, K., and Pampel, F. C. 1990. "Gender Stratification and the Gender Gap in Homicide Victimization." *Social Problems* 37: 593–612.

Gartner, R. and McCarthy, B. 1991. "The Social Distribution of Femicide in Urban Canada, 1921–1988." *Law and Society Review* 25:287–313.

Gatrell, V. A. C. 1980. "The Decline of Theft in Victorian and Edwardian England." In V. A. C. Gatrell, B. Lenman, and G. Parker, eds., *Crime in Western Europe Since 1500*. London: Europa Publications.

Gauthier, D. K. and Bankston, W. B. 1997. "Gender Equality and the Sex Ratio of Intimate Killing." *Criminology* 35:577–600.

Gillis, A. R. 1996. "So Long as They Both Shall Live: Marital Dissolution and the Decline of Domestic Homicide in France, 1852–1909." *American Journal of Sociology* 101:1273–1305.

Giordano, P. C., Kerbel, S., and Dudley, S. 1981. "The Economics of Female Criminality: An Analysis of Police Blotters, 1890–1976." In Lee H. Bowker, ed., *Women and Crime in America*. New York: Macmillan.

Gottfredson, M. and Hirschi, T. 1990. *A General Theory of Crime*. Stanford, CA: Stanford University Press.

Gove, W. R. 1985. "The Effect of Age and Gender on Deviant Behavior: A Biopsychosocial Perspective." In A. R. Rossi, ed., *Gender and the Life Course*. New York: Aldine.

Gurr, T. R. 1981. "Historical Trends in Violent Crime." In N. Morris and M. Tonry, eds., *Crime and Justice: An Annual Review of Research*, Vol. 3. Chicago: University of Chicago Press.

——. 1989. "Historical Trends in Violent Crime: Europe and the United States." In T. R. Gurr, ed., *Violence in America*, Vol. 1. Newbury Park, CA: Sage.

Hagan, J., Simpson, J., and Gillis, A. R. 1987. "Class in the Household: A Power-Control Theory of Gender and Delinquency." *American Journal of Sociology* 92:788–816.

Hanawalt, B. A. 1979. *Crime and Conflict in English Communities, 1300–1348*. Cambridge, MA: Harvard University Press.

Heidensohn, F. 1991. "Women and Crime in Europe." In Frances Heidensohn and Martin Farrell, eds., *Crime in Europe*. London: Routledge.

Hill, G. D. and Crawford, E. M. 1990. "Women, Race and Crime." *Criminology* 28:601–626.

Hirschi, T. 1969. *Causes of Delinquency*. Berkeley, CA: University of California Press.

Hood, K. E. 1996. "Intractable Tangles of Sex and Gender in Women's Aggressive Development: An Optimistic View." In D. M. Stoff and R. B. Cairns, eds., *Aggression and Violence: Genetic, Neurobiological, and Biosocial Perspectives*. Mahwah, NJ: Lawrence Erlbaum Assoc.

Hull, N. E. H. 1987. *Female Felons: Women and Serious Crime in Colonial Massachusetts*. Urbana: University of Illinois Press.

Hyde, J. S. 1986. "Gender Differences in Aggression." In J. S. Hyde and M. C. Linn, eds., *The Psychology of Gender: Advances Through Meta-Analysis*. Baltimore: Johns Hopkins Press.

Inciardi, J. A. and Pottieger, A. E. 1994. "Crack-Cocaine Use and Street Crime." *Journal of Drug Issues* 24:273–292.

Kruttschnitt, C. 1985. "Female Crimes or Legal Labels? The Effect of Deviance Processing Agents on Our Understanding of Female Criminality." In Imogene L. Moyer, ed., *The Changing Roles of Women in the Criminal Justice System*. Prospect Heights, IL: Waveland Press.

——. 1994. "Gender and Interpersonal Violence." In A. J. Reiss and J. A. Roth, eds., *Understanding and Preventing Violence, Vol. 3, Social Influences*. Washington DC: National Academy Press.

——. 1995. "Violence by and Against Women: A Comparative and Cross-National Analysis." In R. B. Ruback and N. A. Weiner, eds., *Interpersonal Violent Behaviors. Social and Cultural Aspects*. New York: Springer Publishing.

——. 1996. "Contributions of Quantitative Methods to the Study of Gender and Crime, or Bootstrapping Our Way into the Theoretical Thicket." *Journal of Quantitative Criminology* 12:135–161.

Lane, R. 1980. "Urban Police and Crime in Nineteenth-Century America." In N. Morris and M. Tonry, eds., *Crime and Justice: Annual Review of Research*, Vol. 2. Chicago: University of Chicago Press.

Laub, J. and McDermott, M. J. 1985. "An Analysis of Serious Crime by Young Black Women." *Criminology* 23:81–99.

Lauritsen, J. L. 1997. "Gender and Risk for Assault: Victimization Patterns from Adolescence Through Young Adulthood." Paper presented at the Annual Meeting of the American Society of Criminology, San Diego, CA.

Lytton, H. and Romney, D. M. 1991. "Parents' Differential Socialization of Boys and Girls: A Meta-Analysis." *Psychological Bulletin* 109:267–296.

Maccoby, E. E. and Jacklin, C. N. 1974. *The Psychology of Sex Differences*. Stanford, CA: Stanford University Press.

——. 1980. "Sex Differences in Aggression: A Rejoinder and Reprise." *Child Development* 51:964–980.

Maher, L. and Daly, K. 1996. "Women in the Street-Level Drug Economy: Continuity or Change?" *Criminology* 34:465–491.

Mann, C. R. 1996. *When Women Kill*. Albany: State University of New York Press.

Maxfield, M. G. 1987. "Household Composition, Routine Activity, and Victimization: A Comparative Analysis." *Journal of Quantitative Criminology* 3:301–320.

——. 1989. "Circumstances in Supplementary Homicide Reports: Variety and Validity." *Criminology* 27:671–695.

Messner, S. F. 1985. "Sex Differences in Arrest Rates for Homicide: An Application of the General Theory of Structured Strain." *Comparative Social Research* 8:187–201.

Miethe, T. D. and Meier, R. F. 1994. *Crime and Its Social Context*. Albany; State University of New York Press.

Phillips, J. A. 1997. "Variation in African-American Homicide Rates: An Assessment of Potential Explanations." *Criminology* 35:527–559.

Polk, K. 1994. *When Men Kill. Scenarios of Masculine Violence*. Cambridge, MA: Cambridge University Press.

Reiss, A. J. and Roth, J. A. 1993. *Understanding and Preventing Violence*. Washington, DC: National Academy Press.

Riley, D. 1987. "Time and Crime: The Link Between Teenager Lifestyle and Delinquency." *Journal of Quantitative Criminology* 3:339–354.

Riley, D. and Shaw, M. 1985. "Parental Supervision and Juvenile Delinquency." Home Office Research Study No. 83, Her Majesty's Stationery Office, London.

Roth, J. A. 1994. *Understanding and Preventing Violence*. National Institute of Justice, Research in Brief. Washington DC: U.S. Department of Justice.

Rude, G. 1985. *Criminal and Victim: Crime and Society in Early Nineteenth-Century England*. Oxford: Clarendon Press.

Sampson, R. J. 1987. "Urban Black Violence: The Effect of Male Joblessness and Family Disruption." *American Journal of Sociology* 93:348–382.

Sampson, R. J. and Lauritsen, J. L. 1994. "Violent Victimization and Offending: Individual-, Situational-, and Community-Level Risk Factors." In Albert J. Reiss, Jr. and Jeffrey A. Roth, eds., *Understanding and Preventing Violence, Vol. 3, Social Influences*. Washington, DC: National Academy Press.

Shoemaker, R. B. 1991. *Prosecution and Punishment: Petty Crime and the Law in London and Rural Middlesex, c. 1600–1725*. Cambridge: Cambridge University Press.

Simon, R. J. 1975. *Women and Crime*. Lexington MA: D.C. Heath.

Simon, R. J. and Baxter, S. 1989. "Gender and Violent Crime." In N. A. Weiner and M. E. Wolfgang, eds., *Violent Crime, Violent Criminals*. Newbury Park CA: Sage.

Simpson, S. 1989. "Feminist Theory, Crime, and Justice." *Criminology* 27:605–632.

Sommers, I. and Baskin, D. R. 1992. "Sex, Race, Age and Violent Offending." *Violence and Victims* 7:191–202.

——. 1993. "The Situational Context of Violent Female Offending." *Journal of Research in Crime and Delinquency* 30:136–162.

Steffensmeier, D. and Allan, E. 1988. "Sex Disparities in Arrests by Residence, Race and Age: An Assessment of the Gender Convergence/Crime Hypothesis." *Justice Quarterly* 5:53–80.

——. 1996. "Gender and Crime: Toward a Gendered Theory of Female Offending." *Annual Review of Sociology* 22:459–487.

Steffensmeier, D., Allan, E. and Streifel, C. 1989. "Development and Female Crime: A Cross-National Test of Alternative Explanations." *Social Forces* 68: 262–283.

Stone, L. 1977. *The Family, Sex and Marriage in England 1500–1800*. New York: Harper and Row.

Straus, M. 1983. "Societal Morphogensis and Intrafamily Violence in Cross-Cultural Perspective." In R. J. Gelles and C. P. Cornell, eds., *International Perspectives on Family Violence*. Lexington, MA: D.C. Heath.

Tieger, T. 1980. "On the Biological Basis of Sex Differences in Aggression." *Child Development* 51:943–963.

Wallace, A. 1986. *Homicide: The Social Reality. New South Wales Bureau of Crime Statistics and Research*. Attorney General's Department. Australia.

White, J. W. 1983. "Sex and Gender Issues in Aggression Research." In R. G. Green and E. I. Donnerstein, eds., *Aggression: Theoretical and Empirical Reviews, Vol. 2, Issues in Research*. New York: Academic Press.

Widom, C. S. 1989. "Child Abuse, Neglect and Violent Criminal Behavior." *Criminology* 27:251–271.

Williams, K. R. and Flewelling, R. L. 1988. "The Social Production of Criminal Homicide: A Comparative Study of Disaggregated Rates in American Cities." *American Sociological Review* 53:421–31.

Wilson, J. Q. and Herrnstein, R. J. 1985. *Crime and Human Nature*. New York: Simon and Schuster.

Wilson, M. I. and Daly, M. 1992. "Who Kills Whom in Spouse Killings? On the Exceptional Sex Ratio of Spousal Homicides in the United States." *Criminology* 30:189–215.

Wolfgang, M. E. 1958. *Patterns in Criminal Homicide*. Philadelphia: University of Pennsylvania Press.

Wolfgang, M. E. and F. Ferracuti. 1967. *The Subculture of Violence*. London: Tavistock.

Zedner, L. 1991. *Women, Crime and Custody in Victorian England*. Oxford: Clarendon Press. ◆

7

Crime and Punishment in the Lives of Women Alcohol and Other Drug (AOD) Users: Exploring the Gender, Lifestyle, and Legal Issues

Richard F. Mancuso
and Brenda A. Miller

This chapter presents a review and exploration of theoretical frameworks that contribute to our understanding of the AOD/crime lifestyle for women. It also identifies prevalence of the AOD problems for women involved in the criminal justice system, discusses risks and consequences for these women, and considers public policies and community initiatives that have specifically affected them. Essential elements needed to break this AOD and offending cycle have not been offered on a wide scale to AOD using women who commit crime. These elements include long-range and intensive AOD treatment that addresses abuse and dependence, the related lifestyle that leads to criminal behavior, cumulative adversities that result from this social context, and failure to acknowledge the larger gender, class, and structural barriers that affect women's lives.

There is an increased awareness that alcohol and other drug (AOD) use is a major correlate of women's offending patterns (Biron,

Brochu, and Desjardins 1995; Browne, Miller, Maguin, forthcoming; El-Bassel et al. 1995; Streifel 1997). Further, drug use in itself is defined as criminal behavior for specific categories of drugs (heroine, cocaine, marijuana). However, the majority of studies and official reports to date have neglected to consider the impact of the AOD/crime lifestyle on women's initiation and maintenance of these deviant behaviors. As defined in this chapter, the AOD/crime lifestyle is the combination of social context and environmental influences that together provide a constellation of interactions and experiences that shape women's experiences. This lifestyle may be conceptualized as consisting of both immediate social contexts, including family, social supports and relationships, and larger macro-level influences of the environment, including social mores and norms of the community, legal and bureaucratic structures, and neighborhood influences.

This lifestyle consists of many behaviors related to both AOD use and criminal behavior. AOD use includes a range of pharmacologic agents, both legal (e.g., alcohol, methadone, prescription drugs) and illegal (e.g., cocaine, heroin, amphetamines, marijuana). AOD use also ranges from occasional to chronic or heavy. Problems associated with AOD use further complicate this picture. These problems may be sufficient to warrant a diagnosis of alcohol or drug abuse/dependence (American Psychiatric Association 1994). This lifestyle is also influenced by the direct pharmacological effects of the substance (Johns 1997); however, our focus will remain on the effects of the lifestyle on the woman's daily life.

Similar issues arise with the concept of criminal behavior. Criminal behavior includes a range of legally proscribed behaviors, from relatively minor crimes (shoplifting, prostitution) to more serious crimes (assaults, robberies, homicides). Criminal behavior can also range from a single occasion of illegal conduct to a full career of crime, spanning the lifetime. Female offenders' use and abuse of AOD is not uniform across criminal behaviors. Differences in the rates of AOD use and the criminal behavior associated with this use are not uniform across geographic regions, ethnic identities, age groups, or economic strata. Unfortunately, prior research has not consistently used the same definitions or concepts for describing these phenomena. Throughout this chapter we will identify how issues related to the lifestyle affect this range of behaviors.

This chapter presents a review and exploration of theoretical frameworks that contribute to our understanding of the AOD/crime lifestyle, identifies the prevalence of AOD problems for women involved in the criminal justice system, discusses the risks and consequences for women involved in this lifestyle, and considers public policies and community initiatives that have specifically affected these women.

Theoretical Framework for Understanding the AOD Lifestyle

Although existing theoretical frameworks relevant to our understanding of the lifestyle have largely been developed to explain male behavior (Anglin and Speckart 1986; Byqvist and Olsson 1998), this work remains important to understanding women's lives as well. Another problem is that most theoretical work focusing on the AOD lifestyle describes solely the drug crime lifestyle. Little attention has been given to legal drugs and how they further influence the lifestyle.

Explaining relationships between AOD and criminal behavior is further complicated by an ongoing debate regarding whether AOD use is a precursor to criminal activity or whether criminal activity is a precursor to AOD use (see for further information, Chaiken and Chaiken 1990; Dembo et al. 1990; Mustaine and Tewksbury 1998; Nurco et al. 1996). These relationships continue to be enmeshed across the life span (or some portion of the life span). Three possible relationships may exist: (1) continued AOD use will exacerbate criminal behavior, (2) criminal behavior will exacerbate AOD use/abuse, and (3) co-occurrences of both criminal and AOD behavior are unrelated but proximal in time.

Earlier work recognized the role of the lifestyle in maintaining behaviors of both AOD use/abuse and criminal activity (Becker 1963; Waldorf 1973; Winick 1967). Accessing drugs, using drugs, and maintaining social connections for these functions evolve to support and sustain drug use and criminal behavior. Becker's (1963) interactionist theory of deviant drug use involves the lifestyle and social practices of marijuana and other drug users being intimately connected to continued deviant activity.

The AOD/crime lifestyle is influenced by both drug using and crime components. First, individuals, through active techniques of rationalization and justification (e.g., Sykes and Matza 1957) make careers out of the lifestyle (Grella and Joshi 1999; Waldorf, 1973). Second, lifestyles are equally influenced by the criminal justice system and by society more generally through labeling both individuals in the lifestyle and the lifestyle itself as deviant. Other explanations focus on social psychological influences (e.g., rational choice, social learning, and cognitive theories) and emphasize interactions of developmental and personal influences within a social context. For instance, Walters (1994, 1999) portrays the AOD/crime lifestyle as involving individual choices, family or peer influences, and cognitive elements such as rationalizations and justifications for continued drug use. Together these three components define a drug-crime lifestyle (Walters, 1994).

Theoretical explanations often focus specifically on the AOD/violence nexus. Goldstein (1985) provides a theoretical framework for understanding the nexus between drugs and violence, identifying three major ways in which these elements are linked in the drug-crime subculture. Two of these explanations focus on aspects of the lifestyle (the third focuses on the direct psychopharmacological effects). Crimes such as shoplifting, prostitution, and robbery are seen as motivated by the financial need to purchase drugs. This is similar to the theoretical perspective offered by earlier work, which saw criminal activity as sustaining drug use but also as evolving out of the larger environmental influences of social policies that criminalize drugs. An even stronger emphasis for the environmental influences can be viewed in Goldstein's description of systemic violence. This explanation for the drug-crime nexus postulates that these relationships emerge as a direct result of interactions in drug distribution networks as either buyers or sellers. For example, the need for establishing "turf" or controlling distribution of drugs can result in violent behavior as individuals pursue their business interests (Inciardi 1992; Johnson et al. 1985; Skolnick et al. 1997). In this theoretical perspective, the drug lifestyle can be seen as emerging in response to larger environmental influences, in which laws and policies are created that criminalize drug use. This criminalization in turn allows related criminal behavior to emerge as part of the process.

This AOD lifestyle takes place within an AOD abusing community, a community largely male controlled and dominated (Dunlap 1992). The highest levels of acquisition within the drug market are often male dominated, and women's roles are predominantly restricted to low-level market activities, such as engaging in prostitution for drug money, holding small amounts of drugs, and often caring for the male partner. An inherent distrust of women exists in this lifestyle, in part, because of women's roles as prostitutes in the drug scene (Mahan 1996; Waldorf 1973). Disagreements over gender roles, stereotyped views of women, and pressures of the larger AOD crime subcultures influence relationships between partners and create incidents of partner violence beyond what is found in the more general population (e.g., Goldstein et al. 1991). Recently, studies have supported stronger female roles in the drug scene, including a case study of a woman who was successful in the drug-crime

business (Dunlap, Johnson, and Manwar 1997). An ethnographic study of methamphetamine dealers who were women (Morgan and Joe 1996), an examination of women in the cocaine world (Fagan 1994), and a study of 149 crack-using women in which one group known as the "Queens of the Scene" financed their use by dealing and working in the crack network (Sterk 1999) have suggested that women may have gained more opportunities in the AOD/crime lifestyle (Morgan and Joe 1996).

Whether women have made status and economic gains in the AOD/crime lifestyle still requires investigation. As Morgan and Joe (1996) note, much of our knowledge about women in AOD/crime lifestyles is limited to those involved in street-level, lower-status criminal activity. Thus, much of what we know is about women caught in the confines of the lower socioeconomic levels of our society. Further, for these women the appearance of more opportunities in the AOD/crime lifestyle has not benefited them. Based on an ethnographic study of women involved in distribution of crack-cocaine in New York City, Maher and Daly (1996) report that "opportunities" were largely afforded to males, not females. Furthermore, conditions for the average AOD/crime-involved woman actually deteriorated (Maher and Daly 1996).

There has been some debate as to whether women engaged in the AOD/crime lifestyle have chosen this lifestyle or have engaged in the lifestyle as a survival strategy to make ends meet (Edin and Lein 1997). Environmental influences, including living in poor, socially disorganized neighborhoods, poor schooling and inadequate job training, and high rates of unemployment in the community or the low wage/temporary employment nature of the work available, may encourage women (as well as men) to enter the AOD/crime lifestyle (Wilson 1996).

Mahan (1996) offers a theoretical perspective that emphasizes the importance of the drug subculture as fulfilling women's unmet personal, economic, and social needs. Her explanations focus on the larger structural inequities and problems created by a sexist, racist, and class-bound society. In this drug lifestyle context, criminal offending (e.g., sex trading, prostitution, theft, violence) is encouraged as part of daily existence. Further complicating this debate between "free will" and "determinism" is the possibility that both conscious and unconscious choices are made at various points in the lifespan and that external events and environmental influences have been present that have provided few, if any, rational choices.

Although environmental influences for the woman AOD offender are similar to the same pressures her male counterpart experiences, women face some additional pressures from societal institutions and communities. Both moral and institutional entrepreneurs (Becker 1963) and pockets of influential agents operating in the criminal justice system (Singer 1996), child protection agencies, (Mancuso 1998) social services, and governmental bureaucracies often classify, label, and stereotype women with AOD and offending histories (Goffman 1961).[1] The organizational and societal view is one in which women who use excessively or who abuse AOD are believed to be deviant. These larger agency and structural messages create the conditions for the AOD-using women who commit crime to be labeled as outsiders by society (Becker 1963; Downs, Robertson and Harrison 1997; Miller and Downs 1995; Sandmaier 1980).

For example, AOD-using and offending women are viewed by society as deviant on three levels (Erickson and Murray 1989; Erickson and Watson 1990): (1) because of their AOD problems—women are not expected to engage in heavy use or to develop AOD problems; (2) because of their means of daily survival—many women engaged in the AOD/crime lifestyle are also involved in prostitution, and (3) due to their offending behavior. This socially constructed view of being deviant on multiple levels is not as prevalent for males and suggests a gender bias even among those in the lifestyle.

Prevalence of AOD Problems Among Women Offenders

A wide range of criminal activity is associated with AOD use/abuse for women, including the exchange of sex for money or drugs, shoplifting, theft, and drug sales/distribution (Inciardi, Pottieger, and Faupel 1982; McElrath, Chitwood, and Comerford 1997; Rosenbaum 1981). The interest in women's crimes associated with AOD use has most typically focused on street crimes such as prostitution, property crimes, and AOD-related offenses by women AOD users (McCoy et al. 1995; Steffensmeier and Allan 1996; U.S. Department of Justice 1997). For example, women commit a high degree of non-AOD-related offenses, such as burglary, prostitution, larceny, and fraud, to fund their drug use (Hser, Chou, and Anglin 1990). By legal definition, much of women's drug use is criminal activity.

An increased incarceration rate for women over the past several years (Bourgois and Dunlap 1993; Beck and Gilliard 1995; Sanchez and Johnson 1987), combined with significant narrowing of the gender gap in drug-offending behavior (Nunesdinis and Weisner 1997), has resulted in the recognition of the importance of the drug problem contributing to the women offender problems (Browne, Miller, and Maguin, forthcoming). According to a nationwide study of incarcerated females and males, the women were very likely to be involved with illegal drugs or with alcohol, and their levels of involvement often surpass those of the men.[2] In selected national sites among the arrestee population, urinalysis testing indicated that 70 percent of females were found with traces of cocaine/crack (compared to 54 percent for male arrestees), 25 percent with heroin (13 percent for males), and 18 percent with methamphetamines (14 percent for males) (U.S. Department of Justice 1997).

When examining prison population data, we find that women are more likely to be incarcerated for drug offenses than males (33 percent versus 21 percent), and this incarceration rate has increased dramatically in the last two decades (U.S. Department of Justice 1995). For example, based on a national survey done by the Sentencing Project, Mauer and Huling (1995) found that the number of women in state prisons for drug offenses increased 433 percent between 1986 and 1991 compared to 283 percent for men. According to a Bureau of Justice Statistics survey of state prison inmates (U.S. Department of Justice 1994), half of the women in the 277 prisons studied reported being under the influence of AOD while committing their offense, and more than half of female state prisoners reported having used drugs in the month prior to their current offense. In addition, Phillips and Harm (1997) report that between 1980 and 1994 the population of women inmates overall increased 386 percent compared to a 214 percent increase in the male prison population. Thus, a greater number of women are being incarcerated, and drug offenses account for much of this increase.

In contrast, the prevalence of women offenders using alcohol is lower than that of men, although the numbers are still substantial. For instance, a national survey of female state prison inmates found that 58 percent of women offenders had used alcohol in the year prior to committing the offense, compared to 73 percent of men (U.S. Department of Justice 1994). In addition, 12 percent of women state inmates and 18 percent of men were under the influence of alcohol at the time of their offenses, and 19 percent of female state prison inmates and 30 percent of male inmates reported daily use of alcohol (U.S. Department of Justice 1994).

In other parts of the criminal justice system, the rates for men and women appear more equal. Based on a national survey completed by the Bureau of Justice Statistics (Bonczar 1997), among probationers, the percentage of women reporting alcohol or drug involvement is similar to that for men. For instance, nearly as many women were sentenced to probation for a drug offense as men (22 percent of men and 20 percent of women). Among women probationers, 67.7 percent report ever having used drugs, as compared to 69.9 percent of males (U.S. Department of Justice 1998). However, when binge drinking (i.e., 20 drinks in a single day) was compared for male and female probationers, men were much more likely to report ever having binges (40.4 percent) as compared to women (16.1 percent) (U.S. Department of Justice 1998).

The high prevalence of AOD involvement among women offenders becomes more salient when rates of AOD involvement in the general population are examined. In the general population, we find that women have lower rates of lifetime and yearly AOD use than men. For example, according to the 1998 National Household Survey on Drug Abuse (NHSDA), lifetime prevalence of any illicit drug use excluding marijuana was 30 percent for females and 39 percent for males (U.S. Department of Health and Human Services 1999). In this same survey, 8 percent of females, as compared to 13 percent of males, reported any illegal drug use during the previous year.

Lifetime drinking was reported by 77 percent of females and 85 percent of males in the general population (U.S. Department of Health and Human Services 1999). Differences between men's and women's drinking patterns are more pronounced with measures of heavy drinking. Heavy drinking, defined as five or more drinks per drinking occasion five or more days in the previous month, was reported by 14 percent of females and 30 percent of males (U.S. Department of Health and Human Services 1997).

Although general population data suggest higher rates of AOD use for men than women, surveys of college students through the young adult years (up to age 32) show more similar rates between males and females for younger age groups that are more comparable to offenders. Results from the 1995 Monitoring the Future study, a national self-report survey, revealed lifetime incidence of any illicit drug use was 35 percent for females and 37 percent for males, and past year rates of illicit drug use (excluding marijuana) were 11 percent for females and 15 percent for males. Prevalence of alcohol use during the past year was 83 percent for women and 86 percent for men. However, prevalence of lifetime heavy drinking, defined as five or more drinks in a row during the previous two-week period, was 35 percent for women and 47 percent for men (Johnston, O'Malley, and Bachman, 1997). Thus, some of the similarities between males and females in drug and alcohol use found in criminal justice populations, which overrepresent younger populations, may be due to less differentiation in AOD use among younger populations. However, the rates of AOD use and abuse in the offender population are still substantially higher than in the general population.

Characteristics and Experiences of Women in the AOD/Crime Lifestyle

Their substance use and criminal activity shape the characteristics and experiences of women in this lifestyle. A number of problems, characteristic of this lifestyle, also contribute to their experiences. For example, psychological problems (depression, suicidal tendencies), physical health conditions (risk of HIV/AIDS, infectious diseases), economic concerns (unemployment, poverty), violence-related incidents (partner violence, child abuse, sexual violence) all contribute to women's experiences in the AOD/crime lifestyle (Wellisch, Prendergast, and Anglin 1994). Women also maintain roles as mothers in this lifestyle (Rosenbaum 1981; Dunlap et al. 1997; Sterk 1999). These characteristics and experiences are important to postulating the risk factors for entering and maintaining the lifestyle within the woman's own lifespan and to transmitting the lifestyle to the next generation.

Influence of the Lifestyle on Medical and Psychological Functioning

Research evidence suggests that women in the AOD/crime lifestyle face a number of medical and mental health problems that may be due in part to the lifestyle. There is evidence that women become addicted to substances more quickly than men do and suffer more harmful physical consequences from various substances. For instance, women are thought to progress to the more severe stages of alcoholism more quickly, a concept that has been described as "telescoping" (Wilsnack, Wilsnack, and Hiller-Sturmhofel 1994; Wilsnack, Wilsnack, and Klassen 1984). They are also at increased risk of becoming addicted and experiencing more harmful physical consequences of hard drugs such as crack cocaine and heroin (Anglin, Hser, and McGlothin 1987; Stephens 1991). Studies have also suggested that women heroin addicts tend to become addicted within one month after first usage and that women in general become addicted in less time than men (Anglin, Hser, and McGlothin 1987).

One way in which the lifestyle may influence this rapid trajectory into AOD involvement is when criminality such as prostitution becomes a major source of support for women's drug use. Prostitution may promote further drug taking simply as a way of handling the stress and negative, pejorative view of their lives, held by the women themselves as well as others. Thus, there becomes a vicious cycle of prostitution to support drug use, and drug use to cope with prostitution. The extent to which rapid involvement in AOD use can be attributed to lifestyle factors versus what aspects of the trajectory are attributable to physiological differences or social influences between men and women needs further investigation.

One of the most serious physical consequences of AOD use for women is the risk of HIV or AIDS. Women in this lifestyle are at increased risk for contracting AIDS as a result of intravenous drug use, sexual activity with an intravenous (IV) drug user or AIDS-infected partner, and sex-for-crack exchanges related to prostitution (e.g., Luxenburg and Guild 1993). In a study of 235 crack and noncrack cocaine users, McCoy, Miles, and Inciardi (1995) found that 65 percent of women crack users exchanged sex for money, and 96 percent of the women who use crack reported having more than one injecting drug user (IDU) as a sexual partner. Thus, the lifestyle places women at high risk for contracting serious health problems.

Lifestyle may also affect these physiological problems, because women in the AOD/crime lifestyle are not likely to receive adequate medical care. Since a majority of women's time is spent using drugs or attempting to get money to support their habits, they tend to ignore their existing medical problems. Their unhealthy lifestyle also tends to include poor nutrition, smoking, violence, and a general lack of health services utilization (Franke 1997; Plichta 1992; Stark and Flitcraft 1996; Windle et al. 1994). In addition, women AOD users often avoid going to the doctor for fear that their addiction will be exposed, which may have both legal and personal consequences.

It is difficult to separate the impact of AOD users' lifestyle on access to health care from their socioeconomic condition, as access to health care for poor women is limited in general (Browne 1992; Nyamathi and Flaskerud 1992). Poor women often access health care through emergency room visits, where the care they receive may be minimal. There have been concerns that women involved in the lifestyle are subjected to discriminatory practices by the health care system. However, one study of women drug users did not find significant evidence that women perceived themselves as discriminated against; only 10 percent of a sample of 157 drug users reported being treated unfairly while at a medical facility such as a clinic, hospital emergency room, or a doctor's office (Miller, Maguin, and Mancuso,

forthcoming). However, discrimination may be more subtly applied and experienced.

In addition to the physical health risks, women AOD-users face significant emotional and mental health problems related to AOD use. Women who are heavily addicted to AOD often experience severe depression, suicidal thoughts or attempts at suicide (e.g., DeLeon 1993), feelings of low self-esteem, loneliness, and isolation due to the persistent nature of addiction (Grant, Hasin, and Dawson 1996; Kandel, Raveis, and Davies 1991; Miller et al. 1996; Weissman et al. 1988). For example, in a study of the psychopathology of cocaine abuse among women and men admitted to a hospital for the treatment of cocaine addiction, Weiss and colleagues (1988) found that 24 percent of women compared with 4 percent of the men were diagnosed with severe depression.

These often co-occurring emotional, physical, and mental health problems associated with AOD use are in part generated by a lifestyle noted for heightened stress levels, limited social support, and limited community resources. Direct experiences of the social context of AOD lifestyles along with the feeling of low self-esteem, depression, and loneliness create cumulative adversities in women's lives.

Violent Victimization Across the Lifespan

Partner violence has been reported as highly associated with the AOD lifestyle (e.g., Downs, Miller, and Gondoli 1987; Miller, Downs, and Gondoli 1989b; Miller, Downs, and Testa 1993) as well as the AOD/crime lifestyle (Blane et al. 1988; El-Bassell et al. 1996). For example, in a study looking at the interrelationships among alcohol, drugs, criminal violence, and domestic violence across three generations (Blane et al. 1988) among 82 male parolees and their partners or spouses, Miller and colleagues (1990) found a significant interaction effect between the women's AOD use, the AOD/

crime lifestyle, and their experiencing spousal or partner violence.

More recently, Miller and colleagues (1993) found that alcoholic women in treatment reported significantly higher levels of verbal aggression in childhood, moderate childhood violence, and severe childhood violence from their father when compared to nonalcoholic women. These early experiences of childhood victimization set the stage for a developmental pathway leading to delinquent activity, AOD use, and involvement in an AOD/crime lifestyle (Miller, Downs, and Gondoli 1989a) .

Violence is also associated with illegal or high-risk behavior associated with obtaining money for drugs or attempting to purchase drugs. The potential for violence involves AOD-using women accessing drugs such as crack or heroin in locations that place them at risk of physical or sexual assault by dealers or strangers (crack houses, drug markets, bars). In Goldstein and colleagues' (1991) work on drug users, they found that men and women experienced nearly equal levels of violence during an eight-week period of reporting. Among 133 female cocaine users, 172 violent episodes were reported, an average of 1.29 episodes per person. In comparison, there were 212 violent incidents among 152 male cocaine users or an average of 1.39 episodes per person (Goldstein et al. 1991).

Women who are heavily involved in the drug lifestyle, particularly using and selling drugs such as cocaine and heroin, often engage in prostitution and sex for drugs or money exchanges in which the threat of violence from pimps, "johns," and partners is high (El-Bassel et al. 1997; Maher and Daly 1996; Simons and Whitbeck 1991; Sommers and Baskin 1994). Maher and Daly (1996) note, for instance, that as a result of the drug, crack, and sexual exchange network making crack the poor person's drug, women have experienced fewer opportunities, more violence, and deteriorating economic conditions related to prostitution and other offending behavior.

Parenting Issues

In general, women AOD users have difficulty parenting. Parental and early family influences, particularly parental AOD and crime problems have been identified as important to subsequent development of a child's criminal behavior (Gendreau, Little, and Goggin 1996; McCord 1979; Viemero 1996) and AOD behavior (Braithwaite and Devine 1993; Cooper, Pierce, and Tidwell 1995; Flanzer 1993; Young 1997). Historically, there has been a glaring gender bias in this research, with most of it focusing on fathers' AOD/crime problems affecting their sons' behaviors (Vellemen 1992). More recently some research has examined the effects of parental AOD problems for daughters (e.g., Benson and Heller 1987; Braithwaite and Devine 1993; Giunta and Compas 1994; Schuckit, Tipp, and Kelmer 1994; Smith et al. 1994). Relatively little has been done, until recently, to examine the role of mothers' AOD problems on either their sons or daughters, except for concerns about AOD use during pregnancy (Miller, Maguin, and Downs 1997).

Intergenerational risk factors for children of AOD-abusing parents have been reported in major reviews of the literature (Lang and Stritzke 1993; Searles and Windle 1990; Steinhausen 1995; Vellemen 1992). These factors include poor growth, physical health, and physical/mental development; risk of mental disorders and mental health problems (depression, low self-esteem, suicidal tendencies); delinquent and criminal behaviors (antisocial behavior, conduct difficulties, and aggression); and difficulties in school (poor academic achievement, truancy problems).

Increased risk for development of AOD/crime lifestyles among children whose parents are involved in the AOD/crime lifestyle is of particular concern. In their ethnographic study of parenting practices among 25 crack-using families, Johnson, Dunlap, and Maher (1998) found, not surprisingly, that children modeled their parents AOD and offending behavior as they moved into adulthood. For instance, the children learned not to raise or financially support their own children. Children also learned not to develop strong attachments with other adults in the family. Because children of AOD and offending parents receive very little parenting training, as adults, they failed to monitor and protect their own children and adolescents from violence. Thus, intergenerational patterns of behavior are learned and subsequently modeled for the next generation. This intergenerational process leads directly to adult AOD abuse, to criminal behaviors such as prostitution, theft, and shoplifting for women, and to the formation of deviant conduct norms (Johnson, Dunlap, and Maher 1998).

Women's AOD use affects their ability to parent their children effectively (Rosenbaum 1981; Smyth and Miller 1998). This parenting dimension falls more heavily on women than men as they have historically been more responsible for child care. Women's AOD use diverts attention away from parenting responsibilities such as protecting young children from abusive situations or seeing to their safety in general. In addition, women who use AOD often fail to engage in active communication and nurturing of young children. Instead, their time is spent either using AOD or finding ways to purchase AOD (Bernardi, Jones, and Tenant 1989; Magura and Laudet 1996; Nurco et al. 1998; Smyth and Miller 1998). AOD-using mothers often leave their kids at home unsupervised while they seek money, acquire drugs, or use drugs (Battle 1990). Some women have friends or acquaintances, also likely to be drug users, watch their children, which can result in children being victimized by the acquaintances. This inattention to parenting responsibilities has especially been noted when women's primary drug is crack. Because of its highly addictive nature, the drug becomes the main focus in a woman's life, and her

children's needs become ignored or forgotten (Battle 1990).

The overall stress of attempting to parent while on AOD is further compounded by constant emotional, financial, psychological, community, and health-related needs of young children. In addition, the stress of the AOD lifestyle, which is often characterized by past and current experiences of violence by parents and partners, may also compromise a woman's ability to cope with the stress inherent in parenting, thereby placing her at higher risk of abusing her children (Smyth and Miller 1998). In fact, research on mothers' alcohol problems and children's victimization has found that women experiencing partner abuse were more likely to abuse their children compared to women without partner violence (Miller et al. 1995). Another unintended result of the women's AOD use and offending behavior is the potential of passing on this lifestyle and these behaviors to their children, and as we have seen, this intergenerational component can result in the women's children facing early AOD use, delinquent behavior, and experiences of childhood and adolescent family and stranger violence that sets in motion their own cycle of AOD and offending behavior.

Social and Legal Responses to the Women in the AOD/Crime Lifestyle

Since the mid-1980s and even dating back to the early 1900s, there has been an increasing awareness of social harms, health problems, and criminal and juvenile behavior associated with both legal (alcohol) and illegal (cocaine, heroin, marijuana) substance use and abuse in the United States (Dembo, Williams, and Schmeidler 1993; Mieczkowski 1996; Mustaine and Tewksbury 1998; Musto 1973). Responses have included the passage of the Food and Drug Act of 1906, the Harrison Narcotics Drug Enforcement Act of 1914, the American Medical Association and the

American Pharmaceutical Association's drug enforcement stance, and the Drug Abuse Act of 1970 (Musto 1973). More recently, social policies have included methadone maintenance programs, needle-exchange programs, drug/DWI courts (Mays, Ryan, and Bejarano 1997), and court-mandated AOD treatment (Fernandez 1998). These social policies have increasingly relied on the criminal justice system, especially since the late 1960s when President Richard Nixon initiated the War on Drugs as part of his law and order domestic program (Baum 1996).

The criminal justice and federal governmental response to women who commit AOD crime has become more severe since the 1980s (Erickson et al. 1994; Hagan 1994). For instance, policies have surfaced that apply to women only, such as criminalization of pregnant AOD users, including the enactment of fetal endangerment statutes and exclusion of pregnant women from drug treatment (Farr 1995; Golden 1991; Mahan 1996; Poland et al. 1993; Reed 1993; Roper 1992). In fact, there has been a concerted effort to criminalize AOD use by pregnant women and more generally to criminalize women and their bodies (e.g., Feinman 1992; see the following Law Reviews for comprehensive overviews: Korver 1991; *New Jersey Law Journal* 1990; Roberts 1991, 1997; Rubenstein 1991; Swenson and Crabbe 1994). The American Civil Liberties Union (ACLU) has identified 51 cases in 19 states in which women have lost custody of infants due to addiction to heroin or other drugs (Paltrow 1990).

This recent shift toward punishing women AOD users can also be seen in laws conceptualized to reduce risks to children from drug-abusing parents. For example, the proposed Child Abuse and Neglect Enforcement Act (CANEA), introduced in the House of Representatives by Susan Molinari (R-NY), requires hospitals to perform drug and alcohol tests on every recently born baby. In addition, the bill would allow child protective services access to sensitive information such as the positive results of the drug test and any prior criminal convictions that the mother may have (H.R. 1419, April 23, 1997). The disproportional focus on women can be seen in the fact that this proposed bill does not drug test or look into the criminal background of fathers. Although the stated goal of this act is to limit the incidence of child maltreatment, if it is enacted into law, women will be punished further. The bill does not offer treatment and assessment to mothers identified as having AOD problems at or near birth, only punitive actions.

In addition, some states, such as Illinois, South Carolina, and Florida, have enacted child protection system measures, such as removing children and placing them in foster care, as well as measures to bring juvenile and adult court prosecutions and arrests against maternal AOD users. These responses have occurred in spite of research suggesting that most AOD-using mothers are mired in poverty, have long-term crack cocaine use history, and have had little drug treatment offered to them prior to or following their pregnancy (Pearson and Thoennes 1996).

At the state level, legislators have approached the problem of drug-exposed children through existing criminal and civil neglect and abuse statutes (Mahan 1996). Some states focus attention on mothers and their drug-exposed infants, while other states have focused efforts on duration of pregnancy (Larson 1991). This movement to punish women drug offenders has further marginalized their status and that of their children.

In a study of 216 low-income women on welfare and 220 homeless women, Bassuk, Browne, and Buckner (1996) found that over 80 percent of the women on welfare had experienced violent physical or sexual victimization over the course of their lives. According to the results of a large-scale study conducted by the Center on Addiction and Substance Abuse (1994), women receiving public assistance were twice as likely (27 percent to 14 percent) to be addicted to AOD than women not receiving public assistance. These studies signify the financial, economic, structural, and psychological effects for women on welfare that will further add to the cumulative stress facing women, their children, and their families. These constellations of events are further compounded for women with AOD and offending histories.

The punitive stance in social policies can be seen in areas where (1) arrests, prosecutions, and sentences for drug users have increased, (2) criminalization of pregnant AOD users has been implemented by state prosecutors, and (3) wide-scale efforts have been made to eliminate women AOD users from welfare rolls (e.g., Beckett 1995; Maher 1992). Combined with the abolition of Aid to Families with Dependent Children (AFDC), which guaranteed federal aid to poor women and their children (Bassuk, Browne, and Buckner 1996), these policies have eliminated safety nets and increased the problems of women involved in the AOD/crime lifestyle.

Concluding Thoughts

Based on our theoretical and social control summaries of the literature, we can identify a number of contextual variables to guide future research, interventions, public policies, and understanding of the AOD/crime lifestyle for women. On social or micro levels, variables that measure the influence of immediate context include family (both in home of origin and current family), parenting practices (home of origin), social support from personal relationships, and experiencing or witnessing violence. On environmental influence or macro levels, variables that measure the impact of larger systems include employment opportunities in the community; the impact of criminal justice system policies and practices; the availability of AOD interventions, policies, and practices; the availability of social service organizations; exposure to violence in the community; drug market activity in the community; and community-level values and expectations about alcohol use.

In this chapter we have emphasized the impact of the social context of the AOD lifestyle on women's lives. Previously, explanations for women's involvement in the AOD/crime lifestyle focused almost exclusively on their continued use of AOD. Many women AOD users engage in crimes (drug selling, prostitution, shoplifting, theft, robbery) in order to continue AOD use, especially for drugs such as crack ("hitting the rock") and heroin ("chasing the dragon") for which the high is intense and immediate (e.g., McCoy et al. 1995; Schuckit 1995). However, it is also the case that more complex and fluid processes are at work that go well beyond the psychopharmacological effects of the drug. In fact, with the exception of a few researchers (see Goldstein 1990; Inciardi and McElrath 1995; Rosenbaum 1995; Mahan 1996), the interrelationship of the AOD use and offending lifestyle with the larger gender, class, sociospatial (Gottdiener 1994) and structural issues (Connors 1996) has been omitted from etiological attention. The essential elements needed to break this AOD and offending cycle have not been offered on a wide scale to AOD-using women who commit crime. These factors include long-range and intensive AOD treatment that addresses the AOD abuse and dependence, the related drug and AOD lifestyle that leads to criminal behavior, the cumulative adversities that result from this social context, and the failure to acknowledge the larger gender, class, and structural barriers that affect women's lives. Despite increases in AOD use among women from the general population and from criminal justice populations, as well as the narrowing gender gap in AOD use and offending activity, women still receive far less treatment than male users.

In addition, little if any recognition is given to the resiliency that these women possess in order to survive, a resilience that may have a positive impact on the next generation. On a structural level, what is needed to break the cycle of chronic poverty and lack of opportunities that permeate women's lives are health and child care, adequate and effective delivery of AOD treatment, and government resources aimed at empowering women.

We conclude by offering a harm-reduction approach to the AOD/crime lifestyle (see Reuter and MacCoun 1995 for an overview of the harm-reduction framework applied to AOD). Under the harm-reduction model, drug and alcohol problems are approached less from a need to reduce and control AOD abuse and more from an attempt to eliminate the harms connected with AOD. These associated harms include childhood and adult victimization, medical and health problems, and the continued criminalization of women because of their AOD use and related offending in order to support the addiction.

Discussion Questions

1. What elements define a drug-crime lifestyle? How do gender roles come into play?

2. What social circumstances and situations surround women's involvement in the drug-crime lifestyle?

3. What are the shortcomings of legislation that addresses criminal behavior resulting from drug abuse?

Endnotes

1. Becker defines *moral entrepreneurs* as those individuals and groups with the power and influence to make and enforce societal rules. The legal and moral rules and laws against drug users and their lifestyle, according to Becker, are the basis for society's view of users, and the AOD users' own view of themselves, as outsiders. This interaction between those who do the labeling and those who are labeled makes up the deviant enterprise.

2. Overall, the percentage and number of women incarcerated has increased at a rate faster than that of men. The number of women in jails grew from 15,900 in

1983 to 51,600 in 1996. This represents a 9.5 percent increase per year compared to 6.2 percent for males (U.S. Department of Justice, 1998).

References

American Psychiatric Association. 1994. *Diagnostic and Statistical Manual of Mental Disorders*, 4th edition (DSM-IV). Washington, DC: Author.

Anglin, M. D., Hser, Y. I., and McGlothin, W. H. 1987. "Sex Differences in Addict Careers: 2. Becoming Addicted." *American Journal of Drug and Alcohol Abuse* 13:59–71.

Anglin, M. D. and Speckart, G. 1986. "Narcotics Use, Property Crime, and Dealing: Structural Dynamics Across the Addiction Career." *Journal of Quantitative Criminology* 2(4):355–375.

Bassuk, E. L., Browne, A., and Buckner, J. C. 1996. "Single Mothers and Welfare." *Scientific American* 275:60–63.

Battle, S. 1990. "Moving Targets: Alcohol, Crack and Black Women." In E. C. White, ed., *The Black Women's Health Book*. Seattle, WA: Seal Press.

Baum, D. 1996. *Smoke and Mirrors: The War on Drugs and the Politics of Failure*. Boston, MA: Little, Brown.

Beck, A. J. and Gilliard, D. K. 1995. "Prisoners in 1994." *Bureau of Justice Statistics Bulletin*. Washington, DC: U.S. Department of Justice.

Becker, H. S. 1963. *Outsiders: Studies in the Sociology of Deviance*. New York: The Free Press.

Beckett, K. 1995. "Fetal rights and 'Crack Moms': Pregnant Women in the War on Drugs." *Contemporary Drug Problems* 22/Winter:587–612.

Benson, C. S. and Heller, K. 1987. "Factors in the Current Adjustment of Young Adult Daughters of Alcoholic and Problem Drinking Fathers." *Journal of Abnormal Psychology*, 96(4):305–312.

Bernardi, E., Jones, M., and Tennant, C. 1989. "Quality of Parenting in Alcoholics and Narcotic Addicts." *British Journal of Psychiatry* 154:677–682.

Biron, L. L., Brochu, S., and Desjardins, L. 1995. "The Issue of Drugs and Crime Among a Sample of Incarcerated Women." *Deviant Behavior: An Interdisciplinary Journal* 16(1):25–43.

Blane, H. T., Miller, B. A., Leonard, K. E., Nochajski, T. H., Bowers, P. M., and Gondoli, D. 1988. *Intra- and Inter-generational Aspects of Serious Domestic Violence and Alcohol and Drugs.* Buffalo, NY: The Research Institute on Addictions.

Bonczar, T. P. 1997. *Characteristics of Adults on Probation, 1995.* Washington, DC: U.S. Department of Justice, Bureau of Justice Statistics.

Bourgois, P. and Dunlap E. 1993. "Exorcising Sex-for-Crack: An Ethnographic Perspective From Harlem." In Mitchell S. Ratner, ed., *Crack as Pimp: An Ethnographic Investigation of Sex-for-Crack Exchanges.* New York: Lexington Books.

Braithwaite, V. and Devine, C. 1993. "Life Satisfaction and Adjustment of Children of Alcoholics: The Effects of Parental Drinking, Family Disorganization and Survival Roles." *British Journal of Clinical Psychology* 32:417–429.

Browne, A. 1992. "Violence Against Women: Relevance for Medical Practitioners." *Journal of the American Medical Association* 267(23):3184–3189.

Browne, A., Miller, B. A., and Maguin, E. (forthcoming). "Prevalence and Severity of Lifetime Physical and Sexual Victimization Among Incarcerated Women." *Justice Quarterly.*

Byqvist, S. and Olsson, B. 1998. "Male Drug Abuse and Subcultural Affiliation in a Career Perspective." *Journal of Psychoactive Drugs* 30(1):53–68.

Center for Addiction and Substance Abuse (CASA) at Columbia University. (June 1994). *Substance Abuse and Women on Welfare.* New York, NY: Author.

Chaiken, J. M. and Chaiken, M. R. 1990. "Drugs and Predatory Crime." In M. Tonry and N. Morris, eds., *Crime and Justice: An Annual Review of the Research,* vol. 12. Chicago, IL: University of Chicago Press.

Connors, M. 1996. "Sex, Drugs, and Sexual Violence: Unraveling the Epidemic Among Poor Women in the United States." In P. Farmer, M. Connors, and J. Simmons, eds., *Women, Poverty, and AIDS: Sex, Drugs, and Structural Violence.* Monroe, ME: Common Courage Press.

Cooper, M. L., Pierce, R. S., and Tidwell, M. 1995. "Parental Drinking Problems and Adolescent Offspring Substance Use: Moderating Effects of Demographic and Familial Factors." *Psychology of Addictive Behaviors* 9(1):36–52.

DeLeon, G. 1993. "Cocaine Abusers in Therapeutic Community Treatment." In F. Tims and C. Leukefeld, eds., *Cocaine Treatment: Research and Clinical Perspectives.* Rockville, MD: National Institute on Drug Abuse.

Dembo, R., Williams, L., and Schmeidler, J. 1993. "Gender Differences in Mental Health Service Needs Among Youths Entering a Juvenile Detention Center." *Journal of Prison and Jail Health* 12(2):73–101.

Dembo, R., Williams, L., Wish, E. D., Berry, E., Getreu, A., Washburn, M., Schmeidler, J. 1990. "Examination of the Relationships Among Drug Use, Emotional/Psychological Problems, and Crime Among Youths Entering a Juvenile Detention Center." *The International Journal of the Addictions* 25(11):1301–1340.

Downs, W. R., Robertson, J. F., and Harrison, L. R. 1997. "Control Theory, Labeling Theory, and the Delivery of Services for Drug Abuse to Adolescents." *Adolescence* 32(125):1–24.

Downs, W. R., Miller, B. A., and Gondoli, D. M. 1987. "Childhood Experiences of Parental Physical Violence for Alcoholic Women as Compared With a Randomly Selected Household Sample of Women." *Violence and Victims* 2:225–240.

Dunlap E. 1992. "The Impact of Drugs on Family Life and Kin Networks in the Inner-city African American Single Parent Household." In Adele Harrell and George Peterson, eds., *Drugs, Crime and Social Isolation.* Washington, DC: Urban Institute Press.

Dunlap, E., Johnson, B. D., and Manwar, A. 1997. "A Successful Female Crack Dealer: Case Study of a Deviant Career." *Drugs, Crime, and Justice: Contemporary Perspectives* 10: 205–226.

Edin, K., and Lein, L. 1997. "Work, Welfare, and Single Mothers' Economic Survival Strategies." *American Sociological Review* 62(2):253–266.

El-Bassel, N., Gilbert, L., Schilling, R. F., Ivanoff, A., Borne, D., Safyer, and S. F. 1996. "Correlates of Crack Abuse Among Drug-using Incarcerated Women: Psychological Trauma, Social

Support, and Coping Behavior." *American Journal of Drug and Alcohol Abuse* 22(1):41–56.

El-Bassel, N., Ivanoff, A., Schilling, R. F., Gilbert, L., and Chen, D. R. 1995. "Correlates of Problem Drinking Among Drug-Using Incarcerated Women." *Addictive Diseases* 20(3):359–369.

El-Bassel, N., Schilling, R. F., Irwin, K. L., Faruque, S., Gilbert, L., Von Bargen, J., Serrano, Y., and Edlin, B. R. 1997. "Sex Trading and Psychological Distress Among Women Recruited From the Streets of Harlem." *American Journal of Public Health* 87:66–70.

Erickson, P. G. and Murray, G. F. 1989. "Sex Differences in Cocaine Use and Experiences: A Double Standard Revived?" *American Journal of Drug and Alcohol Abuse* 15(2):135–152.

Erickson, P. G. and Watson, V. A. 1990. "Women, Illicit Drugs, and Crime." In L. T. Kozlowski, H. M. Annis, H. D. Cappell, F. B. Glaser, M. S. Goodstadt, Y. Israel, H. Kalant, E. M. Sellers, and E. R. Vingilis, eds., *Research Advances in Alcohol and Drug Problems: Volume 10*. New York: Plenum Press.

Erickson, P. G., Adlaf, E. M., Smart, R. G., and Murray, G. F. 1994. *The Steel Drug: Cocaine and Crack in Perspective*. New York: Lexington Books.

Fagan, J. 1994. "Women and Drugs Revisited: Female Participation in the Cocaine Economy." *Journal of Drug Issues* 24(2):179–225.

Farr, K. A. 1995. "Fetal Abuse and the Criminalization of Behavior During Pregnancy." *Crime and Delinquency* 41(2):235–245.

Feinman, C. 1992. "Introduction: The Criminalization of a Women's Body." In C. Feinman, ed., *The Criminalization of a Women's Body*. New York: Haworth Press.

Fernandez, H. 1998. *Heroin*. Center City, MN: Hazelden.

Flanzer, J. P. 1993. "Alcohol and Other Drugs Are Key Causal Agents of Violence." In R. J. Gelles and D. R. Loseke, eds., *Current Controversies on Family Violence*. Newbury Park, CA: Sage.

Franke, N. V. 1997. "African American Women's Health: The Effects of Disease and Chronic Life Stressors." In S. B. Ruzek, U. L. Olesen, and A. Clarke, eds., *Women's Health: Complexities and Differences*. Columbus: Ohio State University Press.

Gendreau, P., Little, T., and Goggin, C. 1996. "A Meta-analysis of the Predictors of Adult Offender Recidivism: What Works." *Criminology* 34:575–607.

Giunta, C. T. and Compas, B. E. 1994. "Adult Daughters of Alcoholics: Are They Unique?" *Journal of Studies on Alcohol* 55:600–606.

Goffman, E. 1961. *Asylums: Essays on the Social Situation of Mental Patients and Other Inmates*. New York: Anchor.

Golden, M. R. 1991. "When Pregnancy Discrimination Is Gender Discrimination: The Constitutionality of Excluding Pregnant Women from Drug Treatment Programs." *New York University Law Review* 66:1832–1880.

Goldstein, P. J. 1985. "The Drugs/Violence Nexus: A Tripartite Conceptual Framework." *Journal of Drug Issues* 493–506.

——. 1990. "The Socio-Cultural Matrix of Alcohol and Drug Use: A Sourcebook of Patterns and Factors." *Interdisciplinary Studies in Alcohol Use and Abuse* 4:319–341.

Goldstein, P. J., Bellucci, P. A., Spunt, B. J., and Miller, T. 1991. "Volume of Cocaine Use and Violence: A Comparison Between Men and Women." *The Journal of Drug Issues* 21:345–367.

Gottdiener, M. 1994. *The New Urban Sociology*. New York: McGraw-Hill.

Grant, B. F., Hasin, D. S., and Dawson, D. A. 1996. "The Relationship Between DSM-IV Alcohol Use Disorders and DSM-IV Major Depression: Examination of the Primary Secondary Distinction in a General Population Sample." *Journal of Affective Disorders* 38:113–128.

Grella, C. E. and Joshi, V. 1999. "Gender Differences in Drug Treatment Careers Among Clients in the National Drug Abuse Treatment Outcome Study." *American Journal of Drug and Alcohol Abuse* 25(3):385–406.

Hagan, J. 1994. *Crime and Disrepute*. Thousand Oaks, CA: Pine Forge Press.

Hser, Y. I., Chou, C., and Anglin, M. D. 1990. "The Criminality of Female Narcotic Addicts: A Causal Modeling Approach." *Journal of Quantitative Criminology* 6(2):201–228.

Inciardi, J. A. 1992. *The War on Drugs*. Mountain View, CA: Mayfield Publishing Co.

Inciardi, J. A., Pottieger, A. E., and Faupal, C. E. 1982. "Black Women, Heroin and Crime: Some Empirical Notes." *Journal of Drug Issues* 241–250.

Inciardi, J. A. and McElrath, K. (eds.) 1995. *The American Drug Scene: An Anthology*. Los Angeles: Roxbury Publishing Company.

Johns, A. 1997. "Substance Misuse—A Primary Risk and a Major Problem of Comorbidity." *International Review of Psychiatry* 9(2-3):233–241.

Johnson, B., Goldstein, P. J., Preble, E., Schmeidler, J., Lipton, D. S., Spunt, B., and Miller, T. 1985. *Taking Care of Business: The Economics of Crime by Heroin Abusers*. Lexington, MA: Lexington Books.

Johnson, B. D., Dunlap, E., and Maher, L. 1998. "Nurturing for Careers in Drug Use and Crime: Conduct Norms for Children and Juveniles in Crack-using Households." *Substance Use and Misuse* 33(7):1511–1541.

Johnston, L. D., O'Malley, P. M., and Bachman, J. G. 1997. *National Survey Results on Drug Use From the Monitoring the Future Study, 1975–1995: Volume II—College Students and Young Adults*. Rockville, MD: National Institute on Drug Abuse. U.S. Department of Health and Human Services.

Kandel, D. B., Raveis, V. H., and Davies, M. 1991. "Suicidal Ideation in Adolescence: Depression, Substance Use, and Other Risk Factors." *Journal of Youth and Adolescence* 20:289–309.

Korver, D. M. 1991. "The Constitutionality of Punishing Pregnant Substance Abusers Under Drug Trafficking Laws: The Criminalization of a Bodily Function." *Boston College Law Review* 32:629–662.

Lang, A. R. and Stritzke, W. G. A. 1993. "Children and Alcohol." In M. Galanter, ed., *Recent Developments in Alcoholism: Ten Years of Progress*. New York: Plenum Press.

Larson, C. S. 1991. "Overview of State Legislative and Judicial Responses." *Future of Children* 1: 72–84.

Luxenburg, J. and Guild, T. E. 1993. "Women, AIDS, and the Criminal Justice System." In R. Muraskin and T. Alleman, eds., *It's A Crime: Women and Justice*. Englewood Cliffs, NJ: Prentice Hall.

Magura, S. and Laudet, A. B. 1996. "Parental Substance Abuse and Child Maltreatment: Review and Implications for Intervention." *Child and Youth Services Review* 18(1/2):193–220.

Mahan, S. 1996. *Crack Cocaine, Crime, and Women: Legal, Social, and Treatment Issues*. Thousand Oaks, CA: Sage.

Maher, L. 1992. "Punishment and Welfare: Crack Cocaine and the Regulation of Mothering." In C. Feinman, ed., *The Criminalization of a Woman's Body*. New York: Haworth Press.

Maher, L. and Daly, K. 1996. "Women in the Street-Level Drug Economy: Continuity or Change?" *Criminology* 34(4):465–491.

Mancuso, R. F. 1998. "With the Best of Intentions: New York State's Child Protection System and the Laws Used to Mask the Real Reasons for Organizational Failure." *Journal of Human Behavior in the Social Environment* 1(4):57–72.

Mauer, M. and Huling, T. 1995. *Young Black Americans and the Criminal Justice System: Five Years Later*. Washington, DC: The Sentencing Project.

Mays, G. L., Ryan, S. G., and Bejarano, C. 1997. "New Mexico Creates a DWI Drug Court." *Judicature* 81(3):122–125.

McCord, J. 1979. "Some Child-Rearing Antecedents of Criminal Behavior in Adult Men." *Journal of Psychiatry and Social Psychology* 37(9): 1477–1486.

McCoy, H. V., Inciardi, J. A., Metsch, L. R., Pottieger, A. E., and Saum, C. A. 1995. "Women, Crack, and Crime: Gender Comparisons of Criminal Activity Among Crack Cocaine Users." *Contemporary Drug Problems* 22:435–451.

McCoy, H. V., Miles, C., and Inciardi, J. A. 1995. "Survival Sex: Inner-City Women and Crack Cocaine." In J. A. Inciardi and K. McElrath, eds., *The American Drug Scene: An Anthology*. Los Angeles: Roxbury Publishing Company.

McElrath, K., Chitwood, D. D., and Comerford, M. 1997. "Crime Victimization Among Injection Drug Users." *Journal of Drug Issues* 27(4): 771–783.

Mieczkowski, T. M. 1996. "The Prevalence of Drug Use in the United States." In M. Tonry, ed., *Crime and Justice: A Review of Research*, vol. 20. Chicago: University of Chicago Press.

Miller, B. A. and Downs, W. R. 1995. "Violent Victimization Among Women With Alcohol Problems." In M. Galanter, ed., *Recent Developments in Alcoholism, Volume 12: Women and Alcoholism.* New York: Plenum Press.

Miller, B. A., Downs, W. R., and Gondoli, D. M. 1989a. "Delinquency, Childhood Violence, and the Development of Alcoholism in Women." *Crime and Delinquency* 35(1):94–108.

——. 1989b. "Spousal Violence Among Alcoholic Women as Compared to a Random Household Sample of Women." *Journal of Studies on Alcohol* 50(6):533–540.

Miller, B. A., Downs, W. R., and Testa, M. 1993. "Interrelationships Between Victimization Experiences and Women's Alcohol Use." *Journal of Studies on Alcohol*, Supplement No.11:109–117.

Miller, B. A., Maguin, E., and Downs, W. R. 1997. "Alcohol, Drugs and Violence in Children's Lives." In M. Galanter, ed., *Recent Developments in Alcoholism, Vol. 13: Alcohol and Violence.* New York: Plenum Press.

Miller, B. A., Maguin, E., and Mancuso, R. F. (forthcoming). *Service Utilization Among Women in Drug Treatment Compared to Women Drug Users in the Community.*

Miller, B. A., Nochajski, T. H., Leonard, K. E., Blane, H. T., Gondoli, D., and Bowers, P. M. 1990. "Spousal Violence and Alcohol/Drug Problems Among Parolees and Their Spouses." *Women and Criminal Justice,* 1(2):55–72.

Miller, B. A., Smyth, N. J., Janicki, P. I., and Mudar, P. J. 1995. *The Impact of Mothers' Alcohol and Drug Problems on Prevention of Violence to Children.* Poster presentation at the Research Society on Alcoholism Meeting, Steamboat Springs, CO.

Miller, N. S., Klamen, D., Hoffmann, N. G., and Flaherty, J. A. 1996. Prevalence of Depression and Alcohol and Other Drug Dependence in Addictions Treatment Populations. *Journal of Psychoactive Drugs* 28:111–124.

Morgan, P. and Joe, K. A. 1996. "Citizens and Outlaws: The Private Lives and Public Lifestyles of Women in the Illicit Drug Economy." *Journal of Drug Issues* 26(1):125–142.

Mustaine, E. E. and Tewksbury, R. 1998. "Specifying the Role of Alcohol in Predatory Victimization." *Deviant Behavior* 19(2):173–199.

Musto, D. F. 1973. *The American Disease: Origins of Narcotic Control.* New Haven, CT: Yale University Press.

New Jersey Law Journal. 1990. "Drugs During Pregnancy: Tragic, but not Criminal." *New Jersey Law Journal* 125(22):p. 9, col. 1.

Nunesdinis, M. C. and Weisner, C. 1997. "Gender Differences in the Relationship of Alcohol and Drug Use to Criminal Behavior in a Sample of Arrestees." *American Journal of Drug and Alcohol Abuse* 23(1):129–141.

Nurco, D. N., Blatchley, R. J., Hanlon, T. E., O'Grady, K. E., and McCarren, M. 1998. "The Family Experiences of Narcotic Addicts and Their Subsequent Parenting Practices." *American Journal of Drug and Alcohol Abuse* 24(1):37–59.

Nurco, D. N., Kinlock, T. W., O'Grady, K. E., and Hanlon, T. E. 1996. "Early Family Adversity as a Precursor to Narcotic Addiction." *Drug and Alcohol Dependency* 43:103–113.

Nyamathi, A. and Flaskerud, J. 1992. "A Community-Based Inventory of Current Concerns of Impoverished Homeless and Drug-Addicted Minority Women." *Research In Nursing and Health* 15:121–129.

Paltrow, L. M. 1990. "When Becoming Pregnant Is a Crime." *Criminal Justice Ethics* Winter/Spring: 41–47.

Pearson, J. and Thoennes, N. 1996. "What Happens to Pregnant Substance Abusers and Their Babies?" *Juvenile and Family Court Journal* 15–28.

Phillips, S. D. and Harm, N. J. 1997. "Women Prisoners—A Contextual Framework." *Women and Therapy* 20(4):1–9.

Plichta, S. 1992. "The Effects of Woman Abuse on Health Care Utilization and Health Status: A Literature Review." *Women's Health Issues* 2(3):154–163.

Poland, M. L., Dombrowski, M. P., Ager, J. W., and Sokol, R. J. 1993. "Punishing Pregnant Drug Users: Enhancing the Flight From Care." *Drug and Alcohol Dependency* 31:199–203.

Reed, S. O. 1993. "The Criminalization of Pregnancy: Drugs, Alcohol, and AIDS." In R. Muraskin and T. Alleman, eds., *It's A Crime: Women and Justice.* Englewood Cliffs, NJ: Prentice Hall.

Reuter, P., and MacCoun, R. J. 1995. "Lessons From the Absence of Harm Reduction in American Drug Policy." *Tobacco Control: An International Journal* 4 (Supplement 2):S28–S32.

Roberts, D. E. 1991. "Punishing Drug Addicts Who Have Babies: Women of Color, Equality, and the Right of Privacy." *Harvard Law Review* 104:1419–1482.

——. 1997. "Unshackling Black Motherhood." *Michigan Law Review* 95:938–964.

Roper, M. E. 1992. "Reaching the Babies Through the Mothers: The Effects of Prosecution on Pregnant Substance Abusers." *Law and Psychology Review* 16:171–188.

Rosenbaum, M. 1981. *Women on Heroin.* New Brunswick, NJ: Rutgers University Press.

——. 1995. "Difficulties in Taking Care of Business." In J. A. Inciardi and K. McElrath, eds., *The American Drug Scene: An Anthology.* Los Angeles: Roxbury Publishing Company.

Rubenstein, L. 1991. "Prosecuting Maternal Substance Abusers: An Unjustified and Ineffective Policy." *Yale Law and Policy Review* 9:130–160.

Sanchez, J. E. and Johnson, B. D. 1987. "Women and the Drugs-Crime Connection: Crime Rates Among Drug Abusing Women at Rikers Island." *Journal of Psychoactive Drugs* 19(2):205–216.

Sandmaier, M. 1980. *The Invisible Alcoholics: Women and Alcohol Abuse in America.* New York: McGraw Hill.

Schuckit, M. A. 1995. "Chasing the Dragon." In J. A. Inciardi and K. McElrath, eds., *The American Drug Scene: An Anthology.* Los Angeles: Roxbury Publishing Company.

Schuckit, M. A., Tipp, J. E., and Kelner, E. 1994. "Are Daughters of Alcoholics More Likely to Marry Alcoholics?" *American Journal of Drug and Alcohol Abuse* 20(2):237–245.

Searles, J. S. and Windle, M. 1990. "Introduction and Overview: Salient Issues in the Children of Alcoholics Literature." In M. Windle and J. S. Searles, eds., *Children of Alcoholics: Critical Perspectives.* New York: Guilford Press.

Simons, R. L. and Whitbeck, L. B. 1991. "Sexual Abuse as a Precursor to Prostitution and Victimization Among Adolescent Homeless Women." *Journal of Family Issues* 12:361–379.

Singer, S. 1996. *Recriminalizing Delinquency: Violent Juvenile Crimes and Juvenile Justice Reform.* Cambridge, England: Cambridge University Press.

Skolnick, J. H., Correl, T., Navarro, E., and Rabb R. 1997. "The Social Structure of Street Drug Dealing." *Drugs, Crime and Justice: Contemporary Perspectives* 8:159–191.

Smith, E. M., Pryzbeck, T. R., Bradford, S. E., Gogineni, A., and Spitznagel, E. L. 1994. "Adult Offspring of Alcoholic Women as Family History Informants." *Alcoholism: Clinical and Experimental Research* 18:1354–1360.

Smyth, N. J. and Miller, B. A. 1998. "Parenting Issues for Substance Abusing Women." In S. L. A. Straussner and E. Zelvin, eds., *Gender Issues in Addiction: Men and Women in Treatment.* New York: Jason Aronson, Inc.

Sommers, I. and Baskin, D. R. 1994. "Factors Related to Female Adolescent Initiation into Violent Street Crime." *Youth and Society* 25(4):468–489.

Stark, E. and Flitcraft, A. 1996. *Women at Risk.* Thousand Oaks, CA: Sage.

Steffensmeier, D. and Allan, E. 1996. "Gender and Crime: Toward a Gendered Theory of Female Offending." *Annual Review of Sociology* 22:459–487.

Steinhausen, H. C. 1995. "Children of Alcoholic Parents: A Review." *European Journal of Child and Adolescent Psychiatry* 4(3):143–152.

Stephens, R. C. 1991. *The Street Addict Role.* Albany: State University of New York Press.

Sterk, C. 1999. *Fast Lives: Women Who Use Crack Cocaine.* Philadelphia: Temple University Press.

Streifel, C. 1997. "Gender, Alcohol Use, and Crime." In R. W. Wilsnack and S. C. Wilsnack, eds., *Gender and Alcohol: Individual and Social Perspectives.* New Brunswick, NJ: Rutgers Center of Alcohol Studies.

Swenson, V. J. and Crabbe, C. 1994. "Pregnant Substance Abusers: A Problem That Won't Go Away." *St. Mary's Law Journal* 25(2):37–42.

Sykes, G. M. and Matza, D. 1957. "Techniques of Neutralization: A Theory of Delinquency." *The American Journal of Sociology* 22:664–670.

U.S. Department of Health and Human Services. June 1997. *National Household Survey on Drug*

Abuse: Population Estimates 1996. Rockville, MD: Substance Abuse and Mental Health Services Administration Office of Applied Studies.

——. August 1999. *National Household Survey on Drug Abuse: Population Estimates 1998.* Rockville, MD: Substance Abuse and Mental Health Services Administration Office of Applied Studies.

U.S. Department of Justice. 1994. *Women in Prison.* Washington, DC: Bureau of Justice Statistics.

——. 1995. *Drugs and Crime Facts, 1994.* Rockville, MD: Office of Justice Programs, Bureau of Justice Statistics.

——. 1997. *1996 Drug Use Forecasting Annual Report on Adult and Juvenile Arrestees.* Washington, DC: Bureau of Justice Statistics.

——. 1998. *Profile of Jail Inmates.* Washington, DC: Bureau of Justice Statistics.

Velleman, R. 1992. "Intergenerational Effects—A Review of Environmentally Oriented Studies Concerning the Relationship Between Parental Alcohol Problems and Family Disharmony in the Genesis of Alcohol and Other Problems, I: The Intergenerational Effects of Alcohol Problems." *The International Journal of the Addictions* 27(3):253–280.

Viemero, V. 1996. "Factors in Childhood that Predict Later Criminal Behavior." *Aggressive Behavior* 22:87–97.

Waldorf. D. 1973. *Careers in Dope.* Englewood Cliffs, NJ: Prentice Hall.

Walters, G. D. 1994. *Drugs and Crime in Lifestyle Perspective.* Thousand Oaks, CA: Sage.

——. 1999. *The Addiction Concept: Working Hypothesis or Self-Fulfilling Prophecy?* Needham Heights, MA: Allyn & Bacon.

Weiss, R. D., Mirin, S. M., Griffin, M. L., and Michael, J. 1988. "Psychopathology in Chronic Cocaine Abusers." *Journal of Nervous and Mental Disorders* 176:719–725.

Weissman, M. M., Leaf, P. J., Bruce, M. L., and Florio, L. 1988. "The Epidemiology of Dysthymia in Five Communities: Rates, Risks, Comorbidity, and Treatment." *American Journal of Psychiatry* 145:815–819.

Wellisch, J., Prendergast, M. L., and Anglin, M. D. 1994. *Drug-abusing Women Offenders: Results of a National Survey.* Washington, DC: U.S. Department of Justice.

Wilsnack, S. C., Wilsnack, R. W., and Hiller-Sturmhofel, S. 1994. "How Women Drink: Epidemiology of Women's Drinking and Problem Drinking." *Alcohol, Health, and Research World* 18(3):173–181.

Wilsnack, S. C., Wilsnack, R. W., and Klassen, A. 1984. "Women's Drinking and Drinking Problems: Patterns From a 1981 National Survey." *American Journal of Public Health* 74(1):1231–1238

Wilson, W. J. 1996. *When Work Disappears: The World of the New Urban Poor.* New York: Vintage.

Windle, M., Carlisle-Frank, P., Azizy, L., and Windle, R. C. 1994. "Women and Health-Related Behaviors." *Drug and Alcohol Abuse Reviews* 5:415–436.

Winick, C. 1967. "Drug Addiction and Crime." *Current History* 52:349–354.

Young, N. 1997. "Alcohol and Other Drugs: The Scope of the Problem Among Pregnant and Parenting Women in California." *Journal of Psychoactive Drugs* 29(1):3–22.

Congressional Bills

104th Congress 1st Session. H.R. 1264 (March 16, 1995). "To amend the Controlled Substances Act and the Controlled Substances Import and Export Act to eliminate certain mandatory minimum penalties relating to crack cocaine offenses."

105th Congress 1st Session. H.R. 1419 (April 23, 1997). "To reduce the incidence of child abuse and neglect, and for other purposes." ✦

8
Explaining Female Offending

*Darrell Steffensmeier
and Lisa Broidy*

Social, biological, economic, and psychological explanations have been combined in various ways to develop theories for why women commit crime, as well as why they commit less crime than men. The number and complexity of these theories have expanded greatly in recent years, as part of the growing body of work on gender both in criminology and in the social sciences more generally. The principal goal of this chapter is to trace the theoretical and empirical development of knowledge regarding female offending.

In this chapter we begin by summarizing key similarities and differences between female and male patterns of offending in order to anticipate what needs to be explained. Next, we present a brief review of early explanations of criminality among women and the gender gap. We then examine the more contemporary period, focusing in particular on two competing theoretical approaches. The first approach attempts to make sense of female crime within the context of mainstream criminological theory; the competing approach consists of efforts to develop new theoretical frameworks with the explicit goal of explaining female offending patterns and the gender gap. Finally, we highlight recent efforts to link these competing approaches by expanding on a gendered paradigm for explaining female (and male) crime. We also set forth a number of recommendations for future theoretical work.

Female (and Male) Offending Patterns

Many sources provide data that permit comparison of male and female offending. Because these findings are described elsewhere in this volume, we will simply highlight the key similarities and differences between female and male patterns of offending. These aggregate and individual patterns raise questions of central import to the development of theories that can account for gender differences in crime as well as for the specific dynamics of both male and female offending.

On the aggregate level, patterns of offending by women and men are notable for both their similarities and their differences. Rates for minor property crime and substance abuse offenses are universally higher than rates for robbery and murder. Still, men offend at higher rates—usually much higher—than women for all crime categories except prostitution. Regardless of the data source, crime type, level of involvement, or measure of participation, the gender gap is greatest for serious crime and least for mild forms of lawbreaking, such as minor property crimes (Kruttschnitt 1994; Steffensmeier and Allan 1995). In addition, the financial and physical losses that result from female thefts, property crimes, drug offenses, and assaults are typically smaller than those for similar offenses committed by males. Macro-level theories of crime need to be able to explain how various historical, structural, and contextual forces differentially affect the offending rates of males and females, leading to similar aggregate-level patterns but distinct rates of offending.

Individual-level crime patterns also display gender similarities and differences. For both males and females, offending peaks during the teen years and gradually declines thereafter. However, while there is evidence that a small, but discernible, percentage of males are "life-course persistent" offenders whose criminal careers start early and continue into adulthood, there is little evidence to suggest that a similar group exists among female offenders. Differences in the course of offending for males and females are especially marked with respect to violence. Violent offending begins and peaks earlier for males than for females. Further, violent female offenders are less likely to recidivate than violent male offenders, and they desist at a greater rate (Weiner 1989). Some evidence suggests the existence of short-term careers in prostitution and minor thefts/fraud (shoplifting, forged checks) among women, but even in these less serious offense categories, long-term careers are anomalous. Female offenders rarely express the strong commitment to and self-identification with crime often found in qualitative studies of male offenders. The overwhelming dominance of males in more organized and highly lucrative crimes, whether based in the underworld or the "upperworld," is further reflection of women's lesser inclination to pursue a criminal lifestyle (Commonwealth of Pennsylvania 1991; Daly 1989; Steffensmeier 1983).

Lack of a strong criminal identity or commitment among female offenders is also reflected in findings concerning differences in the group dynamics of male and female offending. Females are more likely than males to be solo perpetrators or to be part of small, relatively nonpermanent crime groups. When female offenders are involved with others, particularly in more lucrative thefts or other criminal enterprises, they typically act as accomplices to males who both organize and lead the execution of the crime (see Steffensmeier 1983, for a review). This pattern comes through in studies of female gang members as well. Gangs are an overwhelmingly male arena, and female involvement has tended to be limited and typically confined to auxiliary roles in male gangs. Since the 1970s, research suggests that female gangs may be gaining some autonomy, but they remain dependent on male gangs, with female gang members often excluded from most economic criminal activities (Bowker,

Gross, and Klein 1980; Campbell 1984). Further, despite higher levels of violence among female gang members compared to females more generally, female gang members are significantly less violent than their male counterparts (Fagan 1990).

Given women's lesser inclination to identify themselves as criminal, evidence highlighting the importance of situational inducements to crime among females makes sense. A number of studies suggest that women need a higher level of provocation before turning to crime, especially serious crime. For example, in comparison to male offenders, female offenders are more likely to have been physically or sexually abused as children or adults (Chesney-Lind and Shelden 1992; Daly 1994; Gilfus 1992; Widom 1989). Denno (1994), in her analysis of Philadelphia cohort data, reports that although many factors are as predictive of female as male criminality, female offenders are more likely to have had records of neurological and other biological or psychological abnormalities. Likewise, Daly (1994) reports that female offenders (in comparison to male offenders) in a New Haven felony court had greater childhood and adult exposure to abuse. However, she also notes that the female felons were nevertheless more conventional than the males in having greater responsibilities for children, a commitment to education, and legitimate sources of income.

The conventional commitments of female offenders are also reflected in evidence suggesting that the threatened loss of valued relationships may play a greater role in female offending. Although the saying, "She did it all for love" is sometimes overplayed in reference to female criminality, the role of men in initiating women into crime—especially serious crime—is a consistent finding across research (Gilfus 1992; Miller 1986; Pettiway 1987; Steffensmeier 1983; Steffensmeier and Terry 1986). Such findings suggest that women may be as amenable to risk as males but that their risk taking is differentially motivated, with women taking risks that they deem necessary to protect relationships and emotional commitments. While this empathic tendency has been used to explain female offending, it is also a common explanation for women's lower crime rates. Many have argued that an empathic disposition and strong concern for others is what keeps females from engaging in serious, violent crime at rates comparable to those of males.

In sum, at the aggregate level rates of serious crime against property and persons are significantly lower for females than for males. At the individual level, females are less likely to participate in or lead criminal groups. And, when women do commit crime, especially serious crime, it is commonly the result of direct or indirect provocation, such as a history of abuse or the urgings of a criminal male. Nevertheless, females *do* commit crimes, even serious violent crimes, and theories have emerged to explain both between- and within-sex differences in offending. These theories address two key questions: What explains the universal gender gap in crime, and why are some females more likely to violate the law than other females? While theoretically distinct, these questions overlap, and most theories or theoretical treatments aim to explain both sets of issues.

Explaining Female Offending: Early Social Science Views

Early explanations of female crime tended to reflect prevailing views regarding crime and human behavior more generally (see review in Pollock-Byrne 1990). During the late 1800s and early 1900s, theories of human behavior were primarily biologically or socially deterministic. In criminology these biases were apparent in theories attributing crime to either biological or social factors beyond the control of individuals. In the 1930s psychological theories gained prominence and psychological explanations of crime began to emerge. At the same time, major sociological explanations of crime (differential association, anomie/social dis-

organization) were emerging that emphasized the importance of social and cultural factors in accounting for criminality. However, as was the case with biological and psychological theories, the focus and attention of the sociological explanations were primarily on male criminality, with female criminality largely ignored.

Although early treatment of crime focused on male criminality, a few attempts were made to explain female crime. As was the case in criminology more generally, two competing viewpoints dominated writings on female offending in the late nineteenth and early twentieth centuries. One viewpoint emphasized the role of biological and psychological factors in women's and girls' crime, seeing criminal women as exhibiting masculine biological or psychological orientations. The second view stressed the role of social or economic forces and assumed that the social and cultural influences affecting male criminality similarly influence female criminality.

Current interpretations of the history of thought on female crime see a strong "biological" (and psychological) bias in early treatments of female crime. This bias can be seen in early criminological works, which argued that environmental factors are much more predictive of male than female criminality and that females are not affected, or are affected differently, by the macrosocial variables that affect men. Female lawbreakers were viewed as "abnormal," whereas male lawbreaking was seen as a "normal" response to adverse or abnormal economic conditions (for reviews, see Belknap 1996; Rasche 1990; Steffensmeier and Clark 1980). Rita Simon (1975) writes that

Traditionally, most writers on the subject of women in crime have traced female criminality to biological and/or psychological sources, with little or no discussion of such social-structural considerations as the state of the economy, occupational and educational opportunities [etc.]. (p. 4)

Of course, biological and psychological explanations were also provided for male criminality. Lombroso, for example, linked both male and female crime to biological predisposition. And, early sociological explanations, while more often developed to explain male crime, were adopted to explain female crime as well, especially by female criminologists leery of biological determinism (for a summary see chapter 6 in Freedman 1981). These theorists argued that the same social and cultural influences affecting male criminality influence female criminality as well. This view was also prominent in early criminology textbooks (Steffensmeier and Clark 1980). Since the early part of the twentieth century when criminology became a subfield of sociology rather than of the medical-legal profession, the rule among U.S. authors of criminology textbooks has been to provide a sociocultural interpretation of gender differences in crime and to avoid or reject biological explanations. Indeed, by far the most popular criminology text, that of Sutherland, was perhaps the most antagonistic towards biological and psychological (e.g., individual pathology, "deficit" personality) explanations of crime and most forceful in accepting sociogenic views (see review in Steffensmeier and Clark 1980).

It is notable, however, that while a handful of female criminologists at the turn of the century focused their research efforts on explaining female offending, the bulk of criminological theory developed in the late 1800s and early 1900s treated female criminality as an anomaly not worthy of much attention. Steffensmeier and Clark's (1980) review of early criminology textbooks does indicate a tendency to avoid biological explanations of sex differences in crime, emphasizing instead structural and cultural variables. However, in all but two cases, textbook treatments of female crime or of gender differences in offending were limited to seven pages or less. Further, 10 of the 34 textbooks evaluated offered no explanation for gender differences in crime. In short, to the extent that criminologists attempted to explain female offending or gender differences in crime, these explanations were patterned on prevailing explanations of male offending, which were similarly biologically/psychologically or socially/culturally deterministic.

The notion that female offending is an anomaly was further emphasized by early explanations that female criminals were "masculine" in their biological or psychological orientation. Lombroso (1895) for example, viewed female criminals as having an excess of male characteristics. He argued that biologically, criminal females were more similar to normal or criminal males than to normal females. According to Freud (1933), female crime results from a "masculinity complex," stemming from penis envy. He argued that all females suffer from penis envy but that most are able to make a healthy adjustment to the realization that they do not have a penis. Those who cannot successfully resolve their penis envy overidentify with maleness and are likely to act out in criminal ways. Both Lombroso and Freud, then, viewed the female criminal as biologically or psychologically male in orientation.

While some theorists linked female crime to "masculinity," others saw it as distinctly feminine. Eleanor and Shelden Glueck (1934), based on their studies of adult and juvenile delinquents, concluded that female crime reflected the inability of certain women—especially those from disadvantaged neighborhood and family contexts—to control their sexual impulses. The Gluecks also subscribed to the theme of the woman offender as a pathetic creature, a view that characterized much criminological writing in the 1930s:

> The women are themselves on the whole a sorry lot. The major problem involved in the delinquency and criminality of our girls is their lack of control of their sexual impulses. Illicit sex practices are extremely common among them, beginning surprisingly early, and carry in them brain disease, illegitimacy and unhappy matrimony. When we consider the family background of our

women we should rather marvel that a sizable faction of them, by one influence or another, abandoned their misbehavior, than that so many of them continued their delinquencies. (Glueck and Glueck 1934, 96)

Otto Pollack's *The Criminality of Women*, published in 1950, is the most important work on female crime prior to the modern period (for reviews, see Leonard 1982; Simon 1975; Smart 1976). First, the book reviewed and organized previous work on women and crime in the American, British, French, and German literatures. Second, it challenged basic assumptions concerning the extent and quality of women's involvement in criminal behavior. Third, it explained female crime and the gender gap with reference to a mix of biological, psychological, and sociological factors.

According to Pollack, women's crime has a "masked character," and their true crime rate probably approximates that of men. The types of crimes women commit—shoplifting, domestic thefts, thefts by prostitutes, abortions, perjury—are underrepresented in crime statistics. These crimes are easily concealed and seldom reported; even when the crimes are detected and reported, women are less likely than men to be arrested or prosecuted because of the double standard favorable to women and because women usually play accomplice or less overt roles when co-offending with men. Male victims are often too embarrassed to report female offenders, and law enforcement officials are too chivalrous to arrest or prosecute them. Also, when a man and a woman team up to commit crimes, the man is usually the more active partner and thus more likely to be caught and punished. Thus, consistent with some prior criminological writings (see review in Steffensmeier and Clark 1980), Pollack highlighted differences in citizen and law enforcement responses to female as compared to male offending. But he was the first writer to insist that women's participation in crime approaches that of men and is commensurate with their representation in the population.

Pollack emphasized the importance of social or environmental factors as causally related to female crime. He placed particular emphasis on social factors traditionally mentioned in criminology, including poverty, crowded living conditions, broken homes, delinquent companions, and the adverse effects of doing time in reform schools or penitentiaries. Pollack also noted the considerable overlap in causative factors for delinquency among girls and boys, women and men.

> In summary, it is either the criminal association in the home or that resulting from the attempts of girls to compensate for the failure of their home or school, which seems to have a decisive influence upon the causation of juvenile delinquency and professional crime. *This picture is basically the same for girls and boys.* The differential lies only in the role which illicit sex conduct for monetary gain plays in the shaping of the female criminal career, and in the observation that female professional criminals do not specialize in one line as do men. (p. 139, emphasis ours)

Pollack also noted that other social factors—the double standard of sexual morality, the disadvantaged economic and occupational position of women, and the influence of modern advertising—contribute to female crime. These factors foster frustration, resentment, and criminal desires that may lead to perjury or false accusations against men, aggressive behavior toward partners or others, and the temptation to steal (especially in their roles as shoppers and domestics).

On the other hand, a fundamental theme of Pollack's work is the attribution of a biological and physiological basis to female criminality. This theme is reflected in two important elements of his treatment. First, Pollack stressed the inherently deceitful nature of the female sex. He saw this deceitfulness as socially induced to some extent because physical weakness can force a woman to resort to deception and because of other basic facts in a woman's life—including societal pressures to conceal her period of menstruation and expectations that women attract a husband indirectly through wily charm. However, Pollack (1950) saw the primary source of women's deceitfulness as lying in the female physiology, in particular in the passive role assumed by women during sexual intercourse. Pollack considered this inactive role to be biologically, rather than culturally, determined.

> Not enough attention has been paid to the physiological fact that man must achieve an erection in order to perform the sex act and will not be able to hide his failure. His lack of positive emotion in the sexual sphere must become overt to the partner and pretense of sexual response is impossible for him, if it is lacking. Woman's body, however, permits such a pretense to a certain degree and lack of orgasm does not prevent her ability to participate in the sex act. (p. 138)

Second, Pollack reinforced the longstanding idea that the causative influence of biological factors and individual pathology is greater for explaining female than male criminality. In his view, the influences of hormonal and generative phases (e.g., menstruation, pregnancy, and menopause) were particularly significant for female criminality:

> The student of female criminality cannot afford to overlook the generally known and recognized fact that these generative phases are frequently accompanied by psychological disturbances which may upset the need and satisfaction balance of the individual or weaken her internal inhibitions, and thus become causative factors in female crime. (p. 157)

In sum, early theories of criminality tended to include or emphasize biological and psychological factors to a greater extent when explaining female offending than when explaining male offending. Still, despite recent critiques that characterize all

early explanations of female crime as biologically or psychologically deterministic, early sociological explanations of female crime were not entirely absent from the literature. Criminology textbooks and some other writings offered an interpretation of female offending and the gender gap that took into account gender differences in role expectations, socialization patterns and application of social control, opportunities to commit particular offenses, and access to criminally oriented subcultures (see reviews in Chesney-Lind 1986; Steffensmeier and Clark 1980).

A rich and complex literature on female criminality has emerged over the past few decades. Embedded in this literature is an ongoing debate on how best to explain female criminality and the gender gap in offending. One side of the debate views female crime as a function of the same theoretical processes that explain male crime. From this perspective, the gender gap in crime reflects gender differences in levels of exposure to the criminogenic forces identified in mainstream criminological theory. Feminist critics counter this view, arguing that male and female offending are qualitatively distinct, requiring unique theoretical explanations (see Gelsthorpe and Morris 1990; Leonard 1982). More recent explanations have attempted to merge these two camps by recognizing both similarities and differences in the etiology of male and female offending. In the remainder of this chapter we briefly discuss the contributions of traditional criminological frameworks to our understanding of female offending and the gender gap, and point out some of their shortcomings. We then focus on recent theoretical developments that merge these traditional explanations with more gender-specific explanations.

Applying Traditional Sociological Theories to Female Criminality

Despite the oft-raised question of whether female crime can be explained by theories developed mainly by male criminologists to explain male crime, a variety of evidence suggests that these traditional theoretical perspectives do contribute to our understanding of female offending patterns and gender differences in crime. These theories offer defensible accounts of both aggregate and individual level patterns in less serious crimes. However, traditional theories are more problematic when applied to serious female crime and gender differences in serious crime.

Aggregate Level Patterns and Traditional Explanations

Descriptive and correlational studies at the aggregate level suggest a number of similarities between male and female offenders. Offenders of both genders come from similar backgrounds, they have comparable offending patterns (despite differences in levels of offending), and their crime rates are affected by similar structural factors. However, studies also indicate that, despite these similarities, the gender gap in offending, especially serious offending, is largely unaffected by aggregate-level social forces.

Similarity in social backgrounds. In the aggregate, the social backgrounds of female offenders tend to be quite similar to those of male offenders (see reviews in Chesney-Lind and Shelden 1992; Denno 1994; Steffensmeier and Allan 1995). Like male offenders, female offenders (especially those who commit the most serious crimes) are typically of low socioeconomic status, are poorly educated, are under- or unemployed, and are disproportionately from minority groups. The main gender difference in this social profile is the greater presence of dependent children among female offenders.

Regression of female rates on male rates. The extent to which male rates can predict female rates provides indirect evidence of similarity in the etiology of female and male crime (Steffensmeier and Allan, 1988; Steffensmeier, Allan, and Streifel

1989). Groups or societies that have high male rates of crime also have high female rates, whereas groups or societies that have low male rates also have low female rates. When the male rate rises, declines, or holds steady across a specific historical period, the female rate behaves in a similar fashion. Statistically, when the female rates for a given group are regressed on the male rates for the same group, across time or across crime categories, the results for most comparisons do not differ significantly from a prediction of no difference (Steffensmeier and Allan 1988; Steffensmeier and Streifel 1992). Such findings suggest that female rates respond to the same social and legal forces as male rates, independent of any condition unique to women (Boritch and Hagan 1990; Steffensmeier 1980; Steffensmeier and Streifel 1992).

Aggregate analysis. In a rare aggregate study of structural correlates of female crime rates, Steffensmeier and Haynie (2000) report findings similar to those for comparable aggregate studies of male rates. For example, rates of female crime tend to be higher in cities with high levels of economic inequality, poverty, joblessness, and female-headed households. Other structural variables, such as residential stability, structural density, and population size, also have similar effects on rates of female and male offending. Overall, both the direction and the size of the effects of structural disadvantage variables (e.g., poverty) on offending rates are gender-neutral.

Taken together, these findings suggest that similar structural forces affect male and female crime rates. As such, macro-level theories developed to explain crime rates should offer equally adequate explanations of female and male crime rates. The findings lend support to social disorganization and macro-level strain theories as explanations for both male and female crime rates. The "milieu" effects of deleterious social conditions produce frustration, undermine legitimacy, and weaken social bonds in ways that are criminogenic for female as well as male residents. Further, since female criminality is often embedded within the context of male behavior—i.e., co-offending with males (e.g., as accomplices to male-initiated property crime) or responding to male-instigated crime (e.g., violent offending in response to an abusive male)—considerable similarity in social and ecological characteristics of female and male offenders is expected (Bailey and Peterson 1995; Daly 1994; Steffensmeier 1983). Also, gender differences in routine activities might help explain lower overall base rates of offending among women. However, the persistence of the gender gap suggests that, while male and female crime rates respond similarly to universal structural factors, other macro-level forces may work to differentially influence the rates of offending among males and females.

Individual-Level Patterns and Traditional Explanations

Individual-level analyses using self-report data also suggest similarities and differences in the processes that account for male and female offending.

Similarities in causal factors. A number of recent studies have used self-report data to assess the degree to which the theoretical processes that explain male offending also explain female offending. These studies suggest that the causal factors identified by traditional theories of crime, such as anomie, social control, and differential association, are just as applicable to female offending (Akers et al. 1979; Giordano, Cernkovitch, and Pugh 1986; Hagan 1989; Jensen and Eve 1976; Paternoster and Triplett 1988; Smith 1979; Smith and Paternoster 1987; Tittle 1980). Measures of bonds, associations, learning, parental controls, perceptions of risk, and so forth have comparable effects across the genders. However, such findings apply mainly to minor offending, since available self-report data sets do not lend themselves to the study of serious offending—either male or female—because of limited

sample size, question content and format, and other problems.

Individual-level accounts of the gender gap. Mainstream individual-level theories seem better suited than traditional macro-level theories to account for persistent gender differences in offending. Conventional criminological theories, for example, suggest that females offend less than males because they are less subject than males to the cultural emphasis on material success (anomie); because they are less exposed to influence from delinquent peers (differential association/social learning); because they have stronger social bonds and are subjected to greater supervision (social control); or because they are less likely to become involved in gangs (cultural transmission). However, such explanations of the gender gap emphasize quantitative gender differences in levels of exposure to key criminogenic influences to the exclusion of qualitative differences in experiences with these criminogenic influences that are shaped by the dynamics of gender.

Shortcomings of Traditional Theories

Traditional social-structural and individual-level criminological theories are helpful in explaining overall patterns of female and male offending, and they shed some light on why female levels of offending are lower than male levels. However, these approaches are less enlightening in offering explanations for a variety of both subtle and profound differences in female and male offending patterns. Moreover, conventional theories were never designed to tap the encompassing structure and repetitive process of gender as it affects the criminal involvements of either women or men. These theories, for example, offer little insight into such questions as:

- Why are serious crimes against property and against persons so much less a feature of female offending?

- Why are female offenders less likely to participate in or lead criminal groups?
- Why do women seem to need a higher level of provocation before turning to crime, especially serious crime?
- Why does female offending often involve relational concerns?

These and other questions often involve subtle issues of *context* that are not addressed by most traditional and contemporary theories and that tend to be invisible (or nearly so) to quantitative analyses. Fortunately, as we discuss later, contextual issues are illuminated by a wealth of qualitative information to be found both in the traditional criminological literature (Elliott 1952; Reitman 1937) and in the profusion of qualitative research produced by feminist criminologists in recent years.

'New' Theoretical Frameworks and Elaborations of Traditional Theories

The past few decades have witnessed a number of novel attempts to develop causal explanations for women's participation in crime. These explanations typically combine elements of the traditional theories with emerging frameworks in feminism and gender studies. Here we review and critique these explanations.

Macro-Level Explanations

As we have noted, traditional structural explanations for time and space variations in crime tend to ignore the interaction between explanatory structural processes and the dynamics of gender. This neglect has led to the development of macro-level theories aimed specifically at explaining gender differences in crime rates by focusing on time and space variations in gender inequality.

Early opponents of biological explanations of crime cited variations in the ratio of female to male arrests to demonstrate the superiority of sociological explanations of crime (see the review in Steffensmeier and Clark 1980). If the gender gap had a biological basis, it would not vary across time and space. However, recent work suggests that the gender gap does not vary as much across specified groups and times as previously believed. There is some evidence of offense-specific variation in less serious forms of lawbreaking. However, across most offenses, the more systematic analyses of self-report data and official arrest statistics reveal that the gender gap is far more stable than variant across race, age, social class, rural-urban comparisons, and comparisons of less developed and developed nations (Canter 1982; Steffensmeier and Allan 1988; Steffensmeier et al. 1989; Tittle 1980). Even the apparent narrowing of the gender gap during war largely disappears when controls are included for the wartime absence of young men most at risk for crime (Steffensmeier, Shehan, and Rosenthal 1980). The strongest evidence for time-space variations is the narrowing of the gender gap in crime over recent decades in the United States (and some other nations). But, as reviewed elsewhere in this book (see Steffensmeier, chapter 13), this narrowing occurs mainly for less serious forms of lawbreaking.

Unlike the aggregate-level similarities between male and female offenders and offending rates discussed earlier, the relative stability of the gender gap suggests that gender dynamics may have some affect on offending above and beyond other important structural forces. In those instances where the gender gap in crime does vary across societies or population subgroups, the traditional view has been to attribute these variations to differences in gender equality over time and among social groups. The gender gap, it was argued, occurs less in social settings where female roles and statuses are more similar to those of men (e.g., in developed compared to developing countries; in urban rather than in rural settings; among blacks compared to whites; among older ages compared to younger). The gender equality and crime hypothesis attracted widespread public attention in the 1970s, when some criminologists suggested that increases in the female share of arrests could be attributed to gains in gender equality as a result of the women's movement (Adler 1975; Simon 1975). This interpretation of the "dark side" of female liberation was embraced enthusiastically by the media.

Criminologists today question some of the assumptions of the gender equality viewpoint and instead propose that structural forces other than gender equality better explain time-space variations in the gender gap. First, these criminologists point to the peculiarity of considering

> a hypothesis that assumed improving girls' and women's economic conditions would lead to an increase in female crime when almost all the existing criminological literature stresses the role played by discrimination and poverty (and unemployment or underemployment) in the creation of crime. (Chesney-Lind and Shelden 1992, 77)

Second, these criminologists set forth a variety of alternative explanations that appear to provide more plausible and more parsimonious accounts for those differences that do occur in the gender gap. These explanations, for example, emphasize time-space differences in the extent of economic insecurity and community disorganization experienced by women, the extent to which a highly formalized law enforcement apparatus and sanctioning system exists, and the availability of opportunities for "female" type crimes. The female share of offending will be greater in those settings where economic adversity among large subgroups of women is widespread, where opportunities to commit consumer-based crimes such as shoplifting and check fraud are substantial, and where recordkeeping and policing practices are bureaucratized. (For more coverage of alternative explanations of variations in the gender gap, see chapter 13 on female crime trends.)

Hartnagel's (1982; Hartnagel and Mizanudin, 1986) modernization theory focuses on structural factors that affect crime rates generally in conjunction with those that affect female gender roles. This framework is rooted in the argument that understanding gender differences in crime rates necessitates an examination of "social structural variables which may have an impact on both the development of female roles and crime rates" (1982, 478). The hypothesis set forth is that modernization will affect crime rates and that corresponding changes in the female gender role will intervene in the relationship between modernization and female crime rates. However, in empirical analyses, Hartnagel (1982; Hartnagel and Mizanudin, 1986) finds little support for this hypothesis. Measures of modernization and female role participation do not appear to affect female crime. The problem may lie in the theoretical assumption that modernization triggers gender-role convergence. While modernization has led to some changes in female roles and opportunities, significant gender-based differences in status, opportunity, and behavioral expectations remain. Macro-level explanations of female crime and the gender gap need to take into account persistent, structurally reinforced gender differences along with structurally induced convergence.

Lack of empirical support for a link between modernization, changing female roles, and changes in female crime rates suggests that "gender-based inequalities in the distribution of power and wealth may prove a more fruitful avenue to pursue in future attempts to explain cross-national variation in female crime" (Hartnagel and Mizanudin 1986, 12). This statement is reminiscent of Cloward and Piven's (1979) theoretical argument regarding why modernization has not led to significant increases in female crime rates. Despite modernization, gender segregation persists and differentially shapes the form and frequency of male and female deviance. Cloward and Piven's theory, rooted in the strain/anomie tradition, suggests that the adaptations to strain available to females are shaped by their social structural positions. Specifically, limits on women's work force opportunities in conjunction with their more extensive domestic responsibilities limit the deviant adaptations available to women. As a result, "The only models of female deviance which our society encourages or permits women to imagine, emulate and act out are essentially privatized modes of self destruction" (p. 660). Relatedly, Harris (1977) argues that societies are structured such that all behaviors are "type-scripted." These "type-scripts" specify acceptable and unacceptable forms of deviance for various categories of social actors—including men and women. As a result of these type scripts, "It is unlikely or 'impossible' for women to attempt assassination, robbery, or rape" (p. 12). Such behavioral proscriptions against female involvement in externalizing forms of deviance may not be significantly affected by modernization.

Steffensmeier et al.'s (1989) findings further emphasize the inability of gender convergence to account for changes in female crime rates, given enduring proscriptions against certain types of crime for women. They note that gender convergence is one of many possible theoretical explanations for a link between development and increases in female percentage of arrests. Other possibilities are corresponding changes in female economic marginality/insecurity, increased opportunities for "female" crimes (i.e., consumer-based crimes), and increased formalization of social control. They do not find support for a link between gender convergence and increases in female percentage of arrests. However, both increases in opportunities for consumer-based crimes and the formalization of social control mechanisms are associated with increases in the female percentage of arrests associated with development. This finding reinforces the argument that differences rather than similarities in the social structural positions of males and females explain time and space variations in crime rates, both within and between the sexes (Cloward and Piven 1979;

Harris 1977). Increases in female arrests do not appear to be related to increasing similarities between the status of males and females. Rather, development appears to lead to increases in female arrest rates because opportunities for "female" crimes increase, and the formalization of social control mechanisms increases the likelihood of official sanctions against females.

Messershmidt (1986) further explores the relationship between social structural opportunities, behavioral expectations, and the gender gap in offending. He argues that capitalism and patriarchy structure individuals' opportunities and shape their behaviors. He contends that in a capitalist-patriarchal system women will commit the fewest and least serious crimes because most serious crimes are "masculine" in nature (i.e., reinforce male dominance via aggression). Further, in a patriarchal-capitalist system women are more closely supervised than men and have less power in economic, religious, political, and military institutions, thereby limiting their criminal opportunities. This framework helps explain how structural forces shape sex differences in crime rates, but it does not offer an explanation of female crime when it does occur. This lack is, in part, a function of Messershmidt's failure to adequately explore the influence of race and other social structural sources within gender variation that also operate in a capitalist-patriarchal system. It is also a function of the insensitivity of structural explanations of crime to individual-level differences in the influence of structural dynamics on behavioral outcomes. Micro-level theories are often better suited to explaining within-sex variations in offending.

Micro-Level Explanations

The fact that crime is an overwhelmingly male phenomenon has led to theoretical explanations linking offending to gender roles, gender identity, and the assertion of masculinity. Some theorists have suggested that differences in gender roles may explain the gender gap in offending. The assumption here is that the traditional female role is incompatible with offending behavior. As such, the degree to which women subscribe to traditional views of femininity might influence the likelihood that they engage in crime. However, most female (and male) offenders hold traditional gender-role definitions (Bottcher 1995). A few studies report a relationship between nontraditional or masculine gender role attitudes and female delinquency on a given item but not on other items (Heimer 1995; Shover et al 1979; Simpson and Ellis 1995). In fact, the bulk of studies report that traditional rather than nontraditional views are associated with greater delinquency (see reviews in Chesney-Lind and Shelden 1992; Pollock-Byrne 1990; Steffensmeier and Allan 1995).

Some have suggested that gender identity (the degree to which an individual identifies as masculine or feminine), as opposed to beliefs about traditional gender roles, should account for individual-level sex differences in offending. A masculine identity should increase the likelihood of offending and a feminine identity should decrease this likelihood. Horowitz and White (1987) did find evidence to suggest an association between gender identity and styles of pathology. In their analyses, masculinity was associated with delinquency and an absence of masculinity was associated with distress and alcohol and drug problems. However, in their analysis, masculinity and femininity were conceptually distinct, and neither the presence nor absence of femininity was related to delinquency or psychological distress.

Evidence that offending is linked to beliefs about traditional gender roles or to gender identity is inconclusive. A third proposition is that offending is related to the accomplishment of gender as an emergent social construction. In other words, offending represents a way of "doing gender" and, more specifically, of "doing masculinity" (Messerschmidt 1993; Simpson and Ellis 1995). This argument suggests that crime, especially violent crime, is a means for males to validate their masculinity, since it allows them to assert and establish their dominance. Further, gendered behavior norms are such that in certain contexts, violence is socially reinforced for males, whereas it is inconsistent with femininity and socially discouraged in virtually all contexts among females. As such, violent crime as a uniquely masculine pursuit makes sense, since it is clearly inconsistent with "doing femininity."

However, as Miller (1998) notes, this explanation of the link between gender and crime is also problematic since, while accounting for gender differences in violent offending, "it leaves unexplained women's participation in violent street crime, except as an anomaly" (p. 39). She suggests that female offenders may also be "doing gender" when they engage in crime—even violent crime. Her qualitative study of 14 female and 23 male robbers indicate that both males and females "do gender" when they engage in robbery. Despite similar motivations for robbery, the enactment of robbery is shaped by gender. Whereas male robbers typically target other males and use direct confrontation, physical violence, and guns, female robbers often target other females. Further, while females do use violence against other females, they are more likely to forgo weapons or use a knife rather than a gun. However, when women do rob men, they use guns but no physical violence, and they typically rely on sex to make the man vulnerable. Miller concludes that similar structural and cultural factors trigger male and female robbery but that gender is salient in shaping the enactment of robbery, thereby accounting for differences not in "why" males and females rob, but in "how" they rob.

The implication that the processes leading to male and female offending are similar but that the content of their offending is significantly different is also evident in the theoretical framework presented by Broidy and Agnew (1997). They propose an extension of Agnew's general strain theory (1992) that can explain individual-level gender differences in responses to strain and stress. According to Broidy and Agnew, for both males and females crime results when individuals lack the legitimate coping strategies to effectively deal with strain and the negative emotions it engenders. Despite similarities in this process across males and females, the dynamics of gender shape both the types of strains males and females are exposed to and the emotional and behavioral responses available to them, thus leading to distinct outcomes. While aggressive, externalizing behavioral responses are available to males in various environments, such responses are less commonly available to females. As such, female responses to strain are more likely to be nonaggressive or self-destructive. Further, these gender differences in outcomes result not simply from differences in behavioral expectations but in the nature and form of stress males and females experience. Broidy and Agnew note that, while male stress/strain typically results in competitive interactions and environments, female strain more commonly emerges in interpersonal interactions and environments.

Gender differences in the saliency of interpersonal experiences and related strains has implications for both minor and serious female offending that other theories have also highlighted. Caspi et al. (1993) propose a biosocial model of female delinquency that highlights the relationship between biological changes associated with puberty and the social environments in which these changes occur. They argue that early puberty is socially stressful for girls and note that the early onset of menarche "disrupts previously existing social equilibria and presents the adolescent girl with an ambiguous, novel, and uncertain event to which she must now respond" (p. 20). Girls' responses to these physical changes, they argue, are shaped by social and contextual factors. The school is an especially salient social context at this age, since that is where peer affiliations are formed. Caspi et al. hypothesize that early maturing girls in mixed-sex school environments will be at higher risk for delinquency than their counterparts in same-sex schools or than girls who follow normative maturation processes. Their findings support their hypotheses, indicating a link between early maturity and delinquency that is enhanced in mixed-sex school environments via association with older delinquent male peers. The implication is that early maturation is especially stressful for girls because it changes the nature of their social interaction—especially with males.

The interpersonal nature of female strain and its link to more serious forms of female crime and deviance is also highlighted in individual-level explanations of female crime. Chesney-Lind (1997) argues that gender dynamics differentially shape the lives and experiences of boys and girls, even when they grow up in similar structural environments (live in the same neighborhoods, go to the same schools, etc.). Specifically, gender-based socialization patterns set the stage for the sexual victimization and harassment of girls. It is this victimization that triggers girls' entry into delinquency as they try to escape abusive environments. Chesney-Lind argues that girls attempting to run away from abuse often end up in the streets with few legitimate survival options. Resources to help such girls are limited, and they come to perceive crime as their only option for survival.

Gilfus' (1992) work supports this explanation of female crime resulting from interpersonal victimization. Interviews with 20 incarcerated women highlight the blurred boundaries between victimization and offending for these women. The majority of the sample had run away from abusive home environments in their youth, and 16 reported having been victims of rape, assault, or attempted murder. Aside from being victimized in childhood, the bulk of these women (15) had also experienced abusive adult relationships with men. Gilfus suggests that women's victimization experiences place them at risk for offending, which in turn places them at greater risk for future victimization and repeated offending. This dynamic may be especially pervasive for minority and low-income women whose limited resources place them at higher risk for both victimization and offending (Arnold 1995; Richie 1996).

The link between victimization and serious crime among women is also highlighted in Daly's (1994) content analysis of probation officers' reports on 40 women appearing before the felony court in New Haven. Based on her analysis, she developed a typology of serious female offending that highlights four pathways to crime. "Street women" are those who ran away to escape a sexually abusive home environment and turned to prostitution as a way to survive on the streets. "Harmed and harming women" were abused and neglected as children, turned to drugs, and got violent under their influence. "Battered women" use violence as a response to violence directed at them by an intimate partner. Finally, "drug-connected women" use and sell drugs with boyfriends or family members. The majority of the women fit either the street woman or harmed and harming woman characterization, reinforcing the important role of early victimization on violent outcomes for females.

The implication of these qualitative and quantitative micro-level studies and the resulting theoretical frameworks is that individual-level risk factors are experienced in a social structural context that discourages criminal delinquency among females. Nearly all of these theories make explicit reference to the structurally institutionalized gender norms and structurally reinforced opportunity structures and note that it is within this structural context that individual-level factors come into play. These gendered norms and opportunity structures place severe restrictions on women's criminal options. As such, it is not surprising that the individual-level and situational inducements to female crime, especially violent crime, explicated in individual-level qualitative studies are notably traumatic and often threaten or otherwise interfere with women's interpersonal networks/relationships. Female offending is viewed as an extreme response to extreme circumstances—be it precocious matura-

tion, repeated interpersonal and emotional distress, or abusive interactions with others. However, while recognizing the centrality of structural dynamics to explanations of female offending, these theories fail to clearly identify the mechanisms through which the broader structural environment shapes individual-level behavior.

Integrating Macro- and Micro-Level Explanations

The main problems with both macro- and micro-level explanations of female crime and gender differences in offending lie in their inability to account for the precise manner in which individual-level factors interact with structural forces to shape criminal behavior. Some researchers have attempted to merge macro-level explanations of gender differences in crime with micro-level explanations of individual variation in criminal behavior.

Power-control theory (Hagan 1989; Hagan, Gillis and Simpson 1987) explores the impact of macro-level class and gender dynamics and individual-level variations in socialization and social control on delinquent outcomes. Specifically, this theory integrates feminist, conflict, and control theories to explain within- and between-sex differences in offending. Power-control theory accounts for the difference between male and female rates of delinquency by examining the relationship between family structure (patriarchal/egalitarian), class position, and within- and between-sex differences in social control. This theory, then, establishes a link between macro- and micro-level forces by locating it in the family. A family's position in the class structure is hypothesized to influence individual-level socialization patterns. Generally, socialization within the family imposes stronger controls on girls than boys, teaching girls to be risk-adverse and boys to be risk takers. This fact explains why boys are more likely to engage in offending—a risk-taking behavior. But the theory also suggests that this gender-based socialization and control is stronger in "patriarchal" than in "egalitarian" families, helping to explain within-sex differences in offending.

Support for power-control theory is limited. Whereas Hagan (1989) finds support for central power-control theory hypotheses, tests by other researchers have proved less supportive (Cernkovich and Giordano 1987; Jensen and Thompson 1990; Singer and Levine 1988). Specifically, neither gender differences in parental control nor parental class categories help account for the gender gap in delinquency.

Difficulties in integrating macro- and micro-level explanations for female crime and gender differences in offending may stem from the fact that macro- and micro-level forces do not always change in unison. Changes in structural opportunities for women at the macro level, for example, are not necessarily accompanied by individual-level changes in socialization. Steffensmeier (1983) avoids the problems that plague explanations attempting to link broad social structural changes to individual level changes in criminal behavior by focusing particularly on the social structure of the criminal underworld. He suggests that the nature of sex segregation in criminal subcultures and criminal organizations is pervasive and imposes significant restraints on women's criminal involvement. While he acknowledges that such broad structural forces as gendered behavior norms and socialization patterns help explain gender differences in crime, he suggests that these forces are less salient than more immediate structural limitations imposed by gender-segregation within criminal organizations. "Compared to their male counterparts, potential female offenders are at a disadvantage in selection and recruitment into criminal groups, in the range of career paths, and access to them, opened by way of participation in these groups, and in opportunities for tutelage, increased skills, and rewards" (p. 1025). Nonetheless, gender segregation in the underworld, while pervasive, is variable across crime groups and types of crime, helping to account for individual variations in female crime. While sensitive to the dynamics of gender and the way in which they shape gender differences in criminal outcomes, this theoretical account suggests that females' relative lack of involvement in crime is, fundamentally, a reflection of their reduced opportunities for crime at the social structural level. Although the issue of individual-level criminal motivation and the way in which motivation and opportunity interact is not sufficiently explored, Steffensmeier does suggest some connections:

> The availability of concrete opportunities, in turn, helps to explain why among their supposed options, women select criminal behaviors congruent with sex roles (e.g., play sexual media or cover roles). Like male offenders, female offenders gravitate to those activities, which are easily available, are within their skills, provide a satisfactory return, and carry the fewest risks. (p. 1025)

A Gendered Theory of Female Offending and the Gender Gap

We began this chapter by highlighting what we know about female crime and gender differences in offending on both the aggregate and individual levels and by providing an overview of early explanations of these phenomena. We then explored the ability of traditional theories to account for these phenomena, noting that these theories help make sense of the general patterns noted in the data but cannot account for the more subtle dynamics that underlie these patterns. More recent structural and individual-level explanations of the gender gap and female offending show promise but as yet remain fragmented and not well integrated.

Steffensmeier and Allan (1995, 1996) provide the most ambitious attempt to build a unified theoretical framework for explaining female criminality and gender differences in crime. They take the position that both gender-neutral and gender-specific theories contribute to an explanation of female criminality. Traditional gender-neutral theories provide reasonable explanations of less serious forms of female and male criminality and of gender differences in such crime categories. Their principal shortcoming is a lack of information about the specific ways in which differences in the lives of men and women contribute to gender differences in type, frequency, and context of criminal behavior. Gender-specific theories are likely to be even less adequate if they require separate explanations for female crime and male crime. The broad social forces suggested by traditional theories exert general causal influences on both male and female crime. But it is the organization of gender that mediates the manner in which those forces play out into gender differences in types, frequency, and contexts of criminal involvement.

According to Steffensmeier and Allan, a gendered theory of offending should include at least four key elements. First, it should explain how the organization of gender, at the social structural and individual levels, shapes patterns of offending among females *and* males. Second, a gendered approach should account not only for well-documented gender differences in the type and frequency of offending, but for more subtle contextual differences as well. Third, such an approach should illuminate similarities and differences in male and female pathways to crime, recognizing that, especially for serious crime, women's routes to crime may differ substantially from men's. Finally, a gendered perspective should explore the extent to which gender differences in crime derive not only from complex social, historical, and cultural factors but from biological and reproductive differences. In essence, what they call for is an integrated theory of offending, rooted in an understanding of the dynamics of gender. Figure 8.1 is a model of what this gendered paradigm looks like.

The paradigm that Steffensmeier and Allan present (see Steffensmeier and Allan 1996 for a complete summary of their framework) recognizes the important contributions of traditional theory to our understanding of male and female offending. They highlight the influence of social control, self-control, rational choice, criminal opportunities, and criminal motivation. However, they also recognize that the influence of these factors is fundamentally shaped by the dynamics of gender at the social structural and individual levels. As such, gender differences in crime are not merely a function of quantitative differences in exposure to the criminogenic factors identified in traditional theories, but of the interaction between these factors and the macro- and micro-level influence of gender. This interaction creates qualitative differences in the context and nature of male and female offending, triggering significant gender differences in criminal outcomes.

The Steffensmeier/Allan paradigm highlights the ways by which the organization of gender, coupled with differences in physical and sexual characteristics, blunts the probability of crime on the part of women but increases that probability for men. In particular, the framework suggests that the organization of gender shapes male and female crime by reinforcing gender differences in norms, moral development and affiliative concerns, social control, physical strength and aggression, and sexuality. Together, gender differences in these five areas mutually reinforce one another, conditioning gender differences in motivations, criminal opportunities, and contexts of offending. This reinforcement is constant, is cumulative, and occurs in numerous ways. In what follows we provide one example of how these areas might overlap to limit the form and occurrence of female crime.

Role obligations and the presumption of female nurturance ascribed to women via *gender norms* serve to inhibit female criminality. Women, much more than men, are rewarded for building and maintaining relationships and for nurturance of family, and the constraints posed by child-rearing re-

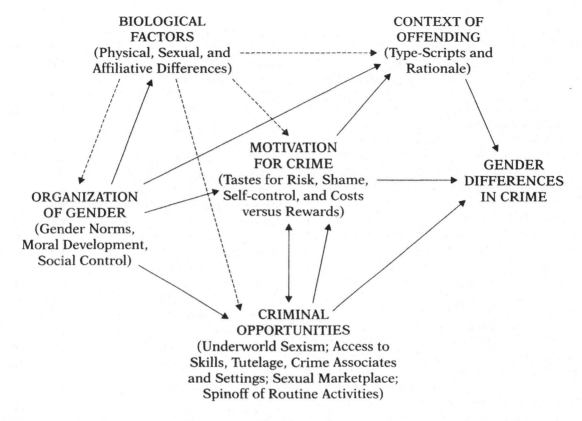

Figure 8.1. Gendered model of female offending and gender differences in crime. *Broken line* indicates weak effect; *solid line* signifies strong effect.

sponsibilities are obvious. These constraints are reinforced by gender differences in *moral development and amenability to affiliation.* Compared to men, women are more likely to refrain from crime because of concern for others. This restraint may result from gender differences in moral development (Gilligan 1982) and from socialization toward greater empathy, sensitivity to the needs of others, and fear of separation from loved ones. From an early age, females are encouraged to cultivate interpersonal skills that will prepare them for their roles as wives and mothers (Beutel and Marinin 1995; Brody 1985; Rossi 1984). This predisposition toward an "ethic of care" restrains women from violence and other behavior that may injure others or cause emotional hurt to those they

love. Such complex concerns also influence the patterns and contexts of crime when women do offend.

Presumptions of female nurturance, along with strong affiliative concerns among women, emerge in the context of gender-specific socialization patterns and *mechanisms of social control.* Particularly during their formative years, females are more closely supervised and their misbehavior discouraged through negative sanctions. Risk-taking behavior, which is rewarded among boys, is censured among girls. Girls' associates are more carefully monitored, reducing the potential for influence by delinquent peers (Giordano, Cernokovich, and Pugh 1986), while attachments to conventional peers and adults are nurtured. Even as adults, women find their freedom to explore worldly temptations constricted (Collins 1992). As such, the ability and willingness of women to commit crime is powerfully constrained not only by internal controls rooted in empathic tendencies, but also by external mechanisms of formal and informal social control.

While gender differences in norms, moral development, and social control shape women's perceived desire to offend, other forces shape their perceived ability to commit crimes. The weakness of women relative to men—whether real or perceived—puts them at a disadvantage in a criminal underworld that places a premium on *physical strength and aggression*. Muscle and physical prowess are functional not only for committing crimes but also for protection, contract enforcement, and recruitment and management of reliable associations.

Females may be perceived by themselves or by others as lacking the violent potential for successful completion of certain types of crime, or for protection of a major "score." This perception can help account for the less serious and less frequent nature of female crime. Female criminals sometimes deliberately restrict themselves to hustling small amounts of money in order not to attract predators. Perceived vulnerability can also help explain female offending patterns, such as women's greater restriction to roles as solo players or to dependent roles as subordinate accomplices, as in the exigencies of prostitute-pimp dependency (James 1977).

Although gender differences in physical size restrict women's access to certain criminal opportunities, their *sexuality* opens other criminal opportunities. The demand for illicit sex creates opportunities for criminal gain through prostitution or quasi-legitimate sexual media activities. These opportunities in turn may reduce the need for women to seek financial returns through serious property crimes, which remain a disproportionately male realm.

At the same time that male stereotypes of female sexuality open certain criminal opportunities for women, within criminal groups these same stereotypes close opportunities for women that are not organized around female attributes. The sexual tensions that may be aroused by the presence of a woman in a criminal group may force her to protect herself through sexual alignment with one man, becoming "his woman."

Together, then, gender differences in norms, moral development and affiliative concerns, social control, physical strength and aggression, and sexuality dictate patterns of female crime by shaping both criminal opportunities and criminal motivations among women. In fact, these factors converge such that, like the upperworld, the underworld has its glass ceiling. The scarcity of women in the top ranks of business and politics limits their chance for involvement in price-fixing conspiracies, financial fraud, and corruption. If anything, women face even greater occupational segregation in underworld crime groups—whether syndicates or more loosely structured organizations (Commonwealth of Pennsylvania 1991, Steffensmeier 1983). Just as in the legitimate world, women face discrimination at every stage, from selection and recruitment to opportunities for mentoring, skill development, and, especially, rewards.

Although motivation is different from opportunity, opportunity can amplify motivation. Being able tends to make one more willing, and vice versa. Female as well as male offenders tend to be drawn to those criminal activities that are easy, within their skill repertoire, and offer a good payoff and low risk. Women's risk-taking preferences and styles differ from those of men (Hagan 1989; Steffensmeier 1980; Steffensmeier and Allan 1995). Whereas men will take risks in order to build status or gain competitive advantage, women may take greater risks to protect loved ones or to sustain relationships. The overall level of criminal motivation is suppressed in women by their greater ability to foresee threats to life chances and by the relative unavailability of female criminal type scripts that could channel their behavior.

Summary and Conclusions

Our knowledge about fundamental issues in the study of gender and crime has expanded greatly with the proliferation of studies over the past several decades, although significant gaps still exist. Our coverage of patterns and etiology of female offending has necessarily been selective and cursory. We conclude by restating and enlarging on some key points.

Women are far less likely to be involved in serious crime, regardless of data source, level of involvement, or measure of participation. The girls and women who make up the bulk of the criminal justice workload involving the female offender (and are the grist of female offender programs) commit ordinary crimes—mostly minor theft and fraud, low-level drug dealing, prostitution, and simple assault against their mate or children. They are likely to have at least one adult conviction for theft, prostitution, or drug/alcohol involvement but return to further crime commission afterward. Some of them commit crime over several years and serve multiple jail or prison terms in the process. But they are not career criminals.

Oftentimes the lives of many of these women are intertwined with the men who are persistent petty criminals or are, in other ways, "losers." Along with their children, these men are the principal focus of these women's lives. The world of these men tends to be an extremely patriarchal one in which women are relegated to subordinate roles. Exploited or treated with indifference by their male partners, the women lead lives that often are miserable and difficult. Routinely, it is they who are left to cope with the consequences of men's unsuccessful escapades and the incarceration these can bring.

Despite some shifts in attitudes toward greater acceptance of women working and combining career and family, the two major focal concerns of women—beauty and sexual virtue and nurturant role obligations—persist. The considerable stability in the gender gap for offending can be explained in part by historical durability of the organization of gender (Walby 1990) and by underlying physical/sexual differences (whether actual or perceived). Human groups, for all their cultural variation, follow basic human forms.

Three key elements should structure future efforts to develop explanations of female offending and the gender gap. These elements also have important implications for developing female offender programs. The first is the need to take into account how the organization of gender deters or shapes delinquency by females but encourages it by males. We use the term "organization of gender" to refer broadly to things gendered—norms, identities, arrangements, institutions, and relations by which human sexual dichotomy is transformed into something physically and socially different. The second is the need to address not only gender differences in type and frequency of crime but also differences in the context of offending. Even when men and women commit the same statutory offense, the "gestalt" of their offending is frequently quite different (Daly 1994). Third, theory and programmatic approaches to female offending need to address several key ways in which women's routes to crime (especially serious crime) may differ from those of men. Building on the work of Daly (1994) and Steffensmeier (1983), such differences include (1) the blurred boundaries between victim and victimization that happen more in women's than men's case histories; (2) women's exclusion from most lucrative crime opportunities; (3) women's ability to exploit sex as an illegal money-making service; (4) the consequences (real or anticipated) of motherhood and child care; (5) the centrality of greater relational concerns among women, and the manner in which they both shape and allow women to be pulled into criminal involvements by men in their lives; and (6) the frequent need of these women for protection from predatory or exploitative males.

In sum, recent theory and research on female offending have added greatly to our understanding of how the lives of delinquent girls and women continue to be powerfully influenced by gender-related conditions of life. Profound sensitivity to these conditions is the key consideration for explanatory frameworks on female offending and is also the bedrock for preventive and remedial programs aimed at female offenders.

Discussion Questions

1. What is the impact of domestic violence and victimization on female offenders?

2. What social factors contribute to women's criminal activities?

3. What do criminologists theorize about the effects of modernization on women and crime?

4. Explain the theory of gender identification as it relates to women and crime.

5. What key elements should a gendered theory of offending include?

References

Adler, F. 1975. *Sisters in Crime*. New York: McGraw-Hill.

Agnew, R. 1992. Foundation for a General Strain Theory of Crime and Delinquency. *Criminology* 30:47–87.

Akers, R. Krohn, M., Lanza-Kaduce, L., and Radosevich, M. 1979. Social Learning Theory and Deviant Behavior: A Specific Test of a General Theory. *American Sociological Review* 44: 298–310.

Arnold, R. 1995. "The Processes of Criminalization of Black Women." In B. Price and N. Sokoloff, eds., *The Criminal Justice System and Women*. New York: McGraw-Hill.

Bailey, W. and Peterson, R. 1995. "Gender Inequality and Violence Against Women: The Case of Murder." In J. Hagan and R. D. Peterson, eds., *Crime and Inequality*. Stanford, CA: Stanford University Press.

Belknap, J. 1996. *The Invisible Woman: Gender, Crime, and Justice*. Belmont, CA: Wadsworth.

Beutel, A. and Marinin, M. 1995. "Gender and Values." *American Sociological Review*, 60: 436–448.

Boritch, H. and Hagan, J. 1990. "A Century of Crime in Toronto: Gender, Class, and Patterns of Social Control 1859–1955." *Criminology* 28: 601–626.

Bottcher, J. 1995. "Gender as Social Control: A Qualitative Study of Incarcerated Youths and Their Siblings in Greater Sacramento." *Justice Quarterly* 12:33–57.

Bowker, L., Gross, H., and Klein, M. 1980. Female Participation in Delinquent Gang Activities. In L. Bowker, ed., *Women and Crime in America*. New York: Macmillan.

Brody, L. R. 1985. "Gender Differences in Emotional Development: A Review of Theories and Research." *Journal of Personality*, 14:102–149.

Broidy, L. and Agnew, R. 1997. "Gender and Crime: A General Strain Theory Perspective." *Journal of Research in Crime and Delinquency* 34:275–306.

Campbell, A. 1984. *The Girls in the Gang*. Oxford: Basil Blackwell.

Canter, R. 1982. "Sex Differences in Delinquency." *Criminology* 20:373–398.

Caspi, A., Lynam, D., Moffitt, T., and Silva, P. 1993. "Unraveling Girls' Delinquency: Biological, Dispositional, and Contextual Contributions to Adolescent Misbehavior." *Developmental Psychology* 29:19–30.

Cernkovich, S. and Giordano, P. 1987. "A Comparative Analysis of Male and Female Delinquency." *Sociological Quarterly* 20:131–145.

Chesney-Lind, M. 1986. "Women and Crime: The Female Offender." *Signs* 12:78–96.

———. 1997. *The Female Offender*. Thousand Oaks, CA: Sage.

Chesney-Lind, M. and Shelden, R. 1992. *Girls, Delinquency, and Juvenile Justice*. Pacific Grove, CA: Brooks/Cole.

Cloward, R., and Piven F. 1979. "Hidden Protest: The Channeling of Female Protest and Resistance." *Signs* 4:651–669.

Collins, R. 1992. "Women and the Production of Status Cultures." In M. Lamont and M. Fournier, eds., *Cultivating Differences*. Chicago: University of Chicago Press.

Commonwealth of Pennsylvania, 1991. *Organized Crime in Pennsylvania: The 1990 Report*. Conshohocken: Pennsylvania Crime Commission.

Daly, K. 1989. "Gender and Varieties of White-Collar Crime." *Criminology* 27:769–794.

———. 1994. *Gender, Crime, and Punishment*. New Haven, CT: Yale University Press.

Denno, D. 1994. "Gender, Crime and the Criminal Law Defenses." *Journal of Criminal Law and Criminology* 85(1):80–180.

Elliott, M. 1952. *Crime in a Modern Society*. New York: Harper & Brothers.

Fagan, J. 1990. "Social Processes of Delinquency and Drug Use Among Urban Gangs." In C. Huff, ed., *Gangs in America*. Newbury Park, CA: Sage.

Freedman, E. 1981. *Their Sisters' Keepers*. Ann Arbor: University of Michigan Press.

Freud, S. 1933. *New Introductory Lectures*. New York: Norton.

Gelsthorpe, L. and Morris, A. (eds.) 1990. *Feminist Perspectives in Criminology*. Philadelphia: Open University Press.

Gilfus, M. 1992. "From Victims to Survivors to Offenders: Women's Routes to Entry and Immersion Into Street Crime." *Women and Criminal Justice* 4:63–89.

Gilligan, C. 1982. *In a Different Voice: Psychological Theory and Women's Development*. Cambridge, MA: Harvard University Press.

Giordano, P., Cernkovich, S., and Pugh, M. 1986. "Friendships and Delinquency." *American Journal of Sociology* 91:1170–1203.

Glueck, S. and Glueck, E. 1934. *Five Hundred Delinquent Women*. New York: Knopf.

Grasmick, H., Hagan, J., Blackwell, B., and Arneklev, B. 1996. "Risk-preferences and Patriarchy: Extending Power-Control Theory." *Social Forces* 75:177–199.

Hagan, J. 1989. *Structural Criminology*. New Brunswick, NJ: Rutgers University Press.

Hagan, J., Gillis, A. R., and Simpson, J. 1987. "Class in the Household: A Power-Control Theory of Gender and Delinquency." *American Journal of Sociology* 90:1151–1178.

Harris, A. 1977. "Sex and Theories of Deviance: Toward a Functional Theory of Deviant Typescripts." *American Sociological Review* 42:3–16.

Hartnagel, T. 1982. "Modernization, Female Social Roles, and Female Crime: A Cross-national Investigation." *Sociological Quarterly* 23:477–490.

Hartnagel, T. and Mizanudin, M. 1986. "Modernization, Gender Role Convergence, and Female Crime: A Further Test." *International Journal of Contemporary Sociology* 27:1–14.

Heimer, K. 1995. "Gender, Race, and Pathways to Delinquency: An Interactionist Explanation." In J. Hagan and R. Peterson, eds., *Crime and Inequality*, Stanford, CA: Stanford University Press.

Horowitz, A. and White, H. 1987. "Gender Role Orientation and Styles of Pathology Among Adolescents." *Journal of Health and Social Behavior* 28:158–170.

James, J. 1977. "Prostitutes and Prostitution." In E. Sagarin and F. Montanino, eds., *Deviants: Voluntary Action in a Hostile World*. New York: Scott, Foresman.

Jensen, G. and Eve, R. 1976. "Sex Differences in Delinquency." *Criminology* 13:427–448.

Jensen, G. and Thompson, K. 1990. "What's Class Got to Do With It? A Further Explanation of Power-Control Theory." *American Journal of Sociology* 95:1009–1023.

Kruttschnitt, C. 1994. "Gender and Interpersonal Violence." In J. Roth, and A. Reiss, eds., *Understanding and Preventing Violence: Social Influences*. Washington, DC: National Academy of Sciences.

Leonard, E. 1982. *Women, Crime and Society*. New York: Longman Inc.

Lombroso, C. and Ferraro, W. 1895. *The Female Offender*. London: Fisher Unwin.

Messerschmidt, J. 1986. *Capitalism, Patriarchy and Crime*. Totowa, NJ: Rowman and Littlefield.

———. 1993. *Masculinities and Crime: Critique and Reconceptualization of Theory*. Totowa, NJ: Rowman and Littlefield.

Miller, E. 1986. *Street Women*. Philadelphia: Temple University Press.

Miller, J. 1998. "Up It Up: Gender and the Accomplishment of Street Robbery." *Criminology* 36:37–65.

Paternoster, R. and Triplett, R. 1988. "Disaggregating Self-reported Delinquency and its Implications for Theory." *Criminology* 26:591–625.

Pettiway, L. 1987. "Participation in Crime Partnerships by Female Drug Users." *Criminology* 25:741–767.

Pollack, O. 1950. *The Criminality of Women*. Philadelphia: University of Pennsylvania Press.

Pollock-Byrne, J. 1990. *Women, Prison, and Crime*. Pacific Grove, CA: Brooks/Cole.

Rasche, C. 1990. "Early Models for Contemporary Thought on Domestic Violence and Women who Kill Their Mates: A Review of the Literature From 1895 to 1970." *Women & Criminal Justice* 1:31–54.

Reitman, B. 1937. *Sisters of the Road: The Autobiography of Box-Car Bertha*. New York: Macauley.

Richie, B. 1996. *Compelled to Crime: The Gendered Entrapment of Battered, Black Women*. New York: Routledge.

Rossi, P. 1984. "Gender and Parenthood." *American Sociological Review*, 49:1–19.

Shover, N., Norland, S., James, J., and Thorton, W. 1979. "Gender Roles and Delinquency." *Social Forces* 58:162–175.

Simon, R. 1975. *The Contemporary Woman and Crime*. Washington, DC: National Institutes of Mental Health.

Simpson, S. and Ellis, L. 1995. "Doing Gender: Sorting Out the Caste and Crime Conundrum." *Criminology* 33:47–77.

Singer, S. and Levine, M. 1988. "Power-Control Theory, Gender, and Delinquency: A Partial Replication With Additional Evidence on the Effects of Peers." *Criminology* 26:627–647.

Smart, C. 1976. *Women, Crime, and Criminology: A Feminist Critique*. London: Routledge & Kegan Paul.

Smith, D. 1979. "Sex and Deviance: An Assessment of Major Sociological Variables." *Sociological Quarterly* 20:183–195.

Smith, D. and Paternoster, R. 1987. "The Gender Gap in Theories of Deviance: Issues and Evidence." *Criminology* 24:140–172.

Steffensmeier, D. 1980. "Sex Differences in Patterns of Adult Crime, 1965–1977: A Review and Assessment." *Social Forces* 58:1080–1108.

——. 1983. "Sex-segregation in the Underworld: Building a Sociological Explanation of Sex Differences in Crime." *Social Forces* 61:1080–1108.

Steffensmeier, D. and Allan, E. 1988. "Sex Disparities in Crime by Population Subgroup: Residence, Race and Age." *Justice Quarterly* 5:53–80.

——. 1995. "Gender, Age, and Crime." In J. Sheley, ed., *Handbook of Contemporary Criminology*. Belmont, CA: Wadsworth.

——. 1996. "Gender and Crime: Toward a Gendered Theory of Female Offending." *Annual Review of Sociology* 22:459–487.

Steffensmeier, D., Allan, E., and Streifel, C. 1989. "Development and Female Crime: A Cross-national Test of Alternative Explanations." *Social Forces* 68:262–283.

Steffensmeier, D. and Clark, R. 1980. "Sociocultural vs. Biological/Sexist Explanations of Sex Differences in Crime: A Survey of American Criminology Textbooks, 1919–1965." *American Sociologist* 15:246–255.

Steffensmeier, D. and Haynie, D. 2000. "Gender, Structural Disadvantage, and Urban Crime: Do Macrosocial Variables Also Explain Female Offending Rates?" *Criminology* 2000, 38:403–438.

Steffensmeier, D., Rosenthal, A. and Shehan, C. 1980. "World War II and its Effect on the Sex Differential in Arrest: An Empirical Test of the Sex-role Equality and Crime Proposition." *Sociological Quarterly* 21:403–416.

Steffensmeier, D. and Streifel, K. 1992. "Time-series Analysis of Female-to-Male Arrests for Property Crimes, 1960–1985: A Test of Alternative Explanations." *Justice Quarterly* 9:78–103.

Steffensmeier, D. and Terry, R. 1986. "Institutional Sexism in the Underworld: A View From the Inside." *Sociological Inquiry* 56:304–323.

Tittle, C. 1980. *Social Structure and Social Deviance*. New York: Praeger.

Walby, S. 1990. *Theorizing Patriarchy*. Cambridge, MA: Basil Blackwell.

Weiner, N. 1989. "Violent Criminal Careers and Violent Career Criminals." In N. Weiner and M. Wolfgang, eds., *Violent Crime, Violent Criminals*. Newbury Park, CA: Sage.

Widom, C. 1989. "Child Abuse, Neglect, and Violent Criminal Behavior." *Criminology* 27:251–271. ✦

Part II
Crimes Against Women

As we pointed out in our introduction to the first section of this book, women are not only less likely than men to be criminals, they are also less likely to be crime victims. For example, about 89 percent of males 12 and older become the victim of a violent crime at least once during their lifetime, whereas 73 percent of women 12 and older are violently victimized. Not surprisingly, however, race and age interact with gender to raise or lower one's risk of criminal victimization. Young men of color, between the ages of 12 and 24, are at greatest risk of violent victimization when compared to any other demographic group.

These figures are based on official statistics, which are considered good overall measures of victimization. However, these victimization statistics may contain gender biases. For instance, women may have difficulty discussing sexual assault or battering by a husband or boyfriend with an interviewer, i.e., a stranger. Yet, these are the types of crime for which women are at greatest risk of victimization.

Women fear crime more than men do, despite their lower rates of victimization. As Stanko pointed out in chapter 2, one reason women fear crime so much is because they are more physically vulnerable than men. At the same time, Stanko argues, women are also afraid because their victimization is more likely to be hidden, overlooked, or trivialized relative to men's victimization.

Women's fear of crime tends to be specific. They are most afraid of sexual assault. Research also indicates that regardless of their age, social class, race, or ethnicity, most women fear strangers more than intimates, and their image of the "dangerous stranger" is typically a poor, uneducated, young black man who is mentally ill or addicted to drugs.

In the chapters in this section, the authors examine common crimes against women. As Ferraro and Allison and Kollenbroich-Shea demonstrate, although women fear being victimized by strangers, they are significantly more likely to experience violent victimization at the hands of an acquaintance, friend, relative, or intimate. (In contrast, men are about as likely to be violently victimized by a stranger as someone they know.)

Rynbrandt and Kramer draw our attention to corporate crime and deviance, an area that, although not overlooked by criminologists, has certainly not been subjected to much gender analysis. Rynbrandt and Kramer provide many examples of women's victimization, both as workers and consumers, by corporate deviance, demonstrating that women have always been victims of corporate crime even if criminologists did not include gender as a central variable in their studies of corporate offending. Rynbrant and Kramer offer a fascinating analysis of the silicone breast implant debacle as a prime example of corporate violence against women.

When most of us think of violence against women, we think of sexual assault and wife battering. Rynbrandt and Kramer's chapter is important for broadening our conceptualization of violence against women. Similarly, Bessant and Cook examine women's violent victimization globally, pointing out that some forms of violence are culturally-specific (e.g., rapes of women during "ethnic cleansing" campaigns, wife burning for failure to produce male offspring or to pay dowry, female genital mutilation). Bessant and Cook consider the usefulness of addressing these diverse forms of violence against women within a universal human rights or international law framework, discussing both the strengths and weaknesses of this approach and critically assessing currently available analytic frameworks and legal remedies.

When reading Bessant and Cook's chapter, one may be struck by a sense of hopelessness: The problem is so large and the potential remedies too limited. However, as the other chapters in this section show, although much remains be to be done significant progress has been made in recent years in improving services for women victims of violent crimes, especially crimes committed by intimates. Feminists have led these reforms and feminists continue to be at the forefront of struggles throughout the world to prevent all forms of violence against women, to aid women who have been victimized, and to hold the victimizers accountable. Although the task is daunting, Bessant and Cook and the other authors in this section challenge us to develop more effective preventions and interventions for the serious problem of crimes against women. ✦

9
Woman Battering: More Than a Family Problem[1]

Kathleen J. Ferraro

Woman battering is more than physical violence against an intimate partner. It is the repeated use of physical, emotional, and psychological abuse in order to establish dominance and control. This chapter examines definitional and measurement problems and presents the results of major studies on incidence. It describes the dynamics of battering relationships, with the caveat that there is no universal "battered woman" or "batterer." A review of criminal justice responses, including the mandatory arrest debate, batterer intervention programs, and coordinated community response networks suggests that although progress has been made, women's safety continues to be marginalized. Finally, the chapter reviews the relationships between women's poverty, welfare reform, and battering, concluding that efforts to enhance women's safety must be integrated with work to empower women if they are to be effective.

> I never considered myself a political person or a feminist, but then there is nothing more politicizing than a fist in the face followed by a little chat with 10 other women with black eyes. (Pence 1996a, 25)

If you are one of the fortunate people who has not had personal experience with battering, your best avenue of education would be to talk with ten women who have. It is difficult to comprehend abuse within an intimate relationship unless one has experienced the confusion, betrayal, fear, and despair that result. Unfortunately, failure to acknowledge women's expertise on this topic has perpetuated a system in which women's safety is marginalized by inappropriate, inadequate, and uncoordinated institutional responses. Grassroots efforts to convince the general public, legislators, social service providers, and criminal justice actors that battering is a serious, pervasive source of danger to women has produced a new category of deviance, "domestic violence."

Like all categories, "domestic violence" helps define similarities in experiences and direct resources to the problem. It also forces complex, multifaceted experiences into a uniform category that severs the lived experience of abuse from institutional responses. "Domestic violence" is unlike other forms of criminal victimization, with the exception of child abuse, in that the victim and perpetrator are involved in an ongoing relationship that has personal, legal, institutional, and social implications. Women who are battered by their partners also share children, households, extended family, financial resources, and emotional bonds with their abusers. "Domestic violence" also differs from stranger violence in that it occurs repeatedly and involves emotional and psychological abuse as well as physical violence. It intersects with all aspects of women's lives, diminishing successful participation in education, employment, mothering, politics, and social relationships.

Women's experiences and responses to battering are also influenced by these other aspects of life, as well as by race, social class, age, physical ability, and personal biography (Crenshaw 1991). Battering is an overwhelming, devastating experience, but it is only one dimension of a woman's life, not her entire identity.

"Domestic violence" is also unlike stranger crime in that it is patterned on a hierarchy of roles inscripted and condoned in the social organization of gender. Men beat their intimate partners to enforce expectations of service and subordination that are normalized by the social institutions of religion, kinship, the economy, and the media. While most men do not use violence to enforce male privilege, the men who do clearly articulate beliefs in legitimate entitlement to women's obedience and loyalty and the right to punish infractions (Ptacek 1988). One of the violent men interviewed by Dobash and Dobash (1998b) explained why he battered his wife:

> [Do you think there is anything (she) could or should do to stop you being violent?] I've battered her that many times, she should know when to stop her crap. She knows when I get annoyed because I sit and clench my teeth. . . Why do I hit her? I don't know. Sometimes she just really nips my head. And it doesn't matter what I say, she won't shut up. . . [Did you feel that you were right to be violent to her?] Yes. She was being cheeky (showing disrespect). . . [When do you think it's okay for a man to hit a woman?] I don't like it. A slap, yes, now and again . . . if it's needed. [What do you mean 'needed'?] If you're sitting in a pub with all your pals and she comes in and gives you a load of cheek. To put her in her place verbally, and if verbally doesn't work, physically. (p. 154)

Until the early 1970s, there was no organized response to domestic violence as a social problem. There were no shelters, hotlines, or laws specific to battering, and the few social science articles were psychiatric analyses of the pathologies of battered women. The development of "domestic violence" discourse in the United States over the past 30 years is a success story because it has transformed women's private suffering to a public social problem. New laws, shelters, organizations, services, and research have helped thousands of women escape from violent, destructive relationships. At the same time, the manner in which "domestic violence" has become part of mainstream consciousness has created new dilemmas and problems (Ferraro 1996). In lieu of a long talk with ten women who have experienced battering, this chapter will provide an over-view of the literature that has been developed from women's experiences. It will also present and discuss the quantitative survey studies that measure battering.

Defining and Measuring Woman Battering

Many terms are used to label the violence women experience at the hands of intimate partners: domestic violence, family violence, woman battering, wife abuse, spousal abuse, partner violence, wife assault, intimate violence, and violence against women. The language selected to describe the problem carries theoretical significance, particularly in regard to the gendered nature of violence. "Domestic violence" is the most common term used in legal categories and is also dominant in popular and social science literature. This term implies a household or family context and the physical violence that occurs between members within that context. It thus directs attention *away* from the gender of victim and perpetrator and also from violence that occurs between intimates who do not share a domestic relationship, such as ex-partners, lovers, and dating partners. Similarly, "family violence," "spousal assault," and "intimate violence" fail to identify the gender of victims and perpetrators, signaling a *gender neutral* analysis. These terms imply that men and women in heterosexual intimate relationships participate equally in a problem that is separate from the larger societal context of patriarchy, sexism, and gender inequality. This perspective has come to be called the "family violence perspective," as sexism is considered only one variable in an array of individual and social structural factors that contribute to violence within families (Anderson 1997).

In contrast, the terms "woman battering," "wife abuse," and "wife assault" make the gendered character of violence explicit and are associated with the "violence against women perspective" (Dobash and Dobash 1992, 264). The violence against women perspective insists that patriarchy, sexism, and gender inequality are the fundamental conditions under which violence against female partners develops (Dobash and Dobash 1979). The influence of race, ethnicity, social class, sexual orientation, and nationality on the use of violence against intimate partners is considered within the context of patriarchy. This chapter is written from the violence against women perspective and uses the term "woman battering."

Unfortunately, all of the language available to address the problem has the consequence of focusing attention on physically violent acts. "Woman battering" deflects focus from the defining characteristic of battering relationships: exertion of power and control over an intimate partner. Physical violence is only one way in which power and control are established. In all battering relationships, even the most severe, physical violence is less commonplace than emotional and psychological abuse. The Power and Control Wheel, developed for use in the Duluth Abuse Intervention Project, has become a useful tool to illustrate the range of abusive behaviors that constitute battering relationships (see Figure 9.1). It is extremely important to understand that slapping, shoving, and throwing things do not necessarily constitute a battering relationship without the behaviors outlined on the power and control wheel. It is the abstraction of individually violent actions from the context of an ongoing process of domination and denigration that has resulted in some of the problems in analyses and social policies addressed to battering (Dobash and Dobash 1998a). Despite this limitation, the term "woman battering" maintains the focus on gender and can be defined to include the nonphysical aspects of battering. "Woman battering" is: the repeated use of physical, emotional, and psychological abuse by a person against a female intimate partner in order to establish dominance and control (Dutton 1992). This definition makes the gender of the abused person explicit but does not exclude lesbian battering. Although much of the following

discussion is relevant to lesbian battering, the focus is on battering in heterosexual relationships; thus, batterers will often be referred to as men.

But what about battered men? One of the most contentious issues in the discussion of battering is the incidence and nature of women's violence against men. This issue is directly linked with methodological problems in the measurement of woman battering. As Dobash and Dobash (1992) point out, the United States is the only country in which the issue of husband battering has engendered serious debate. This is largely the consequence of "a narrow and restricted approach to research and an unswerving reliance on a seriously flawed data collection instrument" (p. 275). Even within the United States, the overwhelming preponderance of evidence indicates that between 90 and 95 percent of all battering victims are women, and most of the small number of men abused by women are either the primary aggressors in the relationship or are abused by male partners. Yet the topic of battered men continues to draw attention, with several scholars and many popular journalists suggesting that it is a problem of equal magnitude with woman battering (Cook 1997; Hoff-Sommers 1994; Pearson 1997). In order to assess the evidence, it is necessary to consider the types of data available on battering and the methodological approaches taken.

Survey Data and Measuring Woman Battering

Two principle forms of survey data are available on woman battering in the United States: the National Family Violence Surveys (NFVS) and the National Crime Victimization Surveys (NCVS). Two sets of NFVS have been conducted, the first in 1975 and the second in 1985 (Straus and Gelles 1986). The surveys were conducted on nationally representative samples of intact families. The first survey was conducted in person, the second by telephone. Respondents were asked about

Figure 9.1. Power and Control Wheel. Reprinted by permission. Originated by the DOMESTIC ABUSE INTERVENTION PROJECT, 202 East Superior Street, Duluth, MN 55802, (218) 722-4134.

conflict in their families and techniques used for resolving conflict.

The data collection tool developed for the surveys is the Conflict Tactics Scale (CTS). A list of 18 items that describe verbal and physical actions ranging from "discussed an issue calmly" to "used a knife or fired a gun." Respondents are asked how often they have en-

gaged in the actions over the prior year and over the course of their relationships. This methodology produced findings indicating a rough parity in male and female use of violence and a decrease in woman battering (and child abuse) in the period between surveys, but an increase in husband battering (Straus and Gelles 1986). The proportion of respondents reporting any use of violence against their intimate partner was 12.1 percent for men and 11.6 percent for women in 1975 and 11.3 percent for men and 12.1 percent for women in 1985.

These studies, funded by the National Institutes of Mental Health, are considered reliable sources of information and are frequently quoted by those wishing to shift attention away from battered women and toward battered men. Yet there are a number of reasons to be cautious about their validity and interpretation that have been acknowledged even by the principal investigators (Gelles 1997; Straus 1993). The accuracy of these data depends on self-reporting of socially unacceptable, criminal conduct. People must report that they were violent toward an intimate partner. We know from work with men in batterers' programs that violent men minimize and deny their abuse (see Ptacek 1988). For example, Ptacek quotes a man attending a court-ordered treatment program as saying, "I never beat my wife. I responded physically to her" (p. 146). We also know that there are systematic gender differences in reporting of marital violence. Szinovacz and Egley (1995) found considerable underreporting of violence, by both men and women, in the National Survey of Family Households. They also report that wives are more likely to be injured in marital violence, a fact corroborated by all research on the topic, and that husbands are not a reliable source of data on violence against wives. Interview data from abusive men and their wives also reveal stark differences between men's and women's accounts of violence, particularly more serious acts and injurious outcomes. Dobash and Dobash (1998b) found that differences between men's and women's reports of injuries were statistically significant in 50 percent of comparison categories.

Another problem with the CTS is that it asks people about strategies used to resolve conflicts in intimate relationships. This approach assumes that violence is the outcome of an argument or conflict. The following introduction to the CTS is read to respondents:

> No matter how well a couple gets along, there are times when they disagree on major decisions, get annoyed about something the other person does, or just have spats or fights because they're in a bad mood or tired or for some other reason. They also use many different ways of trying to settle their differences. I'm going to read a list of some things that you and your (wife/partner) might have done when you had a dispute, and would first like you to tell me for each one how often you did it in the past year. (Straus, Gelles, and Steinmetz 1980, 256)

How different this introduction is from the experiences of constant surveillance and random attacks described by women:

> I realized I was under terrible strain the whole time . . . I'd go into a blind panic about what side the spoon had to be on. It was that sort of detail everyday.
>
> There was too much grease on his breakfast plate and he threw his plate at me. I had a poker thrown at me—just because his tea was too weak—he just takes it for granted, if you're married you'll have to accept it. It's part of being a wife. (Dobash and Dobash 1992, 4).

Although Straus (1993) argues that the CTS does *not* just ask about conflicts, would these women or their abusers think about these instances of violence when asked what they do when they have an argument or spat? CTS questions do not ask about the context of the violent behavior or about the outcome. Throwing a plate, a poker, or a pillow would all be coded the same, as "minor violence," whether throwers missed their target or cut open a face. It is impossible to determine from the NFVS how much violence is committed in self-defense and how much damage is inflicted by the violence. Thus, the finding of "symmetry" in male and female reports of violent behavior in the NFVS cannot be used to determine how much "woman battering" and "husband battering" occurs, but only the number of violent behaviors directed at intimate partners that people are willing to reveal in a survey (see Kurz 1993). Michael Johnson (1995) has labeled this "common couple violence," suggesting that the phenomenon described in the NFVS is a separate phenomenon from the woman battering studied in all other data sources. Johnson argues that the NFVS provides important information about violence in families but that its findings not be confused with the phenomenon of "patriarchal terrorism," or what violence-against-women scholars have termed "woman battering." Distinguishing between the common couple violence described in the NFVS and patriarchal terrorism described in other research clarifies the significance of the context of domination and control that characterizes battering and undermines claims that battering is a gender-neutral phenomenon.

The other main source of survey data on battering is the National Crime Victimization Survey (NCVS). The NCVS is also a random survey, but it focuses on criminal victimization. For years, the NCVS did not specifically cue respondents to include battering as an experience of criminal victimization. In 1992, the NCVS instituted a redesigned methodology that specifically cues about violence committed by intimate partners and thus provides a measure of interpersonal violence that would fit the legal definition of a crime. The NCVS 1992–93 estimates of violence against women report approximately 5 million incidents per year, 29 percent of which were committed by husbands, ex-husbands, boyfriends, or ex-boyfriends. Of all violent incidents against women, over three-quarters were committed by someone known to the victim. Race was not a distinguishing factor, with women of all races reporting similar rates of intimate victimization (Bachman and Saltzman 1995). Data for 1996, however, indicate a higher rate of intimate violence against African American women, 12 per 1,000 versus eight per 1,000 for white women (Greenfeld and Rand 1998). Overall, there was a reduction in intimate violence against women in NCVS

data between 1992 and 1996, with 1.1 million women reporting rape, sexual assault, robbery, aggravated assault, and simple assault perpetrated by a husband, ex-husband, boyfriend or former boyfriend in 1992–93 and 840,000 in 1996 (Greenfeld and Rand 1998).

The NCVS data produce very different results from the NFVS about the gendered nature of intimate violence. The rate of "intimate perpetrated" victimization was found to be six times higher for women than for men in the redesigned NCVS (Bachman and Saltzman 1995). The difference between the finding of near symmetry in the NFVS data and dramatic asymmetry in the NCVS data supports Johnson's contention that two different phenomena are being measured. However, even these much higher rates are probably undercounts of women's victimization rates. The Canadian Violence Against Women Survey (VAWS) was carefully designed to overcome the deficiencies of the Conflict Tactics Scale. The VAWS researchers interviewed a stratified probability sample of 12,300 women 18 and over in 1993 by telephone. They found that 51 percent of women had experienced violence in their lives and that 29 percent of married and ever-married (including common-law) women were victimized by their partners (Johnson 1998).

The most extreme form of intimate violence, homicide, is not measured by the NCVS, but it is measured by the FBI Uniform Crime Reports, National Incident-Based Reporting Program, and Supplementary Homicide Reports. These data indicate a reduction in intimate homicides between 1976 and 1996, from 3,000 to 2,000, accounting for approximately 9 percent of murders (Greenfeld and Rand 1998). Women are much more likely to be murdered by an intimate partner than men. For the period 1976–1996, approximately 30 percent of all women homicide victims were murdered by intimate partners: 18.9 percent by husbands, 1.4 percent by ex-husbands, and 9.4 percent by nonmarital intimate partners. In the same time period, about 6 percent of male homicide victims were murdered by intimate partners: 3.7 percent by wives, 0.2 percent by ex-wives and 2.0 percent by nonmarital partners (Greenfeld and Rand 1998). Overall in this time period, the only group to show an increase in intimate homicides was white females killed by a boyfriend (Greenfeld and Rand 1998). There is evidence, however, of undercounting incidents of intimate homicide. Johnson, De Li, and Websdale's (1998) analysis of Florida homicides found that for 1994, the official count of "domestic fatalities" was 230, while detailed examination of case records revealed 321. Their analysis also found that 95 percent of female domestic homicide victims were killed by men, while only 25 percent of men were killed by women and that when women killed, it was most often in self-defense or defense of their children. Although homicide data may *underreport* murders of women by their intimate partners, all crime victimization survey data indicate that women are by far the most common victims of battering and intimate homicide.

Few random surveys of intimate violence have not been based on the Conflict Tactics Scale, which excludes sexual violence. However, when Diana Russell (1982) conducted a random survey in San Francisco to examine the extent and nature of women's experiences of rape, she found that of the 644 married women in her sample, 12 percent reported rape by their husbands, twice as many as reported rape by strangers. Similar findings were reported by Finkelhor and Yllö (1985), who found that 10 percent of their Boston-area sample reported rape by husbands or partners, and by Straus and Gelles (1986), who found that 8 percent of women in their nationally representative sample were forced to have sex by their husbands and another 5 percent had husbands who *attempted* to force sex (Gelles 1997). Liz Kelly's (1988) research found that most women do not make clear distinctions between sexual and nonsexual violence in their relationships and that women often give in to men's sexual

demands in order to avoid or minimize men's nonsexual assaults. The sexual aspects of battering have been overlooked in most survey data that focus on discrete episodes of physical violence.

Nonrandom Samples and Understanding Woman Battering

We have learned the most about the dynamics of battering relationships from studies in which the samples were selected to maximize respondents with relevant experiences rather than to insure representativeness. These studies found subjects through police and prosecutors' records (Buzawa et al. 1992; Dobash and Dobash 1979; Ferraro 1989), newspaper ads (Bowker 1983), battered women's shelters (Ferraro 1983; Frieze 1979; Gondolf and Fisher 1988; Pagelow 1981), hospital records (Stark and Flitcraft 1996), and snowball sampling, which relies on personal and word-of-mouth contacts (Chang 1996; Lundgren 1998). Violent men have also been studied in such focused samples, for insight into what motivates them to batter and how they conceptualize their behavior (Adams 1988; Dobash and Dobash 1998b; Gondolf and Hanneken 1987; Hamberger and Hastings 1991; Ptacek 1988; Saunders 1993).

Qualitative data provide rich information on the experiences of women and men in violent relationships. Although each individual study may be biased by nonrandom sample selection, multiple studies with different sampling sources that produce similar findings have established a knowledge base that permits some generalizations about the nature of woman battering.

Perhaps the most important thing to recognize is that no single characterization captures all women's experiences with battering. Efforts by scholars and activists to transform destructive, victim-blaming attitudes toward battering have produced language and analyses clarifying that women do *not* precipitate, reciprocate, or enjoy abuse. Today activists emphasize the language of survival rather than of victimization in describing women who have experienced intimate abuse. The term "battered woman" forces women's diverse, multifaceted lives into a constricted category that is not a recognizable representation for most women. It focuses attention on pain, suffering, and domination and makes the strength, joy, intelligence, and resistance of women invisible. Although the term is useful and necessary for discussing, studying, and responding to intimate violence, the complexity it conceals should not be forgotten.

Some of the ideas that emerged in the early part of the battered women's movement reinforced the idea that all women who experience battering have similar characteristics and go through the same reactions. There has also been a tendency to lump all battering behavior—from occasional pushing and slapping to repeated, sadistic rape and torture—into the same category. A number of popularized theories have appeared that are useful for understanding some women's experiences but are not valid for many others. For example, in the 1980s the notion of "the battered woman syndrome" became very popular, particularly in connection with women's self-defense cases, to describe the impact of battering on a woman's perceptions (see Walker 1984, 1989). One aspect of the "syndrome" was the incorporation of "learned helplessness," a concept borrowed from Martin Seligman's (1975) research in animal psychology. The idea that women become conditioned to helplessness through repeated experiences of noncontingency was successful in explaining why women remained in abusive relationships and was helpful in translating women's sense of terror in homicide cases where women killed their abusive partners (Walker 1989). However, the scientific basis for such a "syndrome" does not exist, and the development of learned helplessness is not a universal, or even typical, response to battering. In 1996, the U.S. Department of Justice issued a report stating that "the term 'battered woman syndrome' does not adequately reflect the breadth or nature of the empirical knowledge about battering and its effects," and "the term 'battered woman syndrome' portrays a stereotypic image of battered women as helpless, passive, or psychologically impaired, and battering relationships as matching a single pattern, which might not apply in individual cases" (U.S. Department of Justice 1996, 8; see also Osthoff, this volume). Although rejecting the language of a syndrome, the experts consulted for this report agreed that an immense body of research demonstrates there are consistent patterns of battering and its effects. Each woman's experience of battering is unique and is filtered through her personal background, race, ethnicity, sexual orientation, class, and phase of child rearing as well as her history with a particular batterer (Crenshaw 1991; Rivera 1997). Among the thousands of stories from women who have survived abuse, however, we can see repetitive themes about the dynamics, patterns, and effects of abuse.

The Dynamics of Battering Relationships

The dynamics of battering relationships are based on the central feature of coercive control that a batterer exerts over a partner. One aspect of this control is increasing *isolation* of the woman from family, friends, and work. The isolation is both physical, in terms of keeping a woman from involvement in social arenas outside the relationship, and psychological, through ridiculing and becoming angry and violent over other relationships. Violent men often view other people as a threat to their absolute control of a woman, so they either forbid her from seeing other people or make encounters so unpleasant that both the woman and her acquaintances decide that seeing each other is not worth the trouble.

Another component of control is *extreme possessiveness and jealousy*. Not only are women prevented from interacting with other people, they are continuously scrutinized for evidence of infidelity and routinely accused of imaginary affairs. A phone call from someone dialing the wrong number, a few minutes delay returning home from the grocery store, wearing of makeup or perfume, or an innocent glance at a passerby can be construed by an abuser as a sign that the woman is romantically involved with someone else.

Control also takes the form of *monitoring daily activities*, setting unrealistic and constantly changing standards, and expressing anger, sometimes violently, for failure to meet the man's expectations. As the women quoted above indicate, the mundane tasks of living become tests that women must continuously strive to pass but inevitably fail (Dobash and Dobash 1998b). It is common for an abuser to focus on a woman's deficiencies and to use the most derogatory, insulting language to impress her inferiority on her. It is these nonphysical aspects of control and domination that form the emotional context of battering relationships.

Because the descriptions of battering relationships are so horrific, the most frequently asked question is, "Why do battered women stay in the relationship?" Many authors have criticized this question as misplaced and misogynist. The more appropriate question, they insist, is, "Why do men batter?" Both questions, however, are important in understanding and intervening in battering. The first answer to why women stay is, they don't. Women resist male violence in many ways, and most women attempt to physically leave violent men. Campbell Miller, and Cardwell (1994) found that after two and a half years, 43 percent of the women in their sample had left their abusers and two-thirds were living in nonviolent situations. Leaving a violent relationship is usually a difficult process, however, and Pagelow (1984) found that, on average, the women in her study had left their abusers five or six times before leaving for good. Reasons for returning are complex, but four major factors are the

abuser's retaliation and threats, economic dependency, child custody concerns, and emotional bonding. It is now well known that the period following departure from a violent relationship is a dangerous time for women. Wilson and Daly (1993) report that women are more likely to be murdered by an intimate partner *after* leaving than during the relationship. Many women try to remain in their family household, where their children have school and friends, and attempt to get the abuser to leave. This tack is often unsuccessful, as abusers return to plead, harass, and demand reunion, and orders of protection are not particularly effective (Harrell and Smith 1996).

In addition to fear and refusal of batterers to end the relationship, most women rely on the income of their husband or partner to supplement their own income or as the only source of household income. Although divorce law should provide for the financial security of divorcing women, it does not. The vast majority of divorced women do not receive any kind of alimony or spousal maintenance, and child support payments are low and frequently nonexistent (Kurz 1995). Many studies of battered women report that lack of financial resources and alternative housing are among the top reasons women give for remaining with violent partners (Aguirre 1985; Barnett and Lopez-Real 1985; Ferraro 1983; Pagelow 1981; Roy 1977). Zorza (1991) reports that approximately 50 percent of homeless women have become destitute as a consequence of woman battering.

Although many women are left with full responsibility for caring for and supporting their children, another problem inhibiting dissolution of violent relationships is child custody and visitation awards (Pagelow 1993). Violent men often use the threat of custody battles as a technique of forcing women to stay married, and they are more likely to fight for physical custody of their children than nonviolent men (Taylor 1993). Even men who do not want, or cannot receive, full child custody may receive weekly visitation rights, which make it nearly impossible to cut off contact with the batterer. Women may also fear leaving their children alone with an abusive partner who may physically, sexually, or emotionally abuse them or use the occasion to tear down their mother or make them believe the divorce is all her fault. Many states require judges to hear testimony about battering in child custody hearings, but the fact that a man batters his wife is often insufficient for a judge to limit or eliminate his contact with their children (Chesler 1991). However, if a man inflicts abuse on his children, a woman may lose custody or be charged with child abuse for failure to protect them, even if she has documented evidence of her own victimization (Enos 1996). Women may stay in an abusive relationship to prevent a custody battle they have no money to wage and no guarantee of winning and to protect their children from court ordered unsupervised visitation with their father.

Women battered in lesbian relationships face unique problems with regard to child custody. They must contend not only with an abuser's threats but with a legal system that does not recognize the right of homosexuals to marry or to parent. A lesbian may also face threats from her partner to "out" her to an ex-husband, other family members, or her employer, thus jeopardizing not only child custody agreements but employment and family relationships (Renzetti 1992).

Fear and pragmatic considerations that trap women in battering situations are somewhat more straightforward issues than the more controversial factor of emotional bonding. Recognition of the problems of severing a violent intimate relationship does not necessarily imply victim blaming or the attribution of deviance to battered women, as has been the concern of some writers (Jones 1994; Loseke 1992). Those who work and talk with women who are battered know that enduring emotional bonds and the hope that a batterer will change are as important as external constraints in keeping women in violent relationships. Muldary (quoted in Barnett and LaViolette 1993) coined the

term "learned hopefulness" to describe women's ongoing commitment to the belief that their partners will change. My own research as well as that of many others demonstrates that women's love for their partners does not end automatically because of abuse (Barnett and Lopez-Real 1985; Chang 1996; Ferraro 1983; Frieze 1979; Pagelow 1981; Renzetti 1992). Love may continue even after a woman has killed her partner in self-defense (Browne 1987; Ferraro 1992, 1997).

There have been a number of attempts to explain the continuation of love in spite of battering, including the cycle of violence (Walker 1984), traumatic bonding (Dutton and Painter 1981), and the Stockholm Syndrome (Graham 1994). All three models describe the episodic nature of violence interspersed with affection, contrition, and kindness that kindle hope that the "real man" is not the abuser, but the one who begs for forgiveness.

The three-phase *cycle of violence* first identified by Lenore Walker (1979, 1984, 1989) includes the tension-building stage, an acute battering incident, and the honeymoon or contrition stage. Because the violence is intermittent and followed by a phase of love and remorse, women are "hooked" into a perception of the relationship as potentially positive, and they see the violence as an aberration that can be controlled by their own commitment and his efforts to change. Of all cases studied by Walker, 65 percent showed evidence of a tension-building stage, and 58 percent indicated a phase of loving contrition (1984). When only the last incident of battering was examined, however, the percentages had increased to 71 percent for tension-building and decreased to 42 percent for loving contrition. Dutton (1992) notes that the "cycle theory fails to account for all stages of the cycle as different forms of controlling behavior," since the phase of loving contrition is an effort to control the woman's commitment to the batterer, and that "the sequence of physical, sexual, psychological, and property assaults by some perpetrators seem to deny a characteristic cycle of violence" (p. 24). Although the cycle helps to understand that battering occurs in a pattern, the simple three-phase model does not accurately describe the continuity of controlling behavior, the range of patterns that exist, or the diminution of contrite, loving behavior once domination has become established through violence.

The effects of battering on women are also variable, and there is no single profile of "the battered woman." Beyond the form and severity of abuse, the impact of and reactions to battering depend on a number of factors discussed by Dutton (1992) including: "(1) tangible resources and social support, (2) institutional response, (3) personal strengths/inner resources, (4) other current stressors in addition to the abuse, (5) vulnerability factors, and (6) positive and negative aspects of the relationship in which the abuse occurs" (p. 10). Obviously, women with the most external and internal resources, the most positive institutional responses, the least stress and vulnerability, the fewest positive links to the relationship, and the least infrequent and less damaging forms of abuse will not develop the same level of trauma as women with the opposite set of characteristics. For many women, the effects of battering are similar to other forms of trauma and include psychological distress, relational disturbances, and changes in cognitive schema (Dutton 1992).

There are also significant differences among men who batter. According to Healey, Smith, and O'Sullivan (1998), program directors and probation officers working with batterers see "no *one* type of batterer and (find) no *one* intervention or treatment to be effective with all batterers" (p. 57). Several researchers have developed typologies of batterers, although no one typology has been agreed upon. Gondolf and Fisher (1988) developed a four-part typology based on interviews with 525 battered women: sociopathic, antisocial, chronic, and sporadic batterers. However, Gondolf's current, unpublished research with violent men is producing differ-

ent results based on administration of the Millon Clinical Multiaxial Inventory III. Of the men in the research "25 percent showed evidence of a severe mental disorder; 25 percent showed narcissistic personality traits; 24 percent showed passive-aggressive traits; and 19 percent were clinically depressed" (Healey et al. 1998, 58). This is a much higher level of psychological disturbance than previous researchers had reported. Another typology includes the following groups:

(1) The Family Only batterer is characterized as rigid, perfectionist, and conforming, with limited social skills. The family-only batterer did not experience much physical abuse in childhood and is mildly to moderately violent toward his family.

(2) The Dysphoric/Borderline batterer is very emotional, experienced parental rejection and fears abandonment, and is extremely abusive psychologically but not severely violent physically.

(3) The Generally Violent/Antisocial batterer tends to abuse alcohol, lacks empathy, has rigid gender role attitudes, and is narcissistic—that is, expects special treatment and deference. He was physically abused in childhood and engages in other crimes, viewing violence as the appropriate method of solving problems (Healey et al. 1998, 58).

Recognition of the various types of batterers helps in the development of criminal justice and social service interventions. It is to these institutional responses that we now turn.

The Criminal Justice Response to Battering

Traditionally, the criminal justice system has responded to woman battering as a private issue, excluded from the constitutional responsibility to provide equal protection under the law and the moral and civic responsibility to provide safety to all citizens. An 1864 North Carolina court ruled that the state "will not invade the domestic forum or go behind the curtain" except in cases of permanent injury or an "excess of violence" (Dobash and Dobash 1979, 62). Despite formal laws against wife beating and occasional campaigns to "bring back the whipping post" for batterers, the de facto practice was to exclude battering from the criminal justice domain (Martin 1976; Pleck 1987). When the battered women's movement took shape in the early 1970s, one of the first demands was that police, prosecutors, and judges begin to respond to women's requests for intervention. Since that time, the demand that domestic violence "be treated as a crime" has become a major focus of scholarship and activism in the United States (Ferraro 1989, 1996). There is now a huge body of literature on this topic alone, which cannot be comprehensively examined in the space of this chapter. The issues that have generated the most discussion, the police response and diversion programs, will be addressed, as well as the innovative work by the Duluth Abuse Intervention Project and Ellen Pence on safety audits.

The Police Response

The police are the first agency contacted by most people who are victimized by crimes. Yet, according to the Bureau of Justice Statistics, only about half of incidents of intimate violence are reported to police by women. Reasons for nonreporting include the belief that the incident was a personal matter, fear of retaliation, or the perception that the police would be ineffective (Greenfeld and Rand 1998). Despite women's reluctance to call police, there has been a national effort to increase responsiveness through enhanced arrest powers, mandatory arrest policies, and coordinated community response networks.

One of the more controversial issues regarding policing woman battering is mandatory arrest (American Bar Association 1998). In the early 1980s, several factors coalesced to result in widespread adoption of presumptive or mandatory arrest policies in most large urban police departments (Ferraro

1993). The Sherman and Berk Minneapolis Domestic Violence Police Experiment was the first field-based, controlled experiment to test the deterrent effect of arrest, separation, or mediation in domestic violence misdemeanor incidents. The finding that arrest was a significantly more effective deterrent to future assaults than either mediation or separation was widely hailed and celebrated as scientific evidence that battered women's activists were correct in demanding arrest and punishment of batterers. Before other research, or even analysis of the original findings, could take place, 47 urban police departments adopted mandatory or presumptive arrest policies (Crime Control Institute 1986). The Attorney General's Task Force on Family Violence in 1984 heard expert testimony on domestic violence and the results of the Minneapolis study. Its first recommendation for the justice system was "family violence should be recognized and responded to as a criminal activity" (U.S. Attorney General 1984, p.10), and law enforcement agencies were encouraged to adopt presumptive arrest policies. That same year, Tracy Thurman won a $2.3 million settlement against the City of Torrington because of police failure to intervene while her husband assaulted and permanently paralyzed her. The scientific evidence, the political mandate, and the threat of civil suits produced nearly unanimous agreement that arrest was the best policy for domestic violence.

The National Institute of Justice funded six replication studies in other cities, including Metro-Dade (Miami), Colorado Springs, Milwaukee, Charlotte, Omaha, and Minneapolis. The results of these studies are less clear about the relative superiority of arrest in deterring future violence (Buzawa and Buzawa 1996). Results from Omaha, Charlotte, and Milwaukee found that arrest increased recidivism (Schmidt and Sherman 1996). One of the original researchers, Lawrence Sherman, now argues that mandatory arrest laws should be repealed and that arrest is effective only for men with a "stake in conformity,"—that is, a job (Schmidt and Sherman 1996).

Despite the lack of evidence that arrest deters battering, many experts maintain that arrest should be the preferred action for domestic violence cases. Stark (1996) and Zorza (1994) argue that the experiments were poorly designed and did not consider external factors, such as the political climate in site cities and the economic cycle in the late 1980s. The 1994 Violence Against Women Act, the American Bar Association, the National Coalition Against Domestic Violence, and most battered women's advocates support a strong pro-arrest policy. The many dilemmas and problems resulting from mandatory arrest policies, such as failure to implement, mutual arrests, and harassment of men of color, are recognized. However, as Pence (1996a) notes, it is not practically possible for the battered women's movement to choose whether to engage law enforcement. The question is rather one of strategy, constant vigil, and pressure, and the development of coordinated responses to create safety for women.

Diversion of Violent Men

One outcome of enhanced police response to battering is an increase in the number of offenders processed through the court system. The expense of incarceration, plus the recognition that jail does not reform the vast majority of batterers, has led to the creation of diversion programs in most large urban areas. In addition, many battered women express the desire that their partners "get help" and prefer diversion outcomes to jail sentences (Ferraro and Boychuk 1992). Typically, diversion programs are for first-time, misdemeanor offenders and offer participation in batterer programs in lieu of prosecution. Participation in batterer intervention programs may also be a condition of probation.

The range of programs is tremendous, reflecting variations in ideology, required training for leaders, length of time, and link-age to victim services. All 50 states and the District of Columbia have developed or are in the process of developing standards for programs to insure that men are diverted to programs that adhere to existing knowledge of what works (Healey et al. 1998). Unfortunately, current evaluations of the effectiveness of batterer intervention programs are not encouraging. Harrell's quasi-experimental study of 193 male offenders found not only that the treatment did not reduce the prevalence or frequency of violence but that men who were *not* in treatment were significantly *less likely* to assault their partners than those in treatment (Harrell 1991). Preliminary results from Gondolf's four-site study indicate that men who drop out at intake have similar reoffense rates to men who complete programs (Harrell 1991).

Lack of evidence that intervention programs reduce men's violence or their coercive control over women raises serious questions about their impact on women's safety. This situation is particularly worrisome, because women are more likely to continue relationships with men who are in a program, believing that they are finally "getting help." Programs that are not embedded in a well-coordinated response system, in which batterers are monitored during participation and women are provided with support, are likely to reduce women's safety. As Andrew Klein, chief probation officer of the Quincy, Massachusetts, District Court Model Domestic Abuse Program argues, "You can't separate batterer treatment from its [criminal justice] context. You can't study the effectiveness of treatment without studying the quality of force which supports it" (quoted in Healey et al. 1998, 10).

Coordinated Community Response and Safety Audits

Advocates have long recognized that the criminal justice system will only increase women's safety when all parts of the system, and the actors within them, are coordinated to respond to battering based on women's experiences and needs. Many participants have been struggling in this uphill battle, but the group that has been most persistent, creative and successful in developing a coordinated community response is the Duluth Abuse Intervention Project (DAIP), with inspiration from Ellen Pence. The DAIP coordinates a comprehensive approach to battering that includes police, prosecutors, probation officers, judges, a batterer intervention program, and services and support to women (Pence 1996a; Pence and Shepard 1988). The program has been so successful that it has become a model in the United States and other countries and has influenced the Department of Justice to award grants to other cities for the purpose of developing coordinated community response networks.

A coordinated community response means more than developing a board with representatives from each agency and writing policies for processing "domestic violence" cases. Many initiatives have failed to incorporate the most important component, "creating a coherent philosophical approach centralizing victim safety" (Pence 1996a, 47). Abrahams and Bruns (1998), comparing a feminist and a gender-neutral coordinated community response network, found that the gender-neutral network perpetuated victim-blaming practices, focused on individualistic causes of violence, and did not empower women. As one judge in this network said, "The system works but women abuse it" (p. 12). According to Pence, however, even a feminist-based network can marginalize women's safety because of incompatible discourses of law and women's lives (Pence 1996b). In response to the difficulties she observed in Duluth, Pence has developed the concept of a safety audit.

A safety audit, similar to a financial audit, is a way of examining the bureaucratic practices of each segment of the criminal justice process to discover mechanisms that tend to compromise and marginalize women's safety. As soon as a woman dials 911 for help, she begins an elaborate process that may involve 40 or more people in a variety of agencies. A safety audit examines each step of this process through technologies, resources, procedures, and texts, and accounts for the context of violence in terms of: the pattern of abuse, power differentials, the particulars of the case, potential dangers to a victim of a fragmented response, victim perception of danger, the differences in women's lives, and the presence of imminent danger (Pence 1996a). A safety audit requires resources for people to be able to gather all the data on specific cases and may create resistance in those whose work is being audited. Pence notes, however, that the focus of the audit is institutional *processes* rather than *individual actions*, thereby shifting attention and blame from individual actors to organizational processes. The audit is a method for implementing social change in patriarchal institutions while keeping women's experiences and needs as the central focus.

Conclusion: Integrating Resistance to Battering and Empowerment Efforts

The tremendous gains of the battered women's movement have also engendered some costs that are now being addressed. The creation of "domestic violence" discourse that individualizes and neutralizes the gender dimensions of battering has also resulted in a detachment of woman battering from the larger context of women's lives. In 1994, the landmark Violence Against Women Act (VAWA) was signed into law and authorized over $1.6 billion over six years in funding for police, prosecution, prevention, and victim service initiatives (U.S. State Department 1998). The act also provided resources to establish a national domestic violence hotline, made it a federal crime to cross state borders for the purpose of committing domestic violence, and mandated various forms of research and evaluation.

Passage of VAWA was an important victory for battered women. Unfortunately, two years later, in 1996, the Personal Responsibility and Work Opportunity Reconciliation Act (PRWORA) was passed ending welfare as it had existed in the United States since the establishment of Aid to Families with Dependent Children (AFDC) in 1935. PRWORA established a lifetime limit of five years for Temporary Assistance to Needy Families (TANF) benefits and requires work for all recipients. The Family Violence Option (FVO) does give the states the option of granting waivers to bona fide victims of domestic violence, but this is hardly a substitute for the social safety net required to empower women.

Recent scholarship has begun to focus more broadly on the aspects of women's lives that increase their vulnerability to battering. A number of recent studies have demonstrated that large portions of women on welfare, from 33.8 percent (Lloyd 1997) to 61 percent (Browne and Bassuk 1997), have experienced battering in their relationships. Kenney and Brown (1997), Kurz (1998), and Raphael (1996) detail the ways in which violent men produce poverty for women: by prohibiting or sabotaging work efforts, stalking, causing permanent injuries, refusing to care for children or pay child support, and inflicting emotional damage that interferes with women's capacities to work and succeed. Battering is a major cause of women's poverty, and poverty helps trap women in abusive relationships. Obviously, "domestic violence" is not a phenomenon that can be successfully eliminated without addressing the larger issues of women's subordination in a patriarchal society.

While enhanced criminal justice responses to battering incidents may increase women's safety if they are modeled on the recommendations outlined by Pence, women's empowerment must also include access to education, careers, child care, health care, and reproductive freedom. A program in Kentucky evaluated by Websdale and Johnson (1997), which provided all of these services to battered women in addition to criminal justice intervention, found that 82 percent experienced no revictimization. This is certainly a greater success rate than any of the arrest or treatment interventions have been able to produce. If the United States were to adopt these basic human services, available to women in all other developed countries, perhaps there would be a reduced demand on the criminal justice system. Activists in issues that have been somewhat compartmentalized, including welfare rights, children's rights, homelessness, and battering, are now linking their efforts to develop more comprehensive approaches to women's empowerment.

Woman battering has also gained recognition as a human rights issue by the United Nations. In 1992, the United Nations adopted the Declaration on the Elimination of Violence Against Women, which includes violence in the family, violence in the general community, and violence perpetrated or condoned by the state (McWilliams 1998). U.N. reports document high levels of battering in every country examined, including countries in Latin America, Southeast Asia, the Far East, the Caribbean, Africa, and Europe. Some reports emphasize the role of women's status in the levels of violence against them. In particular, structural adjustment programs, required by the International Monetary Fund and World Bank for loans to developing countries, have "reversed many of the gains made in women's legal rights, access to education, health and participation in decision-making" (United Nations 1995, 1). When "domestic violence" is divorced from the context of women's lives, national and international agencies can promote policies that undermine women's empowerment and simultaneously condemn domestic violence and fund law enforcement interventions. As women seek legal and governmental aid in national and global movements to end battering and all violence against women, the links between woman battering and woman empowerment must remain at the forefront.

Discussion Questions

1. Define the family violence and violence against women perspectives on studying woman battering. Discuss the possibilities and problems for integrating the two perspectives.

2. Explain the two main sources of quantitative data on the incidence of woman battering in the United States. Why do you think the National Family Violence Surveys find that men and women are equally violent while the National Crime Victimization Surveys find that women are much more likely to be victims of intimate violence?

3. Discuss the dynamics of battering relationships, and use the Power and Control Wheel to describe the emotional context of physical violence as well as the role of patriarchal values in woman battering.

4. What were the mandatory arrest experiments, what did they find, and what conclusions have been drawn from this research? Articulate your own position on the appropriateness of mandatory arrest for "domestic violence."

5. Develop a model for action to eliminate woman battering that incorporates the scholarship presented in this chapter. Explain how the components of your model reflect current knowledge about woman battering.

Endnote

1. This chapter was completed prior to the release of results from the National Violence Against Women Survey. Patricia Tjaden and Nancy Thoennes, "Prevalence, Incidence, and Consequences of Violence Against Women: Findings From the National Violence Against Women Survey," *Research in Brief*, National Institute of Justice and Centers for Disease Control and Prevention. NCJ 172837. November, 1998.

References

Abrahams, N. and Bruns, M. 1998. "Gendered Violence, Gendered Response: Coordinated Community Response Networks and the Battered Women's Movement." Paper presented at the Annual Meeting of the Pacific Sociological Association, San Francisco, CA.

Adams, D. 1988. "Treatment Models of Men Who Batter: A Profeminist Analysis." In Kersti Yllö and Michele Bograd (eds.), *Feminist Perspectives on Wife Abuse*. Newbury Park, CA: Sage.

Aguirre, B. E. 1985. "Why Do They Return? Abused Wives in Shelters." *Social Work* 30: 350–354.

American Bar Association. 1998. *Legal Interventions in Family Violence: Research Findings and Policy Implications*. Washington, DC: U.S. Department of Justice.

Anderson, K. L. 1997. "Gender, Status, and Domestic Violence: An Integration of Feminist and Family Violence Approaches." *Journal of Marriage and the Family* 59:655–669.

Bachman, R. and Saltzman, L. E. 1995. *Violence Against Women: Estimates from the Redesigned Survey*. Washington, DC: U.S. Department of Justice.

Barnett, O. W. and Lopez-Real, D. I. 1985. "Women's Reactions to Battering and Why They Stay." Paper presented at the Annual Meeting of the American Society of Criminology, San Diego, CA.

Barnett, O. W. and LaViolette, A. D. 1993. *It Could Happen to Anyone*. Newbury Park, CA. Sage.

Bowker, L. H. 1983. *Beating Wife-Beating*. Lexington, MA. Lexington Books.

Browne, A. 1987. *When Battered Women Kill*. New York: Free Press.

Browne, A. and Bassuk, S. S. 1997. "Intimate Violence in the Lives of Homeless and Poor Housed Women: Prevalence and Patterns in an Ethnically Diverse Sample." *American Journal of Orthopsychiatry* 67(2):261–278.

Buzawa, E. S. and Buzawa, C. G. (eds.) 1996. *Do Arrests and Restraining Orders Work?* Thousand Oaks, CA: Sage.

Buzawa, E. S., Austin, T. L., Bannon, J., and Buzawa, C. G. 1992. "Role of Victim Preference in Determining Police Response to Victims of Domestic Violence." In Eve S. Buzawa and Carl G. Buzawa, eds., *Domestic Violence: The Changing Criminal Justice Response*. Westport, CT: Auburn House.

Campbell, J., Miller, P. and Cardwell, M. M. 1994. "Relationship Status of Battered Women Over Time." *Journal of Family Violence* 9(2):99–111.

Chang, V. N. 1996. *I Just Lost Myself*. Westport, CT: Praeger.

Chesler, P. 1991. *Mothers on Trial: The Battle for Children and Custody*. New York: McGraw-Hill.

Cook, P. W. 1997. *Abused Men: The Hidden Side of Domestic Violence*. Westport, CT: Praeger.

Crenshaw, K. 1991. "Mapping the Margins: Intersectionality, Identity Politics, and Violence Against Women of Color." *Stanford Law Review* 43:1241–99.

Crime Control Institute. 1986. "Police Domestic Violence Policy Change." *Response* 9(2):16.

Dobash, R. E. and Dobash, R. P. 1979. *Violence Against Wives*. New York: Free Press.

——. 1992. *Women, Violence and Social Change*. New York: Routledge.

——. (eds.) 1998a. *Rethinking Violence Against Women*. Thousand Oaks, CA: Sage.

——. 1998b. "Violent Men and Violent Contexts." In R. E. Dobash and R. P. Dobash, eds., *Rethinking Violence Against Women*. Thousand Oaks, CA: Sage.

Dutton, D. and S. Painter. 1981. "Traumatic Bonding: The Development of Emotional Attachments in Battered Women and Other Relationships of Intermittent Abuse." *Victimology* 6:139–155.

Dutton, M. A. 1992. *Empowering and Healing the Battered Woman*. New York: Springer.

Enos, V. P. 1996. "Prosecuting Battered Mothers: State Laws' Failure to Protect Battered Women and Abused Children." *Harvard Women's Law Journal* 19:229–268.

Ferraro, K. J. 1981. *Battered Women and the Shelter Movement*. Unpublished Ph.D. dissertation, Arizona State University, Tempe, AZ.

——. 1983. "The Rationalization Process: How Battered Women Stay." *Victimology* 8(34):203–214.

——. 1989. "The Legal Response to Battering in the U.S." In M. Hanmer, J. Radford, and E. Stanko, eds., *Women, Policing and Male Violence: International Perspectives*. London: Routledge.

——. 1992. "Crazy Bilagaana and Spider Woman Visit the Land of White and Black." Paper presented at the Annual Meeting of the Society for the Study of Social Problems, Pittsburgh, PA.

——. 1993. "Cops, Courts, and Battering." In E. Moran, P. Bart and P. Miller, eds., *Women and Male Violence*. Newbury Park, CA: Sage.

——. 1996. "The Dance of Dependency: A Genealogy of Domestic Violence Discourse." *Hypatia* 11(4):77–91.

——. 1997. "Battered Women: Strategies for Survival." In A. Carderelli (ed.), *Violence Among Intimate Partners: Patterns, Causes and Effects*. Boston: Allyn and Bacon.

Ferraro, K. J., and Boychuk, T. 1992. "The Court's Response to Interpersonal Violence: A Comparison of Intimate and Nonintimate Assault." In E. Buzawa and C. G. Buzawa, eds., *Domestic Violence: The Changing Criminal Justice Response*. Westport, CT: Auburn.

Finkelhor, D. and Yllö, K. 1985. *License to Rape*. New York: Holt, Rinehart and Winston.

Frieze, I. H. 1979. "Perceptions of Battered Wives." In I. H. Frieze, D. Bar-Tal, and J. S. Caroll, eds., *New Approaches to Social Problems*. San Francisco: Jossey-Bass.

Gelles, R. J. 1997. *Intimate Violence in Families*. 3d ed. Thousand Oaks, CA:Sage.

Gondolf, E. W. and Fisher, E. R. 1988. *Battered Women as Survivors*. Lexington, MA: Lexington.

Gondolf, E. W. and Hanneken, J. 1987. "The Gender Warrior: Reformed Batterers on Abuse, Treatment, and Change." *Journal of Family Violence*. 2(2):177–191.

Graham, D., with Rawlings, E. I. and Rigsby, R. K. 1994. *Loving to Survive: Sexual Terror, Men's Violence and Women's Lives*. New York: New York University Press.

Greenfeld, L. A. and Rand, M. R. 1998. *Violence by Intimates*. Washington, DC: U.S. Department of Justice.

Hamberger, L. K. and Hastings, J. E. 1991. "Personality Correlates of Men Who Abuse Their Partners: A Cross-Validation Study." *Journal of Family Violence* 1:323–341.

Harrell, A. 1991. *Evaluation of Court Ordered Treatment for Domestic Violence Offenders [Final Report]*. Washington, DC: Urban Institute.

Harrell, A. and Smith, B. E. 1996. "Effects of Restraining Orders on Domestic Violence Victims." In E. S. Buzawa and Carl G. Buzawa, eds., *Do Arrests and Restraining Orders Work?* Thousand Oaks, CA: Sage.

Healey, K., Smith, C., and O'Sullivan, C. 1998. *Batterer Intervention: Program Approaches and Criminal Justice Strategies*. Washington, DC: U.S. Department of Justice.

Hoff-Sommers, C. 1994. *Who Stole Feminism?* New York: Simon & Schuster.

Johnson, B., Li, D., and Websdale, N. 1998. "Florida Mortality Review Project: Executive Summary." In American Bar Association, ed., *Legal Interventions in Family Violence*. Washington, DC: U.S. Department of Justice.

Johnson, H. 1998. "Rethinking Survey Research on Violence Against Women." In R. E. Dobash and R. P. Dobash, eds., *Rethinking Violence Against Women*. Thousand Oaks, CA: Sage.

Johnson, M. P. 1995. "Patriarchal Terrorism and Common Couple Violence: Two Forms of Violence Against Women." *Journal of Marriage and the Family* 57:283–294.

Jones, A. 1994. *Next Time She'll Be Dead*. Boston: Beacon.

Kelly, L. 1988. *Surviving Sexual Violence*. Cambridge: Polity.

Kenney, C. T. and Brown, K. R. 1997. *The Impact of Violence on Poor Women*. New York: NOW Legal Defense Fund.

Kurz, D. 1993. "Physical Assaults by Husbands: A Major Social Problem." In R. Gelles and D. Loseke, eds., *Current Controversies on Family Violence*. Newbury Park, CA: Sage.

———. 1995. *For Richer, For Poorer: Mothers Confront Divorce*. New York: Routledge.

———. 1998. "Women, Welfare, and Domestic Violence." *Social Justice* 25(1):105–122.

Lloyd, S. 1997. "The Effects of Violence on Women's Employment." Paper presented at the Trapped in Poverty/Trapped by Abuse Conference, Evanston, IL.

Loseke, D. R. 1992. *The Battered Woman and Shelters*. Albany: State University of New York Press.

Lundgren, E. 1998. "The Hand That Strikes and Comforts: Gender Construction and the Tension Between Body and Symbol." In R. Dobash and P. Dobash, eds., *Rethinking Violence Against Women*. Thousand Oaks, CA: Sage.

Martin, D. 1976. *Battered Wives*. San Francisco: Glide.

McWilliams, M. 1998. "Violence Against Women in Societies Under Stress." In R. E. Dobash and R. P. Dobash, eds., *Rethinking Violence Against Women*. Thousand Oaks, CA: Sage.

Pagelow, M. D. 1981. *Woman-Battering: Victims and Their Experiences*. Beverly Hills, CA: Sage.

———. 1984. *Family Violence*. New York: Praeger.

———. 1993. "Justice for Victims of Spouse Abuse in Divorce and Child Custody Cases." *Violence and Victims* 8(1):69–83.

Pearson, P. 1997. *When She Was Bad: Violent Women and the Myth of Innocence*. New York: Viking.

Pence, E. L. 1996a. *Safety for Battered Women in a Textually Mediated Legal System*. Unpublished Ph.D. Dissertation, University of Toronto.

———. 1996b. *Coordinated Community Response to Domestic Assault Cases: A Guide for Policy Development*. Duluth: Minnesota Program Development, Inc.

Pence, E. L. and Shepard, M. 1988. "Integrating Feminist Theory and Practice: The Challenge of the Battered Women's Movement." In K. Ylö and M. Bograd, eds., *Feminist Perspectives on Wife Abuse*. Newbury Park, CA: Sage.

Pleck, E. 1987. *Domestic Tyranny: The Making of Social Policy Against Family Violence from Colonial Times to the Present*. New York: Oxford.

Ptacek, J. 1988. "Why Do Men Batter Their Wives?" In K. Ylö and M. Bograd, eds., *Feminist Perspectives on Wife Abuse*. Newbury Park, CA: Sage.

Raphael, J. 1996. *Prisoners of Abuse: Domestic Violence and Welfare Receipt*. Chicago: Taylor Institute.

Renzetti, C. M. 1992. *Violent Betrayal: Partner Abuse in Lesbian Relationships.* Newbury Park, CA: Sage.

Rivera, J. 1997. "Domestic Violence Against Latinas by Latino Males: An Analysis of Race, National Origin, and Gender Differentials." In A. K. Wing, ed., *Critical Race Feminism.* New York: New York University.

Roy, M. 1977. "A Research Project Probing a Cross-Section of Battered Women." In Maria Roy, ed., *Battered Women.* New York: Van Nostrand Reinhold.

Russell, D. E. H. 1982. *Rape in Marriage.* New York: Macmillan.

Saunders, D. 1993. "Husbands Who Assault: Multiple Profiles Requiring Multiple Responses." In Z. Hilton, ed., *Legal Responses to Wife Assault.* Newbury Park, CA: Sage.

Schechter, S. 1982. *Women and Male Violence.* Boston: South End.

Schmidt, J. D. and Sherman, L. W. 1996. "Does Arrest Deter Domestic Violence?" In E. S. Buzawa and Carl G. Buzawa, eds., *Do Arrest and Restraining Orders Work?.* Thousand Oaks, CA: Sage.

Seligman, M. E. P. 1975. *Helplessness: On Depression, Development, and Death.* San Francisco: W. H. Freeman.

Stark, E. 1996. "Mandatory Arrest of Batterers: A Reply to Its Critics." In E. S. Buzawa and C. G. Buzawa, eds., *Do Arrest and Restraining Orders Work?* Thousand Oaks, CA: Sage.

Stark, E. and Flitcraft, A. 1996. *Women at Risk.* Thousand Oaks, CA: Sage.

Straus, M. A. 1993. "Physical Assaults by Wives: A Major Social Problem." In R. J. Gelles and D. R. Loseke, eds., *Current Controversies on Family Violence.* Thousand Oaks, CA: Sage.

Straus, M. A. and Gelles, R. J. 1986. "Societal Change and Family Violence from 1975–1985 as Revealed by Two National Surveys." *Journal of Marriage and the Family* 48:465–479.

Straus, M. A., Gelles, R. J., and Steinmetz, S. K. 1980. *Behind Closed Doors: Violence in the American Family.* Garden City, NY: Anchor Press/Doubleday.

Szinovacz, M. E. and Egley, L. C. 1995. "Comparing One-Partner and Couple Data on Sensitive Marital Behaviors: The Case of Marital Violence." *Journal of Marriage and the Family* 57 (4):995–1010.

Taylor, G. 1993. "Child Custody and Access." *Vis à Vis: National Newsletter on Family Violence* 10(3).

United Nations. 1995. *Report on the Fourth World Conference on Women, Beijing,* 8th meeting. Web document. Gopher://gopher.un.org/00/conf/fwcw/conf/pre/

U.S. Attorney General. 1984, September. *Attorney General's Task Force on Family Violence. Final Report.* Washington, DC: U.S. Department of Justice.

U.S. Department of Justice. 1996. *Battering and Its Effects: The Validity and Use of Evidence Concerning Battering and Its Effects in Criminal Trials.* Washington, DC: Author.

U.S. Department of State. 1998. *Violence Against Women.* Web document. (www.state/www/global/women/fs_980310_women_violence.html.)

Walker, L. E. 1979. *The Battered Woman.* New York: Harper & Row.

———. 1984. *The Battered Woman Syndrome.* New York: Springer.

———. 1989. *Terrifying Love.* New York: Harper & Row.

Websdale, N. and Johnson, B. 1997. "Reducing Woman Battering: The Role of Structural Approaches." *Social Justice* 24(1):54–81.

Wilson, M. and Daly, M. 1993. "Spousal Homicide Risk and Estrangement." *Violence and Victims* 8:3–16.

Zorza, J. 1991. "Woman Battering: A Major Cause of Homelessness." *Clearinghouse Review* 25: 421.

———. 1994. "Must We Stop Arresting Batterers? Analysis and Policy Implications of New Police Domestic Violence Studies." *New England Law Review* 28:929. ✦

10
Sexual Assault

Julie Allison and
Irene Kollenbroich-Shea

This chapter provides a general overview of
the problems of sexual assault and rape. The
chapter begins by introducing the statistical
realities of the overwhelming incidence and
prevalence rates of sexual assault. To help explain the staggering rate of rapes, the chapter
next examines attitudes toward rape and sexual assault. Many myths about rape and sexual assault result in the perpetuation of these
crimes, including those regarding the motivations underlying sexual assault. Contrary to
the beliefs of many, rape is not motivated by
sex but rather by a combination of anger,
power, and sadistic motives. The chapter concludes with a discussion of the consequences
of rape and of ways in which sexual assault
may be prevented.

Before you finish reading this page, another woman will be raped in the United
States.

Consider the following statement:

> Somewhere in America, a woman is raped
> every two minutes. (U.S. Department of
> Justice 1994)

In 1995, 355,300 women were the victims of
an attempted or completed rape or sexual assault (U.S. Department of Justice 1997). An
estimated 77 out of every 100,000 females in
the United States were raped in 1994 (Federal Bureau of Investigation 1997).

The Scope of Rape

Statistics like these led Senator Joseph R.
Biden, Jr. to declare, in a Majority Staff Re-

port, that "American women are in greater
peril now from attack than they have ever
been in the history of our nation" (1991, ii).
This report, offered by Biden to the Committee on the Judiciary of the United States Senate, found that the incidence of rape has
been increasing steadily since governmental
data have been collected on the issue.

Now, consider that these recent government survey figures represent only reported
crimes. Research conducted by Koss and her
colleagues (Koss, Gidycz, and Wisniewski
1987) suggests that when unreported rapes
are included, these statistics rise enor-
mously. Their research, the most comprehensive to date on incidence and prevalence
rates of rape and sexual assault, found that,
on average, one out of eight women attending higher education institutions all across
the nation reported having been raped. Furthermore, one out of four women reported
having experienced some form of sexual assault, including attempted rape. These findings suggest that the actual incidence rate of
sexual assault is much higher than Justice
Department statistics maintain—as much as
10 to 15 times higher. If these statistics represented a medical disease, sexual assault in
our country would be declared an epidemic.[1]

In fact, rape is probably the *most underreported violent crime in* the United States
(Lonsway and Fitzgerald 1994; Ullman
1997). The FBI recently estimated that 37
percent of all rapes are reported to law enforcement officials, and the Department of
Justice found that only 26 percent of all
rapes or attempted rapes are reported to authorities (Rape, Abuse and Incest National
Network 1996). Again, however, research
suggests that these governmental statistics
are overly optimistic. Some research pro-
jects that utilize more sensitive measures of
victimization find meager reporting rates of
5 percent and lower (Finkelson and Oswalt
1995; Koss 1985; Mynatt and Allgeier 1990).

Why the discrepancy between incidence
rates of sexual assault and reports of such
crimes? To be sure, there is no single answer
to this question. Rather, the answers lie

woven among an entangled web of false assumptions and attitudes about sexual assault and an oftentimes cruel reality regarding the aftermath of sexual victimization for those who do report. For example, reporting a rape to the police may mean intrusive and painful medical examinations, embarrassment and humiliation during police questioning or while giving testimony in court, and social isolation from some family and friends.

Rape Myths

It is the false assumptions and attitudes about rape that have the most insidious effects on survivors of rape, friends and family members of rape victims, and society in general. Oftentimes referred to as rape myths (Burt 1980; Lonsway and Fitzgerald 1995), these attitudes serve both to perpetuate the staggering numbers of sexual assaults that take place every year and to trivialize the very nature of rape with all of its devastating effects. And as long as rape myths are adhered to, rape will remain a misunderstood crime (Allison and Wrightsman 1993).

Date or Acquaintance Rape

One very specific rape myth concerns the relationship between the victim and the perpetrator. When people think of rape, they generally conjure up pictures of a strange man—insane, sex-starved, or both—lurking behind bushes waiting for his victim to arrive. In reality, few rapes actually occur in this manner. To the contrary, most rapes occur between individuals who know each other—they could be neighbors, coworkers, friends, or lovers. In the research described earlier by Koss and her colleagues (1987), 84 percent of the rape or attempted rape victims knew their attacker. Finn (1995) suggests that "in every classroom with 50 female students, there are, on average, six to seven women who, in the past year, have been victims of rape or attempted rape *by someone they know*" (p. 12, our emphasis).

Through adherence to rape myths, we are faced with a situation in which *beliefs* about rape are vastly different from the *reality* of rape. The consequences of such a difference are clear. When a discrepancy exists between an actual rape and the stereotype of rape, the trivialization process of rape begins, and the very real experience of rape is now perceived as something less than a "real rape" (see Estrich 1987). Victims may be disinclined to label their experience as rape yet still experience the negative consequences of having been raped (Koss et al., 1987), or they may find fault in themselves for the incident. Those of us who are told about such incidents may be similarly inclined to trivialize the incident and engage in victim blaming.

Other Myths

Other myths concerning rape may take one of three general forms: (1) Women cannot be raped against their will, (2) Women secretly wish to be raped, and (3) Most accusations of rape are false (Brownmiller 1975). These rape myths do not just reflect social attitudes—their existence may also be found in our legal system.

Myth: Women cannot be raped against their will. The idea expressed is that any woman who doesn't really want to be raped can be successful in her resistance to the rapist. This myth actually serves to nullify the very existence of rape.

Myth: Women secretly wish to be raped. This myth rests on the assumption that women may find pleasure and satisfaction from being forced to engage in sexual behaviors. Indeed, it is believed by those who accept this myth as reality that women actually fantasize about being raped. The idea that women secretly desire rape has been codified into our legal system; in 1952 the *Yale Law Journal* asserted, "A woman's need for sexual satisfaction may lead to the unconscious desire for forceful penetration." (Estrich 1987, 39). And the *Stanford Law Review* reiterated this view in 1966 when it was written that "a woman may note a man's brutal nature and be attracted to him rather than repulsed" (Note, 1966, p. 682). In 1988, one rapist was caught and convicted only after he called his victim, promising to return the jewelry he had stolen from her if she would go on a date with him (Allison and Wrightsman 1993).

Myth: Most accusations of rape are false. This belief was developed as a mechanism that would serve to protect men from false accusations on both a social and a legal level. Such fears of being falsely accused are long-standing, as illustrated by a statement of the seventeenth century English jurist Lord Chief Justice Matthew Hale (1680):

> It is true, rape is a most detestable crime, and therefore ought severely and impartially to be punished with death, but it must be remembered that it is an accusation easily to be made and hard to be proved; and harder to be defended by the party accused tho ever so innocent. (p. 635)

In 1904, a Georgia appellate court asserted that "every man is in danger of being prosecuted and convicted on the testimony of a base woman, in whose testimony there is no truth" (*Davis v. State* 1904, 181). Indeed, many states still impose a resistance requirement on the victim, in order to legally prove that a rape occurred (Largen 1988). Hence, rape is the only crime that actually requires that the behavior of the victim be examined to determine the guilt of the defendant in a court of law. In actuality, false accusations occur no more often for rape than for any other crime, about 2 percent (Bienen 1983).

Rape Myths and Victim Responsibility

As long as there is an acceptance of rape myths, rape will continue to be a problem of epidemic proportions. Rape myths serve to perpetuate the very existence of rape by encouraging the placement of responsibility for rape on the victims. When victims of rape are held responsible for their own victimization, we justify the behavior of rapists,

essentially letting them off the hook. Indeed, our society is notoriously bad about holding rapists accountable for their behavior; only an estimated 2 to 5 percent of rapists are convicted of their crimes.

One startling example of the justification of rape comes from the work of Goodchilds et al. (1988). In this research, adolescent boys and girls were asked "Under what circumstances is it okay for a guy to hold a girl down and force her to have sexual intercourse?" When provided with a series of nine statements describing possible circumstances, 66 percent of the participants indicated agreement that some circumstances legitimized the use of force in sex. This means that two-thirds of adolescents in this study believed that rape was justifiable under certain circumstances. These circumstances ranged from "when a girl gets a guy sexually excited" to "when they have dated for a long time, or when she is stoned or drunk."

Rape Myths and Rapists

Rape myths also provide one explanation for why rapists rape: They provide a rationale for the behavior. In fact, research suggests that such rape-supportive attitudes are one of the few variables that may discriminate men who are sexually aggressive from men who are not (Burkhart and Fromuth 1991; Koss 1985; Lonsway and Fitzgerald 1995; Malamuth 1986). One rapist described how two of his rape victims "brought the rape on themselves" (Sussman and Bordwell 1981):

> I was robbing this one person's apartment, she came in on me, I told her not to be afraid, to sit down, she did sit down, and the next thing I knew she was coming out of the apartment screaming for help. I ran out after her, and caught her took her back to the apartment. If she wouldn't have ran, that wouldn't have happened.
>
> And in the other case, I would say I was more the victim in this case, this person came to the door, dressed with a towel wrapped around them. I told the person to

go and get some clothes on, she went into her bedroom to put some clothes on, but she put the clothes on so I could see her. I was in the other room watching her more or less so she couldn't do nothing funny, and when she started putting on clothes, there she was right in front of my eyes. (p. 198)

Motivations for Rape

The fact that adherence to rape myths encourages sexual aggression is not surprising. At the core of these beliefs is the false belief that rape is motivated by sex. To be sure, rape involves the act of sexual intercourse, and sexual assault by definition includes sexual behavior. However, rape and sexual assault use sexual behavior to express aggression, not sexuality (Groth 1979, 1983).

Nicholas Groth, a leading researcher in the area of motivations for rape, has collected data on over 500 convicted rapists. Based on these data, Groth (1979) developed a tripartite typology of the motivations of the rapist, which include power, anger, and sadism. Groth argues that although all three motivations are present in every rapist, they may be categorized by which of the three serves as the most powerful motivator.

Power Rape

Power is the most common motivation for rapists. Generally the psychology of the power rapist includes deep feelings of insecurity and inadequacy. Rape becomes the means of compensating for these feelings by providing feelings of strength and control, power and mastery. One power rapist told Groth:

All my life I felt I was being controlled, particularly by my parents, that people used me without any regard for my feelings, for my needs, and in my rapes the important part was not the sexual part, but putting someone else in the position in which they were totally helpless. I bound and gagged and tied up my victims and made them do something they didn't want to do, which was exactly the way I felt in my life. I felt helpless, very helpless in that I couldn't do anything about the satisfaction I wanted. Well, I decided I'm going to put them in a position where they can't do anything about what I want to do. They can't refuse me. They can't reject me. They're going to have no say in the matter. I'm in charge now. (1979, 30)

The goals of the power rapist are not to harm and humiliate but to conquer and possess another, and sex becomes the means of establishing this kind of power. The power rapist uses force only to the extent that is necessary to achieve these goals. But while his rapes are not characterized by the marked brutality found in anger rapes, they may last longer. The feelings of power and mastery gained by the power rapist last only as long as the rape.

Anger Rape

Anger rapes are the result of pent-up hostilities that at some point erupt. Such anger may dwell within the rapist for days, months, or years, until some identifiable and external stressful event triggers an explosion of rage for which rape is the expression. Through rape, the anger is released, at least temporarily. Predictably, anger rapists follow a pattern of allowing their anger and hostilities to build until another explosion—and another rape. As one rapist told Groth,

I felt relieved of the tension and anger for a while, but then it would start to build up again, little things, but I couldn't shake them off. (1979, 15)

The anger rape lasts only as long as is necessary to release the anger. However, anger rapes may be particularly brutal. The goal of the anger rapist is to harm and humiliate the victim, and he chooses sex as the manner in which to express his anger because he finds it to be the best way to reach his goal. Victims of anger rape are often forced to perform sexual acts that the rapist finds particularly demeaning, such as oral or anal sex.

Sadistic Rape

In the mind of the sadistic rapist, sex and violence become indistinguishable. Violent behavior is sexually arousing to the sadistic rapist, and the more violent, the more sexually arousing. The sadistic rapist derives great pleasure from tormenting his victim and watching her suffer in agony. This type of assault is generally premeditated and often involves acts of calculated torture. While a statistical rarity, the sadistic rape is more likely than any other to result in murder.

The sadistic rapist is the least common of the three identified by Groth. However, it is the rapist motivated by sadism who inspires the most fear. As a result, this type of rape receives the most attention from the media, and hence the public. And it is the sadistic rape and all the attention it receives that helps perpetuate many of the myths surrounding rape.

Note that the data on which Groth's model is based came from convicted rapists who were currently serving time in prison. Given that only a small minority—2 to 5 percent—of all rapists are ever convicted, one concern about this research is the generalizability of the data. Those who are convicted of rape and sentenced to prison are more likely to be particularly violent in their acts and are more likely to have raped women whom they did not know (characteristics perceived to be better indicators of guilt in rape cases). Is it appropriate, therefore, to conclude that the same motivations found in these rapists will generalize to the date rapist whose most common strategy is to hold his victim down while ignoring her pleas (Koss et al. 1988)? Research attempting to answer this question has found that the same elements found to motivate the rapists in Groth's sample also serve as primary motivators for those who rape victims they know (Lisak and Roth 1988).

The Consequences of Rape

Ultimately, the specific characteristics or motivations associated with rape that inves-

tigators tease out for the purposes of research do not matter for the victim of rape. Whether a victim is raped by a complete stranger or by a friend she has known for years, she has been violated in the most personal of ways. Whether she is also assaulted with physical blows to the body or is left without any visible signs of attack, the rape victim is faced with a recovery process that may take months or years. All victims of rape show signs of psychological trauma and face a long road toward recovery.

Georgette was a first-year college student when she was raped.[2] Her rapist was the resident adviser of her dorm. She had been standing in the hall when he started making advances. Despite her rejections, he dragged her into the room nearby and raped her. She described her experience to Warshaw (1988):

> I didn't tell anyone. In fact, I wouldn't even admit it to myself until about four months later when the guilt and fear that had been eating at me became too much to hide and I came very close to a nervous breakdown. I tried to kill myself but fortunately I chickened out at the last minute.
>
> There's no way to describe what was going on inside me. I was losing control and I'd never been so terrified and helpless in my life. I felt as if my whole world had been kicked out from under me and I had been left to grope all alone in the darkness. I had horrible nightmares in which I relived the rape and others which were even worse. I was terrified of being with people and terrified of being alone. I couldn't concentrate on anything and began failing several classes. Deciding what to wear in the morning was enough to make me panic and cry uncontrollably. I was convinced I was going crazy, and I'm still convinced I almost did. (p. 84)

Georgette's reactions, both emotional and behavioral, are common. As stated earlier, no matter what the specifics of the rape, all victims face a long road toward recovery. For the victim of rape, the act can never be undone; she will never *not* be a rape victim. However, a rape victim can, through the recovery process and hopefully with the support of her family and friends, become a rape survivor.

Rape Trauma Syndrome

In 1974, the term *rape trauma syndrome* was coined by Burgess and Holmstrom to describe a collection of common symptoms found among victims of rape. According to Burgess and Holmstrom, the question is not whether a rape victim will experience rape trauma syndrome, but rather which specific symptoms will manifest themselves and to what extent. The rape trauma syndrome can be divided into two phases, the acute crisis phase and long-term reactions.

Phase I: The Acute Crisis Phase. Within the context of recovery, the acute crisis phase does not last long, generally from a few days to several weeks. However, the symptoms that appear during this phase may be quite strong. Note the words that Georgette used to describe what she was experiencing after her rape: *guilt, fear, terrified, horrible*. These reactions are common. In fact, many of the consequences that victims experience during this phase revolve around fear and anxiety. Other immediate reactions include denial and shock, guilt and self-blame, regression, and distorted perceptions. In one study, victims of rape were asked to identify their symptoms only hours after their attack (Veronen, Kilpatrick, and Resick 1979).

96 percent reported feeling scared

96 percent reported shaking or trembling

92 percent reported feeling terrified

92 percent reported feeling confused

80 percent reported having racing thoughts

80 percent reported a racing heart

72 percent reported feeling pain

68 percent reported tight muscles

64 percent reported rapid breathing

60 percent reported experiencing numbness

Phase II: Long-Term Reactions. Once the acute crisis phase has passed, the rape victim is faced with the daunting task of putting the pieces of her life back together again. During this second phase of recovery, the victim must somehow find a new order to her life and bring back a sense of control (Burgess and Holmstrom 1985). And she must somehow accomplish this task while still experiencing symptoms of trauma. Major symptoms of this phase include phobias, disturbances in physical functioning, and changes in lifestyle.

A *phobia* is an irrational fear that interferes with general functioning. Recall that Georgette described being terrified of both being with other people and being alone. Experiencing such fear in particular situations, or with objects associated with the rape, is common. Rape victims will go to great lengths to avoid the object of their fear. One victim described her fear-based dilemma as a no-win situation:

> Jon and I had known for months that he would have to make a business trip to California in December. Originally, before things had changed, we had all planned to go. I loved California, I wanted to go away with Jon, I didn't want to be left alone, but as the trip approached we had to face the reality . . . I didn't think I could leave the little security I found in my house, for strange motels. Camping was out of the question. We gave up the idea and I tried not to think about how I would survive a week without Jon.

Disturbances in general functioning often revolve around eating and sleeping. Victims may alternate between not eating and binging. Sleep may follow a similar pattern—victims may either not be able to sleep at all or may find that they can't get out of bed. One woman reported:

> At first, I had no appetite. I didn't eat anything for three whole days. It hurt to swallow for some reason. Then I began to eat a lot, you know, and gained weight. I don't think I slept for the same three days that I didn't eat. I remember not going to bed the first two nights. After that I couldn't sleep more than a couple of hours at a time for a

week or so, and that still happens two or three times a week. (Rowland 1985, 146)

Changes in sexual relationships may also accompany this phase of recovery. Although research finds that victims may still have sexual relations with their partners, the quality of these experiences is negatively affected by the rape (Feldman-Summers, Gordon and Meagher 1979). Victims of rape also report reduced desire for sexual activity (Becker, et al., 1984).

Changes in lifestyle may represent the most drastic of alterations that occur in the aftermath of rape. These include changes in everyday activities, appearance, or home. It is not uncommon for a victim raped in her home to move, or for a college student to change universities. Additionally, many victims' relationships end as a consequence of rape.

It is important to note that similarities exist between rape trauma syndrome and posttraumatic stress disorder (PTSD), identified by the DSM-IV (*Diagnostic and Statistical Manual of Mental Disorders*) of the American Psychiatric Association. Researchers find that for most rape victims, a diagnosis of PTSD is both common and appropriate (cf. Allison and Wrightsman 1993).

How long does recovery take? This question is still being investigated. First and foremost, it must be understood that individual differences are the rule here—no two victims will respond in exactly the same way, and each rape victim will recover in her own unique way, and in her own time. Although some victims may report symptoms many years afterward (Kilpatrick, Veronen, and Best 1985), about one out of four victims report no symptoms one year after the event. Most improvement seems to take place within the first three months following the rape (Kilpatrick, Resick, and Veronen 1981).

Supporting the Raped Woman

While many victims of rape do not tell anyone about their experience, those who do disclose their very personal victimization are taking an important step toward recovery by seeking out the social support of their loved ones. The reactions of those entrusted with this personal information is therefore crucial. Reacting with suspicion, blame, or anger may catalyze the victim's recovery process to a regressed state, causing recovery to be both harder and longer. Rape victims have a hard enough time dealing with the trauma of the event; negative reactions only serve to retraumatize them.

Friends and family members can help by providing an atmosphere based on acceptance, empathy, and support (Bard 1982; Koss and Harvey 1991). Paying attention to her story will help her feel accepted and heard. Acknowledging her words by restating what she has said may help reinforce this feeling of acceptance. Empathy involves viewing her story from her personal perspective, without expressing vengeance. One powerful means of providing support to the victim is validating the victim's reactions at the time of the attack by letting her know that she neither caused nor deserved the assault. Finally, it is of utmost importance for the victim to be assured that rape is *survivable*. A woman who has been victimized does not have to be a victim forever—she can feel safe and in control again.

Preventing Rape

It is nothing less than sad that, despite increased research and vast educational efforts in the area of sexual aggression, the rates of rape and sexual assault continue to rise. We believe that one of the reasons for this paradox has to do with the focus of educational efforts. That is, the focus of most strategies for rape prevention tends to be solely on the behavior of females and what they can do to prevent rape. It is of course important for women to know ways to reduce their chances of being raped. However, rape is caused by rapists, not victims. And while most men are not rapists, most rapists are men. Thus, until the behavior of men is addressed, rape will continue to occur at alarming rates. For centuries, society has attempted to control the behavior of women in its efforts to stop sexual assault, and it simply has not worked.

Given this situation, research has found that some strategies for avoiding rape are better than others. However, there is no strategy or set of strategies that guarantees that one will not be raped. And no one can second-guess how a victim will respond to an attack.

In a review of empirical-based rape avoidance studies, Ullman (1997) found that forceful physical resistance (scratching, punching, biting), forceful verbal resistance (screaming, threatening the offender) and nonforceful physical resistance (fleeing, pulling away from the rapist) strategies are all likely to be effective for avoiding rape. Nonforceful verbal resistance strategies (pleading, talking, crying) do not seem to be effective. Ullman (1997) also found that when responses were immediate and determined, rape avoidance was more likely. Allison and Wrightsman's (1993) review of the research led them to succinctly state, "Doing something is better than doing nothing" (p. 251). This advice apparently still holds true.

Some studies (Block and Skogan 1986; Prentky, Burgess, and Carter 1986; Ruback and Ivie 1988) have found that using forceful physical resistance may also be related to an increased risk of physical injury. However, Ullman (1997) has suggested that more research is needed to more closely examine the sequential relationship between attack, resistance strategy, and physical injury.

Rape prevention also requires knowledge of the role of alcohol and drugs in many rapes. The prevalent use of alcohol by the victim or the perpetrator prior to sexual attack has been a consistent research finding for decades (Abbey 1991; Amir 1971; Koss and Dinero 1989; Pernanen 1991; Rada 1975; Russell 1984). It is thought that alcohol consumption by the victim may inhibit her ability to resist (Allison and Wrightsman

1993: Harrington and Leitenberg 1994) and therefore increase the likelihood of a completed rape by either a stranger or an acquaintance (Ullman and Innight 1993). Alcohol use by the perpetrator also appears to be positively related to severity of sexual violence (Ullman and Innight 1993), thus aggravating victim physical injuries.

In the past few years, sedatives, in particular Rohypnol (flunitrazepam) and gamma hydroxy butyrate (GHB) have frequently been used illegally by rapists to render their targeted victim sluggish and vulnerable. Colorless, tasteless, and odorless, these drugs dissolve quickly into drinks and are unlikely to be detected. In addition to sluggishness, the victim may also experience difficulty with motor and verbal skills (e.g., walking and talking) and experience amnesia and blackouts.

What can be done about these dangerous drugs, often referred to as "date rape drugs"? According to a June 1997 report from the National Victim Center, if the victim reports the crime or seeks medical attention shortly afterward, medical personnel can determine the presence of these drugs through urine tests and the collection of evidence of sexual intercourse. In addition, several states have made possession of Rohypnol illegal. Furthermore, in 1996 President Clinton signed the Drug-Induced Rape Prevention and Punishment Act, which "imposes a prison sentence of up to 20 years for distributing illicit drugs to others without their knowledge or consent in order to commit sexual assault." (National Victim Center, 1997, 12).

As stated earlier, responsibility for the prevention of rape and sexual assault cannot lie solely in the hands of women. Rape is a societal problem because we live in a society that accepts, condones, and even rewards sexual aggression. Nagayama-Hall and Barongan (1997) have suggested that rape prevention efforts should include the adoption of multicultural and feminine socialization in place of traditional male-dominant cultural patterns. In addition, it is suggested that men need to take an active and committed role against the crimes of rape and sexual assault. Rape is a men's issue, too.

Discussion Questions

1. Explain why discrepancies exist between governmental statistics on rape and sexual assault, and data obtained from scientific research. Which statistics are more accurate, and why?
2. Identify three basic rape myths. What are the consequences of adherence to rape myths?
3. Discuss the three motivations for rape identified by Groth.
4. Describe the consequences of rape for victims. What can others do to be supportive of rape victims?

Endnotes

1. The authors wish to acknowledge the seriousness of the problem of rape for male victims. However, this chapter will focus primarily on female victims and male perpetrators, as this is the most prevalent type of sexual assault.
2. It is, in fact, the first few weeks of college when women are particularly vulnerable to being sexually assaulted.

References

Abbey, A. 1991. "Misperception as an Antecedent of Acquaintance Rape: A Consequence of Ambiguity in Communication Between Women and Men." In A. Parrot and L. Bechhofer, eds., *Acquaintance Rape: The Hidden Crime*. New York: Wiley.

Allison, J. A. and Wrightsman, L. S. 1993. *Rape: The Misunderstood Crime*. Newbury Park, CA: Sage.

Amir, M. 1971. *Patterns in Forcible Rape*. Chicago: University of Chicago Press.

Bard, M. 1982. [Testimony presented at a public hearing of the President's Task Force on Victims of Crime.] Washington, DC, September, 1982.

Becker, J., Skinner, L., Abel, G. G., Axelrod, R., and Treacy, E. C. 1984. "Depressive Symptoms Associated With Sexual Assault." *Journal of Sex and Marital Therapy* 10:185–192.

Bienen, L. 1983. "Rape Reform Legislation in the United States: A Look at Some Practical Effects." *Victimology: An International Journal* 8: 139–151.

Block, R. and Skogan, W. C. 1986. "Resistance and Nonfatal Outcomes in Stranger-to-Stranger Predatory Crime." *Violence and Victims* 4:241–253.

Brownmiller, S. 1975. *Against Our Will: Men, Women, and Rape*. New York: Simon & Schuster.

Burgess, A. W., and Holmstrom, L. L. 1974. "Rape Trauma Syndrome." *American Journal of Psychiatry* 131:981–999.

——. 1985. "Rape Trauma Syndrome and Post-traumatic Stress Response." In A. W. Burgess, ed., *Research Handbook on Rape and Sexual Assault*. New York: Garland.

Burkhart, B. R. and Fromuth, M. E. 1991. "Individual and Social Psychological Understanding of Sexual Coercion." In E. Gruerholz and M. A. Koralewski, eds., *Sexual Coercion: A Sourcebook on its Nature, Causes, and Prevention*. Lexington, MA: Lexington.

Burt, 1980. "Cultural Myths and Supports for Rape." *Journal of Personality and Social Psychology* 38:217–230.

Committee on the Judiciary United States Senate. 1991. *Violence Against Women: The Increase of Rape in America 1990*. March 21.

Davis v. State, 120 Ga. 433, 48 S. E. 180 1904).

Estrich, S. 1987. *Real Rape*. Cambridge, MA: Harvard University Press.

Federal Bureau of Investigation, 1997. *Crime in the United States*. Washington, DC: U.S. Government Printing Office.

Feldman-Summers, S., Gordon, P. E., and Meagher, J. R. 1979. "The Impact of Rape on Sexual Satisfaction." *Journal of Abnormal Psychology* 88:101–105.

Finkelson, L. and Oswalt, R. 1995, October. "College Date Rape: Incidence and Reporting." *Psychological Reports* 77(2):526.

Finn, P. 1995. *Preventing Alcohol-Related Problems on Campus: Acquaintance Rape*. (ED/

0PE95-7). Washington, DC: U.S. Government Printing Office.

Goodchilds, J. D., Zellman, G., Johnson, P. B., and Giarrusso, R. 1988. "Adolescents and Their Perceptions of Sexual Interaction Outcomes." In A. W. Burgess, ed., *Sexual Assault*, Vol.2. New York: Garland.

Groth, N. 1979. *Men Who Rape*. New York: Plenum.

———. 1983. "Treatment of the Sexual Offender in a Correctional Institution." In J. O. Greer and I. R. Stuart, eds., *The Sexual Aggressor: Current perspectives on treatment*. New York: Van Nostrand Reinhold.

Hale, M. 1680. *History of the Pleas of the Crown* (Vol 1). (Emlyn ed., 1847).

Harrington, N. T. and Leitenberg, H. 1994. "Relationship Between Alcohol Consumption and Victim Behaviors Immediately Preceding Sexual Aggression by an Acquaintance." *Violence and Victims* 9:315–324.

Kilpatrick, D. G., Resick, P., and Veronen, L. 1981. "Effects of a Rape Experience: A Longitudinal Study." *Journal of Social Issues* 37(4): 105–112.

Kilpatrick, D. G., Veronen, L. J., and Best, C. L. 1985. "Factors Predicting Psychological Distress Among Rape Victims." In C. R. Figley, ed., *Trauma and its Wake*. New York: Brunner/Mazel.

Koss, M. P. 1985. "The Hidden Rape Victim: Personality, Attitudinal, and Situational Characteristics." *Psychology of Women Quarterly* 9: 193–212.

Koss, M. P., and Dinero, T. E. 1989. "Discriminant Analysis of Risk Factors for Sexual Victimization Among a National Sample of College Women." *Journal of Consulting and Clinical Psychology* 57:242–250

Koss, M. P., Dinero, T. E., Seibel, C. A., and Cox, S. L. 1988. "Stranger and Acquaintance Rape: Are There Differences in the Victim's Experience?" *Psychology of Women Quarterly* 12:1–24.

Koss, M. P., Gidycz, C. A. and Wisniewski, N. 1987. "The Scope of Rape: Incidence and Prevalence of Sexual Aggression and Victimization in a National Sample of Higher Education Students." *Journal of Consulting and Clinical Psychology* 55:162–170.

Koss, M. P. and Harvey, M. R. 1991. *The Rape Victim: Clinical and Community Interventions* (2nd ed.). Newbury Park, CA: Sage.

Largen, M. A. 1988. "Rape-Law Reform: An Analysis." In A. W. Burgess (Ed.), *Rape and Sexual Assault*, Vol. 2. New York: Garland.

Lisak, D. and Roth, S. 1988. "Motivational Factors in Nonincarcerated Sexually Agressive Men." *Journal of Personality and Social Psychology* 55(5):795–802.

Lonsway, K. A. and Fitzgerald, L. F. 1994. "Rape Myths." *Psychology of Women Quarterly* 18: 133–164.

———. 1995. "Attitudinal Antecedents of Rape Myth Acceptance: A Theoretical and Empirical Reexamination." *Journal of Personality and Social Psychology* 68(4):704–711.

Malamuth, N. M. 1986. "Predictors of Naturalistic Sexual Aggression." *Journal of Personality and Social Psychology* 50:953–962.

Mynatt, C. R. and Allgeier, E. R. 1990. "Risk Factors, Self-Attributions, and Adjustment Problems Among Victims of Sexual Coercion." *Journal of Applied Sociology* 20:130–153.

Nagayama-Hall, O. and Barongan, C. 1997. "Prevention of Sexual Aggression: Sociocultural Risk and Protective Factors." *American Psychologist* 52(1):5–14.

National Victim Center. 1997, June. "The Danger of Date Rape Drugs." *Networks* 12(2).

Note. 1966. "The Resistance Standard in Rape Legislature." *Stanford Law Review* 18:682.

Pernanen, K. 1991. *Alcohol in Human Violence*. New York: Guilford Press.

Prentky, R., Burgess, A., and Carter, D. 1986. "Victim Response by Rapist Type: An Empirical and Clinical Analysis." *Journal of Interpersonal Violence* 1:688–695.

Rada, T. 1975. "Alcohol and Rape." *Medical Aspects of Human Sexuality* 9:48–65.

Rape, Abuse and Incest National Network. 1996. *Before You Finish Reading This, Another Woman Will Be Raped* [brochure]. Washington, DC: Author.

Rowland, J. 1985. *The Ultimate Violation*. Garden City, NY: Doubleday.

Ruback, R. B. and Ivie, D. L. 1988. "Prior Relationship, Resistance, and Injury in Rapes: An

Analysis of Crisis Center Records." *Violence and Victims* 3:99–111.

Russell, D. E. H. 1984. *Sexual Exploitation: Rape, Child Sexual Abuse, and Workplace Harassment*. Beverly Hills, CA: Sage.

Sussman, L. and Bordwell, S. 1981. *The Rapist File*. New York: Chelsea House.

Ullman, S. 1997. "Review and Critique of Empirical Studies of Rape Avoidance." *Criminal Justice and Behavior* 24(2):177–204.

Ullman, S. and Innight, R. 1993. "The Efficacy of Women's Resistance Strategies in Rape Situations." *Psychology of Women Quarterly* 17:23–38.

Veronen, L. J., Kilpatrick, D. G., and Resick, P. A. 1979. "Treatment of Fear and Anxiety in Rape Victims: Implications for the Criminal Justice System." In W. H. Parsonage, ed., *Perspectives in Victimology*. Beverly Hills, CA: Sage.

U.S. Department of Justice. 1994, January. *Violence Against Women: A National Crime Victimization Survey Report* (HHS Publication No. NCJ-145325). Washington, DC: U.S. Government Printing Office.

———. 1997, February. *Sex Offenses and Sex Offenders: An Analysis of Data on Rape and Sexual Assault* (HHS Publication No. NCJ-163392). Washington DC: U.S. Government Printing Office.

Warshaw, R. 1988. *I Never Called It Rape*. New York: Harper & Row. ✦

11
Corporate Violence Against Women

*Linda Rynbrandt and
Ronald C. Kramer*

Corporate violence against women is an emerging issue in criminology. Traditionally, women as victims of domestic violence formed a major focus within the discipline. More recent literature expands the concept of violence against women to women harmed by corporate deviance as well. In this chapter we define corporate crime and violence. Then, we specifically address corporate violence against women as workers and consumers. We use the silicone breast implant controversy as a case study in which to examine corporate violence against women in greater detail. Finally, we evaluate future prospects regarding women and corporate violence.

Joan received the bad news in 1977: Her breasts must be removed because of precancerous tumors. The good news, however, was that reconstructive surgery was possible. She received silicone implants and again looked forward to life as a busy young woman with a family and a career. Soon, however, she suffered from extreme fatigue and arthritis. Often she was so ill that she could not leave her bed. Joan was forced to quit her job, and her family had to learn to function without her. This caused the entire family great emotional distress. Joan eventually suspected that her ill health was linked to her silicone implants and had them replaced with saline implants in 1993. Although her health has improved somewhat, she is still unable to

work. Because of concerns about saline implants, Joan is seriously considering removing them as well, in what she calls her "third mastectomy" in less than two decades.[1]

Betsy was born with a physical deformity of her breasts. After the trauma of being different/deformed her entire life, she decided on silicone breast implants in 1981 to correct the problem. Painful breasts and an x-ray that showed a possible rupture led Betsy to have the silicone implants removed and replaced with saline implants in 1993. Betsy's health problems continue even after removal of the silicone implants. She experiences severe fatigue, serious joint and muscle pain, headaches, and memory loss. Although she formerly functioned as the co-owner and office manager of her own business, she is now wary of leaving home alone for fear she will become confused and lost.

Joan and Betsy are examples of the approximately 2 million women in the United States who have received silicone breast implants since they were introduced in 1964. While some women claim to be satisfied with their implants, many believe that their health has been severely damaged by the corporate actions of Dow Corning and other silicone implant manufacturers. They have suffered from such physical symptoms as hardening of breast tissue, leakage, autoimmune reactions, infections, and possibly even cancer (Purvis 1991).

The emotional toll on many of these women has also been dramatic. Those with health problems they associate with silicone implants stress the psychological strain they endure. Uncertainty regarding the current and future health impact of the implants causes emotional distress for the women and their families. In addition, the condescending way in which these women have been treated by physicians, lawyers, the media, and the implant makers has accounted for a great deal of tension.

Have these women experienced corporate violence? Before we can address that question, we must first define corporate crime and violence more thoroughly. We will then examine corporate violence against women both historically and today. Using the case study of the silicone breast implant controversy, we then examine corporate abuse of women in greater detail. Finally, we evaluate future prospects concerning corporate violence and women.

Corporate Crime and Violence

Corporate crime is a type of white-collar crime. The concept of white-collar crime generally refers to the crimes committed by respected, trusted, and powerful individuals and organizations. The term was created by criminologist Edwin Sutherland in 1939. Although he was not the first to call attention to elite wrongdoing and the crimes of the powerful, his work popularized the concept and gave it a sociological perspective (Sutherland, 1940, 1949).

Sutherland's definition of white-collar crime, and his inconsistent use of the term, however, caused some confusion among criminologists and led to various attempts to refine and redefine the concept (Kramer 1982). Today, most criminologists regard white-collar crime as a generic concept and break it down into various types. The two types of white-collar crime that are most often recognized are occupational crime and corporate crime (Clinard and Quinney 1973; Friedrichs 1996).

Occupational crime is a crime committed by individuals during the course of their occupation for their own personal gain. Embezzlement and fraud by professionals would be examples of this type of white-collar crime. Corporate crime, on the other hand, is an offense of the corporate organization itself to achieve organizational goals. With corporate crime, the organization is viewed as a social actor in its own right, capable of violating the law. Price-fixing by two or more firms and environmental pollution by a business are two examples of this form of white-collar crime.

Actually, most of the research in Sutherland's book, *White-Collar Crime*, was on the various law violations of major corporations (Sutherland 1949, 1983). And in the 1970s and 1980s, many criminologists began to focus more and more on organizational crime in general and corporate crime specifically (Clinard and Yeager 1980; Schrager and Short 1978). The growing recognition of corporate crime as an area for sociological research reflected, in part, the increased public concern about corporate wrongdoing in the 1960s and 1970s.

One important aspect of that growing public and criminological concern was the recognition that corporate wrongdoing imposes physical as well as economic costs on society. As Gil Geis (1973, 183) noted, "Corporate crime kills and maims." Thus, some criminologists began to isolate corporate violence as one specific form of corporate crime (Frank and Lynch 1992; Hills 1987; Kramer 1983; Mokhiber 1988). Kramer (1983) defines corporate violence this way:

> corporate behavior which produces an unreasonable risk of physical harm to employees, the general public, and consumers, which is the result of deliberate decision-making by persons who occupy positions as corporate managers or executives, which is organizationally based, and which is intended to benefit the corporation itself. (p. 166)

This definition makes several important points. First, it directs our attention to the corporate organization itself as the social and legal entity that is criminally involved. It also points out that even though a corporation can only act through the persons who occupy positions within the organization, the work-related thoughts and actions of these persons are shaped by organizational norms and procedures. This definition also explicitly recognizes the various categories of victims of corporate violence: workers, consumers, and the general public.

Finally, this definition does not restrict corporate violence to only those acts that violate the criminal law. It uses the unreasonable risk of physical harm standard to classify corporate behavior as violence for the purpose of study. Beginning with Sutherland, many criminologists who have studied white-collar crime have broadened the concept to cover acts that are not defined as a violation of criminal law but that violate broader legal or social standards of one kind or another (Michalowski and Kramer 1987; Schwendinger and Schwendinger 1970). Furthermore, the failure of the government to protect society from corporate violence can itself be viewed as a type of political crime (Caulfield and Wonders 1993; Chambliss 1989; Tunnell 1993).

Corporate crime and violence have thus become an important area of study within criminology. However, the media, the law enforcement community, and the public to some extent, are still reluctant to view these acts as major crimes that need to be dealt with. As Frank and Lynch (1992) note,

> Where harms are indirect, where violence is accomplished without traditionally recognized weapons (e.g., with consumer products rather than guns and knives), where organizations rather than individuals are the responsible actors, when powerful, upper-class persons are the offenders, we seem to be unwilling to label the act as serious violence. (pp. 2–3)

And this is even more so the case when the victims of corporate violence are women.

Corporate Violence Against Women

Even criminologists who have done work in the area of corporate violence have often overlooked women as a special category of victim (DeKeseredy and Goff 1992; Gerber and Weeks 1992). Recent work, however, has begun to acknowledge the crucial connection between corporate violence and women (Rynbrandt and Kramer 1995; Szockyj and Fox 1996). Both criminologists and the gen-

eral public must become as aware of the gendered nature of the corporate abuse of women as they are of the impact of domestic violence on women.

Recognition of the concept of corporate violence against women is fairly recent, but it is not new. Women as employees and consumers have long been special targets of corporate indifference, greed, and arrogance. From the infamous Triangle Shirtwaist fire in 1911, in which 146 women employees died for corporate profits (Newman 1991), to the latest assaults on women's bodies by Dow Corning in the name of corporate expediency, gendered threads of social, economic, and cultural values tie these otherwise disparate events together.

Further, corporations in the United States, both past and present, do not act in a political vacuum. Their corporate power is often enhanced by governmental policies that promote, or at least tacitly facilitate, corporate abuse of women. State support for policies which champion patriarchy and capitalism place women in jeopardy (Caulfield and Wonders 1993; Kramer 1992).

A socialist-feminist approach to corporate abuse of women posits that women were and are especially vulnerable because of their subordinate position in the social structure. Although all workers and consumers are potentially at risk in a society that extols profit at all costs, women face unique problems. Women's relatively low economic position and segregation in the secondary labor market create a situation in which they are particularly at risk for dangerous employment environments. The Triangle Shirtwaist fire, in which many poor women died because they were forced by economic necessity to work behind locked doors in an unsafe environment, was tragic. However, the fact that many poor women died in a similar event at the Imperial Food Products plant in 1991 (Aulette and Michalowski 1993) underscores the ongoing nature of corporate violence against women workers.[2]

As consumers, women also face unique risks of corporate harm because of their special biological and cultural roles in society. Women's reproductive role places them at risk for unsafe products in connection with sexuality, pregnancy, and childbirth. Cultural prescriptions concerning women's appearance increases their potential for risk from unnecessary products and procedures intended to enhance their appearance to conform with cultural norms of beauty. Again, while both women and men are at risk from poorly tested or underregulated drugs, women are unique in that medicine has long attempted to control women's health and reproductive function (Ehrenreich and English 1978). Medicine has also encouraged women to improve their mood and enhance their bodies through surgery and prescription drugs (Faludi 1991; Wolf 1991). Ironically, when these products or procedures ultimately prove harmful to women, medicine and science do not accept responsibility, but rather blame women for their own victimization.

Women and the Pharmaceutical Industry

Pharmaceutical companies and the government have a long history of insufficiently tested and regulated products that eventually harm women or their children. DES (diethylstilbestrol), IUDs (intrauterine contraceptive devices), toxic shock syndrome associated with highly absorbent tampons, and silicone breast implants are only the best-known examples of harmful products associated with women's sexuality or reproduction.

DES, a synthetic estrogen, was prescribed to pregnant women in the 1950–1960s to prevent miscarriage. Although studies questioned the effectiveness and safety of this product, pharmaceutical companies continued to push it and physicians continued to prescribe it until over 2 million women and 500,000 of their children were exposed. Ultimately, it became apparent that daughters of women treated with DES were more likely to develop a rare form of cancer. After some delay, the Food and Drug Administration (FDA) finally withdrew approval of DES for use by pregnant women in 1971. Today DES daughters continue to fight for recognition and restitution against such corporate giants as Eli Lilly, Abbot Labs, and Squibb (Findley 1996; Meyers 1983).

The Dalkon Shield debacle is a classic case of corporate indifference and greed at the expense of women's health and wellbeing (Mintz 1987; Perry and Dawson 1987). In 1971, A. H. Robins Company marketed its new IUD, the Dalkon Shield, as a safe and effective birth control device. In reality, it was neither safe nor effective. Women using the device developed infections called PID (pelvic inflammatory disease), which were sometimes fatal and often resulted in infertility. Also, about 5 percent of women became pregnant while using this purportedly effective birth control device. Many experienced miscarriages or gave birth to children with birth defects. These problems convinced the FDA to suspend U.S. sales in 1974. However, A. H. Robins continued to sell its lucrative product abroad. The IUD, despite known health hazards, was not subject to recall until 1984. During this time, many women in the United States and around the world continued to be harmed.

Despite the fact that A. H. Robins suppressed scientific studies, did not report health hazards to physicians, consumers, or governmental agencies, and valued women outside of the United States even less than those at home, it still maintained its innocence regarding any harmful or criminal actions toward women. The FDA was also slow to protect women from the Dalkon Shield as A. H. Robins stonewalled and continued to market its profitable, albeit highly harmful, product. Eventually, courts awarded large financial settlements to some women harmed by the Dalkon Shield, and the largest class-action suit to date was brought against A. H. Robins. The corporation responded by filing for bankruptcy in 1985 and through legal appeals delayed compensation for women injured by their product for years. In the end, many women settled for far less than they were entitled to. A. H. Robins served as an excellent role model for Dow Corning, when it found itself in a similar sticky situation regarding silicone breast implants.

The revised edition of Ermann and Lundman's (1996) anthology on corporate/governmental deviance substitutes a chapter on superabsorbent tampons and toxic shock syndrome (Swasy 1996) for a chapter on the Dalkon Shield (Perry and Dawson 1987) that was in an earlier edition. While the harmful product changes, the beat goes on. In the 1970s, Procter & Gamble attempted to increase its share of the tampon market with a new superabsorbent product called, ironically, Rely. It became increasingly clear that this supertampon, which was being aggressively promoted by P&G, might be linked to toxic shock syndrome, a sometimes fatal bacterial disease.

Despite growing concern by women consumers and the Centers for Disease Control, P&G did not issue any warnings to physicians or consumers and continued to push its product. Even after Rely tampons were recalled in 1980, under pressure from the FDA, P&G did not acknowledge the tampons were dangerous or warn women against use of the product. Concerns about legal liability, giving an advantage to their competition, and its own corporate image were greater than considerations regarding the health of women (Swasy 1996). Yet again, corporate self-interest superseded corporate responsibility and accountability.

Dow Corning: The Battle Over Breasts

The anatomy of the battle for women's health moved from the vagina to the breasts when silicone breast implants appeared on the market in 1964. What could be better? Not only could women who had "lost" their femininity after mastectomies regain the appearance of a real woman, but even wom-

en who suffered from the scourge of small breasts could become sexually attractive through the addition of some strategically placed silicone. Women could seize the chance to choose from a menu of breast sizes. What autonomy!

Over 150,000 women a year in the United States took advantage of this opportunity. Most were under age 35, and approximately 80 percent of the implants were done for cosmetic reasons (Smart 1991). No doubt, women assumed that the product had been tested for safety, while in reality silicone breast implants had been inadequately tested and unregulated by the FDA until 1967. Women who were concerned about safety were assured by their physicians that the implants were safe and would last for a lifetime (Byrne 1996).

While some women were pleased with their implants, many others began to develop health problems that they eventually associated with their silicone implants. As with other cases of corporate crime, potential victims may not realize they are endangered, as a number of the possible health problems associated with silicone implants might not appear immediately. For this reason, some have called the implants "time bombs" as their actual effects on the body may not be known for years (Purvis 1991, 70).

Word began to spread concerning potential health concerns, ranging from hardening of the breast tissue to possibly even cancer (Park and Brown 1991). Concerned women, consumer groups, and congressional committees finally forced the FDA to investigate the safety of silicone implants. Although serious concern had been raised within the FDA in 1982 regarding implant safety, it did not call for an investigation and require implant makers to submit proof of product safety until 1991 (Fischer 1991).

Why did the FDA delay so long when women's health and safety were at stake? Perhaps the answer may be found in the fact that silicone breast implant surgery was a $450 million a year industry in the United

States (Smart 1991). This was a lucrative product for Dow Corning and other corporations, as they fought for a piece of the market that was growing every year. Plastic surgeons joined implant manufacturers in a multimillion-dollar crusade against any restrictions on silicone implants (Caplan 1991).

It is telling that in an FDA hearing in 1991 to determine whether to remove silicone implants from the market, the FDA's own advisory panel's opinion that the implant makers had not proven product safety was ignored. Despite that fact that safety tests done by the implant makers were judged to be inadequate, the FDA allowed silicone implants to remain on the market because they were deemed to be a public health necessity for both reconstructive and cosmetic surgery (Hilts 1991).

While the FDA was slow to act to protect women from potentially dangerous silicone implants, women who took their cases to court were awarded millions in damages as juries found implant makers Dow Corning and Bristol-Meyers guilty of fraud, defective products, and failure to warn women of health risks (Seligmann, Cowley, and Springen 1992). Then internal Dow Corning documents revealing that the corporation had long been aware that the implants were not as safe as they publicly claimed were leaked to the FDA. These internal memos disclosed that, because of market pressures, Dow Corning put off research studies for years, even though scientists within the corporation warned of possible corporate liability. Even the little research that *was* done was inadequate and incomplete (Hilts 1992).

In January 1992, in the largest-ever moratorium on a medical device, the FDA called for a voluntary moratorium on the manufacture and sale of silicone implants. Although implant makers and plastic surgeons reluctantly agreed to the moratorium, some corporations continued to sell their product abroad (Rose 1992). The American Medical Association contended that the FDA's decision would unnecessarily frighten women with implants, and the AMA blamed consumer groups and greedy lawyers for the triumph of hysteria over science and reason. Even though the product was now off the market, the controversy continued to be waged in the media. Dow Corning worked at damage control and, after an initial period of stonewalling, changed tactics and began to cooperate with the FDA. Ironically, while Dow Corning's silicone implants had been inadequately tested because of market pressures and competition from other implant makers, in the end the greatest loss Dow experienced was not to its bottom line, but to its reputation.

Eventually, in 1992 the FDA allowed silicone implants for reconstructive surgery and ordered intensive research on the safety of implants. Conclusive results of those tests will not be available for years, and conflicting test results lead to continued anxiety and uncertainty for women with silicone implants. Dow Corning withdrew from the implant market in 1992, and later that year a report was released indicating that Dow Corning employees had faked reports and provided the FDA with incomplete data for years (Burton 1992).

Corporate control over the FDA was so powerful that Congress was forced to intervene before decisive action was finally taken. Dow Corning and other implant manufacturers did not act alone; they had the invaluable assistance of a nearly impotent FDA in their quest for profit and growth at the expense of women's health (Kolata 1992).

When the silicone implants were finally recalled from the market, it appeared that women and other consumer groups concerned about the safety of implants had finally been vindicated. It seemed that the emerging social movement against corporate crime and governmental complicity had won a major victory. Even beyond the moral victory, financial compensation for women injured by silicone implants also appeared to be forthcoming. Dow Corning announced in 1992 that it had $250 million in insurance to cover product liability costs. However, by 1993 so many suits had been filed against implant makers that a class-action suit appeared to be the only viable option. Implant makers offered $4.5 billion to settle implant claims. This global settlement fell apart in 1994 when nearly 100,000 claims exceeded the resources of the settlement fund. Under the weight of massive liability claims, Dow Corning filed for bankruptcy in 1995.

Since that time, class-action trials and corporate offers and counteroffers to plaintiffs continue. Controversy over implant safety also continues to be debated, with some recent studies suggesting there is no link between silicone implants and disease. Research findings that support the contention of implant makers that their product is not responsible for health problems in women will likely influence future class-action and individual liability suits against Dow Corning and other manufacturers.

Meanwhile, verdicts such as the 1997 Louisiana class-action decision that found Dow Corning guilty of negligent research and knowingly deceiving women about health risks of silicone (Burton 1997) encourage women in their quest for compensation and justice. Still, the legal battle is far from over. It now seems likely that, as in the case of the Dalkon Shield, women will ultimately receive little financial compensation or moral restitution.

Conclusion

The silicone breast implant case illustrates the dilemma of women and corporate victimization. How is it possible to acknowledge the grave harm inflicted on women by corporate malfeasance and governmental inaction without representing women as helpless victims? The extreme power differential between an individual woman harmed by silicone implants and a giant corporation such as Dow Corning immediately places the woman in a vulnerable legal, economic, and social position.

In addition to this structural disadvantage, women are often blamed for their own

victimization when the product in question relates to women's sexuality. As is frequently the case in rape trials, the woman finds that she, rather than the corporation, is on trial. She is forced to defend her choices and even her reputation. Women are divided into worthy and "unworthy" victims, and justice is distributed accordingly. This was often the situation with implants. Women who received implants for reconstructive purposes after cancer surgery were worthy victims, while women who chose implants for cosmetic reasons were suspect. If these later women experienced health problems from their implants, it was considered to be their own fault.

The notion that women "freely" chose to augment their breasts obscures the fact that in a culture such as our own large breasts are the cultural icon of feminine sexuality. In such a cultural milieu, many women feel compelled to enhance their appearance to conform to cultural standards for critical economic and social reasons. It is also questionable that women actually were able to give their "informed consent" to the procedure when factual health and safety data regarding silicone implants were deliberately withheld and misrepresented by Dow Corning and other implant makers.

The issue of choice was often used by interest groups concerned with keeping silicone implants on the market, and feminists found themselves in the ironic position of appearing to be against free choice for women as they argued to remove silicone implants from the market (Ehrenreich 1992; Wolf 1992).

Future Prospects

Women attempted to overcome the power differences between corporations and individuals harmed by implants by forming support groups and by joining global class-action lawsuits against implant makers (Rynbrandt and Mullendore 1996). Support groups cut both ways. Alone, women are no match for Dow Corning, but even the strongest support group faces challenges. Initially, groups were formed with enthusiasm and hope for mutual support and compensation. Now not only are groups challenged by the need to retain motivation and solidarity in the face of frustration and long periods of delay, but the women are fragmented in other ways as well. Divisions center on whether women had the surgery for reconstructive or cosmetic reasons and whether women should file individual claims or join the global suit. Dow Corning's strategies of delay and "divide and conquer" tactics have taken their toll on women individually and collectively. Also, it is becoming increasingly clear that our present legal system is inadequate to meet the needs of women harmed by corporate violence (Findley 1996; Peppin 1995). The impasse that has been reached in this mass tort litigation bodes poorly for the chances of a settlement ever being reached that can adequately address the needs of the individual claimants and also be acceptable to defendant Dow Corning.

The problems encountered in the ultimate resolution of this case highlight the inadequacy of our current governmental and judicial system to adjudicate these controversial issues and may well lead to new approaches in the ongoing mediation between consumers and corporations in our capitalist society (Birnbaum and Jackson 1994).

Paradoxically, for Dow Corning to survive and continue as a profitable corporate enterprise enabling it to settle the claims of women injured by their product, Dow must minimize its losses through the bankruptcy process, which means that the women who have suffered will not be completely compensated (Rynbrandt and Mullendore 1996).

There has been a growing movement against corporate and governmental crime, and publicity regarding corporate misconduct has become an important deterrent to corporate deviance. Still, a backlash against regulation to protect consumers and calls for tort reform challenge any gains that may have been made in the battle for consumer

protection. As this chapter has demonstrated, this is especially problematic for women as they are uniquely at risk for many forms of corporate violence.

The silicone breast implant case illustrates not only the potency of cultural values of beauty but also the ability of powerful corporations to exploit those social values to their own benefit. The demand for breast implants remains high, with rates that have nearly rebounded to premoratorium levels (Rios 1997). This demand, as well as the fact that Dow Corning has been able to avert restitution to women harmed by silicone implants, does not bode well for the future. The promise of high profits, along with the doubtful retribution for any wrongdoing in the pursuit of those profits, gives the green light to corporations to go ahead with business as usual. As history reveals, this encourages corporate violence against women, which is likely to continue into the future.

Discussion Questions

1. Does the silicone breast implant case meet the definition of corporate violence offered in the chapter? Why or why not?

2. What role did government agencies play in the various cases of corporate violence against women discussed in the chapter?

3. Why are women often blamed for their own victimization when a product in question relates to women's sexuality?

4. Do you think the women harmed in these cases freely chose to use the products in question such as breast implants? Why or why not?

Endnotes

1. In this, "Joan" is not unusual. A study published in the *New England Journal of Medicine* found that 25 percent of all women with implants required a second surgery. This was especially true for women who received implants after cancer surgery. This group had a 35 percent

chance of needing a second, or even third, operation (Gabriel et al. 1997)

2. Sally Simpson and Lori Elis (1996) astutely point out that race was a crucial factor in the Imperial Food fire, as the poor, black women who lost their lives were especially vulnerable because of the social and political intersections among race, class, and gender. The women in the Triangle Shirtwaist fire were also predominantly ethnic minority immigrants (Newman 1991).

References

Aulette, J. R. and Michalowski, R. 1993. "The Fire in Hamlet: A Case Study of a State-Corporate Crime." In K. Tunnell, ed., *Political Crime in Contemporary America*. New York: Garland.

Birnham, S. and Jackson, J. 1994 (September 19). "Recent Multibillion-dollar Settlements Could Serve as Models for the Resolution of Mass Products Liability and Toxic Tort Litigation." *National Law Journal* 17(3):B4, B6.

Burton, T. 1992 (November 3). "Dow Corning Employees Falsified Data on Breast Implants, Counsel Concludes." *Wall Street Journal*, p. A3.

———. 1996a (February 28). "Breast-implant Study Is Fresh Fuel for Debate." *Wall Street Journal*, p. B1.

———. 1996b (April 15). "FDA Says Data Linking Breast Implants to Immune-system Illness Not Definitive." *Wall Street Journal*, p. B9.

———. 1997 (August 19). "Dow Chemical Erred on Silicone, Jury Finds." *Wall Street Journal*, p. A3.

Byrne, J. 1996. *Informed Consent*. New York: McGraw-Hill.

Caplan, A. 1991 (November 26). "Safety Must Rule in Debate Over Breast Implants." *Detroit Free Press* p. B2.

Caulfield, S. and Wonders, N. 1993. "Personal and Political: Violence Against Women and the Role of the State." In K. Tunnell, ed., *Political Crime in Contemporary America*. New York: Garland.

Chambliss, W. J. 1989. "State-organized Crime." *Criminology* 27 (No. 3):183-208.

Clinard, M. B. and Quinney, R. 1973. *Criminal Behavior Systems: A Typology*, 2nd ed. New York: Holt, Rinehart and Winston.

Clinard, M. B. and Yeager, P. C. 1980. *Corporate Crime*. New York: The Free Press.

DeKeseredy, W. and Goff, C. 1992 (Autumn). "Corporate Violence Against Canadian Women: Assessing Left-realist Research and Policy." *Journal of Human Justice* 4:55–70.

Ehrenreich, B. 1992 (February 17). "Stamping Out a Dread Scourge." *Time* p. 88.

Ehrenreich, B., and English, D. 1978. *For Her Own Good*. Garden City, NY: Anchor Books.

Ermann, D., and Lundman, R. (eds.) 1996. *Corporate and Governmental Deviance*, 5th ed. New York: Oxford University Press.

Faludi, S. 1991. *Backlash: The Undeclared War Against American Women*. New York: Crown.

Findley, L. 1996. "The Pharmaceutical Industry and Women's Reproductive Health." In E. Szockyj and J. Fox, eds., *Corporate Victimization of Women*. Boston: Northeastern University Press.

Fischer, A. 1991 (September). "A Body to Die For." *Redbook*, pp. 96–99, 173–174.

Flanders, L. 1996 (January/February). "Beware: P. R. Implants in News Coverage." *Extra*, pp. 8–11.

Frank, N. K. and Lynch, M. J. 1992. *Corporate Crime Corporate Violence: A Primer*. New York: Harrow & Heston.

Friedrichs, D. O. 1996. *Trusted Criminals: White-collar Crime in Contemporary Society*. Belmont, CA: Wadsworth.

Geis, G. 1973. "Deterring Corporate Crime." In R. Nader and M. Green, eds., *Corporate Power in America*. New York: Grossman.

Gabriel, S., O'Fallon, M., Kurland, L., Beard, M., Woods, J., and Melton, L. J. 1994. "Risk of Connective-tissue Diseases After Breast Implantation." *New England Journal of Medicine* 330(24):1697–1702.

———. 1997 (March 6). "Complications Leading to Surgery After Breast Implantations." *New England Journal of Medicine* 336(10):677–682.

Gerber, J., and Weeks, S. 1992. "Women as victims of Corporate Crime: A Call for Research on a Neglected Topic." *Deviant Behavior: An Interdisciplinary Journal* 13:325–347.

Hills, S. L. (ed.) 1987. *Corporate Violence: Injury and Death for Profit*. Totowa, NJ: Rowman & Littlefield.

Hilts, P. 1991 (November 15). "FDA Panel Cites Need to Keep Breast Implants." *New York Times* p. A8.

———. 1992 (January 13). "Maker of Implants Balked at Tests, Its Records Show." *New York Times* p. A1 and B10.

Kolata, G. 1992 (January 26). "Questions Raised on Ability of FDA to Protect Public." *New York Times* p. A1.

Kramer, R. C. 1982. "Corporate Criminality: The Development of an Idea." In E. Hochstedler, ed., *Corporations as Criminal*. Beverly Hills, CA: Sage.

———. 1983 (May). "A Prolegomenon to the Study of Corporate Violence." *Humanity and Society* pp. 149–178.

———. 1992. "The Space Shuttle *Challenger* Explosion: A Case Study of State-Corporate Crime." In K. Schlegel and D. Weisburd, eds., *White-collar Crime Reconsidered*. Boston: Northeastern University Press.

Lilliston, B. 1995 (November 13). "The Enemy Within." *In These Times*, pp. 14–18.

Meyers, R. 1983. *DES: The Bitter Pill*. New York: Seaview/Putnam.

Michalowski, R. J. and Kramer, R. C. 1987. "The Space Between Laws: The Problem of Corporate Crime in a Transnational Context." *Social Problems* 34:34–53.

Mintz, M. 1987. "At any Cost: Corporate Greed, Women and the Dalkon Shield." In S. Hills, ed., *Corporate Violence: Injury and Death for Profit*. Savage, MD: Rowman & Littlefield.

Mokhiber, R. 1988. *Corporate Crime and Violence: Big Business, Power and the Abuse of the Public Trust*. San Francisco, CA: Sierra Club Books.

Nemecek, S. 1996. "Augmenting Discord." *Scientific American* 247(4):36–38.

Newman, P. 1991. "The Triangle Shirtwaist Factory." In L. Kerber and S. DeHart, eds., *Women's America: Refocusing the Past*, 3rd ed. New York: Oxford.

Park, P. and Brown, P. 1991 (May 11). "Compound From Breast Implants Linked to Cancer." *New Scientist* p. 14.

Peppin P. 1995. "Feminism, Law, and the Pharmaceutical Industry." In F. Pearce and L. Snider, eds., *Corporate Crime: Contemporary Debates*. Toronto: University of Toronto Press.

Perry, S. and Dawson, J. 1987. "Nightmare: Women and the Dalkon Shield." In M.D. Ermann and R. Lundman, eds., *Corporate and Governmental Deviance*, 3d ed. New York: Oxford University Press.

Purvis, A. 1991 (April 29). "Time Bombs in the Breasts?" *Time* p. 70.

Rios, D. 1997 (September 17). "Building an Image." *The Grand Rapids Press*, pp. F1, F2.

Rose, R. 1992 (March 4). "Breast Implants Still Being Sold Outside," *Wall Street Journal* p. B1.

Rynbrandt, L. and Kramer, R. 1995. "Hybrid Non-women and Corporate Violence: The Silicone Breast Implant Case." *Violence Against Women* 1(3):206–217.

Rynbrandt, L. and Mullendore, K. 1996. *Beauty, Business and Bankruptcy: The Silicone Implant Wars Continue*. Paper presented at the Annual Meetings of the American Society of Criminology.

Sanchez-Guerrero, J., Colditz, G., Karlson, E., Hunter, D., Speizer, F., and Liang, M. 1995. "Silicone Breast Implants and the Risk of Connective Tissue Diseases and Symptoms." *New England Journal of Medicine* 332(25):1666–1670.

Schrager, L. S. and Short, J. F. 1978. "Toward a Sociology of Organizational Crime." *Social Problems* 25:407–419.

Schwendinger, H. and Schwendinger, J. 1970. "Defenders of Order or Guardians of Human Rights?" *Issues in Criminology* 5:123–157.

Segal, M. 1995 (November). "A Status Report on Breast Implant Safety." *FDA Consumer* 29(9): 11–16.

Seligmann, J., Cowley, G., and Springen, K. 1992 (January 6). "Another Blow to Implants." *Newsweek* p. 45.

"Silicone Link to Disease Called 'Largely Settled.'" 1996 (June 6). *Wall Street Journal* p. B6.

Simpson, S. and Elis, L. 1996. "Theoretical Perspectives on the Corporate Victimization of Women." In E. Szockyj and J. Fox, ed., *Corporate Victimization of Women*. Boston: Northeastern University Press.

Smart, T. 1991 (June 10). "Breast Implants: What Did the Industry Know, and When?" *Business Week* pp. 94–95.

Sutherland, E. H. 1940 (February). "White-Collar Criminality." *American Sociological Review* 5: 1–12.

——. 1949. *White-Collar Crime*. New York: Dryden. (Reissued by Holt, Rinehart & Winston, New York 1961).

——. 1983. *White-Collar Crime: The Uncut Version*. New Haven, CT: Yale University Press.

Swasy, A. 1996. "Rely Tampons and Toxic Shock Syndrome: Proctor & Gamble's Responses." In M. D. Erdmann and R. Lundman, eds., *Corporate and Governmental Deviance*. New York: Oxford University Press.

Szockyj, E. and Fox, J. (eds.) 1996. *Corporate Victimization of Women*. Boston: Northeastern University Press.

Tunnell, K. D. (ed.) 1993. *Political Crime in Contemporary America: A Critical Approach*. New York: Garland.

Washburn, J. 1996 (March/April). "Reality Check: Can 400,000 Women be Wrong?" *Ms.* pp. 51–57.

Wolf, N. 1991. *The Beauty Myth: How Images of Beauty Are Used Against Women*. New York: Doubleday.

——. 1992 (January 23). "Keep Them Implanted and Ignorant." *Wall Street Journal*, p. A17. ✦

12
Understanding Violence Against Women: Universal Human Rights and International Law

*Judith Bessant
and Sandy Cook*

Despite advances in human civilization and human relationships, women continue to be subjected to violence—physical, sexual, and emotional—in social institutions and intimate relationships. This chapter offers a comprehensive definition of "violence" and then examines the correlation between violence and inequality, the role of personal and public rights in protecting women from violence, and the implication of culture for the understanding and application of human rights. The authors also examine the framework of universal and international law concerning human rights and highlights its strengths and weaknesses in effectively protecting women around the world from violence.

Violence against women has been a serious problem in most societies throughout history. Sometimes the scale of that violence has been terrifying in its enormity. In the Ottoman (Turkish) Empire, hundreds of thousands of Armenian women, in what was called Armenia, were savaged, raped, and starved to death between 1915 and 1917 (Hovannisian 1986). Similarly in the process of "'ethnic cleansing" that took place

between 1991 and 1993, the Serbian government and military forces in Bosnia-Herzegovina systematically raped, tortured, and starved thousands of Muslim women in secret concentration camps like Omarska (Allen 1997; Cigar 1997).

The scale of the violence against women is smaller elsewhere, although the violence is no less appalling. In East Pakistan today, hundreds of young wives who have failed to produce male children or who in some other way have offended their husband or his family are burned with petrol. Several hundred die each year, while the survivors are permanently scarred. Meanwhile, Pakistani police and other authorities close their eyes, as victims and perpetrators describe the violence as "cooking accidents."

In most societies, many women continue to be subject to the threat and actuality of sexual, physical, and emotional violence. This problem is especially prevalent in the family, where high levels of domestic violence ridicule the notion of the family as a safe haven, a place of emotional intimacy, and personal security. For a long time, women and children around the world have been victims of domestic violence, servitude, and physical, sexual, and emotional abuse. In the 1980s, the Papua-New Guinea Law Reform Commission found that 67 percent of women in Papua-New Guinea had experienced marital violence. Commenting on findings like this, Chapman (1990) argued that

> Police statistics are considered to represent only the tip of the iceberg, but they show that violence against women, from assault to homicide, represents a significant source of crime all over the world. Homicide statistics in the United States and all other countries show that large numbers of murder victims are women killed by their husbands and boyfriends. (p. 55)

The streets of most cities around the world continue to be unsafe, causing many women in places like the United States, Canada, and Australia to establish marches to "reclaim the night." In many paid work organizations in "advanced" and "developing" societies, despite the legislative systems and sanctions and counseling services, many women continue being subjected to overt sexual harassment, as well as to more subtle forms of violence that often deny them employment, promotion, and work satisfaction.

As we suggest in this chapter, identifying violence in all its diverse forms and indicating the magnitude of violence that women in most societies and cultures experience in their daily lives is easier than finding solutions. We also argue that many forms of violence are not recognized because the behavior is not labeled violence. The extent of "the problem" of violence against women depends in part on how violence is defined.

Thus, we begin by discussing what we mean by violence. We then ask whether international law offers a framework of protection for women against the various forms of violence they confront. This is an important question, given that much violence against women is institutionalized (in the family, major church organizations, educational systems, the workplace) and also given that it is often sanctioned by local custom and sometimes by local community or national legal systems.

At first it *seems* attractive to have a framework of universal rights or international law that addresses the problem of violence against women, especially when such a framework involves lifting women from their local customs and local laws that victimize them. We argue that

1. Many of the statements of human rights promulgated since 1947 by the United Nations are benchmarks that outline normative approaches to women's rights and that clearly define as unacceptable (under any circumstance) activities such as rape, torture, murder, and physical assault.

2. The lack of effective power to enforce the conventions and principles of human rights and international laws has been and continues to be a major weakness. So too is the refusal of nation-states to surrender sovereignty to bodies such as the United Nations or the International Court of Justice.

3. Some of the specifications of women's rights are dubious or ambiguous because (a) they rely on male standards and criteria that fail to address specifically female issues or conditions of existence, or (b) they impose spuriously universal criteria that ignore or override legitimate local practices and the agency of women.

Theorizing Violence

Violence has a long history, and what exactly constitutes violence has generated considerable controversy (see Flanagan 1972, 271–278; Wolff 1971). Part of the problem in defining violence is that it is a normative as well as a descriptive concept. Typically, when we use the term "violence" to identify an action or describe an event, we are "naming" an action *as well as* evaluating that action in moral or legal terms (Holmes 1993).

It is reasonable to suppose that most people understand violence to mean some activity that causes harm, injury, or death to another human or to a group of people or that causes destruction to property or harm, injury, or death to other forms of life.

Problems in trying to define violence often begin when some people want to draw a distinction between nonphysical activities such as speaking, writing, or gesturing at another person, and physical activities, such as shooting, stabbing, raping, or hurting another person and to use this distinction to suggest that physical violence is more real and more harmful than emotional or psychological violence. Those who argue for this distinction seem to believe that "physical" violence is more serious than nonphysical violence. However, this assumption ignores the possibility that some apparently nonphysical activities can cause a severe bodily response in the victim. It also ignores the well-researched emotional effects of physical violence (Keegan 1987).

There are indeed many forms of violence other than those that produce physical destruction of life or loss of bodily integrity. Imprisonment, harassment, surveillance, interrogation, emotional or religious persecution, and verbal intimidation all constitute violence. Such violence may appear less frightening and dangerous than direct physical harm, but the general patterns of inequitable power relations between men and women mean that women are disproportionately subject to both overt and opaque violence. One way of broadening the concept of violence is to recognize the links between violence and inequality. As Finlay et al. (1997) note: "A violent relationship is an extreme example of power imbalance between the individuals involved" (p. 541).

We do not draw a distinction between "physical" and "nonphysical" violence, although we appreciate that some forms of violence are more severe or distressing than others. Establishing which forms of violence are more serious than others does, however, need to be grounded in specific analysis and evaluation.

A further problem with defining violence relates to attempts to distinguish between legitimate and illegitimate forms of violence. Some people distinguish, for example, between shooting someone dead on the street, which in most societies is a crime, and killing someone on a battlefield, which may be an act of heroism or evidence of a devotion to duty and patriotism. In other words, depending on who is doing the defining, some violent activities are defined as acceptable, even morally deserving, while the same acts done by other people or in other settings, are morally or legally reprehensible. What we argue is that such a distinction should not alter the fact that violence is violence.

Here Max Weber's account of how violence is often legitimated is useful. Weber described the state as an organization that endeavors to secure a legitimate monopoly over the means of violence; modern nation-states want to claim that an act is morally and legally acceptable when they do it, but not when some others do it. Typically, when other organizations or people do what states do, those actions are not legitimate and are defined as homicide or terrorism.

Those who attempt to draw distinctions between legitimate and illegitimate violence often try to conceal the fact that states have been involved in major criminal acts. Governments have been responsible for large-scale homicide, systematic torture, rape, unjust routine imprisonment, and assault, the magnitude of which makes the crimes of even the most notorious criminal organizations seem petty in comparison. The fact that governments and the elites who hold power within them are men, and that they also try to justify certain forms of violence as acceptable (such as rape in marriage) in specific or local moral, legal, or cultural settings, indicates why reference to larger external international or universal definitions of rights and principles is important. We need a strong conceptualization of violence that does not permit these kind of defenses by governments and their agents, or by moral or religious leaders of communities, or by those many men around the world who continue to regard women as their "property."

Definition and Discussion of Violence

We use violence to describe any act that is informed by the intention to cause harm or to destroy the physical or emotional integrity and agency of people and that then produces that harm. The *intention* to cause harm is central to any satisfactory account of violence, because some attempts to justify violence often ignore the intention to cause harm by focusing on the local "religious," "traditional," or "legal" justifications for certain violent activities against women. We do not object to defenses that refer to custom or practice as long as they do not attempt to defend practices in which the intention to cause harm is crucial to the practice or activity.

Such a definition of violence is comprehensive because it takes into account the activities of individuals and of organizations in the private, community, and state sectors. It also includes various sporadic and institutional forms of incarceration, policing, surveillance, and harassment. Violence can be overtly physical, but it can also be emotional or psychological. Whatever form violence takes, the question of intentionality is usually central. For many women, discussions about violence have been problematic because popular and legal accounts have excluded many forms of violent behaviors in which the intention to cause harm has been apparent.

Our approach to understanding violence also acknowledges the use of force or authoritative (legal) constraints that cause harm by requiring obedience to certain moral values in ways that deny agency to the victim/survivor. It is, however, obvious that denying agency to individuals "for their own good," as we do when we prevent a child from placing his hand on a fire, is quite different from claiming that it is "for the woman's own good" to beat her because she was seen talking to other men, or to take her children away from her because she is poor or young or black or single.

Women experience many things as violence that are not usually identified as such. These activities are often ones seldom or never experienced by men. Examples include infanticide of female babies, gender-specific abortions, infibulation (the removal of the labia and stitching up of the vagina, leaving only a small hole for bodily fluid to pass through), clitordectomy, and nontherapeutic hysterectomies. Such actions may also include demanding that a person keep secrets about pregnancies, sexual violations, and other forms of physical abuse. Demanding obedience and the keeping of certain secrets may on some occasions be a compassionate, benevolent, and beneficial act— indeed, it is not difficult to cite examples when a prohibition on certain behaviors is defensible. However, when certain groups institute practices in order to establish and safeguard their own notion of social order that violates the legitimate entitlements of those required to conform, violence is taking place. Examples of this situation include pedophilia, incest, the organization of child prostitution, various forms of blackmail, and a multitude of other strategies to secure compliance. When groups of people or an individual use certain techniques to maintain power and authority, or to defend what they think is right, by infringing in unjustifiable ways on others' rights to pursue their lives in relative freedom, then we are talking about violence.

Causing harm and intending to cause it are central to understanding violence: Requiring obedience or coercing obedience from someone may or may not be good for a particular individual. Typically we use these arguments in relation to certain kinds of people such as small children or young people who are "our" dependents and in our care. With children and some young people, there is often a legitimate basis for believing they may not be fully aware of the risks to their lives or well-being from certain actions.

It is true that some perpetrators of violence believe they did not intend to cause harm. This is the typical kind of justification given by many pedophiles who say they simply want to "love" children. However, such "justifications" evade recognition of the fact that their actions do cause a variety of physical and emotional harms to their victims/survivors. It is in this context that we need to treat minor forms of sexual harassment, such as demeaning comments about women's appearance, morality, or behaviors, as forms of opaque violence.

Violence is often pervasive, subtle, and systemic in many traditional and modern societies. Opaque violence is also often discriminatory because it disproportionately affects women. In other words, it is women who are typically the targets of such violence. Some forms of violence are rooted in well-established practices, such as sexual violence, forced pregnancy, and gender-selective abortions. Other systemic forms of officially sanctioned violence, such as the abduction of children from indigenous women or working-class mothers and young single women need to be identified in a more inclusive treatment of violence. In many cases the pain, suffering, and sense of loss for both mother and child have resulted in lifelong, irreparable pain and injury. The loss of family and the denial of cultural and personal identity is a brutal act of violence, which many women have suffered even in "advanced" societies like the United States, Canada, and Australia.

Culturally embedded, institutionalized, and pervasive forms of violence have destructive effects on the lives of many women and girls. The denial of women's access to certain resources (such as money, other members of their family), bullying, and the often discreet but powerful acts of dominance and oppression are patterns of brutality that characterize the lives of generations of women. The often indirect and pervasive nature of such behaviors and the ways they are made invisible are obfuscated, or are even encouraged by custom, language, and law means that both recognizing and naming "violence" as violence and then responding to it as such is difficult.

Finally, our approach to violence means not accepting as legitimate the defense that some forms of violence against women are acceptable because some women accept that violence is right (i.e., marital rape, domestic violence, and other types of punishment). Our focus is on whether there is an intention to cause harm or to destroy the physical and emotional integrity and agency of people. This focus is important for understanding violence; it also means that no one has a right to kill, incapacitate, torture, or rape another person. Further, we argue that no one has a right to be a willing victim of such violence (rape, torture, homicide).

With this clarification of the concept of violence, we now turn to international law and human rights and ask whether formal international laws and declarations, such as the

United Nations Declaration of Human Rights (UNDHR) and the International Covenant on Civil and Political Rights (1966), adequately safeguard the human rights of women, particularly when they are the victims of violence.

Human Rights and International Law

In the international arena, human rights declarations and law reflect admirable aspirations and have achieved considerable successes in protecting women from violence and the violation of their basic rights. In the modern era, the Declaration of Human Rights promulgated by the United Nations in 1948 made an important procedural innovation with its claim that all people, by virtue of their humanity, have legitimate and equal claims to cultural, social, political, and civil rights, including protection from unlawful violence.

"Rights talk" (Dworkin 1977) has provided the basis for a degree of empowerment and has been a vital part of discourses within the women's movement and other social movements. Demands for rights also provide the basis for many claims against states and organizations that have improved the lives of many women. However, international conventions still do not adequately protect the rights of many women experiencing violence.

The United Nations' attempt to define a set of universal rights needs to be understood in the context of a reality in which many people are relatively powerless, weak, and susceptible to fear, violence, and exploitation. Furthermore, large numbers of people most at risk of becoming the victims of terror, violence, and exploitation include women, children, the poor, and ethnic minorities overwhelmed by ethnic majorities. Indeed, one critical factor that puts many people at risk of being subject to violence is their sex—being female. Ethnic cleansing exercises and political purging have targeted women and children, particularly with the use of rape and forced pregnancy (with "the enemy's child") as a means of diluting the "bloodline."

A conception of human rights that protects women (and female children) requires an appreciation of the types of relationships in which many women live. Protective mechanisms need to recognize the reality that many women find themselves in relationships characterized by *inequality*, with females subordinate to males. Disparities in power and lack of access to money, time, education, and legal representation mean that women are regularly at risk of having their human rights violated. Thus, consideration has to be given to the potential consequences of inequitable power relationships between men and women both in the personal realm and in wider institutional and social spheres. Respect for differences in terms of power and the vulnerability of many women compared to men needs to be recognized in international law if legislation is to be effective in addressing the problem of violence against women as a human rights issue.

Two sets of issues need to be raised when considering the effectiveness of international law: One is practical and the other is conceptual:

1. In a context where nation-states retain considerable power, issues about the *practical effect* that can be given in the administration of international law and human rights remain in question.

2. If international law is to be effective when addressing problems of violence against women, then greater *conceptual clarity* is needed in relation to what counts as violence against women.

Neither of these tasks is simple or easy.

Ensuring Practical Effect Is Given to International Law

There has been increasing dissatisfaction about the capacity of the United Nations to enforce its declarations. With allegations that the original UNDHR (1948) failed to recognize the gendered nature of the problems facing many women, the United Nations subsequently enacted the International Covenant on Civil and Political Rights (1966), and in 1980 it passed the Convention for the Elimination of Discrimination Against Women, or what has been referred to as the "Women's Human Rights Convention." The 1996 Covenant established an international obligation imposed by treaty on signatory states. States party to the Convention were required to perform acts in accordance with, or refrain from acts inconsistent with, the Covenant. By 1976 all signatories were required by law to act in accordance with its provisions. The question remains, however, as to how effective the obligations created by the International Covenant on Civil and Political Rights have been. Australia's response illustrates a broader problem.

Australia, an advanced modern society with a strong women's movement and a federal system of government and law, signed the Covenant in 1972 but did not ratify it until 1980. Moreover, the Australian/Federal government made a number of reservations and declarations in 1980 that minimized the effectiveness of the Covenant. (Making things worse, it withdrew a number of those declarations in 1984.) The Covenant appears now as a schedule to the Australian government's Human Rights and Equal Opportunity Act of 1986. As late as 1997 it did not form part of the domestic law of Australia, and all state governments have been able to claim exemption from the effect of the Covenant. If Australian statutory law gives ambiguous support to the Covenant, how well does Australia's common law handle the issue of rights? The answer is that according to Australia's common law system, the idea of fundamental rights inherent in all people by virtue of their humanity has been accepted.

The problem with the international framework of human rights is that, *it is difficult if not impossible to establish appropriate sanctions and coercive powers that can compel sovereign states to give effect to their international obligations on human rights*, even when nations have become signatories to these declarations and covenants. We extend our concerns by asking: Even if the United Nations had effective sanctions, would the right of women to live free from violence be safeguarded?

Recognizing the Gendered Nature of Violence Against Women

Apart from the question of the effectiveness (or ineffectiveness) of the United Nations as a body capable of compelling sovereign states to execute their human rights obligations, a number of practical and discursive problems weaken the ability of these admirable rights statements to work effectively in women's interests. The problems we refer to include: (1) the implicit distinction foundational to most Anglo-American legal and political systems between a public domain in which civic rights are defined and protected, and a private realm in which rights are neither protected nor recognized; (2) the problem of specifying when a particular set of practices or behaviors constitutes an offense against a universal right; and (3) the problem of determining when it is appropriate to exempt a local or specific practice from the obligations of universal rights and/or international law.

The public and private distinction. Foucault (1977) claimed that the greatest power anyone can ever have is the capacity to define reality. All laws, according to Foucault, may be deconstructed, laying bare the existence of certain power relationships between those defining the law and those subject to the law.

What are identified as legitimate rights reflect the perceptions and interests of powerful alliances involved in the processes of defining problems and framing rights-based solutions. Men's interests and perspectives were embedded in the foundation of Western political theory and in the national legal systems of countries like Britain, the United

States, and Australia as well as international law and rights theory. Some feminists argue that Western liberal political theory, including the liberal state and its preoccupation with individual and civic rights and obligations, constitutes an important component in discourses in which the primary business has been to legitimize male superiority in public life (Pateman 1990). Moreover, that discursive architecture of the liberal state relies on a long tradition of Western political theory that maintains the dominant patriarchal institutional prerogatives of men. MacKinnon (1989) offers this explanation:

> the liberal state coercively and authoritatively constitutes the social order in the interest of men as a gender—through its legitimating norms, forms, relations to society, and substantive policies. (p. 162)

MacKinnon traced the genealogy of contemporary human rights, pointing out how they were derived from eighteenth century statements like the American Declaration of Independence and the French Declaration of the Rights of Man, which identified the male-citizen as the citizen for whom such constitutional specifications were written. Foundational to this conceptualization of rights was the old, male-centered assumptions found in Aristotle's *Politics* that politics, power, and rights were all created and developed in the public sphere, a sphere of action in which only men acted and thought.

Discussion and specification of universal rights at the United Nations in 1948 assumed that rights are primarily *civil rights* and that traditionally these rights belonged in the "public sphere." (This was exemplified in statements like "The inherent dignity and equal and inalienable rights of all is the foundation of freedom, justice and peace.") The conception of civil rights developed in these international conventions assumed a precedent and a quite traditional gendered distinction between public and private realms. McBride Stetson (1995) argues,

Western human rights theory accepts, without question, the patriarchal assumptions that the modern state must protect and further the liberties of citizens in the public sphere, but that the private sphere of the family and sexuality is outside of its concern. (p. 72)

Chapman (1990) takes this further, reinforcing the point we made earlier. She maintains that some violence against women such as "wife beating . . . far from being a rupture in the social order, is, in fact, an affirmation of a particular social order" (p. 56).

Thus, the central concern in current human rights theory to identify and protect rights in public civil life ignores the many violations of women's human rights that occur in the private realm of home (Bahar 1996; MacKinnon 1989; McBride Stetson 1995; Otto 1993; Rowland 1995).

The Western liberal state constitutes a social order in which the interests of men are reaffirmed and protected through its legitimization of masculine norms, masculine defined relations to society, and policies (McBride Stetson 1995). This has meant exclusion from its jurisdiction of private domestic space, typically the domain of women. Moreover, the privileging of civil rights embargoes interventions aimed at securing women's human rights in the home/family and also strengthens notions of the sanctity of the home as a place of retreat and privacy. Bahar (1996) made the point:

Many human rights violations against women, including domestic violence, female genital mutilation, sexual slavery, forced pregnancies, and sterilization, are committed within the family and by private individuals and organizations. (p. 105)

The private nature of the home means domestic violence and other forms of violence against women remain a private matter. And, as a private issue in a private place, this violence is not subject to public gaze and scrutiny in the same ways violations against a person's civil rights, such as their right to a fair trial, are.

Women, many of whom experience large parts of their lives within the home/family, are subject to definitions of human rights that do not include violence in the home as a violation or as part of its jurisdiction. Human rights documents drafted by those who take primary responsibility for child care and domestic life may require additional and new sets of human rights that are not just universal but could set new and additional definitions of rights that are specific and sensitive to the relationships, cultural context, and emotional life of people who spend much of their time in the "private sphere."

Reliance on universalizing principles. "Human rights talk" works effectively when it spells out in unambiguous ways a range of core and genuinely universal rights such as the right to be free from violence such as rape, assault, murder, and torture based on gendered assumptions and practices.

Categories like "human" are also crucial to documents like the Universal Declaration of Human Rights. Such a category is intended to be all-encompassing, pointing to an assumed basic nature said to be shared by all people. Current mainstream theorizations of universal human rights are based on the idea that membership in the category "human" assumes the prior existence of certain shared needs or interests.

Universal declarations and covenants on human rights do not protect many women's human rights because they ignore the task of specifying what particular sets of practices or behaviors constitute offenses against a universal right. As we have already indicated, the actual forms of violence done to women go beyond the usual or accepted definition of violence from which women need to be protected.

Take the example of slavery. Article Four of the UNDHR maintains that "no one shall be held in slavery or servitude; slavery and the slave trade shall be prohibited in all their forms." (See also the International Convention on Civil and Political Rights, Article 8.) This may appear to be a worthwhile declaration because it seems to be unequivocal in its condemnation of slavery. However, the practice of subordinating a person to the control or ownership of another and accompanying that control with forced labor is descriptive of many women's lives, as they are denied both self-autonomy and their liberty. Many women are subject to domestic servitude but because such slavery usually occurs in the privacy of the home, it is either not seen or, if seen, is typically not recognized as a denial of the woman's human rights. (One may also question whether domicile dependence constitutes a denial of a woman's human rights.)

Similarly Article Four fails to recognize as servitude the situation of many women and girls "employed" in the global "hospitality/ sex trade." The globalization of the world's economy has seen women and female children-as-products bought (and sometimes even kidnapped) in places such as Latin America, Burma, and Africa from where they are shipped to places such as Japan, Thailand, and Europe to be sold or forced to endure indentures in brothels. Mirkinson (1994) made the observation that in 1993,

> 200,000 women have been sent from Bangladesh to Pakistan. . . . One of the lures for business and for their employees is the promise of available women. . . . It's got . . . to the point where entire villages in northern Thailand and southern Burma are being decimated of their girl children. (pp. 2–3)

Although it is important to focus on the discursive capacities of universal rights in international law to recognize and redress problems of violence facing women, it is just as important to consider whether the United Nations can in practical ways give effect to its covenants.

Universal rights and divergent philosophical cultural traditions. There is also the question of determining when, if ever, it is appropriate to exempt a local or specific practice from being brought under the obligations of universal rights or international law. As indicated earlier, the notion of *uni-*

versal human rights carries with it ideas of totality and commonality: that all people have legitimate claims to universal human rights as specified. The issue we now turn to is the contradiction between cultural specificity and universal rights.

The problem relates to *the contradiction between the universalizing intention of international law and universal rights talk and the extent to which specific practices shaped by gender, political systems, science, custom, or legal definitions are either exempted from or not seen as breaches of these rights.*

The idea that rights are innate and an intrinsic feature of being human is based in part on a Lockean conception of innate rights. According to this formulation, found for example in the American Declaration of Independence, certain truths are held to be self-evident: that "all men" were created equal and are endowed by their Creator with certain unalienable rights, including the right to life, liberty and the pursuit of happiness. Moreover, the claim is made that the state ought not violate a person's natural rights. This claim results in, among other things, an emphasis on protecting the individual's autonomy and personal or private freedoms against an "invasive" state. Western notions of rights draw on a liberal tradition, functionalist metaphors, and faith in the Enlightenment project grounded in the privileging of rationality and individualism.

The first problem is that, dependent on the time, the place, and who is doing the defining, a wide range of activities can be (and are) defined either as acceptable or as breaches of universal rights. For example, in "civilized" countries like Australia, during the 1930s sterilization for certain "types" of girls was a common practice. Similarly, procedures such as clitoridectomies were performed on young girls in kindergarten and defined as best practice in the area of psychiatric medicine. Now, however, such interventions are seen as barbaric and atrocious offenses against the intention of Article Five, which states, "No one shall be subjected to torture or to cruel, inhumane or degrading treatment or punishment."

Furthermore, there is a problem of how to respond to claims of universal rights being a form of ideological camouflage. Post-colonialist writers and feminist critics of the United Nations rights talk argue that the universalizing intentions of the UNDHR cannot disguise the fact that such documents are actually specific expressions of white, affluent, middle-class male interests and prejudices. There are a number of worrying implications of this criticism. The first is that if we accept the criticism, no universal statements can be derived that do not in some way carry the interests and prejudices of the originators. This may mean that

- we should always be suspicious of universal principles, or
- we should refuse to pursue "the fantasy" of universalism and stop the search for a universal rule of law or a universal ethic, or
- we should attempt to apply, on top of the already established universal rights, further layers that take into account the gender-specific nature of violence and the specific conditions in which many women live.

Another implication is that if universal claims about rights are just pseudo-universal claims, we could say that it is best if the local and the relative take precedence over any apparent universal claims. However, we would then confront a plethora of diverse practices, customs, and norms that each have validity for those who practice or believe them (even if they result in horrific violence against women). The problem is that this path provides no ground for disapproving of practices such as gender-selective infanticide or female circumcision.

The claim to universality is indeed problematic given the tremendous diversity of cultures to which such fundamental principles are meant to have application. It is also problematic in relation to safeguarding a woman's agency, or her right to self-determination (i.e., what if a woman's choice is to kill her newborn baby because it is female; or what if a woman wants to seriously damage herself in some way?). *Do you stand by and protect the woman's agency (her right to self-autonomy and her cultural heritage) by not intervening when, for example, she self-mutilates or insists that she or her daughter have a clitoridectomy? Or do you claim ground by identifying the act as a violation of universal human rights?*

Safeguarding human rights means comparing the behaviors women are subjected to (or that they subject themselves to). As just explained, such comparison is not always easy, and often strategies that allow for differences are required. Comparability across cultures and time is a further limiting factor in the development and application of human rights because it requires comparisons between people who are not like each other; that is, a 30-year-old Nigerian, black, poor, heterosexual, pregnant Catholic woman must be compared to a 60-year-old English, white, affluent, lesbian, atheist woman. As Thornton (1990) explains in her discussion of the issue of discrimination:

> confusion is inevitable with the concept of comparability . . . how should differences associated with women and minority groups be dealt with? Should they be dismissed as irrelevant in accordance with a strict application of the equal treatment of standards, or should they be celebrated? This sameness/difference dilemma continues to worry feminists and minority group members alike, particularly as there is a need to be treated the same on some occasions but differently on other occasions. (pp. 1–2)

For international law to be effective in protecting women against violence and safeguarding their basic human rights, it is necessary to recognize the need for both approaches. *Strategies are required that allow for the recognition of both difference and equal-*

ity and that also identify the need for both differential treatment and equal treatment.

Attempts to deal with violence against women and the notion of universal human rights must take into account the fact that meanings of human rights vary according to the specific cultural context. In other words, the notion of human rights is observed and endorsed in various and often different ways. As Cassese (1994) explains,

> universality is, at least for the present, a myth. Not only are human rights observed differently—certainly to differing degree—in different countries; but they are also conceived of differently. (p 51)

There are major divergences in how human rights are understood. However, if we agree with Cassese's insight, does that mean we then agree that in places where the local culture approves of wife beating that this behavior is acceptable? Beyani (1995) offers this argument:

> Traditional and cultural assumptions about gender roles within society are used to justify continued oppression and subordination of women, as are various religious doctrines. Challenging these is seen as socially destabilizing, and as a threat to family and social cohesion. Women accept violence as part of their life: it is just the way it is. (p. 24)

All this raises a number of complex and challenging issues for those interested in women's human rights. As mentioned earlier, arguing that *all* women *should* or *must* enjoy particular "rights" and "freedoms" can actually result in a denial of their human rights (such as the right to self-determination and the right to participate or not participate in decision making on matters that affect them). Such declarations may be interpreted by those being spoken about as a denial of their agency (their right to self-determination) and an act as oppressive as that which it is intended to redress.

Conclusion: Social Theory and Feminism

We have argued that power and violence are linked aspects of the same problem. Given the prevalence of male-centered social institutions in most communities across the globe, most women, regardless of their cultural context, do not as a group enjoy economic, political, social, or cultural equality in relation to men. Although power impinges in direct and at times brutal and physical ways in the lives of both men and women, we emphasize the fact that power as it relates to violence against women is not merely a personal and private business, but a matter of public concern. Power is not just exercised in a personal or physical way; it is also given effect through technical and moral means, notably through control over knowledge, norms, and moralizing judgments. The exercise of power over women, which can shift easily into violence, occurs in the public and private sphere, taking place in the home, workplaces, schools, and other everyday settings.

Discussion Questions

1. Give examples of acts of violence against women that are not generally characterized as violent acts.

2. What experiences must be considered when crafting an international law to safeguard women's human rights?

3. When considering the history of law—from Plato to Thomas Jefferson—in light of women's experience, what are the two major areas of concern?

References

Allen, B. 1997. *Rape Warfare: The Hidden Genocide in Bosnia-Herzegovina and Croatia.* Minneapolis: University of Minnesota Press.

Bahar, S. 1996. "Human Rights are Women's Rights: Amnesty International and the Family." *Hypatia* 11(1):105–134.

Beyani, C. 1995. "The Needs of Refugee Women: A Human Rights Perspective." *Gender and Development* 3(2):29–30.

Cassese. A. 1994. *Human Rights in a Changing World.* Cambridge: Polity Press.

Chapman, J. 1990. "Violence Against Women as a Violation of Human Rights." *Social Justice* 17(2):54–69.

Cigar, N. 1997. *Genocide in Bosnia: The Policy of Ethnic Cleansing,* Houston: Texas A & M Press.

Dworkin, R. 1977. *Taking Rights Seriously.* Cambridge: Harvard University Press.

Finlay, H., Bailey-Harris, R., and Otlowski, M. 1997. *Family Law in Australia,* 5th ed. Sydney: Butterworths.

Flanagan, P. 1972. "Wolff on Violence." *Australasian Journal of Philosophy* 3(50):271–278.

Foucault, M. 1977. *Discipline and Punish: The Birth of the Prison.* London: Penguin.

Holmes, R. 1993. *On War and Morality.* Princeton: Princeton University Press.

Hovannisian, R. (ed.) 1986. *The Armenian Genocide in Perspective.* New Brunswick, NJ: Transaction Publishers.

Keegan, J. 1987. *The Face of War.* London: McGibbon.

MacKinnon, C. 1989. *Toward a Feminist Theory of the State.* Cambridge, MA: Harvard University Press.

McBride Stetson, D. 1995. "Human Rights for Women: Interpersonal Compliance with a Feminist Standard." *Women and Politics* 15(3): 71–92.

Mirkinson, J. 1994. *The Global Trafficking of Women.* (lpease@netcom.com.)

Otto, D. 1993. "Violence Against Women, Something Other Than a Violation of Human Rights." *The Australian Feminist Law Journal* 1:159–162.

Pateman, C. 1990. *The Disorder of Women: Democracy, Feminism, and Political Theory.* Stanford, CA: Stanford University Press.

Rowland, R. 1995. "Human Rights Discourses and Women: Challenging the Rhetoric With Reality." *Australian New Zealand Journal of Sociology* 31:8–25.

Thornton, M. 1990. *The Liberal Promise: Antidiscrimination Legislation in Australia.* Melbourne: Oxford University Press.

United Nations. 1948. "The Universal Declaration of Human Rights." In A. Cassese, 1994, *Human Rights in a Changing World.* Cambridge: Polity Press.

Wade, F. 1971. "On Violence." *Journal of Philosophy* 68:369–377.

Wolff, R. P. 1971. "Violence and the Law." In R. Wolff, ed., *The Rule of Law.* New York: Simon & Schuster. ✦

Part III

Gender, Law, and Criminal Justice

Probably every reader of this book has seen the statue or a picture of it: a woman draped in a flowing cloth, holding a sword in one hand and scales in another, wearing a blindfold. It is Lady Justice. When the Division on Women and Crime (DWC) of the American Society of Criminology was looking for a logo, division members considered Lady Justice. She was eventually adopted as the logo, but without the blindfold. Why? Because as feminists (and for some, people of color), the DWC members knew well that our justice system certainly is not blind. Our justice system is gendered—and raced, classed, and aged. Our justice system also has a heterosexual bias.

In this third and final section of the book, we offer seven chapters that examine gendered (and other) inequalities within law and the criminal justice system. Steffensmeier begins with an overview of female crime trends spanning a 35-year period, from 1960 to 1995. Steffensmeier's chapter gives us perspective on the "female crime problem" to which the criminal justice system is responding.

With Steffensmeier's data in mind, we turn to Bernat's chapter, which analyzes the gendered nature of law and how law reproduces established gender norms and relations. Bernat discusses many of the gender stereotypes underlying the law and its application in the courts, showing how these stereotypes inform decisions about the constitutionality of sex-based laws, the disposition

of criminal cases, and gender differences in sentencing.

Gilbert extends Bernat's analysis by examining how gender and race biases interact in the criminal justice system to produce specific outcomes. Gilbert's data reveal that women and men of color are consistently treated more harshly within the criminal justice system. It is hardly surprising after reading Gilbert's analysis that people of color, especially African Americans, are also disproportionately represented in our nation's prisons and jails.

Osthoff also examines gender stereotypes. In her chapter, Osthoff, an advocate on behalf of battered women charged with crimes, discusses how stereotypes of the "real" battered woman and the "good" battered woman operate against battered women who have killed their abusers. The media have popularized these images, and the general public who sees them on television or reads about them in newspapers, magazines, and books sometimes end up on juries, hearing a case involving a battered woman charged with murdering her abusive partner. One of the most valuable contributions of Osthoff's chapter is her discussion of battered woman syndrome, about which there is widespread misunderstanding, particularly regarding its usefulness in court.

Osthoff emphasizes that most battered women charged with crimes are convicted and given long prison sentences. Owen picks up on this point in her chapter when she discusses the reasons more women are in prison. A large percentage of incarcerated women, regardless of the crimes they've committed, have a history of abuse. However, Owen also shows that much of the increase in women's incarceration is due to the "war on drugs," a point that echoes Mancuso and Miller's concerns in chapter 7. Through her interviews with incarcerated women, Owen gives us insight into women's prison culture. If we compare her findings with those of other researchers who have studied men's prison culture, we see clear gender differences, particularly with regard to the development of personal relationships of support and care. But although more women than ever before are being sentenced to prison and most are doing their time peacefully, little is being done by the corrections system to improve the lives of these women once they are released. Job training, substance abuse treatment, and similar programs are nearly nonexistent or grossly inadequate in most women's prisons. Owen leaves us wondering what the future holds for these women if their unique problems are not addressed during incarceration.

Women are involved in the criminal justice system not only as offenders but also as professionals. Miller's chapter traces the history of women in policing and the contemporary experiences of female police officers in this traditionally male-dominated occupa-

tion. In particular, Miller examines the role of women in community policing, noting how the philosophy underlying this policing model is more in tune with traits traditionally associated with femininity rather than masculinity.

Jurik and Martin continue the discussion of women's experiences in criminal justice professions, expanding the analysis from policing to corrections. Jurik and Martin examine how gender, along with race, class, and sexual orientation, have influenced work in the criminal justice professions. Their analysis shows that women and people of color have made significant inroads into many criminal justice occupations, but they also highlight the barriers that remain.

Thus, this book ends much the same way it began: emphasizing that criminology and the criminal justice system itself have not been untouched by feminism, but rather have yielded, even if at a painfully slow pace, to feminist activists' demands for reform in a number of significant areas. Yet, although much has changed, much remains the same, and some is worse. Our hope is that this book challenges readers to take up the struggles outlined by the authors so that in a few years we can publish a revised edition that highlights the considerable progress made in addressing the problems raised here. ✦

13
Female Crime Trends, 1960–1995[1]

Darrell Steffensmeier

This chapter provides a statistical portrait and assessment of female crime trends over the past several decades, focusing in particular on female offending patterns as revealed in the FBI's Uniform Crime Reports. Alternative sources of information also provide both quantitative and qualitative evidence on female criminality, on the status of women in American society, and on changes in crime statistics and criminal opportunities. The author first reviews female arrest trends from 1960 to 1995 and then outlines various explanations of the trends. He then connects the explanations to arrest trends for specific offenses where notable increases and decreases in the female percentage of arrests have occurred and concludes by proposing future topics of research on trends in female crime.

Trends in female criminality have created a lively debate in both social science and popular commentary during the past several decades. Four questions have stirred the most interest:

1. Has female crime been changing in recent decades and, if so, in what ways?

2. Are the changes similar to or distinct from those occurring among males?

3. Are the changes greater among some age groups (e.g., adolescent females)?

4. Why have the changes occurred?

The debate has drawn evidence primarily from nationwide arrest statistics compiled in the FBI's Uniform Crime Reports and has been shaped by the interpretation of these statistics in two works published in the mid-1970s, by Freda Adler (1975) and Rita Simon (1975). Both concluded that changing gender roles and the women's movement had a significant impact on female crime. They argued that as women gained self-esteem, confidence, and self-sufficiency (especially via paid employment), female crime rates increased, and the character of female crime shifted toward more "masculine" kinds of law breaking.[2] Whereas Adler accented the growth in violent crimes by women, Simon stressed the rise in white-collar and occupational crimes.

A number of criminologists (Box and Hale 1984; Chesney-Lind 1986; Miller 1986; Steffensmeier 1980) have taken issue with Adler's and Simon's interpretations of the UCR data and their claims of robust changes in female criminality during the 1960s to mid-1970s period when significant numbers of women in the United States (and indeed throughout the industrialized world) took on new work roles and a new consciousness concerning themselves and their place in society. Supplementing the UCR data with other sources of information on crime and female offending, these criminologists drew the following conclusions about female arrest trends:

1. Except for substantial increases in the female percentage of arrests for minor property crimes such as larceny and fraud, the female-to-male share of offending has not undergone significant change (i.e., across most offenses, the female percentage has held steady or has risen only slightly).

2. Women have not shifted toward greater involvement in violent crimes but rather have become more involved (both absolutely and relative to men) in minor property crimes.

3. The women arrested for larceny and fraud typically have committed a *non*occupa-

tional crime, such as shoplifting or writing bad checks.

4. Sociological factors other than women's liberation better explain the changes in female arrest patterns.

After reviewing arrest trends from the early 1960s to mid-1970s, I noted

> Whatever changes [in female arrest patterns] have occurred appear due to changing law enforcement practices, market consumption trends, and the worsening economic position of many females in the U.S. rather than changing sex roles or the improved occupational, educational, and economic position of women. (Steffensmeier 1978, 580)

Nonetheless, some criminologists and many popular writers continue to believe that female criminality has been undergoing major changes, that its character is approaching that of male criminality, and that these changes are best explained by changing gender roles and the greater "masculinization" of women. The "liberation thesis" linking women's paid employment and overall emancipation to increased rates of female crime is longstanding in criminology (dating back to at least the 1870s) and intuitively appealing. It appeals to contemporary criminologists because it asserts the importance of social variables and downplays biological or physical differences between the sexes. The assumption is that socialization and social participation are the predominant social processes that cause women to behave like men as women take on the roles traditionally held by men. In addition, the emancipation perspective offers an uncomplicated picture of social change and female criminality that is easily understood, remembered, and reported.

But skepticism, even rejection, of the emancipation perspective does not call into question the relevance and importance of social variables for explaining female arrest trends. Nor does it imply that female crime is driven by biology. To the contrary, the view that there are sociological factors other than women's liberation that better account for female arrest trends may substantially improve our ability to develop an accurate explanation of the trends.

UCR Arrest Statistics by Gender

The Uniform Crime Reports are the only long-term continuous source of annual data on sex- and age-specific arrests categorized by offense. Arrest rates are calculated on all the UCR offense categories except forcible rape and runaways/curfew violations. The rates are calculated for the population as a whole, as well as for adults and juveniles. Two principal methods of measuring change are used. One is the *female percentage of arrests* (FP/A), adjusting for the sex composition of the population at large. The other is the *offender-profile percentage*, which is defined as the percentage of all arrests within each sex that are arrests for that particular offense. This part of the analysis examines the distribution of offenses committed by females to determine whether the profile of the female offender has changed (e.g., toward more violence).

Using UCR arrest data for gender comparisons over time is risky for two reasons: one involves the issue of *reliability*, the other concerns the *meaning* of the statistics per se. First, several factors have artifactually increased the arrest probabilities of females relative to males over the past few decades (see later discussion). Second, the UCR offense categories are *broad* and are derived from a heterogeneous collection of criminal acts. For example, the offense category of larceny-theft includes shoplifting a $10 item, theft of a radio from a parked auto, theft of merchandise by an employee, and cargo theft amounting to thousands of dollars. The broad offense category of fraud includes passing bad checks of small amounts and stock frauds involving large sums of money. Burglary includes both safecracking and unlawful entry into an ex-spouse's apartment to retrieve merchandise. Further, arrests are not distinguished in terms of whether the suspect is the sole or major perpetrator. Many females arrested for robbery or burglary act as accomplices to male offenders (Covington 1985; Steffensmeier and Terry 1986), and many females arrested for homicide or assault act in response to considerable provocation (Browne 1992).

These characteristics of UCR data are aggravated by the tendency of researchers to ignore secondary data sources and localized studies of arrests, court referrals, and so forth as supplemental evidence to interpret the UCR statistics. As a result, inaccurate conclusions are easily drawn, such as the mistaken claim that female arrests for larceny and fraud involve occupational crimes. This crucial point is iterated throughout the chapter.

Table 13.1 summarizes a variety of information drawn from 1995 (also 1960 and 1980) male and female arrest data for all FBI offense categories except rape (a male crime) and runaway and curfew (juvenile offenses). This information includes male and female arrest rates per 100,000 population (columns 3, 6), the female percent of arrests (column 9), and the offending profiles of males and females (columns 11, 13). All calculations in Table 13.1 adjust for the sex composition in the population as a whole and are based on all ages (versus, for example, using ages 10–64 as the population most at risk for criminal behavior). In describing the female offending patterns, I focus on the most recent period (1995) and compare its patterns to the earlier periods.

Trends in Arrest Rates

The first six columns of Table 13.1 show male and female arrest rates per 100,000 population for 1960, 1980, and 1990. For both males and females, 1995 arrest rates were higher for less serious offenses. Female rates were highest for minor property crimes such as larceny and fraud and for substance abuse (DUI, drugs, and liquor law violations). Arrest rates for prostitution-type offenses were comparatively smaller, a pattern that largely reflects nonenforcement police practices. Other data sources indicate that prostitution continues to be a chief form of female offending, especially on the part of drug-dependent women and women facing adverse economic circumstances.

In general, the pattern of change over the 1960–95 period was similar for both sexes, with large increases occurring only for larceny, fraud, driving under the influence, drug violations, and assault; and decreases in arrest rates for public drunkenness, sex offenses, vagrancy, suspicion, and gambling. This suggests that similar social and legal forces influence the arrest rates for both sexes, independent of any condition unique to women.

Trends in the Female Percentage of Arrests

The middle columns (7, 8, 9) in Table 13.1 show the female percentage of arrests (FP/A) for various offenses. In 1995 the female share of arrests for most categories was 15 percent or less and was typically smallest for the most serious offenses. The female share of arrests was the largest for prostitution (including disorderly conduct and vagrancy statutes used in arresting females for prostitution) and for minor property crimes (larceny, fraud, forgery, and embezzlement).

Several important trends in female-to-male offending patterns are revealed in Table 13.1. Note that an increase in the FP/A occurred if female rates increased more than male rates, if female rates were constant but male rates declined, or if female rates declined less than male rates.

When total arrests across all offenses are considered, the female percentage rose substantially—from 11 percent in 1960 to 15 percent in 1980 and to 19 percent in 1990. (The bulk of that rise, as discussed below, was due to the sharp increase in the numbers

Table 13.1

Male and Female Arrest Rates/100,000 (all ages), Female Percentage of Arrests, and Male and Female Arrest Profiles (1960–1995 *Uniform Crime Reports*)

Offense	Male Rates			Female Rates			Female Percentage (of arrests)			Offender-Profile Percentage[a]			
										Males		Females	
	1960 (1)	1980 (2)	1995 (3)	1960 (4)	1980 (5)	1995 (6)	1960 (7)	1980 (8)	1995 (9)	1960 (10)	1995 (11)	1960 (12)	1995 (13)
Against Persons													
Homicide	8.7	15.3	16.6	1.8	2.3	1.7	17.2	12.8	9.2	0.1	0.2	0.2	0.1
Aggravated Assault	99.5	215.7	367.5	16.0	29.2	70.3	13.8	11.9	16.0	1.4	3.9	1.9	3.2
Weapons	68.2	135.3	190.5	4.1	10.2	15.6	5.7	7.0	7.6	1.0	2.0	0.5	0.7
Simple Assault	263.7	368.2	790.7	28.8	55.4	174.0	9.9	13.1	18.0	3.8	8.5	3.5	7.8
Major Property													
Robbery	64.2	123.5	132.0	3.2	9.0	15.6	4.8	6.8	8.7	0.9	1.4	0.4	0.6
Burglary	268.8	428.4	281.7	8.8	27.0	31.4	3.2	5.9	10.0	3.9	3.0	1.1	1.4
Stolen Property	21.1	96.2	114.0	1.9	11.0	17.0	8.2	10.2	12.9	0.3	1.2	0.2	0.8
Minor Property													
Larceny-Theft	390.6	728.1	810.1	77.8	300.7	381.8	16.6	29.2	32.0	5.6	8.7	9.4	17.3
Fraud	69.3	146.2	195.2	12.6	90.2	125.8	15.4	38.2	39.2	1.0	2.1	1.5	5.7
Forgery	43.0	47.8	58.8	8.1	19.8	30.8	15.9	29.4	34.4	0.6	0.6	1.0	1.4
Embezzlement	—	5.6	6.6	—	1.9	4.5	—	25.3	40.6	—	0.1	—	0.2
Malicious Mischief													
Auto Theft	122.2	125.4	140.4	4.7	11.2	19.0	3.7	8.2	11.9	1.8	1.5	0.6	0.9
Vandalism	—	202.1	217.5	—	17.7	30.6	—	8.0	12.3	—	2.3	—	1.4
Arson	—	15.3	13.5	—	2.0	2.3	—	11.3	14.5	—	0.1	—	0.1
Drinking/Drugs													
Public Drunkenness	2499.5	946.0	499.2	207.8	72.3	62.0	7.7	7.1	11.0	35.9	5.4	25.1	2.8
DUI	340.8	1078.5	948.4	21.2	99.1	150.8	5.9	8.4	13.7	4.9	10.2	2.6	6.8
Liquor Laws	182.7	316.3	342.8		28.0	51.8	78.0	13.3	14.1	18.5	2.6	3.7	3.4
Drug Abuse	48.5	456.2	897.5	8.2	67.6	168.8	14.5	12.9	15.8	0.7	9.6	1.0	7.6
Sex/Sex Related													
Prostitution	13.6	26.2	32.1	35.9	52.7	50.5	72.6	66.9	61.1	0.2	0.3	4.3	2.3
Sex Offenses	80.5	56.3	73.4	16.2	4.5	6.4	16.8	7.3	8.0	1.2	0.8	2.0	0.3
Disorderly Conduct	744.7	566.5	462.7	113.5	99.8	118.2	13.2	15.0	20.4	10.7	5.0	13.7	5.3
Vagrancy	251.8	27.6	18.3	22.1	8.1	3.6	8.1	21.2	16.8	3.6	0.2	2.7	0.2
Suspicion	206.9	14.3	9.1	26.4	2.2	1.6	11.3	13.2	14.8	3.0	0.1	3.2	0.1
Miscellaneous													
Against Family	88.1	44.6	76.1	8.1	4.7	18.3	8.4	9.6	19.3	1.3	0.8	1.0	0.8
Gambling	193.0	44.3	13.3	17.0	4.4	2.2	8.0	9.1	14.1	2.8	0.1	2.0	0.1
Other (except traffic)	867.4	1382.7	2418.9	154.0	222.3	509.4	15.1	13.9	17.4	12.5	26.0	18.6	23.0
Indices													
Violent	188.4	387.4	545.1	21.1	40.6	85.0	10.0	9.5	13.5	2.7	5.9	2.5	3.8
Property	781.6	1286.4	1245.8	91.3	339.5	434.5	10.5	20.8	25.9	11.2	13.4	11.1	19.6
Index	974.0	1668.2	1790.9	112.7	380.1	519.4	10.4	18.5	22.5	14.0	19.3	13.6	23.5
Total													
All Offenses	6956.8	7757.1	9305.6	826.7	1372.7	2214.1	10.6	15.0	19.2	—	—	—	—

a) 1960 columns do not quite add up to 100% because rape (a male offense) is omitted. 1995 columns do not add up to 100% because runaways and curfew/loitering also are omitted; prior to 1964 (i.e., including 1960) the UCR lumped arrests for these two juvenile-status offenses into "Other (except traffic)."

of women arrested for minor property crimes such as larceny and fraud.)

Second, for the majority of offenses, the female percentage of arrests inched upward (about 1 to 2 percent each interval); see, for example, arrests for simple assaults and burglary. The increase in the FP/A for burglary since the mid-1970s is attributable to sharply declining rates among males, as compared to stable or slightly rising burglary rates among females. Also, the FP/A for DUI, after holding steady for two decades, nearly doubled between 1980 and 1995. (Note, however, that the base rate for females arrested for burglary and DUI is small, so even a doubling of the FP/A is not that large an absolute increase.)

Third, for a number of offenses, the female percentages held steady or declined slightly, including arrests for drug law violations and homicide. The female share of homicide arrests is now about 10 percent, compared to about 17 percent in 1960.

Fourth, the female percentage of arrests narrowed considerably for larceny-theft, fraud, and forgery. The female share of all larceny arrests increased from 17 percent in 1960 to about 32 percent in 1995, while the female share of fraud and forgery arrests increased from about 15 percent to 40 percent and 34 percent, respectively. Some research suggests that much of the increase in the FP/A for larceny was due to disproportionate numbers of females arrested for shoplifting (Giordano, Kerbel, and Dudley 1981; Klemke 1992; Silverman, Vega, and Gray 1976; Watson 1993), whereas much of the increase in fraud arrests involved larger numbers of women being arrested for credit-based currency crimes such as bad checks, forged credit cards, and nonpayment of services. The female share of embezzlement arrests has also been rising (from about 25 percent in 1980 to 37 percent in 1990), but since very few females or males are arrested for this crime, arrest rates are of little significance in terms of overall male/female arrest trends. Finally, note that the FP/A's for larceny, fraud, and forgery have held fairly steady since 1980, partly because continued gains are harder to come by once the female rate approaches the male rate (i.e., female gains were more possible in earlier years when the female rate was much smaller than the male rate).

Because the volume of larceny arrests is sizable, female gains in larceny have contributed to a large increase in the FP/A for serious or index crimes (homicide, aggravated assault, forcible rape, robbery, burglary, motor vehicle theft, and larceny-theft). The FP/A for index crimes climbed from 10 percent in 1960 to 22 percent in 1995. Also, 13 percent of all female arrests were for index crimes in 1960, compared to 24 percent in 1995. For males, arrests for index crimes increased more modestly, from 14 percent in 1960 to 19 percent in 1995. The remaining increase in the FP/A for index crimes is attributable to a sharp drop in male burglary rates since the mid-1970s and to a more rapid rise in female than male arrest rates for aggravated assault since the early 1990s (see later discussion).

Trends in Offender Profiles

Table 13.1 also compares the 1960 and 1995 arrest profiles of male and female offenders (columns 10–13). The profiles represent the percentage of all within each sex that are for that particular offense. The homicide figures for 1995 of .18 for men and .08 for women indicate that only two-tenths of 1 percent of all male arrests were for homicide, and only one-tenth of 1 percent of all female arrests were for homicide. In comparison, a whopping 26 percent of all male arrests and 23 percent of female arrests were for "other except traffic"—a residual category that includes mostly criminal mischief, harassment, public disorder, local ordinance violations, and assorted minor crimes.

The similarities between the male and female profiles and their arrest trends are considerable. For both males and females, the five most common arrest categories in 1995 were "other except traffic," driving under the influence (DUI), larceny-theft, drug abuse, and other assaults. As I discuss later, the offense category "other assaults" (also called misdemeanor assault) includes mostly minor, even trivial, incidents of threat or physical attack against another person, such as scratching, biting, throwing objects, shoving, hitting, or kicking. Because of growing citizen concerns about violence and aggression in U.S. society, enhanced reporting and policing have resulted in rising rates of arrests of both males and females for misdemeanor assault (also, aggravated assault) in recent years. Together, these five offenses account for 63 percent of all male arrests and 62 percent of all female arrests. Note, however, that after "other except traffic," larceny arrests are the highest category (17 percent in 1995) for females; but that DUI arrests are more important for males (10 percent). Arrests for murder, arson, and embezzlement are relatively rare for males and females alike, while arrests for offenses such as liquor law violations (mostly underage drinking), simple assault, and disorderly conduct represent "middling ranks" for both sexes.

The most important gender differences in arrest profiles are the relatively greater involvement of females in minor property crimes such as larceny and fraud (about 25 percent of all female arrests in 1995, compared to 12 percent of male arrests) and in prostitution, and the relatively greater involvement of males in crimes against persons and major property crimes (17 percent of all male arrests versus 11 percent of all female arrests). These patterns are similar to those found in other comparisons of gender differences in crime (see review by Steffensmeier and Allan 1990).

The distribution of offenses for which both men and women are arrested has shifted a fair amount over the past forty years, but the patterns of shifts for males and females are comparable. Of all persons arrested in 1995 versus 1960, a larger share of *both* male and female arrests were for DUI, larceny, fraud/forgery, drug law violations, and assault, while a smaller share were for public drunkenness and disorderly conduct. I also rank-ordered by size the male and female rates

and found parallel shifts in rank except that the rank for fraud jumped much more among female than male arrestees whereas the rank for prostitution and vagrancy dropped more among female arrestees. Rank-order correlations performed on the 1960 and 1995 ranking of offenses (as reflected in the profile percentages) confirms that female arrest patterns have undergone moderate change, as have male patterns (Rho = .57 and .60 respectively). Some convergence has occurred between the sexes in the kinds of crimes for which they are arrested: the male-to-female rank-order correlation is .76 for 1960 and .88 for 1995. However, when sex-related offenses (e.g., vagrancy) are removed, the male-to-female rank-order correlation is .89 for 1960 and .87 for 1995. Relative to men, therefore, the profile of the female offender has not changed.

Juvenile Versus Adult Trends in the Female Percentage of Arrests

It is plausible that shifting gender-role ideologies and other structural changes have had more of an effect on younger women than older women, so that the rise in offending by young women may be especially acute (see the review in Steffensmeier and Streifel, 1992). In general, the FP/A's across the three decades are quite similar for youths and adults. For example, the FP/A for larceny in 1990 is 27.7 for youth and 32.2 for adults. The major difference in arrest patterns between the two age groups occurs for fraud and forgery, where the increase in the female percentage of arrests is much greater among adults than juveniles. The change among adults is 31 percentage points for fraud and 19 percentage points for forgery, compared to changes of 17 percentage points for fraud and 9 percentage points for forgery among youth. These differences reflect expanding opportunities for credit-based currency crimes (writing bad checks, defrauding an innkeeper, forging credit cards, nonpayment of services) that intertwine more with adult than juvenile lives.

Other Evidence on Female Crime Trends

Evidence from other sources corroborates the relatively low female involvement in serious offending and also shows more stability than change in female crime relative to male crime over the past several decades. Data from the *National Crime Victimization Survey* (NCVS)—in which victims of personal crimes, such as robbery and assault are asked the sex of the offender—reveal female-to-male totals quite close to but slightly smaller than those found in UCR data (Bureau of Justice Statistics 1994). In 1994, for example, women were reported to be responsible for about 8 percent of robberies, 12 percent of aggravated assaults, 15 percent of simple assaults, 5 percent of burglaries, and 5 percent of motor vehicle thefts reported by victims. These percentages have held unchanged since the NCVS began in the mid-1970s.

The pattern of a higher female share of offending for mild forms of law breaking and a much lower share for serious offenses is confirmed by the numerous *self-report* studies in which persons (generally juveniles) have been asked to report their own offenses (Steffensmeier and Allan 1996). These results hold both for prevalence of offending (the percent of the male and female samples that report any offending) and for the frequency of offending (the number of crimes an active offender commits in a given period). Gender differences are smallest for offenses such as shoplifting and minor drug use.

Notably, the National Youth Survey, generally recognized as the best of the self-report delinquency studies, provides information on delinquency trends for male and female adolescents from the late 1960s to the early 1980s. The survey finds increases in some delinquent behaviors (alcohol and drug use) among both male and female ado-

lescents and decreases in others (theft and assault), but stable gender differences in delinquency. After reviewing the data, Delbert Elliott and associates (1987) concluded that during this time frame, the self-report data "show no significant decline in the [male-to-female] sex ratios on eight specific offenses" (pp. 13–14).

Statistics on males and females incarcerated in state and federal prisons reveal that from roughly the mid-1920s to the present, the female percentage of the total prison population has varied between 3 percent and 6 percent. The percentage was about 5 percent in the 1920s, was about 3 percent in the 1960s, and is about 6 percent today. As with male incarceration rates, female rates have risen sharply—more than tripled—over the past two decades. Most women in prison today were convicted of homicide and assault (usually against spouse, lover, or child) and for drug offenses or for property crimes that are often drug related. A much larger percentage of female than male new court commitments are entering prison today for a drug offense. Also, a higher percentage of female prison inmates were under the influence of drugs or alcohol at the time of the offense (Greenfeld and Minor-Harper 1991).

Statistics on males and females convicted of felony offenses in state courts are available for 1988 and 1994, and include a breakdown by type of offense (Brown and Langan 1998). The key results are as follows. First, the conviction data are consistent with arrest and self-report data in documenting the much greater involvement of males in violent and serious property crimes, as well as the much smaller gender gap for minor property offenses and drug offenses. Second, the female share of involvement in violent and serious property crime is less than the share reported in UCR arrest data. This difference reflects the tendency of the police to cast a wider net and overcharge suspects when making arrests, whereas court practices operate to ferret out weak cases and better align the conviction offense with actual criminal behavior. Third, although both sexes were more likely to be convicted for drug offenses in 1994 than 1988, the shift in the offender profile is somewhat greater among females.

Finally, female involvement in professional and organized crime has not increased and continues to lag far behind male involvement. Women continue to be hugely underrepresented in traditionally male-dominated associations that engage in safecracking, fencing operations, gambling operations, and racketeering. In 1991 the Commonwealth of Pennsylvania released its 1990 report on organized crime and racketeering activities in the state during the 1980s. That report identified only a handful of women who were major players in large-scale gambling and racketeering, and their involvement was a direct spinoff of association with a male figure (i.e., the woman was a daughter, spouse, or sister). The 1990 report also noted that the extent and character of women's involvement in the 1980s was comparable to their involvement during the 1970s.

Of anecdotal pertinence are the responses of 215 lower-court judges (128 male and 87 female judges) in Pennsylvania who, as part of a larger survey of the minor judiciary in the state, were asked to assess trends in female crime. Some judges had been in office more than 25 years. The judges uniformly responded that crime remains essentially a male phenomenon. This response from a female magistrate was typical: "Most of my caseload is male, very much so. The only real female crime that stands out in my mind is retail theft and harassment. And checks. I am seeing more women for that because there's a big shopping mall in my district."

Explaining Female Arrest Trends

There are at least six plausible explanations for these trends and patterns in female arrests that I group under the following headings: law and the organizational management of crime; gender equality; economic adversity of females and increased inner-city community disorganization; expanded opportunities for female-type crimes; shifts in the underworld; and trends in drug dependency. Each should be viewed as a series of hypotheses in need of empirical testing.

Organizational Management of Crime: Enhanced 'Visibility' of Female Offending

The arrest rate, similar to any official measure of crime, is a function of behaviors defined as criminal and control measures established to deal with these behaviors. Some of the increase in the female percentage of *arrests* may reflect changes in laws, in policing, or in record keeping that have raised female arrest rates relative to male rates in recent decades. That bureaucratization and more formal policing tend to increase official ratios of female-to-male criminality is consistent with alternative sources of data on female crime.

For example, computerization and improved record keeping in police departments have increased the accuracy in recording suspects' sex. This improvement has reduced the level of hidden female crime, because an "unknown" is tabulated as a male arrestee in published tables. This refinement in record keeping probably had its greatest impact on female arrest trends during the 1960s (Steffensmeier 1980). More bureaucratization in policing has also introduced more universal standards of decision making, thus reducing the effects of gender on probability of arrest (Visher 1983). Additionally, the expanded use of informants has increased the use of female suspects charged with offenses as a pressure point for gaining incriminating evidence against male offenders with whom they are associated (Pennsylvania Crime Commission 1991; Steffensmeier and Terry 1986). Finally, changes in laws and enforcement toward targeting less serious forms of lawbreaking (e.g., lowering the blood alcohol content in arrests for DUI; filing "assault" charges for harassment or minor physical attacks) have increased the risk of arrest for female offenders. The ability of the authorities to dip more deeply into the pool of offenders will increase the female share of arrests, because females tend to be involved disproportionately in the less serious forms of law-breaking even within a specific offense category.

The reduced tolerance and increased *criminalization* of "deviant" behavior has caused a rise in some types of crime—DUI, assault, and so on—among both males and females. A noteworthy example is in the area of assault and aggravated assault—what once was viewed as harassment or disorderly conduct is today increasingly treated as an assault, even an aggravated assault. Note that the NCVS shows no overall rise in aggravated assault and no change in the female-to-male percentage.

Gender Equality

Both the popular press and some social scientists have linked recent trends in arrests to female emancipation and the improved status of women (Simon and Landis 1991). Less traditional gender-role attitudes and greater opportunities in the economic sphere, especially female advances in the paid workforce, are believed to have resulted in higher levels of female crime. Most notably, the increase in arrests of women for larceny and fraud is attributed to more women being in the workforce and is interpreted as evidence that women are catching up with males in involvement in white-collar and corporate crimes.

Consistent with this perspective is changes in arrests for some offenses that appear to have clear connections to changes in women's roles and activities. For example, the rise in the female percentage of arrests for DUI can be attributed, in part, both to women's greater participation in the public sphere (e.g., going to college, working, traveling) and to more women driving automobiles. However, it is debatable whether the expand-

ing use of the automobile by women is better explained as a fundamental role change or as a society-wide diffusion of a technological necessity (i.e., a required mode of transportation). The latter interpretation suggests a different type of explanation from the "female emancipation" account.

Also, many writers argue that it is theoretically unwarranted to assume that the effect of equalization of gender roles is necessarily criminogenic, as greater female social participation may reduce stress, increase self-esteem, and in other ways positively affect what are often described in the criminological literature as the causes of crime (see review in Steffensmeier and Allan 1996).

The major difficulty with the liberation thesis, however, is that it is *inconsistent* with much of what is known about both female crime and contemporary gender roles. Five types of evidence support this claim. First, the changes in the female percentage of arrests prior to the women's movement (beginning around 1970) were as great or greater than in subsequent years when female labor force participation and other "status of women" indicators accelerated (Bianci and Spain 1986). Second, the female percentage of arrests is comparable across age groups both for the entire period (1960–1990) and for individual decades. This contradicts the expectation that trends in female employment and women's status should have a greater impact on the criminality of young adult and middle-aged women than adolescent and elderly women (Steffensmeier and Streifel 1992). Third, increases in the female percentage of embezzlement arrests are as large among juveniles as adults, which conflicts with Simon's version of the emancipation thesis. Fourth, female offenders typically bear little resemblance to the "liberated female crook" described by some commentators. Instead, these offenders typically are unemployed women working at low-paying jobs, or minority women drawn from backgrounds of profound poverty (Chesney-Lind 1986; Steffensmeier and Allan 1996). Finally, recent time-series and cross-sectional analyses indicate that higher female-to-male arrest levels are linked to structural conditions in which women face adverse rather than favorable economic circumstances (Streifel 1990; Steffensmeier and Streifel 1992).

Increased Economic Adversity of Women and Community Disorganization

One of the better predictors of involvement in criminal activity is economic hardship (Allan and Steffensmeier 1989). A larger segment of the female population faces greater economic insecurity today than 30 years ago, even though some women have become more emancipated and have moved into formerly male professions. Rising rates of divorce, illegitimacy, and female-headed households, coupled with continued segregation of women in low-paying occupations, have aggravated the economic pressures on women and have left them more responsible for child care than they were two or three decades ago. Growing economic adversity increases the pressures to commit consumer-based crimes such as shoplifting, check fraud, theft of services, and welfare fraud.

The economic adversity thesis is consistent with studies of the characteristics of female offenders and with recent cross-sectional and time-series research on structural correlates of the female percentage of property-crime arrests (Steffensmeier and Streifel 1992; Streifel 1990). These studies show that the higher female-to-male arrest levels are linked to social conditions in which women face adverse rather than favorable economic circumstances, such as greater occupational segregation, more female-headed households, higher rates of illegitimacy, and higher rates of female unemployment. The adversity thesis also predicts female arrest gains in *all* the property crimes, which in fact has occurred.

Research on the urban "underclass" suggests a growing detachment on the part of many inner-city minorities (particularly blacks) from mainstream social institutions such as marriage, education, and employment. The complex set of "disarticulation" processes leading to this detachment include the lack of employment opportunities caused by industrial restructuring, the exodus of the black middle class from inner-city neighborhoods, and racial discrimination. Industrial restructuring, in particular, has contributed to a reduction in demand for workers with low levels of skill and education in those geographic areas where low-income blacks are most likely to live (Brown 1997). The economic disadvantage affects attitudes and aspirations, spawning and sustaining an underclass subculture that rejects traditional norms regarding marriage, educational attainment, and employment on the one hand, while fostering violent and drug-using behavior on the other.

The same disarticulation processes (e.g., labor market disadvantage) facing black men also affect black women. Inner-city black women are increasingly concentrated in geographic areas with less favorable employment opportunities, higher levels of poverty, and higher prevalence of female-headed households. Some evidence suggests that the lesser supervision and weakened social controls characterizing these areas affects on female crime/delinquency as much as or more than male delinquency. Truancy, street-corner "hanging" by teenage gangs, drug involvement, and violence may be seen as adaptive strategies by female (and male) inner-city residents to a social context that includes poor schools, unemployment, crime, family disruption, and weak community organizations (Sommers and Baskin 1992). It appears that the social and institutional transformation of the inner city has created opportunities and facilitated entry of minority women into crime in ways that have escalated their criminal offending as much as or more than that of minority males. In turn, this escalation has swamping effects that elevate female offending levels for the population as a whole.

Expanded Opportunities for Female-Type Crimes

Because female offenders (similar to male offenders) gravitate toward activities that are easily available and within their skills, the level and character of female crime in a given society will be strongly affected by the availability of crime opportunities suited to female interests and abilities. Changes in American society since World War II have created more opportunities for fraud and dishonesty, and related offenses that "everywoman" (or everyman) can commit (Steffensmeier 1980; Weisburd et al. 1991). They do not require the physical skills and dexterity of many forms of street crime, nor the skills of professional con artists. These crimes typically require little more than "the ability to read, write, and fill out forms, along with some minimum level of presentation of a respectable self" (Weisburd et al. 1991, 182). Moreover, while collusion may often be present, many of these crimes can be committed on one's own.

Changing patterns of productive activity in at least five areas have created opportunities for the commission of new forms of crime, such as minor thefts and frauds, that favor female involvement: (1) production, merchandising, and marketing of goods; (2) the credit economy; (3) a welfare state and its programs; (4) the importance of credentials for job placement and social status; and (5) consumerism and the message of consumption.[3]

Important conditions leading to more opportunities for theft and fraud include the credit economy and the increases in shopping malls, self-service marketing, and small, portable products. Lines of credit and credit cards produce paper frauds such as credit fraud, bad checks, coupon fraud, and fraudulent theft of services. This last typically involves failure to make payment for rental property (e.g., videocassettes) or for contracted services such as shelter, water, heat, cable TV, and telephone. The growth in shopping malls and portable products enhances the opportunities (and incentives) for shoplifting, theft from parked automobiles, and the like.

Various programs of the welfare state also create the conditions for the commission of fraud and theft. Student loans, Social Security, Medicaid, and other programs depend on written materials, and all involve the potential for fraudulent applications. There is also potential for theft of government checks from mailboxes and delivery trucks. At the same time, society's increasing reliance on formal credentials creates opportunities to falsify identification in the preparation of application forms or to fake the data. The emphasis on grades, graduation, awards, and job experience soon elicits "pressures to inflate the credentials, or to make them up when they do not exist" (Weisburd et al. 1991, 183).

These changes are reinforced by the media's message of consumption that encourages excessive spending and buying on credit. The message to "consume" goods encourages theft (including shoplifting) and chiseling to stretch the paycheck or upgrade one's car, home, appearance, or lifestyle. The rise in female property crime in particular can be seen as a by-product of opportunities created by the evolution of productive activity (e.g., transportation, merchandising, currency) rather than to changes in female motivation or in their social and economic position. Although these changes have expanded crime opportunities for both sexes, on balance the opportunities for traditional types of female crime have been expanding at a faster pace than those for traditional male crimes. Analogously, American society has become more "target rich" for property crimes that favor middle-class involvement (Weisburd et al. 1991).

Changes in the Criminal Underworld

The criminal underworld has undergone important changes in recent decades that, on balance, appear to have contributed to higher rates of female offending. The changes include (1) emergence of drug trafficking as the dominant criminal market; (2) a decline in some forms of professional crime; (3) shifts in ethnic composition; (4) an increase in "instrumental" forms of violence (which would increase male violence); and (5) a reduced supply of male crime partners because of increased incarceration rates.

Subtle shifts in the underworld may raise or dampen the prospects for female involvement. Given the male dominance of the underworld and the sexism characterizing it, female crime opportunities are partly dependent on whether male criminals find females to be useful. For example, in recent years women have become useful for successful drug trafficking because they are more likely to have clean records, create less suspicion, and can conceal drugs more easily. Also, rising incarceration rates have reduced the supply of males for recruitment into drug or other crime networks, thus enhancing or necessitating the recruitment of women into such networks.

At the same time, the underworld appears to be younger, more amateurish, and less professional today. My research suggests that professional crime groups are less likely to admit women or to allow them to play fairly active roles (Steffensmeier 1983; Steffensmeier and Terry 1986). Also, some forms of professional crime that historically involved a preponderance of male offenders have declined (e.g., safecracking). Would-be recruits into these traditionally male crimes are being drawn instead into other forms of theft (e.g., theft from parked motor vehicles) or drug trafficking (Shover 1991; Steffensmeier 1986).

Meanwhile, demographic shifts in the large urban areas of America where the bulk of reported crime occurs have affected both underworld crime and female law-breaking. In particular there has been an increase in Hispanic and black populations that tend to have comparatively high levels of female-to-male offending, especially in drug trafficking (Anglin, Hser, and McGlothin 1987; Pennsylvania Crime Commission 1991; Steffensmeier and Allan 1988).

The other major change in the underworld involves the greater use of violence for instrumental or materialistic ends. An increasing proportion of all homicides are perpetrated for instrumental rather than expressive purposes. Males disproportionately commit instrumental-type killings, which helps explain the decline in the FP/A for homicide.

Drug Dependency/Addiction

Rising levels of illicit drug use by females over the past two or three decades may also help account for female crime trends. Drug addiction amplifies income-generating crimes of both sexes but more so for females than males (Anglin et al. 1987; Inciardi, Lockwood, and Pottieger 1993). Because females face greater constraints against crime (it is more stigmatizing for them), they may need greater motivational pressures before they will commit a crime. Female involvement in burglary and robbery, in particular, typically occurs during addiction and is likely to be abandoned when drug use ceases (Anglin et al 1987). Drug use is also more likely to initiate females into the underworld and criminal subcultures and to connect them to drug-dependent males who use them as crime accomplices or exploit them as "old ladies" to support their addiction (Covington 1985; Miller 1986; Steffensmeier and Terry 1986). In these and other ways, the rise in drug dependency would have a greater impact on female criminality, even though female drug arrests have not outpaced male arrests since 1960.

Application of Framework to Select Crimes

The preceding discussion can provide an account for offenses such as homicide, in which the female share of arrests has declined, and for offenses such as larceny and DUI in which notable increases have occurred in the female share of arrests. The following examination of trends in several crime categories is somewhat speculative and is intended to raise issues for future research.

Homicide

The female percentage of homicide arrests decreased steadily over the three decades, from 17 percent in 1960 to 9 percent in 1995. This downward trend is due largely to a proportionate increase in felony-murders and stranger killings (from about 7 percent of all homicides in 1960 to about 20 percent in 1995). Males are overwhelmingly the offenders in instrumental, felony-related killings (e.g., a contract murder or a homicide committed while carrying out a robbery or a drug deal), whereas homicides involving female perpetrators almost always occur during non-criminal activity (e.g., domestic dispute). The increase in instrumental murders appears to be due to several factors: the growth in convenience stores and similar establishments that are more suitable targets for robbery; the escalating availability of more lethal firearms; the growth in violent youth gangs; and the strong consumer appetite for hard drugs that has fostered a violent drug trade (especially in large urban areas).

Another factor that may have contributed to the decline in the FP/A for homicide, particularly during the 1980s, is the growth of shelters and other services for abused women. This growth may have enabled abused women to escape from abusive males, instead of killing them. Browne (1992) reports a 20 percent decrease in the number of women killing male partners over the 1976–1987 period, about the time domestic violence legislation and extralegal resources for abused women were coming into place. (Over half of the victims of female homicides are male intimate partners. The presence of avenues for escape or protection for women threatened by male partners may have averted at least a portion of those homicides that occur in desperation or self-defense. Browne reports that this downward trend in partner homicides by women was not matched, however, by a similar trend in partner homicides by men.

Burglary

The female percentage of burglary arrests has inched upward, especially during the 1980s. The major force pushing up the female percentage has been a fairly steep drop in the male burglary rate since the mid-1970s (while female rates have held fairly steady). The drop in the male rate reflects a paper decrease brought on by a change in reporting procedures, together with a real decrease in male burglary rates due to shifts in the underworld away from burglary toward drug dealing and other theft offenses as more attractive money-making options (Shover 1991; Steffensmeier 1986; Steffensmeier and Harer 1999).

The paper decrease in burglary has occurred because, contrary to instructions from the Uniform Crime Reporting Program, many police departments categorize "theft from a motor vehicle" (e.g., breaking into a parked automobile and stealing a CD player) as a burglary rather than a larceny-theft. In response to UCR pressures, the trend today is for individual police departments to classify a theft from a motor vehicle as a larceny-theft. This change has also pushed up male arrest rates for larceny-theft rates since the mid-1970s.

Meanwhile, major developments in crime opportunities on the one hand and in crime-control measures on the other have contributed to a decline in burglaries committed by males. First, there appears to be a *substitution effect* whereby the decline in an index crime like burglary is made at the expense of an increase in nonindex criminal behaviors such as drug violations, fraud offenses, and theft from motor vehicles (classified as larceny-theft in the UCR). Enhanced opportunities for thefts from cars or vans and for frauds such as credit card fraud or bad checks provide "replacement" crimes for dampening burglary involvement. Second, the abundance of popular consumer items (e.g., TV, VCR, camera) has cut demand and street prices for many stolen household goods (Cohen 1998), prompting some thieves to turn to crimes like robbery and drug dealing that are more immediately rewarding than breaking and entering. Third, the most important change, perhaps, is the emergence of drug trafficking as the dominant criminal market—it offers a more open and easier (e.g., requires less skill) crime route than burglary. Simultaneously, in neighborhoods characterized by heavy drug dependency, the money to be made through burglary has dwindled because addicts already flood the stolen goods market with jewelry, guns, and consumer electronic goods (Baumer et al. 1998). Finally, major improvements in domestic and commercial security (better lighting, better safes, alarm systems) may have deterred would-be burglars, just as enforcement programs targeted at career offenders may have reduced the number of active or "professional" burglars who commit many burglaries and also recruit younger thieves for burglary involvement.

Together, these changes in illegal markets and crime opportunities over the past couple of decades have lessened the attractiveness of burglary as a crime option and have eroded the subcultural elements and recruitment processes for the establishment of burglary networks and careers. But these changes have mainly affected would-be male burglars. Other factors have produced stable or slightly rising female burglary rates, including: a growth in burglary targets that are more suitable for female involvement (such as houses or apartments that are unoccupied during the daytime); an increase in drug-related burglaries (and robberies) that involve women as solo perpetrators or as accomplices of male offenders; the expanding role of the informant system within law enforcement that leads to arrests of females for testimony against male offenders; and a trend toward younger, more reckless criminals who

appear more willing than their older, more professional counterparts to admit women into their groups or to exploit them for criminal purposes. (Some of these factors have also contributed to rising arrest rates of females for other property crimes.)

For example, the growth in suburban housing and the greater numbers of women at work have exposed households to greater risk because family members are away or because there are fewer neighbors to look after property while residents are away from home. When women burglarize, they prefer daytime crimes in unoccupied houses or apartments. One female ex-burglar told me:

> The women I met in prison who were involved in burglary did it because they were dopers, or did it for a boyfriend who wanted them to scout a place, or both. My involvement came from selling real estate. A couple of the homes I was showing left money laying around. I was very short of money at the time. I had the keys, so I went back later. Did it twice and got caught. It amounted to $844 in all. But the papers blew it all out of proportion, called me the 'real estate lady-burglar,' like I was some kind of new feminist freak.

Driving Under the Influence

A combination of factors help explain the rise in the female percentage of arrests for DUI, from 6 percent in 1960 to 14 percent in 1995. First, DUI statutes now require a smaller amount of alcohol consumption or blood-alcohol content as a criterion for intoxication. In addition, DUI enforcement practices have toughened. Both factors have contributed to arrests of less intoxicated violators, particularly women drivers. Second, the proportion of drivers who are female has increased. This trend reflects the growing reliance on the automobile in modern American society, especially among women as they carry out their work roles, fulfill their family responsibilities, and pursue their leisure activities. Third, women have greater freedom of movement and experience greater acceptance of their drinking in public places. Fourth, there is now a larger pool of single, separated, or divorced females, a group that is at comparatively greater risk for driving under the influence at night, when enforcement accelerates and most arrests are made (McCormack 1985; Shore et al. 1988). Single or divorced women are more likely than married women to drink at bars, private clubs, and other social gatherings.

The significance of these factors for trends in female DUI arrests is reflected in responses drawn from recent interviews of lower-court magistrates in Pennsylvania. This judge's comment is typical:

> DUI cases are still mainly male but we are seeing more women. The reasons are not that complex, really. There are more women who drive nowadays and the law's a lot stricter. You can get hammered [arrested] for just a couple of drinks now. The women are out to socialize, have a drink with some lady friends or to meet guys, at a bar or private club. A lot of these gals are single or divorced, in their twenties and thirties. They're out for a good time—have a couple of drinks, dance, party a little, and head for home. Oops! The cops pull them over.

Larceny-Theft

Since 1960, females have made sizable gains in arrests for larceny, fraud, and forgery. The FP/A rose from about 15 percent in 1960, to about 30 percent in 1980, to about 35 percent in 1995 (thus, most of the female gains occurred in the sixties and seventies). Most arrests of women in these offense categories are for shoplifting, passing bad checks, credit card fraud, theft of services, welfare fraud, and small con games (Giordano et al. 1981; Klemke 1992; Silverman et al. 1976; Steffensmeier 1980; Watson 1993). These kinds of law-breaking represent extensions of female domestic and consumer role activities, rather than new role patterns. Males also engage in such crimes and in larger numbers, but the proportion of male crime accounted for by these crimes is lower than

the proportion for females (Klemke 1992). Recent changes in currency and consumerism have affected the theft/fraud opportunities for both sexes, but more for females than males. Simultaneously, the greater economic adversity facing large subgroups of women may have heightened their incentive and risk-taking aptitude for theft and fraud.

Note also that the female percentage of arrests for larceny, fraud, and forgery more than doubled between 1960 and 1980 but subsequently leveled off or only inched upward. Quite simply, more rapid female gains were attainable in earlier years because base rates for female offending were so much smaller than male base rates. These gains have leveled off as female base rates have become larger and the gender gap has narrowed. Once the female share of arrests for specific crimes reaches 35–40 percent, additional gains are unlikely as that would require catching up or even surpassing male levels.

Several interrelated factors also help explain the rapid rise and subsequent plateau in the FP/A for larceny. First, increased opportunities for shoplifting—a female-type crime—occurred across the three decades but especially in the 1960s when the rapid growth in shopping malls, self-service marketing, and small, portable products outpaced protection-against-theft measures. Second, that trend has been countered in recent years by increased opportunities for larcenies such as bicycle theft and theft from parked automobiles that overwhelmingly are committed by male offenders. Third, fluctuations both in the law and in enforcement practices have affected arrest trends for larceny.

In the 1960s and early 1970s, the enforcement trend was toward a stricter, more formal handling of shoplifters (which would lead to more arrests of females). In recent years, stores have become less willing to prosecute shoplifters (leading to proportionately fewer larceny arrests of females). In fact, many states now have "civil recovery" laws that allow store officials to impose a civil penalty (e.g., return the merchandise and pay a $50 recovery fee) on apprehended shoplifters instead of arresting or initiating formal charges against them (Klemke 1992). In some localities there are even nonarrest alternatives whereby first-time shoplifters are allowed to participate in shoplifting prevention programs in place of a formal arrest. At the same time, the reclassification of a theft from a motor vehicle to a larceny (rather than a burglary) has increased male larceny arrests. Thus, countervailing trends in opportunities and enforcement practices brought about a rise in female larceny arrests in the 1960s but have dampened arrest gains in the 1980s. (Some similar developments in law enforcement have also affected arrest probabilities for check or credit card fraud, etc.)

In her interpretation of UCR arrest trends, Simon (1975; Simon and Landis 1991) argues that an increase in women in the paid workplace has resulted in more female employee theft and white-collar crime, and consequently more arrests of women for larceny and fraud. (See Darrow [1922] for an earlier statement of this view). It is reasonable to assume that at least some proportion of the increasing number of working women have capitalized on their opportunities for work-related thefts and frauds, so that employee theft and white-collar crime involving women is greater today than a decade or two ago. There is, in this regard, considerable similarity between the current situation and that of the late nineteenth century when female involvement in domestic theft (also an occupational crime) was unusually high as a result of work roles then available to women.

But because the crime categories of larceny and fraud are poor indicators of white-collar offenses, it is a mistake to conclude that recent trends in female employment have had much of an impact on female arrest trends. The typical arrestee in these offense categories has committed a *non*occupational crime such as shoplifting or passing bad checks. Jennifer Watson and I recently examined the case files of all arrests for mi-

nor property crimes in an SMSA county in central Pennsylvania for three randomly selected months in each of the years 1989 and 1990 (Watson 1993). In both years there were about 600 minor property crime arrests (for larceny, fraud, forgery, and embezzlement). We did not find a single arrest for an occupational crime in the 1989 data, and only four arrests for an occupational crime in 1990. These arrests were a male and a female arrested for misappropriation of funds by a local government official; a female arrested for pilfering clothes from a local department store; and a male arrested for stealing carpentry tools from his employer. An earlier study conducted in 1981 at the same site had uncovered only four cases of employee theft or fraud, out of a total of 311 arrests. Two of these four arrests involved domestic theft by self-employed cleaning ladies. Further, we also questioned a number of police officials responsible for record keeping in other localities of Pennsylvania; all agreed that arrests for occupational or employee-type crimes are infrequent. Noted one police official:

> My acquaintances in business are always complaining to me about their employees stealing from them. I tell them, why don't you report it, call the police. They say [that] they prefer to fire them and leave it at that. Less hassle I guess.

Arrests for employee theft or other occupational crimes, therefore, are rare events. There is probably more, perhaps much more, employee theft by women today than in the past, but that increase cannot be extrapolated from or determined by UCR arrest statistics. Moreover, UCR data on embezzlement arrests are not of much value for understanding occupational crime, because embezzlement makes an insignificant contribution to overall occupational crime patterns. Embezzlement statistics also make up some amount of nonoccupational embezzlements (e.g., the club treasurer who embezzles). In addition, the increase in the female percentage of arrests for embezzlement is as large among juveniles as among adults, who have been most affected by recent employment trends. More important, so few persons—whether female or male—are arrested for embezzlement that its overall significance is trivial (it has the smallest arrest rate of all UCR crimes).

There are also important errors in Simon's rejection of any link between the economic adversity thesis and female gains in minor property crimes. She writes, "The economic marginalization thesis would argue that as women move into more responsible positions, their propensities to commit property offenses will decline. The data show that the reverse has occurred. There is a positive relationship between female occupational mobility and higher female property crime, especially white-collar, arrest rates" (Simon and Landis 1991, 11). Leaving aside the "ecological fallacy" problem, Simon misses the point of the economic marginalization thesis—that, while some women have achieved occupational mobility, another segment of the female population has encountered economic marginalization. Simultaneous trends describe women's economic status, one of upward mobility and the other of greater economic adversity. Second, the Simon/Landis view of female upward mobility predicts increases in female arrests for larceny and fraud only, but the female percentage has also risen for burglary and robbery. The latter increases are consistent with the economic marginalization thesis, since it predicts increases in *all* property crimes (see Steffensmeier and Streifel 1992). Third, female arrest gains for larceny peaked in the mid-1970s and have held steady since, despite continued employment gains by females in the 1980s.

Conclusion

Three general conclusions can be drawn about recent trends in female arrests. First, the distribution of offenses for which both males and females are arrested has changed

but, relative to males, the profile of the female offender has not changed. Both sexes are arrested largely for minor crimes (i.e., theft, fraud, drugs, drinking) but the female profile is slanted more toward minor theft/fraud and prostitution offending, although the male profile is slanted more toward violent and serious property offending. Second, females have made arrest gains (mostly small gains) in many UCR offense categories but the most significant change in the female percentage of arrests involves the overall rise in property crime, especially minor thefts and frauds. Third, female-to-male involvement in serious or violent crime has held steady since 1960 (FP/A dropped for homicide, was constant for aggravated assault, and increased slightly for robbery). Evidence from other sources on crime trends also shows both stability and change in female crime relative to male crime over the past several decades.

These patterns parallel those described in earlier analyses that covered the period of the 1960s and 1970s (Steffensmeier 1980), with two exceptions. After holding steady during the 1960s and 1970s, the female percentage of DUI arrests rose sharply during the late 1980s. Second, the female share of burglary and robbery arrests rose more rapidly in the 1980s than in prior decades. As holds true for trends in the FP/A for other crimes, the increase in the FP/A for burglary (and robbery) can be attributed to the interplay of several factors. These include a decline in male burglary (because of changes in reporting procedures and because of males selecting drug trafficking as an alternative criminal activity), greater opportunities for female "kinds" of burglary, greater police targeting of female "co-offenders" to inform on male offenders, declining professionalism within the ranks of burglary and the underworld more generally, and increased drug dependency among women.

Gender differences in quantity and quality of crimes continue to be consistent with traditional gender-role expectations, behaviors, and opportunities. Indeed, substantial changes in the illegitimate activities of women would be surprising. Attitudes have shifted toward greater acceptance of women in the workforce, combining career and family, and the gender-role system favors more individual latitude. But little change has occurred in many aspects of gender roles: in gender typing in children's play activities and play groups (Fagot and Leinbach 1983; Stoneman, Brody, and MacKinnon 1984; Thorne 1992), in gender differences in conversational styles (Tannen 1991; Weaner-Davis 1992), in the kinds of personality characteristics that both men and women associate with each gender (Bergen and Williams 1991; Maccoby 1985), in the expectation that women will be the gatekeepers of male sexuality (Rubin 1983), in the importance placed on physical attractiveness of women and their pressures to conform to an ideal of beauty or "femininity" (Mazur 1985), and in female responsibilities for child rearing and for nurturing activities such as caring for the sick and the elderly (Himes 1992).

Female economic participation per se does not necessarily lead to greater female criminality, just as improved economic opportunities and higher educational achievement do not lead to greater male criminality. This does not mean that changes in the family and economy have not had an impact on female patterns of offending. As noted earlier, recent changes in the household economy and family have resulted in greater participation of women in economic production and the public sphere. This greater participation provides more opportunities for certain kinds of crime. Yet, at the same time, it leads to fewer familial or private social controls in some aspects of women's lives but more legal controls, including arrest and official sanctioning. Increases in female arrests for minor property crime and DUI, for example, reflect those trends.

It also is possible that greater numbers of working women increase female crime by contributing to a sense of relative deprivation among women who are being paid less than their male colleagues or even among women who are not working outside the home. Viewed this way, the female employment thesis may converge in some ways with the economic adversity hypothesis. There might be other, less obvious links between female employment and crime, such as the circuitous path by which female employment gains may contribute to female arrests for fraud and forgery. Employment enhances the prospects for acquiring credit and securing loans, so that working women may have greater opportunities to commit credit-based frauds such as nonpayment of services and fraudulent unemployment claims (see Steffensmeier and Streifel 1992). This is obviously a very different causal path than that suggested by Simon.

Other possible contributors to female crime trends include the changing ethnic/racial composition of urban areas. For historical and cultural reasons, female-to-male involvement in some forms of crime (gang delinquency, drug dealing, serious property crimes) appears to be somewhat greater among blacks and Hispanics than among whites or Asians (Anglin et. al. 1987; Pennsylvania Crime Commission 1991). If this is so, then the disproportionate influx of blacks and Hispanics into the large urban centers with high crime rates would tend to increase the female share of offending, all other factors being equal. The impact of this population change may also be exacerbated by heightened community disorganization in many urban neighborhoods.

Finally, female arrest gains in some crime categories may partly reflect a sort of diffusion process spawned by widespread involvement. In some areas of deviance (e.g., alcohol, tobacco, and drugs), it appears that once involvement has become widespread, and presumably less deviant, the female percentage increases. In other words, sex ratios of deviance vary inversely with rates of deviance (Ferrence and Whitehead 1980). In addition, males tend to be the early participants in new forms of deviance, and peak levels of female involvement lag behind those of males. So too, many forms of fraud, minor theft, employee pilferage, and even drug dealing have become widespread and increasingly diffuse throughout large segments of the population. Media attention on female crime or violence may contribute to this diffusion process and encourage girls and women to copycat the "new female offender."

My goal has been to place female crime trends within a broad multivariate framework and to show how some large-scale societal changes have influenced female offending and female-to-male arrest trends. Unbundling and then tying together the alternative forces that are driving those trends has the additional benefit of adding to our understanding of male offending.

Discussion Questions

1. What is the most significant gender difference in the arrest process?
2. How have changes in productivity patterns affected women and crime?
3. What main factor contributed to the decrease in female homicide arrests over the last three decades?

Endnotes

1. This chapter is a major revision of an earlier treatment that appeared in the *Journal of Quantitative Criminology*, 9 (1993): 411–441.
2. Some commentators have classified Adler's approach as "subjectivist," where the emphasis is on attitudes and identities, and Simon's as "objectivist," where the emphasis is on opportunities. I disagree. Some differences between Adler's and Simon's perspectives do exist, but their interpretations overlap considerably. Alder places considerable emphasis on the criminogenic effects of women's liberation on female crime opportunities, while Simon emphasizes the criminogenic effects of changes toward nontradi-

tional attitudes and self-definitions of women.
3. In presenting these changes, I borrow heavily from my earlier work (Steffensmeier 1980, 1983) and from Weisburd et al (1991). While my focus has been on the disproportionate increase in opportunities for female-type crimes, their emphasis is on the increase in crime opportunities for middle-class persons.

References

Alder, F. 1975. *Sisters in Crime*. New York: McGraw-Hill.

Allan, E. and Steffensmeier, D. 1989. "Youth, Underemployment, and Property Crime: Effects of the Quantity and the Quality of Job Opportunities on Juvenile and Young Adult Arrest Rates." *American Sociological Review* 54:107–123.

Anglin, D, Hser, Y. and McGlothin, W. 1987. "Sex Differences in Addict Careers." *American Journal of Drug and Alcohol Abuse.* 13:59–71.

Baumer, E., Lauristen, J., Rosenfeld, R., and Wright, R. 1998. "The Influence of Crack Cocaine on Robbery, Burglary, and Homicide Rates: A Cross-City Longitudinal Analysis." *Journal of Research in Crime & Delinquency* 35: 295–315.

Bergen, D. and Williams, J. 1991. "Sex Stereotypes in the United States Revisited:1972–1988. *Sex Roles* 24:413–423.

Bianci, S. and Spain, D. 1986. *American Women in Transition*. New York: Russell Sage Foundation.

Bishop, C. 1931. *Women and Crime*. London: Chatto & Windus.

Boritch, H. and Hagan, J. 1990. "A Century of Crime in Toronto: Gender, Class, and Patterns of Social Control, 1859 to 1955." *Criminology* 28:567–599.

Box, S. and Hale, C. 1984. "Liberation/Emancipation, Economic Marginalization, or Less Chivalry: The Relevance of Three Theoretical Arguments to Female Crime Patterns in England and Wales, 1951–1980." Criminology 22:473–98.

Brown, I. 1997. "Explaining the Black-White Gap in Labor Force Participation Among Women

Heading Households." *American Sociological Review* 62:236–252.

Brown, J. and Langan, P. 1998. *State Court Sentencing of Convicted Felons, 1994*. Washington, DC: Bureau of Justice Statistics.

Browne, A. 1992. "Violence Against Women" *Journal of the American Medical Association* 267:3184–3195.

Chesney-Lind, M. 1986. "Women and Crime: The Female Offender." *Signs* 12:78–96.

Cohen, W. 1998. "Crime Rates Down." *U.S. News & World Report*, May 25, pp. 39–40.

Covington, J. 1985. "Gender Differences in Criminality Among Heroin Users." *Journal of Research in Crime and Delinquency* 22:329–353.

Daly, K. and Chesney-Lind, M. 1988. "Feminism and Criminology." *Justice Quarterly* 5:497–538.

Darrow, C. 1922. *Crime: Its Causes and Treatment*. Montclair, NJ: Patterson-Smith.

Elliott, D., Ageton, S., and Huizinga, D. 1987. "Social Correlates of Delinquent Behavior." Unpublished paper.

Fagot, B. and Leinbach, M. 1983. "Play Styles in Early Childhood: Social Consequences for Boys and Girls." In M. Liss, ed., *Social and Cognitive Skills: Sex Roles and Children's Play*. New York: Academic Press.

Feree, M. 1990. "Beyond Separate Spheres: Feminism and Family Research." *Journal of Marriage and the Family* 52:866–884.

Ferrence, R. and Whitehead, P. 1980. "Sex Differences in Psychoactive Drug Use." In Orina Kalant, ed., *Alcohol and Drug Problems in Women*. New York: Plenum.

Giordano, P., Kerbel, S., and Dudley, S. 1981. "The Economics of Female Criminality: An Analysis of Police Blotters, 1890–1976." In Lee H. Bowker, ed., *Women and Crime in America*. New York: Macmillan.

Greenfeld, L. and Minor-Harper, S. 1991. <IWomen in Prison. Bureau of Justice Statistics, Special Report. Washington, DC.: U.S. Department of Justice.

Himes, C. 1992. "Future Caregivers: Projected Family Structures of Older Persons." *Journal of Gerontology* 47:517–26.

Inciardi, J., Lockwood, D., and Pottieger, A. 1993. *Women and Crack-Cocaine*. New York: Macmillan.

Klemke, L. 1992. *The Sociology of Shoplifting: Boosters and Snitches Today*. Westport, CT: Praeger.

Maccoby, E. 1985. "Social Groupings in Childhood: Their Relationship to Prosocial and Antisocial Behavior in Boys and Girls." In Dan Olweus, Jack Block, and Marian Radke-Yarrow, eds., *Development of Antisocial and Prosocial Behavior: Theories, Research and Issues*. Academic Press.

Mazur, A. 1986. "U.S. Trends in Feminine Beauty and Overadaptation." *Journal of Sex Research* 22:281–303.

McCormack, A. 1985. "Risk for Alcohol-Related Accidents in Divorced and Separated Women." *Journal of Studies on Alcohol* 46:240–243.

Miller, E. 1986. *Street Women*. Philadelphia: Temple University Press.

Ridgeway, C. 1997. "Interaction and the Conservation of Gender Inequality: Considering Employment." *American Sociological Review* 62: 218–235.

Rubin, L. 1983. *Blue Collar Wives*. New York: Harper & Row.

Shore, E. R., McCoy, M., Toonen, T. and Kuntz, E. 1988. "Arrest of Women for Driving Under the Influence." *Journal of Studies on Alcohol* 49:7–10.

Shover, N. 1991. "Burglary." In M. Tonry, ed., *Crime and Justice: A Review of Research*. Chicago: University of Chicago Press.

Silverman, I., Vega, M., and Gray, L. A. 1976. "Female Criminality in a Southern City: A Comparison over the Decade 1962–1972." Paper presented at the Annual Meeting of the American Society of Criminology, Tuscon, AZ.

Simon, R. 1975. *The Contemporary Woman and Crime*. Washington, DC: National Institutes of Mental Health.

Simon, R. and Landis, J. 1991. *The Crimes Women Commit, The Punishments They Receive*. Lexington, MA: Lexington Books.

Sommers, I. and Baskin, D. 1992. "Sex, Race, Age, and Violent Offending." *Violence and Victims* 7: 191–201.

Steffensmeier, D. 1978. "Crime and the Contemporary Woman: An Analysis of Changing Levels of Female Property Crime, 1960–75." *Social Forces* 57:566–584.

——. 1980. "Sex Differences in Patterns of Adult Crime, 1965–77: A Review and Assessment." *Social Forces* 58:1080–1108.

——. 1983. "Organization Properties and Sex-Segregation in the Underworld: Building a Sociological Theory of Sex Differences in Crime." *Social Forces* 61:1010–1032.

——. 1986. *The Fence: In the Shadow of Two Worlds.* Lanham, MD: Rowman and Littlefield.

Steffensmeier, D. and Allan, E. 1988. "Sex Disparities in Arrests by Residence, Race, and Age: An Assessment of the Gender Convergence/Crime Hypothesis." *Justice Quarterly* 5:53–80.

——. 1990. "Gender, Age, and Crime." In Joseph Sheley, ed., *Handbook of Contemporary Criminology.* New York: Macmillan.

——. 1996. "Gender and Crime: Toward a Gendered Theory of Female Offending." *Annual Review of Sociology* 22:459–87.

Steffensmeier, D., Allan, E., and Streifel, C. 1989. "Development and Female Crime: A Cross-National Test of Alternative Explanations." *Social Forces* 68:263–283.

Steffensmeier, D. and Harer, M. 1999. "Making Sense of Recent U.S. Crime Trends, 1980–98: Age Composition Effects and Other Explanations." *Journal of Research in Crime & Delinquency* 36:235–274.

Steffensmeier, D. and Streifel, C. 1992. "Time-Series Analysis of the Female Percentage of Arrests for Property Crimes, 1960–85: A Test of Alternative Explanations." *Justice Quarterly* 9:77–103.

Steffensmeier, D. and Terry, R. 1986. "Institutional Sexism in the Underworld: A View from the Inside." *Sociological Inquiry* 56:304–323.

Stoneman, A., Brody, G., and MacKinnon, C. 1984. "Naturalistic Observations of Children's Activities and Roles While Playing With Their Siblings and Friends." *Child Development* 55:617–627.

Streifel, C. 1990. *Cross-sectional Analysis of the Female Percentage of Arrests.* Ph.D. dissertation. University Park: The Pennsylvania State University.

Tannen, D. 1991. *You Just Don't Understand: Women and Men in Conversations.* New York: Morrow.

Thorne, B. 1992. *Gender Play: Girls and Boys in School.* New Brunswick, NJ: Rutgers University Press.

U.S. Department of Justice. 1960–1992. *Uniform Crime Reports.* Washington, DC: U.S. Government Printing Office.

Visher, C. 1983. "Police Arrest Decisions and Notions of Chivalry." *Social Problems* 21:5–23.

Watson, J. 1993. "Gender Differences in Crime and Disposition in Pennsylvania Lower-Courts." Undergraduate honors thesis, Sociology Department, The Pennsylvania State University.

Weaner-Davis. 1992. *Divorce-Busting.* New York: Summit Books.

Weisburd, D., Wheeler, S., Waring, E. and Bode, N. 1991. *Crimes of the Middle Classes: White-Collar Offenders in the Federal Courts.* New Haven, CT: Yale University Press.

Weitzman, L. 1985. *The Marriage Contract: Spouses, Lovers, and the Law.* New York: Free Press.

Zeitz, D. 1981. *Women Who Embezzle or Defraud: A Study of Convicted Felons.* New York: Praeger. ✦

14
Gender and Law

Frances Bernat

When women's biological nature is used by the legal system as a justification for disparate treatment and the perpetuation of gender stereotypes, women are ultimately disadvantaged. In order to understand this dynamic, this chapter analyzes how gender works in law and how law works to produce gender. In addition, the chapter examines the ways gender stereotypes continue to influence criminal law practices. The balance of this chapter focuses on understanding the manner in which courts determine: (a) the constitutionality of sex-based statutes, and (b) the level of gender bias in the disposition of criminal cases, as well as gender-based sentencing disparity.

Understanding the law and its relationship to gender is a difficult enterprise. Throughout much of U.S. history, women had no legal status or rights. Many early feminists believed that if women could obtain suffrage, it would follow that women would have equal rights with men and that laws and practices that discriminated against women would be abolished (Bernat 1992). Once the right to vote was obtained in 1920, however, legal rules and practices did not automatically change to provide women with equal rights or opportunities. Consequently, in 1972 the U. S. Senate and House of Representatives passed the Equal Rights Amendment (ERA) and submitted it to the individual states for ratification.[1] It was thought that a federal constitutional amendment was needed to recognize women's legal status as "equal" to men and to end discrimination. Subsequent debate on the ERA focused on changing the formal processes so that women's lives and status would be improved. Although the ERA was not ratified by the states, legal practices, both formal and informal, that affect women's equality and equitable treatment were openly reviewed and challenged—and some of these legal practices were changed. Understanding the gendered nature of law and its impact on women has been a subject of inquiry for feminist legal scholars and is the focus of this chapter.

Feminist Jurisprudence

Feminist jurisprudence analyzes law within the context of the reality of women's experiences and concerns (Belknap 1996; Pruitt 1994; Schneider et al. 1991). Some feminist legal scholars analyze women's lives and the law by focusing on issues pertaining to "sex discrimination," while other scholars focus on women's "gendered lives." The explanatory power of feminist scholarship, and hence feminist jurisprudence, is in its ability to understand women's lives in an ever-changing social, cultural, and legal system (Daly and Maher 1998). Traditionally, law has been defined in male terms and has been derived from men's experiences (Finley 1997; Smart 1998). Feminist jurisprudence exposes the traditional view of law as being gender-neutral, rather than as an objectification of male views and power (Loyola of Los Angeles Law Review 1995). The struggle for feminist legal scholars is to determine whether there are any differences between men and women that should be legally relevant considerations (Scales 1995). Consequently, feminist legal theory attempts not only to describe women's experiences but also to provide a prescriptive analysis of women and the law (Siegel 1993). Smart (1998) contends that the law is gendered. She states that feminist legal scholars need to analyze how gender works in law and how law works to produce gender.

Feminist scholars who have focused on gender relationships in our society have generally used Carol Gilligan's (1982) work on differences between males' and females' ethical decision-making processes. In her groundbreaking work, Gilligan found that when faced with an ethical dilemma, females attempt to balance reciprocal responsibilities between individuals (an "ethic of care") rather than to rank-order ethical choices (an "ethic of justice") as the males she studied had done (Siegel 1993). Gilligan noted that male voices are usually characterized as exhibiting a higher order of reasoning than female voices in our society. Consequently, Gilligan aimed to challenge the view that female ethical decisions are inferior or less sound than those of males.

Gilligan's work is used to understand the normative stratification of women in our society. However, her work does not analyze gender relationships as they intersect with race and class concerns. Feminist legal scholars who use Gilligan's theory as a framework for analyzing law and gender issues are faced with the problem of oversimplifying differences among women in order to challenge disparate gender-based practices that favor males over females within a social system of male domination (Angelari 1994; Scales 1995).[2] Pruitt (1994) contends, for example, that a gender-oriented approach may perpetuate gender stereotypes about women along feminine-masculine lines and result in a static concept about women through the creation of gender labels. Rice (1990) also observes that feminism usually analyzes women's experience from a white woman's perspective rather than from the experiences of various racial/ethnic women's perspectives. In this regard, Rice notes that even within racial groups, women's experiences may vary.

Feminist scholarship that analyzes sex discrimination places women's lives within the context of a social hierarchy that legally values males over females, white people over people of color, and the rich over the poor.

Under a patriarchal system, however, the law is constructed in such a way as to justify and define "male" behavior as the norm (Belknap 1996). Sex equality is thus viewed as a method for achieving parity for women in our social and legal systems.[3] Catherine MacKinnon (1987), for example, argues that if women were equal to men, women would not be marginalized or exploited. Postmodern deconstructionists have sought to expose the sexual hierarchy by inverting the logic that underlies a social reality. Feminist jurisprudence that uses a deconstructionist method seeks to expose the "truth" that a preference of one object (male) over another (female) is a socially biased construct (Loyola of Los Angeles Law Review 1995). As Scales (1995) states, "The issue is not freedom to be treated without regard to sex; the issue is freedom from systematic subordination because of sex" (p. 1395).

Perhaps problematically, a deconstructionist method for feminist jurisprudence may break down the origins and impact of women's oppression to such a degree that the "objective reality" found in our use of language hides the "abject reality" within which women live (Higgins 1995; Loyola of Los Angeles Law Review 1995). Klein's (1995) comments regarding feminist criminology are instructive for understanding feminist jurisprudence as well:

> It is far easier to identify what feminist criminology is not than to describe what it is or should be. This is not merely because of the newness of the project or the scarcity of exemplary studies. It is also because, perhaps, inherent in feminist thinking and in the deconstructive critique is the caution that we should not be creating universal feminist questions. Rather, they will arise out of interactions and observations, and we will need to be constantly self-reflexive concerning our own assumptions. Perhaps only after the fact will we see what our problematics and theories have in common. (p. 230)

Klein concludes with a challenge for us to move to a point where we make concrete our abstract ideas that can make an intellectual and political difference for women in the United States.

Legal Issues Pertaining to Gender Discrimination

Despite the fact that the ERA failed to pass in 1983, gender-based criminal laws and sentencing schemes in the United States have not proliferated. The equal protection clause of the Fourteenth Amendment, coupled with the existence of equal rights amendments in many state constitutions, succeeded in eliminating virtually all formalized, or *de jure*, sex-based legal discrimination in the criminal laws. In general, equal protection under the Fourteenth Amendment requires states to treat similarly situated groups alike. To do otherwise results in unconstitutional state action. Generally, the only criminal law areas where states may continue to define unlawful conduct along sex lines are crimes dealing with the sexually related offenses of rape and pandering.

Some state legislatures have sought, so far unsuccessfully, to create another area of sex-based legislation. In recent years, efforts have been mounted in several states to criminalize behaviors committed by females with respect to their pregnancies. As a result, a new and emerging area of sex-based criminal legislation and gender discrimination is arising as we enter the twenty-first century.

However, gender stereotypes continue to influence criminal law practices. Judges with broad discretion in sentencing continue to mete out systematically different sentences to male and female defendants convicted of the same crime. Eliminating *de facto* discrimination, or discrimination based on decision-making practices that derive from the broad discretionary powers of criminal justice personnel, is extremely difficult. The remainder of this chapter focuses on understanding the manner in which courts determine (a) the constitutionality of sex-based statutes, and (b) the level of gender bias in the disposition of criminal cases.

The Equal Protection Clause and Sexually Discriminatory Statutes

The equal protection clause of the Fourteenth Amendment has been an effective tool in preventing states from enacting statutes that either criminalize behavior or impose differential sanctions on the basis of sex. The significant step toward this end occurred in 1976 when the U.S. Supreme Court issued its landmark ruling in *Craig v. Boren* [429 U.S. 190 (1976)]. In *Craig*, the Court determined that sex-based laws would be constitutional only if the state's gender classification bore a "substantial relationship" to "legitimate state objectives." This ruling raised the constitutional standard by which sex-based statutes would be evaluated—from a minimal to an intermediate standard. As Higgins (1995) notes, the *Craig* Court questioned a reliance on "social facts as a foundation between law and the social order of gender" (p. 1547). The Court, in general, dismissed the idea that disparate treatment between men and women is justified by social differences that exist between the sexes. The Court had been moving toward creating a middle-tier of constitutionality for gender-based classifications prior to its *Craig* ruling [see *Reed v. Reed*, 404 U.S. 71 (1971) and *Frontiero v. Richardson*, 411 U.S. 677 (1972)]. In *Craig*, however, the court clearly articulated the middle-tier test for the Fourteenth Amendment analysis when gender-based laws (and classifications) are challenged. Previously, there were only two equal protection tests: a *strict scrutiny* test for classifications based on race, national origin, or alienage, and a *rational basis test for all other classifications*. The *Craig* test would render gender-based laws unconstitutional if a state is unable to show that the law is substantially related to a legitimate state interest. Of course, state interests can vary depending on the law and its stated purposes.

As the U.S. Supreme Court was moving toward a position that would make it more difficult for states to justify and defend sex-based laws, states had to respond to constitutional challenges to their sex-based statutes. In Pennsylvania, for example, the state's Muncy Act (so called because it created the state's first female prison in the town of Muncy) provided for harsher punishments for female offenders than the state law imposed on male offenders. The Pennsylvania Supreme Court held that the Muncy Act's sentencing provisions were unconstitutional on the basis of both the Fourteenth Amendment's equal protection clause and the state's own equal rights amendment [*Commonwealth v. Butler*, 328 A 2d 851 (1974); *Commonwealth v. Daniels*, 243 A 2d 400 (1968); *Commonwealth v. Sanders*, 331 A 2d 193 (1975)]. Consequently, the state amended its sentencing law and eliminated the sex-based sentencing provisions in 1974. Other states facing similar challenges to their discriminatory sentencing laws began to rescind or revise them in the 1970s. Today, sex-neutral sentencing laws are in place throughout the United States. Pennsylvania's Muncy Act was revised and the offending language was removed in 1974 (61 Pennsylvania Statutes Annotated Section 566). New Jersey's statutes were repealed in 1979 (New Jersey Statutes Annotated Sections 2A: 164–17, 30:4–155). Nonetheless, gender bias in the legal system is an ongoing concern.

Sex-Based Criminal Statutes and Equal Protection

Not all statutes that have explicit sex-based classifications violate the equal protection clause. In the last decade, a number of courts have found criminal laws that punish one sex for behavior that is not illegal if committed by the other sex to be constitutional even when they applied the *Craig* test. The statutes challenged include California's [4] and Iowa's[5] statutory rape laws, [see *Michael M. v. Superior Court of Sonoma County*,430 U.S. 464 (1981)]; Georgia's pandering law,[6] [see *Fluker v. State*, 282 S.E. 2d 112 (1981)] ; *Navedo v. Preisser* 630 F 2d 636 (8th Cir. 1980), and New York's first degree rape and sodomy laws[7] [see *People v. Liberta*, 474 N.E. 2d 567 (1984)]. The courts, faced with these challenges, have generally affirmed the defendants' convictions and sentences. Because these sex-based laws primarily concern rape legislation, the equal protection challenges of male-based rape laws require further analysis. Currently, there are no gender-based criminal statutes that punish females for behavior but exempt males. Nonetheless, some states are considering whether to enact such explicit gender-based laws in order to punish pregnant women who use drugs or alcohol. States that seek to impose punishments on such women currently attempt to do so by applying existing gender-neutral laws. This issue is discussed in greater detail later in this chapter.

By the late 1980s, over 70 percent of states had replaced sex-based statutory language in their rape laws with gender-neutral terminology (Searles and Berger 1987). This reform reflects pressure placed on state legislatures to enhance prosecutions and convictions in rape cases on behalf of all rape victims—young and old, male and female. The remaining states retained traditional common law definitions of rape in their statutes and thereby maintained gender-based definitions of rape. In 1981, the U.S. Supreme Court issued a significant ruling on an equal protection challenge to one such traditional rape statute. Many states have attempted to proscribe marital rape. However, the degree to which the traditional marital exemption to rape has been abrogated by these statutes varies greatly from state to state. In addition, the number of arrests, prosecutions, and convictions of persons who rape their spouses is relatively small.

In *Michael M. v. Superior Court of Sonoma County* [450 U.S. 464 (1981)], the Supreme Court upheld California's statutory rape law prohibiting a male from having sex with a female under the age of 18. Under California law, females were not prohibited from having sex with males who were under the age of 18. The Court determined that a reasonable state purpose for establishing a sex-based statute was to prevent illegitimate pregnancy. The Court reasoned that young women should be deterred from early sexual experiences because by nature they bear the risk of pregnancy. Thus, in order to "'equalize' the deterrents on the sexes, a state could solely punish males for having sex with females under the age of consent"[8] (450 U.S. 464, 473).

In this ruling, the Court allowed for the continuation of the sex-based statute by construing the sex-based law as a manifestation of the biological differences between males and females. The *Michael M.* decision rekindled turn-of-the-century reasoning that young women are both "naturally" weaker than young men and too immature to understand the nature of the sex act; thus, only females require state protection for the proper maintenance of their social roles and chastity. The court's holding that a valid purpose underlying statutory rape laws is to prevent illegitimate pregnancies reflects these outmoded norms as well as stereotypical beliefs that women alone face the demands of birth and child care. Chused (1990) asserts that this opinion reflects confusion as to the proper spheres men and women share when a young woman becomes a single mother.

Rape is a crime shaped by social definitions of sex and sexuality. Rape law engenders these definitions by legitimating women's sexual subordination to men and making it difficult for women to adjudicate their sexual victimization when sexual aggression is a biological given for men (Pendo 1994).

De Facto Gender-Based Discrimination in Sentencing

Historically, theorists argued that women received a "chivalrous" advantage on the basis of gender when they came before a sentencing judge. By assigning women more lenient sentences, judges were thought to be sparing vulnerable and fragile women the pain, stigma, and trauma associated with long prison terms. However, the relationship between gender and sentencing is a complex one. The sentencing laws that mandated harsher penalties for women than for men, as we have already discussed, are long gone (Baer 1991; Belknap 1996). However, disparate treatment in sentencing has continued despite an end to these laws. Sentencing judges continue to make distinctions between male and female offenders when imposing a sentence—usually to the disadvantage of women.

Over the past two decades, extensive empirical research has been conducted in both the United States and Great Britain on gender-based sentencing disparity (see Julian 1993). A cursory review of these results might lead a reader to conclude that women offenders receive less severe sentences than similarly situated men (Boritch 1992; Chesney-Lind 1987; Hutton, Pommersheim, and Feimer 1989; Morris 1988). A number of explanations have been advanced to account for the gender differences found, and a clearer picture of the extent and nature of informal gender-based sentencing practices is beginning to emerge. Lenient treatment is not extended to all women offenders, nor does it occur equally at all stages in the criminal process. Chesney-Lind (1987) notes that preferential treatment for female defendants is found only among women charged with serious crimes and occurs only at the sentencing stage. Thus, the vast majority of women in court for minor offenses do not receive preferential treatment (Bernat 1984, 1985; Ghali and Chesney-Lind 1986). A recent study on gender bias in Florida's criminal justice system revealed that while women who committed serious offenses were not sentenced as harshly as men, the reverse was true when it came to less serious offenses (Florida Law Review 1990). It was also determined that women who are incarcerated have less access than men to work release and rehabilitative programs. In addition, because of overcrowded conditions in male facilities, men are likely to be released early, whereas women, often serving their time in less crowded prisons, must serve out their full terms. Similarly, gender bias has been found in California where female inmates are confined in facilities far from their homes and children and have much less access to services and programs than male inmates (Tripodi II 1991).

Among serious female offenders, lenient sentences appear to be reserved for those women who conform to conventional feminine stereotypes. Sentencing judges have been shown to consider personal characteristics—for example, marital status (Nagel 1981) and family background (Farrington and Morris 1983)—when sentencing women but not when sentencing men. Researchers also note that this paternalism is extended to women who are considered "good mothers" or who exhibit other "commendable" attributes (Hutton et al. 1989; Morris 1988). Kruttschnitt (1982), for instance, found that "respectable" women (i.e., women with good employment records, women without alcohol or drug problems, women without psychiatric histories) received less severe sentences than women considered "disreputable." Not surprisingly, then, a New Jersey task force empaneled to study gender bias in the state's legal system found that information about a female offender's marital and familial status was routinely provided to sentencing judges by defense attorneys. While it was not clear that such information contributed to gender disparity in sentencing, judges and attorneys believed that it could (Wikler and Schafran 1991; Women's Rights Law Reporter 1986).

African-American women have been greatly affected by recent trends in the criminal justice system and are treated more harshly than white women (Gelsthorpe 1989; Johnson 1995). According to Johnson (1995):

> In contemporary times, as in the past, poverty is the major correlative in African-American women's involvement in criminality. Relatedly, and particularly characteristic of the modern era, state and federal emphasis on mandatory and guideline sentencing schemes, coupled with the nation's 'war on drugs,' has resulted in a substantial increase in African-American women's incarceration. Women are much more likely than men to be serving sentences for drug offenses and other nonviolent crimes with economic motives. In 1991, almost 64 percent of females in federal institutions were serving sentences for a drug-related offense. (p. 7)

Drug-offense sentencing has a profound impact on African Americans and is the principal reason for their incarceration in recent years (Johnson 1995). For example, Angela Thompson, a 17-year-old African-American woman with no prior criminal record, was convicted of selling crack cocaine to an undercover police officer in 1988 [*New York versus Thompson*, 633 N.E. 2nd 1074 (1994), rev'g 596 NVS 2d 421 (1993)]. Although the trial and intermediate appellate courts determined that the state's mandatory law should not be applied to Thompson, New York State's highest court resentenced Thompson to the mandatory minimum of 15 years to life (Johnson 1995).

Judges have also been known to be more punitive toward women convicted of certain crimes of violence considered to have been carried out in an "unfeminine" fashion (Nagel 1981; Nagel, Cardascia, and Ross 1982). At the close of the twentieth century, women made up only 1.5 percent of inmates on death row (*CNN Interactive* 1998). However, if the homicide a woman committed was extraordinarily violent, and the court (jury) viewed her as having exhibited "shockingly 'unladylike' behavior," she received the death penalty (Streib 1990, 878). The execution of Karla Faye Tucker in Texas on February 3,

1998, highlights this point. She had been convicted of killing two people with a pick-axe in 1983. Her execution was only the second of a woman in Texas since the Civil War (*CNN Interactive* 1998).

Punishment Based on Women's Reproductive Capacities

States have recently begun to confine or punish women for certain behaviors committed during pregnancy (Kasinsky 1993). These state actions have occurred within the context of conservative political agendas designed to protect the rights of the fetus over the right of women to control their reproductive lives. In some states, a woman can be confined (hospitalized) under court order if the court determines that she is not taking care of herself during her pregnancy and thus may be harming the fetus. Usually, these orders are issued in the woman's third trimester of pregnancy, when a court believes that her body will not successfully carry the fetus to term without such hospitalization (Notes 1989). A Massachusetts court in 1986, for example, determined that

> the right to life of a 32-week-old fetus invoked a compelling state interest strong enough to override the pregnant woman's liberty and privacy rights. (Notes 1989, 215)

Women in two other states, Colorado and Illinois, have been similarly confined under court orders to protect their fetuses (Notes 1989).

Other women are being criminally prosecuted as child abusers for taking drugs (cocaine or heroine) in their third trimester of pregnancy (Kasinsky 1993). Prosecutors have argued drugs used during pregnancy endanger the health of the soon-to-be-born child. These prosecutors have sought to apply gender-neutral laws (e.g., child endangerment, child abuse, distribution of a controlled substance to a minor) to the actions of these women in the hopes of securing criminal convictions and sanctions. Generally,

however, higher courts have not supported the prosecutions [for example, in Ohio see *State v. Gray*, 584 N.E. 2d 710 (1990); in Florida, see *State v. Gethers*, 585 So. 2d 1140 (1990)]. One court reasoned that public policy requires that such women not be prosecuted insofar as (1) the family would be disrupted or destroyed by separating a mother from her child; (2) addicted women might consider abortion or not receive prenatal care in order to avoid detection and prosecution; and (3) prosecution could deter women from seeking drug treatment (585 So. 2d 1140, 1143).

Nevertheless, such prosecutions are likely to continue, and state legislatures have themselves looked to enact explicit laws to criminalize taking drugs or drinking alcohol during pregnancy. Recently, the U.S. Supreme Court ruled that states may enact laws that limit the reproductive freedom of pregnant women [*(Carey v. Population Services).*, 431 U.S. 670 (1977)]. Although the Carey decision did not overrule *Roe v. Wade* [410 U.S. 113 (1973)], the decision provides states with greater latitude to regulate abortion and, thereby, protect fetal rights. In light of the *Michael M.* decision, such laws, should they be enacted, might be upheld as constitutional.

Conclusion

Legal paternalism is evidenced in court decisions which assume that a state can legitimately exercise its powers for the purpose of protecting female sex-role identities (chastity) and in state attempts to criminalize the actions of women who take drugs or drink alcohol during pregnancy. When women's biological nature is used by the legal system as a justification for disparate treatment and the perpetuation of gender stereotypes, women are ultimately disadvantaged. The invidiousness of gender bias in the legal system is in the perpetuation of traditional female gender roles that fail to take into account the realities of women's lives in patriarchal social and legal systems.[9] Consequently, it is important for feminist scholars to move to a point where macro and micro analyses of women's experiences in the legal system are joined together. Finding the intersection is not easy. It will take great effort for feminist legal scholars and lawyers seeking to end gender bias and discrimination to hold onto the conflicting realities within which women live. The law is gendered and corresponds to male characteristics at the expense of females. But to challenge legal discrimination, we must recognize that the law is not monolithic and immutable.

Discussion Questions

1. What is the significance of rape laws when considering gender and the law?
2. Give evidence of gender biasing in the sentencing process.
3. Describe the experience of African-American women in the criminal process and highlight the ways in which their experience differs from that of other criminals, both men and women.

Endnotes

1. The ERA was introduced into the U.S. Congress in 1923 by Alice Paul and was passed by Congress in 1972. However, an amendment to the U.S. Constitution requires ratification by three-fourths (38) of the states. Although Congress extended the deadline for the states to ratify the amendment from 1979 to 1983, proponents were not able to secure the requisite number of states, falling three votes shy of ratification.
2. Smart (1998) indicates that Gilligan's work focuses on females' social-psychological processes. Consequently, according to Smart, this work may be misconstrued as being reductionist as the framework of her study necessarily focuses on the individual.
3. Danner (1996) argues, however, that in societies where there is great inequity between men and women, there is less need to criminalize the behaviors of women because other social forces maintain control over them. In societies with greater equality between the sexes, there is a greater need to resort to the criminal justice system to control women.
4. California Penal Code Annotated Section 261. 5. See *Michael M. v. Superior Court of Sonoma County*, 450 U. S. 464 (1981).
5. Iowa Code Section 698. 1 (1975). See *Navedo v. Preisser*, 630 F. 2d 636 (8th Cir. 1980).
6. Georgia Code Annotated Section 26-2016 (1968, 1970). See *Fluker v. State*, 282 S. E. 2d 112 (1981).
7. McKinney's Penal Law Section 130. 35. See *People v. Liberta*, 474 N. E. 2d 567 (1984).
8. 450 U. S. 464, 473. Some people may be concerned that if a court finds a gender-based criminal statute (e.g. , a traditional rape law) unconstitutional, the crime would be unprosecutable until such time as the state legislature enacted a statute that did not violate the equal protection clause. However, a court could hold that although the Fourteenth Amendment was violated by the gender-based statute, in the interests of justice, the statute is now to be read as including the previously exempted gender. Thus, if the statutory rape law in *Michael M.* was held to violate the equal protection clause, the court could simply hold that the statute is now to be read as applying to the behaviors of both males and females.
9. A full discussion of this point is beyond the scope of this chapter. For an elaboration, see Smart (1998).

References

Angelari, M. 1994. "Hate Crime Statutes: A Promising Tool for Fighting Violence Against Women." *American University Journal of Gender and the Law* 2:63–105.

Armstrong, G. 1980. "Females Under the Law: 'Protected' but Unequal." In B. R. Price and N. J. Sokoloff, eds., *The Criminal Justice System and Women*. New York: Clark Boardman.

Baer, J. A. 1991. *Women in American Law: The Struggle Toward Equality From the New Deal to the Present*. New York: Holmes and Meier.

Belknap, J. 1996. *The Invisible Woman: Gender, Crime and Justice*. Belmont, CA: Wadsworth.

Bernat, F. P. 1984. "Gender Disparity in the Setting of Bail: Prostitution Offenses, New York 1977–1979." *Journal of Offender Services and Rehabilitation* 9:21–47.

——. 1985. "New York State's Prostitution Statute: Case Study of the Discriminatory Application of a Gender-Neutral Law." In C. Schweber and C. Feinman, eds., *Criminal Justice Politics and Women: The Aftermath of Legally Mandated Change*. New York: Haworth.

——. 1992. "Women in the Legal Profession." In I. L. Moyer, ed., *The Changing Roles of Women in the Criminal Justice System*. Prospect Heights, IL: Waveland.

Bortich, H. 1992. "Gender and Criminal Court Outcomes: An Historical Analysis." *Criminology* 30:293–325.

Chesney-Lind, M. 1987. "Female Offenders: Paternalism Reexamined." In L. L. Crites and W. L. Hepperle, eds., *Women, the Courts and Equality*. Newbury Park, CA: Sage.

Chused, R. H. 1990. "Gendered Space." *Florida Law Review* 42:125–161.

CNN Interactive. 1998, February 3. "Texas Executes Tucker for '83 Pickax Murders." Available online at: http://cnn.com/US/9802/03/tucker. execution. 2/omdex. html.

Daly, K. and Maher, L. 1998. "Crossroads and Intersections: Building From Feminist Critique." In K. Daly and L. Maher, eds., *Criminology at the Crossroads: Feminist Readings in Crime and Justice*. New York: Oxford University Press.

Danner, M. J. E. 1996. "Gender Inequality and Criminalization: A Socialist Feminist Perspective on the Legal Social Control of Women." In M. D. Schwartz and D. Milovanovic, eds., *Race, Gender and Class in Criminology: The Intersection*. New York: Garland.

Farrington, D. , and Morris, A. 1983. "Sex, Sentencing and Reconviction." *British Journal of Criminology* 23:229–248.

Finley, L. 1997. "Breaking Women's Silence in Law: The Dilemma of the Gendered Nature of Legal Reasoning." In H. Barnett, ed., *Sourcebook on Feminist Jurisprudence*. London: Cavendish.

Florida Law Review. 1990. "Florida Supreme Court Gender Bias Study, III: Gender Bias in the Criminal Justice System." 42:836–917.

Gelsthorpe, L. 1989. *Sexism and the Female Offender*. Aldershot, England: Gower.

Ghali, M. and Chesney-Lind, M. 1986. "Gender Bias and the Criminal Justice System: An Empirical Investigation." *Sociology and Social Research* 70:164–171.

Gilligan, C. 1982. *In a Different Voice*. London: Harvester.

Higgins, T. E. 1995. " 'By Reason of Their Sex': Feminist Theory, Postmodernism, and Justice." *Cornell Law Review* 80:1536–1594.

Hutton, C., Pommersheim, F., and Feimer, S. 1989. " 'I Fought the Law and the Law Won': A Report on Women and Disparate Sentencing in South Dakota." *Criminal and Civil Confinement* 15:177–220.

Johnson, P. C. 1995. "At the Intersection of Justice: Experiences of African American Women in Crime and Sentencing." *American University Journal of Gender and the Law* 4:1–76.

Julian, F. H. 1993. "Gender and Crime: Different Sex, Different Treatment?" In C. C. Culliver, ed., *Female Criminality: The State of the Art*. New York: Garland.

Kasinsky, R. G. 1993. "Criminalizing of Pregnant Women Drug Abusers." In C. C. Culliver, ed., *Female Criminality: The State of the Art*. New York: Garland.

Klein, D. 1995. "Crime Through Gender's Prism: Feminist Criminology in the United States." In N. H. Rafter and F. Heidensohn, eds., *International Feminist Perspectives in Criminology: Engendering a Discipline*. Buckingham, England: Open University Press.

Kruttschnitt, C. 1982. "Women, Crime and Dependency." *Criminology* 19:495–513.

Loyola of Los Angeles Law Review. 1995. "Demanding Justice Without Truth: The Difficulty of Postmodern Feminist Legal Theory." 28, 1197–1250.

MacKinnon, C. 1987. *Feminism Unmodified.* Cambridge, MA: Harvard University Press.

Morris, A. 1987. *Women, Crime and Criminal Justice.* London: Basil Blackwell.

——. 1988. "Sex and Sentencing." *Criminal Law Review* pp. 162–171.

Nagel, I. 1981. "Sex Differences in the Processing of Criminal Defendants." In A. Morris and L. Gelsthorpe, eds., *Women and Crime.* Cambridge: Cambridge Institute of Criminology.

Nagel, I., Cardascia, J., and Ross, C. E. 1982. "Sex Differences in the Processing of Criminal Defendants." In D K. Wesiberg, ed., *Women and the Law: A Social Historical Perspective,* Vol. I. Cambridge, MA: Schenkman.

Notes. 1989. "Court-Ordered Confinement of Pregnant Women." *Criminal and Civil Confinement* 15, 203–223.

Pendo, E. 1994. "Recognizing Violence Against Women: Gender and Hate Crimes Statistics Act." *Harvard Women's Law Journal* 17:157–183.

Pruitt, L. 1994. "A Survey of Feminist Jurisprudence." *University of Arkansas at Little Rock Law Journal* 16:183–210.

Rice, M. 1990. "Challenging Orthodoxies in Feminist Theory: A Black Feminist Critique." In L. Gelsthorpe and A. Morris, eds., *Feminist Perspectives in Criminology.* Buckingham, England: Open University Press.

Scales, A. C. 1995. "The Emergence of Feminist Jurisprudence: An Essay." *Yale Law Journal* 95: 1373–1403.

Schneider, E. M., Finley, L., Clauss, C., and Bertin, J. 1991. " 'Feminist Jurisprudence': The 1990 Myra Bradwell Day Panel." *Columbia Journal of Gender and the Law* 1:5–46.

Searles, P., and Berger, R. 1987. "The Current Status of Rape Reform Legislation: An Examination of State Statutes." Women's *Rights Law Reporter* 10:25–43.

Siegel, M. 1993, September/October. "A Practitioner's Guide to Feminist Jurisprudence." *Boston Bar Journal,* pp. 6ff.

Smart, C. 1989. *Feminism and the Power of Law.* London: Routledge.

——. 1998. "The Woman of Legal Discourse." In K. Daly and L. Maher, eds., *Criminology at the Crossroads: Feminist Readings in Crime and Justice.* New York: Oxford University Press.

Streib, V. L. 1990. "Death Penalty for Female Offenders." *Cincinnati Law Review* 58, 845–880.

Tripodi II, P. D. 1991. "Achieving Equal Justice for Women in the Courts." *UCLA Women's Law Journal* 1, 209–220.

Wikler, N. J. and Schafran, L. H. 1991. "Learning From the New Jersey Supreme Court Task Force on Women in the Courts: Evaluation, Recommendations and Implications for Other States." *Women's Rights Law Reporter* 12:313–385.

Women's Rights Law Reporter. 1986. "The First Year Report of the New Jersey Supreme Court Task Force on Women in the Courts—June 1984." 9:129–177. ✦

15
Women, Race, and Criminal Justice Processing

Evelyn Gilbert

While discrimination has been postulated as a crucial factor in the overrepresentation of racial minorities in the criminal justice system, the evidence for and against this assertion has focused primarily on males, not females. The focus of this inquiry is whether women are differentially processed based on race. Despite the increasing number of women processed in the criminal justice system, it appears that women of color are more likely to undergo formal processing. Available data and published work suggest a rethinking of theoretical perspectives premised on a homogeneous gender category explanatory of all women offenders.

Our knowledge of women in the criminal justice system has grown steadily since the 1960s. Although the system still processes more male than female offenders, the victimization of women, inside and outside of the home, has been elevated to a criminal justice issue. Similarly, explanations about the criminality of women have advanced beyond biological archetypes—women offenders as diminutive masculinities is a *passe* ideology. Similarly, descriptions of screening out of women are no longer recitations of beliefs about the place of women in society. Women in prison are characteristically single parents who have experienced abuse at the hands of a partner, which emphasizes that violence against women is not solely a domestic or familial issue.

Despite the emergent body of work on women in the criminal justice system, the public perception of female offenders (which is often reflected in the response of prosecutors, judges, and juries) still relies on narrowly defined appropriate behavior for women. Events of recent years are indicative. The War on Drugs, mandatory sentences, and sentencing guidelines have cast a wide net that is not blind to gender.

The number of women processed in the criminal justice system has been increasing. Data from the U.S. Bureau of Justice Statistics (1994) show a 75 percent increase between 1986 and 1991. Whether this increase has negated the stereotypes[1] of women that advantaged them in the criminal justice system is not known. These stereotypes have been used to explain the justice system's reluctance to exact the full weight of the law on women offenders or to deny the victimization of women.[2] However, these stereotypes do not incorporate the racial factor.[3] Among women who were federal prisoners in 1997, whites numbered 3,665 and blacks numbered 2,466.

Although women offenders are no longer "invisible" in the criminal justice system, diversity among women and its impact on processing is obscured. There has been no argument among theorists and researchers that class and race are important risk factors in being processed in the criminal justice system. Among women, disparate backgrounds, lifestyles, experiences, and opportunities may translate into differential processing of offenders (Morris 1987). The question for criminologists, professionals, and theorists is what role differential treatment in criminal justice processing plays in the high crime figures of African-American women. Some feel that it has been firmly established that disparate processing plays a minuscule role in the overrepresentation of racial minorities in the criminal justice system. Others suggest that racial and discriminatory bias are the factors contributing to the disproportionate involvement of racial/ethnic minorities in the criminal justice system.

The discussion that follows examines research on women offenders from time of arrest to sentencing. The findings are explored for indications of differential processing based on race. At each stage of processing under review, questions are put forward whose answers have implications for racial bias. Finally, theoretical and practical implications of ignoring racial bias among a group already disadvantaged in the criminal justice system are probed.

Extent and Nature of Female Offending

In 1996 women represented 21 percent of all arrests; a 3 percent increase over 1995 and the same amount of increase over 1986 (U.S. Bureau of Justice Statistics 1997). These arrests were not limited to urban areas; the pattern was repeated in suburban and rural areas. The main offenses that brought women into the criminal justice system were arrest for larceny-theft, simple assaults, drug violations, DUI, fraud, and disorderly conduct. Among these crimes, arrests for larceny-theft and drug violations showed the smallest increase over 1995 (less than 1 percent). Drug use among the women arrested was more common than not, with cocaine more widespread than either marijuana or opiates. Interestingly, white women were more likely to test positive for drug use than black women. Black women were more likely to test positive for marijuana; white women were more likely to test positive for opiates; and both black and white women were equally likely to test positive for cocaine use.

The increase in arrests of women seems to have stabilized during the last decade. The dynamics occur after arrest. In 1996 and 1997, women made up 10 percent of all jail inmates. The offenses of women jail inmates were somewhat different from those of arrestees: property (larceny-theft and fraud), drug, public order (obstruction of justice, drunkenness, and DUI), and violent (assault) offenses. More specifically, women were more likely than men to be in jail for drug,

fraud, and theft offenses, and whites were half as likely as blacks to be in jail for drug offenses.

Conviction offenses for women are very instructive. In the 10-year period ending in 1995, felony convictions for violent crimes dropped by three-fourths. During the same period of time, property convictions decreased by half but jumped in 1995 resulting in a 3 percent overall increase. As for drug offenses, convictions increased by 21 percent at the midpoint of the 10-year period, but a 16 percent decline followed, resulting in a 4 percent increase for the entire period.

While women remain primarily property offenders, they are quickly becoming identified as drug offenders. The sharpest decline in convictions for violent crimes (24 percent) occurred between 1991 and 1994; for property crimes between 1986 and 1991 (13 percent); and for drug offenses between 1991 and 1994 (16 percent). However, huge increases in convictions for property crimes (24 percent) occurred during a one-year period (1994–1995). In 1994, women made up 15 percent of felony offenders convicted in state courts (US. Department of Justice 1997), with most convictions being for property offenses, followed by drug offenses. The period between 1986 and 1991 registered the largest increase in drug convictions. This extraordinary activity in the processing of property and drug offenses is no doubt due to sentencing guidelines. It appears that the sharp increases and decreases in convictions represented transition, adjustment, and correction phases brought on by the implementation of mandatory and sentencing guidelines.

Correctional supervision of women again reveals a willingness to process women. In 1995, women made up 26 percent of all adults on probation under federal jurisdiction and 16 percent under state jurisdiction. For parole, the comparable numbers are 14 percent and 9 percent. They were on probation for property offenses (43 percent), public order offenses (27 percent), and drug offenses (20 percent). The practices in federal jurisdictions are instructive. In 1997, 71 percent of women committed to federal prisons were there for drug offenses. While whites make up the largest group of women in federal prisons (58 percent versus 39 percent for African Americans), African Americans constitute the largest group of women in federal prisons for drug offenses (see Table 15.1). Although these numbers do not necessarily reflect a change in the criminality of women, the racial composition of imprisoned women may reflect prosecutorial and judicial disparate views of the female stereotype.

Table 15.1
1997 Commitment Offenses of Females Federal Inmates by Percent

	Violent	Property	Drug
White	1.4%	5.7%	68.1%
Black	1.3	5.3	73.2

Preadjudication Processing

The police represent the first point of the criminal justice system at which differential processing may occur. Having wide latitude in the performance of law enforcement duties, police may exercise discretion in such a way that more minorities enter the criminal justice system. For African Americans, the prevailing evidence suggests that police rely less on gender in deciding to arrest and more on legal and situational factors, community standards, and agency policies (Klein and Kress 1986; Young 1986; Patterson and Lynch 1991). However, reliance on community values and attitudes is problematic because the police are not usually part of the community (notwithstanding community-oriented policing) in which they enforce the law. Gangs and drug-related activities in poverty-stricken urban areas make them areas high in violence, as well as undesirable patrol assignments for officers. The street crime witnessed by police officers may con-firm stereotypes of African-American involvement in criminal activity.

There is reason to believe that police manipulation of arrest charges adversely affects African Americans. Bail is one area that is prone to manipulation. A study examining whether police comply with or deviate from the bail schedule demonstrates manipulation that adversely affects African Americans. Patterson and Lynch (1991) found that bail amounts tended to be excessive for both white and black women. However, white females were more likely to receive less bail than that provided for by the bail guidelines, a benefit not afforded African-American women. According to Patterson and Lynch, reduced bail for white females demonstrates bias in the early stages of criminal justice processing, at the hands of police.

When processing moves from police to judges, gender and race interact with nonlegal and legal factors to produce outcomes that resemble racial effects. Katz and Spohn (1995) found that the pecking order of release prior to trial is white females, black females, and white males. They observed that African-American women charged with assault were more likely to be released than black men charged with less serious crimes. The higher incidence of pretrial release for black women (second only to white women) is because of lower bail imposed by the judge. Katz and Spohn conclude that economics, not race, accounts for pretrial release decisions. Daly's (1989) two-city study of pretrial release is more definitive in attributing race effects. Daly found nonlegal factors placed African-American women at an advantage. Being married and having dependents were factors that increased the likelihood of being released prior to trial. Daly specifically found that in New York married African-American women, with or without dependents, were more likely to be released; in Seattle, having a dependent was more advantageous for African-American women.

While family responsibilities appear to be an important nonlegal factor in processing decisions, some factors (dependents under the age of 18, residing with dependents, two-parent household) appear to be more predictive of how African-American women are processed. Rather than a unidimensional demographic characteristic, family responsibilities represent a complexity of factors. To adequately assess how much this demographic factor contributes to disparate pretrial release decisions, different combinations of family factors must be examined.

The importance of release pending further processing is well known. A favorable disposition is more likely to result from pretrial release of the accused. Many decisions are made prior to adjudication that may adversely affect racial minorities. Formal charging is a critical stage and may strengthen the decisions made by police at the beginning of criminal justice processing. Pleading is another important decision stage that may have detrimental outcomes for racial minorities. These and other decision stages are examined in the next section.

Disposition

The discretion exercised by prosecutors is, by and large, unchecked in determining charges. The prosecutor alone decides whether to dismiss, *nolle prosequi*, or accept a case. If the decision is to proceed with a case, the outcome sought is a guilty plea. No doubt, pleading opportunities are equally available to whites and racial minorities. In overcharging, however, prosecutors build in leverage to coax defendants to plead guilty. Overcharging is usually in the form of multiple charges. The carrot held out by the prosecutor is reduced charges or a favorable sentencing recommendation to the court or both. Farnworth and Teske (1995) found that African-American males, but not African-American females, were less likely than whites or Hispanics to receive charge reductions. When these researchers compared women charged with assault, they discovered that "white females were about twice as likely as minority

females to have assault charges at arrest changed to nonassault charges at final sentencing" (p. 38). Farnworth, Teske, and Thurman (1991) reported both gender and racial differences in charge reduction. Female defendants received reduced charges more often than male defendants. Among women, whites were more likely to receive reduced charges, while blacks had a greater chance of receiving probation. They found evidence that African Americans had their charges reduced less often than whites

When defendants cannot make bail, they may feel pressured to accept a plea bargain offered by the prosecutor. Spohn and Cederblom (1991) found that pretrial detention increased the chance of incarceration and that African Americans were more likely than whites to be detained prior to trial. So, even with weak cases, prosecutors may induce defendants with inadequate economic resources to plead guilty. For some defendants, release from detention at any cost is preferable to the uncertainty of the outcome of a trial (jury or bench). The reward for pleading guilty is a less severe sentence. The tendency, however, is for blacks to be tried by a jury, with a prison term and long sentence (Spohn and Cederblom 1991). In the Farnworth and Teske (1995) study, female offenders with no charge reduction tended to be sentenced to jail or probation; those with charges reduced to misdemeanors received probation. Drawing on the female stereotype of women who deviate, lenient outcomes such as probation or jail sentences are to be expected.

An important aspect of the prosecuter's charging and sentencing decisions is the impact of mandatory minimum sentences and drug prohibition laws. In drug-related cases, African-American defendants are less likely than white defendants to plea bargain (U.S. Sentencing Commission 1991). What this means is "no plea, no sentence reduction." At the state level, the pattern is not clearly discernible. Zatz's (1984) examination of determinate sentencing revealed no racial effect. Rather, the evidence is that the type of plea is predictive of short sentences. Of the types of pleas examined (no contest, guilty, change to plea of guilty), African Americans pleading no contest received the shortest sentences. One would expect that offenders with prior histories would be adept at the "pleading game" but that first-time offenders would be at the mercy of the prosecution. There is much to be learned by exploring racial patterns of pleading among women.

Given the prominent role of the prosecutor in deciding charges, accepting pleas, and recommending sentences, the judge's role has been virtually neutralized under mandatory minimum sentences. Before their introduction, sentencing guidelines gave judges much more discretion in fashioning a sentence. The judge makes two decisions: how long the sentence should be and whether or not to imprison. Judges customarily consider legal factors such as conviction offense and prior record to lengthen sentences, and they look to offender characteristics to shorten sentences (Keil and Vito 1989; Unnever and Hembroff 1987). Some offender characteristics that may contribute to longer sentences, include urban residence, unemployment, and receipt of public assistance, but race is the most studied characteristic.

Research in this area shows that race interacts with prior record to disadvantage African Americans. Welch et al. (1984) studied various measures of prior record to determine whether a race effect existed. Their measures of prior record included felony conviction, imprisonment, number of prison terms, incarceration for more than one year, and number of felony convictions. They found that African Americans with a prior history were more likely than whites to receive a harsh sentence and to be sent to prison. Specifically, a harsh sentence was related to a prior record consisting of multiple felony convictions and multiple prison terms, while incarceration was associated with any prior imprisonment.

Early studies reported gender effects on imprisonment (Frazier, Block, and Henrietta 1983; Gruhl et al. 1984; Spohn, Gruhl, and Welch 1985; Myers and Talarico 1986; Daly 1987; Johnston, Kennedy, and Shuman 1987). More recently, Farnworth and Teske (1995) found that females were more likely than males to be sentenced leniently: less chance of incarceration and less chance of a jail sentence with no prior record. Moreover, probation was more often given to females than to males. Comparisons of women with no prior records reveal lenient sentences. As reported by Farnworth et al. (1991), black women were more likely than white women to be sentenced to probation. Incarceration is a more severe penalty and in recent years has become more characteristic of female sentences.

Spohn and Cederblom (1991) reported that judges had a tendency to use nonlegal factors in the decision to incarcerate African Americans convicted of less serious offenses. In their examination of the racial effect on sentencing, the crimes of robbery, assault, murder, and rape were ranked according to seriousness: absence of a gun, victim injury, victim/offender acquaintance, and prior violent crime conviction. Race was found to be a significant predictor of incarceration. African Americans with no prior record had a greater chance of incarceration for a nongun assault or robbery of an acquaintance (less serious crimes) than those convicted of a more serious assault (gun used, victim was a stranger) or whites who robbed acquaintances. As expected, blacks were more likely to be sent to prison for the more serious crime of rape of a stranger.

The intraracial character of most crimes committed by African Americans is another complex issue that warrants further attention. The leniency afforded offenders in black-on-black crimes may be explained by color (Mann 1993). Additional study is warranted to determine what aspect of race is predictive of differential processing of interracial versus intraracial crimes.

Similarly, early research provided evidence that race and gender interact to produce bias in sentencing for African-American women (Foley and Rasche 1979; Klein and Kress 1976; Kruttschnitt 1980–81). More recent studies support the early work. When Steffensmeier et al. (1993) compared the sentences of black and white women they found harsher treatment of black offenders. The average prison sentence for white defendants was three months less than that of black defendants. The race and gender interaction effects parallel that of race effects. Race appears to be more indicative of type of sentence rather than length of sentence. Kramer and Steffensmeier (1993) observed that the imposition of sentences that depart from statutory requirements generally favored white defendants. The departure sentence was usually probation; black defendants were sentenced to jail or prison. Prior record and offense seriousness were found to be more important than race in determining length of sentence and type of sentence.

The nature of prior history should be examined further to pinpoint the specific offenses that may contribute to less harsh sentences. For women, the examination must begin with "traditional" crimes such as prostitution, theft, and fraud. There is reason to believe that African-American and white women are different in that the prior history of African Americans is more likely to consist of theft and fraud crimes. While the crimes are "traditional" female crimes, the female stereotype may not be equally attached to the crimes.

Such selective imaging ignores the different life chances of African-American women. Poverty, abuse, and limited economic opportunities shape the lives of most female offenders, making them marginal in society. However, African-American women also suffer intraracial gender oppression and class oppression. These additional burdens acknowledge their marginality in society but mask their marginality among women offenders. The impact of multiple marginalities is succinctly described by Belknap (1996): "As a rule, women of color, poor women, and

younger women are afforded less leniency than other females" (p. 174).

Implications for Differential Processing

The United States has historically had a disproportionate number of African Americans in its prisons (Binkley-Jackson, Carter, and Rolinson 1993; Free 1996; French 1983; Mann 1993; Sari 1987). According to Mauer (1995), African-American women have experienced the greatest increase in criminal justice involvement of all demographic groups, with their rate of criminal justice control rising 78 percent from 1989 to 1994. This disparity continues today and is more pronounced when the conviction offense is drug related (Mauer and Huling 1995). The increasing incarceration of drug law violators has a disproportionate effect on women, African Americans, and Hispanics. In the federal system, drug law violators serve average sentences of three to five years. The long sentences are prescribed by the sentencing guidelines and mandatory minimum sentences that took effect in the mid-1980s and the early part of the 1990s. The gender benefit-of-the-doubt in sentencing is not apparent, given the number of women sentenced for drug-related crimes. Perhaps there is a gender benefit, but it is for whites only. According to Temin (1976), judges reserve the harshest sentences for women who commit masculine-type offenses—crimes that are serious and depart greatly from traditional female gender-role expectations. Because more African-American women in prison have drug-related convictions, it may be argued that judges' sentences are punitive and not paternal, as in the case of white women (Klein and Kress 1976).

Twenty-five years ago the differential processing of African-American women was attributed to their criminality. That is, the crimes they committed were more similar to those of men than those of women (Adler

1975). Fifteen years ago, we discovered that the crimes committed by African-American women were similar to those committed by white women (Young 1986). In the past, the female stereotype of offenders permitted the characterization of women as less dangerous and the practice of fewer arrests and incarceration for less serious offenses (Muraskin and Alleman 1993; Pollock 1997). The conviction crimes of women today sustain the historical characterizations and practices when the offender is not a person of color.

The evidence on disparate processing of women of color is not clear. What exists, however, cautions that race-gender interaction depicted by enumerations of arrestees, convictions, and prisoners limits our knowledge. The race-gender interaction has complex dimensions that must be explored to fully account for statistical evidence showing similarities in the crimes of white and black women but disparities in the way they are processed. On the basis of current statistical findings, differential discretion resulting in disparity occurs at formal and informal decision points. First, the crime charged by police is likely to reflect disparity based on gender-race interaction. Overpolicing and excessive surveillance in African-American neighborhoods leads to increased police-citizen contacts that result in arrest. Aggressive patrol practices coupled with departmental policies emphasizing proactive policing and drug prohibition law enforcement strategies result in large numbers of arrests for crimes feared most by the public. Gender is not a mitigation for African Americans.

A second decision point is bail. Whether arrestees can avail themselves of departures from bail limits depends upon the economic resources they have at their disposal. In the case of poor women, differential treatment is evident because even reasonable bail may not be an assurance that the arrestee will be released prior to further processing. The decision points under the control of the prosecutor begin with bail determination and continue to sentence determination.

Prosecutorial charging is a third decision point. Plea negotiations offer opportunities for differential treatment. Low-level offenders are at greater risk of prosecutorial excess and abuse of discretion. In drug-related cases, prosecutors offer lenient charges and sentences to induce offender cooperation in identifying persons higher up in the drug trade. Users, lookouts, and street-level dealers with no useful information are at a distinct disadvantage in bargaining for reduced charges. Persons who are mere users have no advantage in bargaining.

Conviction offense is the fourth decision point that may yield differential gender disparity by race. Drug convictions are problematic. Under the federal system, incarceration sentences are 80 percent longer for trafficking offenders than for possession offenders. While the number of women incarcerated for drug-related crimes has increased for both whites and African Americans, careful attention should be paid to the type of conviction offense. Police effect drug-related arrests of African Americans through saturation at the street level. Trafficking is characteristically not a street-level enterprise. Therefore, one would expect, absent racial bias, that whites would serve the longer sentences. However, the crack/powder cocaine anomaly under federal sentencing sends many street-level offenders to prison. African Americans "use crack" and are more likely to be prosecuted for crack offenses. The mandatory minimums are triggered for five grams of crack and 500 grams of powder. Since convictions will continue under the mandatory minimums into the foreseeable future,[4] attention should focus on the gap in time served between racial minorities and whites.

The sentence is an important decision point. There is every reason to believe that judge-and-jury imposed sentences (notwithstanding guidelines and mandatory sentences) are sources of gender-race disparity. Whether the most important considerations are formal or informal remains to be determined.

Discussion Questions

1. What recent changes in the law have contributed to increased numbers of women in prison?
2. Identify formal and informal decision points in criminal justice processing.
3. Are traditional female stereotypes applicable to African-American women? Explain.
4. At what decision point in criminal justice processing are African-American women at the greatest disadvantage?

Endnotes

1. Rafter and Stanko (1982) proposed a typology consisting of five images of women. These images represented deviations from the "natural" role of women: women as the pawn of biology; women as impulsive and nonanalytical; women as passive and weak; women as impressionable and in need of protection; active women as masculine; and criminal women as purely evil.
2. Society's image of women as shallow is represented by Feinman's (1986) typology: madonna or whore.
3. Young (1986) offers a different typology for African-American women that connotes society's perception that they are not deserving of consideration: Amazon, sinister sapphire, mammy, and seductress.
4. In 1995 Congress chose not to legislatively reduce the disparity in penalties for crack cocaine and powder cocaine. ✦

References

Adler, F. 1975. *Sisters in Crime: The Rise of the New Female Criminal*. New York: McGraw Hill.

Belknap, J. 1996. *The Invisible Woman: Gender, Crime, and Justice*. Belmont, CA: Wadsworth Publishing.

Binkley-Jackson, D., Carter, V. L., and Rolison, G. L. 1993. "African-American Women in Prison." In B. R. Fletcher, L. D. Shaver, and D. B. Moon, eds., *Women Prisoners: A Forgotten Population*. Westport, CT: Praeger.

Daly, K. 1987. "Discrimination in the Criminal Courts: Family, Gender, and the Problem of Equal Treatment." *Social Forces* 66:152–75.

———. 1989. "Neither Conflict nor Labeling nor Paternalism Will Suffice: Interactions of Race, Ethnicity, Gender, and Family in Criminal Court Decisions." *Crime & Delinquency* 35: 136–168.

Farnworth, M. and Teske, R. 1995. "Gender Differences in Felony Court Processing: Three Hypotheses of Disparity." *Women & Criminal Justice* 6:23–44.

Farnworth, M., Teske, R., and Thurman, G. 1991. "Ethnic Racial, and Minority Disparity in Felony Court Processing." In M Lynch and E. Paterson, eds., *Race and Criminal Justice*. New York: Harrow and Heston.

Feinman, C. 1986. *Women in the Criminal Justice System*, 2nd ed. New York: Praeger.

Foley, L. and Rasche, C. 1979. "The Effect of Race on Sentence: Actual Time Served and Final Disposition." In John Conley, ed., *Theory and Research in Criminal Justice: Current Perspectives*. Cincinnati: Anderson Publishing.

Frazier, C., Block, E., and Henrietta, J. 1983. "The Role of Probation Officers in Determining Gender Differences in Sentencing Severity." *Sociological Quarterly* 24:305–318.

Free, M. D. 1996. *African Americans and the Criminal Justice System*. New York: Garland Press.

French, L. 1983. "A Profile of the Incarcerated Black Female Offender." *Prison Journal* 63: 80–87.

Gruhl, J., Welch, S., and Spohn, C. 1984. "Women as Criminal Defendants: A Test for Paternalism." *Western Political Quarterly* 37:456–467.

Johnston, J., Kennedy, T., and Shuman, I. G. 1987. "Gender Differences in the Sentencing of Felony Offenders." *Federal Probation* 51:49–55.

Katz, C. and Spohn, C. 1995. "The Effect of Race and Gender on Bail Outcomes: A Test of an Interactive Model," *American Journal of Criminal Justice* 19:161–184.

Keil, T. and Vito, G. 1989. "Race, Homicide Severity, and Application of the Death Penalty: A Consideration of the Barnett Scale," *Criminology* 27:511–31.

Klein, D. and Kress, J. 1976. "Any Woman's Blues." *Crime and Social Justice* 5:34–49.

Kramer, J. and Steffensmeier, D. 1993. "Race and Imprisonment Decisions," *Sociological Quarterly* 34:357–376.

Kruttschnitt, C. 1980–81. "Social Status and Sentences of Female Offenders." *Law and Society Review* 15:247–265.

Mann, C. 1993. *Unequal Justice: A Question of Color.* Bloomington, IN: Indiana University Press.

Mauer, M. 1995, October 16. "Disparate Justice Imperils a Community," *Legal Times.*

Mauer, M. and Huling, T. 1995. *Young Black Americans and the Criminal Justice System.* Washington, DC: The Sentencing Project.

Morris, A. 1987. *Women, Crime, and Criminal Justice.* Oxford: Basil Blackwell.

Muraskin, R. and Alleman, T. 1993. *It's a Crime: Women and Justice.* Englewood Cliffs, NJ: Regents-Prentice Hall.

Myers, M. and Talarico, S. 1986. "The Social Contexts of Racial Discrimination in Sentencing." *Social Problems* 33:236–51.

Patterson, E. and Lynch, M. 1991. "Bias in Formalized Bail Procedures." In M. Lynch and E. Paterson, eds., *Race and Criminal Justice.* New York: Harrow and Heston.

Pollock, J. 1997. *Prisons: Today and Tomorrow.* Gaithersburg, MD: Aspen Publishers

Rafter, N. and Stanko, E. 1982. "Introduction." In Nicole Rafter and E. Stanko, eds., *Judge, Lawyer, Victim, Thief: Women, Gender Roles and Criminal Justice.* Stoughton, MA: Northeastern University Press.

Sari, R. 1987. "Unequal Protection Under the Law: Women and the Criminal Justice System." In J. Figueira-McDonouth and R. Sari, eds., *The Trapped Woman: Catch 22 in Deviance and Control.* Newbury Park, CA: Sage.

Spohn, C. and Cederblom, J. 1991. "Race and Disparities in Sentencing: A Test of the Liberation Hypothesis," *Justice Quarterly* 8:305–327

Spohn, C., Gruhl, J., and Welch, S. 1985. "Women Defendants in Court: The Interaction Between Sex and Race in Convicting and Sentencing." *Social Science Quarterly* 66:178–85.

Steffensmeier, D., Kramer, J., and Streifel, C. 1993. "Gender and Imprisonment Decisions." *Criminology* 31:411–446.

Temin, C. 1976. "Discriminatory Sentencing of Women Offenders: The Argument for ERA in a Nutshell." In Laura Crites, ed., *The Female Offenders.* Beverly Hills, CA: Sage.

Unnever, J. and Hembroff, L. 1987. "The Prediction of Racial/Ethnic Sentencing Disparities: An Expectation States Approach," *Crime and Delinquency* 25:53–82.

U.S. Bureau of Justice Statistics. January 1994. *Violence Against Women: A National Crime Victimization Survey Report.* Washington, DC: U.S. Department of Justice.

——. 1995. *National Crime Victimization Survey.* Washington, DC: U.S. Department of Justice.

——. 1997. *Prison and Jail Inmates at Midyear 1996.* Washington, DC: U.S. Department of Justice.

——. 1997. *Compendium of Federal Justice Statistics, 1994.* Washington, DC: U.S. Department of Justice.

——. 1998. *Compendium of Federal Justice Statistics, 1995.* Washington, DC: U.S. Department of Justice.

U.S. Bureau of Justice Statistics Executive Summary. 1998. *Felony Defendants in Large Urban Counties, 1994.* Washington, DC: U.S. Department of Justice.

U.S. Bureau of Justice Statistics Special Report. 1994. *Survey of State Prison Inmates, 1991: Women in Prison.* Washington, DC: U.S. Department of Justice

——. 1997. *Characteristics of Adults on Probation, 1995.* Washington, DC: U.S. Department of Justice.

——. 1998. *Profile of Jail Inmates 1996.* Washington, DC: U.S. Department of Justice.

U.S. Department of Justice. 1997. *Sourcebook of Criminal Justice Statistics.* Washington DC: Author.

U.S. Sentencing Commission. 1991. *Federal Sentencing Guidelines: A Report on the Operation of the Guidelines System and Short-Term Impacts on Disparity of Sentencing, Use of Incarceration and Prosecutorial Discretion and Plea Bargaining.* Washington, DC: Author.

Welch, S., Gruhl, J., and Spohn, C. 1984. "Sentencing—The Influence of Alternative Measures of Prior Record." *Criminology* 22:215–227.

Young, V. 1986. "Gender Expectations and Their Impact on Black Female Offenders and Victims." *Justice Quarterly* 3:305–327.

Zatz, M. 1984. "Race, Ethnicity, and Determinate Sentencing." *Criminology* 22:147–171. ✦

16
When Victims Become Defendants: Battered Women Charged With Crimes

Sue Osthoff

This chapter examines what happens in court to battered women charged with crimes, including the murder of their abusive partners. Starting with a discussion of several stereotypes and myths about battered women in general—including the stereotypical "real battered woman"—and, in particular, battered women who kill, the chapter analyzes how these popular misconceptions (commonly held by the general public, judges, prosecutors, and even defense attorneys) may be used against battered women charged with crimes and how they impact on the women's legal defense. It concludes by discussing the important legal issues of the use of the battered woman syndrome in court, drawing attention to the fact that there is no "battered woman's defense."

What happens to a battered woman who, after years of mental and physical abuse, kills or assaults her abusive partner? Or to a battered woman who is coerced into crime or is unable to protect her children from her batterer? The fact is that the same criminal justice system that often ignored her pleas for assistance now vigorously prosecutes her as a criminal. Even today, she faces monumental obstacles that make it difficult for her to receive services or get a strong legal defense at her trial. Despite increasing public discourse during the last 10 years about domestic violence issues generally and battered women charged with crimes specifically, there continue to be many misunderstandings and misconceptions about battered women defendants and about their legal defenses. These misconceptions—held by many defense attorneys, judges, expert witnesses, advocates, and jurors and exploited by many prosecutors—get in the way of women receiving the support they need and the appropriate legal defenses.

Many attorneys do not understand how best to defend battered women defendants and how to use expert witnesses appropriately. Experts themselves often use outdated concepts when discussing the experiences of battered women and undermine their own effectiveness in cases involving battered women. Yet, as we embark on a new century, battered women charged with crimes continue to face many difficulties, and even some new problems they did not necessarily face earlier.

When Battered Women Kill

The book *The Burning Bed* told the story of Francine Hughes, a Michigan woman who was severely battered and who eventually killed her abuser by setting his bed on fire while he slept (McNulty 1980). It was made into a television movie that aired for the first time in 1984 and featured Farrah Fawcett as Francine. In the movie, Francine does everything "right," but despite her heroic efforts to escape her abuser, she cannot. Eventually, she packs her kids into the car, pours gasoline over her sleeping husband and his bed, sets the bed on fire, and drives away with her children. The movie ends with Francine being found not guilty in the death of her husband.[1]

Although this movie was instrumental in bringing the issue of domestic violence into households across the country, it also helped create certain key stereotypes about battered women who kill. Based in part on this movie, many people concluded that when battered women kill, they go to court, tell their story, and are acquitted and that when battered women kill they do so when their partners are sleeping or when there is a lull in the violence. Others concluded that battered women simply "cannot take it" any longer or "simply snap" and then go and kill the man as he sleeps.

Francine Hughes' situation was not typical in many respects. She was acquitted, which, as we will discuss shortly, is unusual.[2] She also killed her abuser while he was passed out. It is true that some battered women do kill their abusers while they are asleep or passed out, or during some other lull in the violence. And some women do hire someone or ask others to hurt or kill their abusers. But most battered women kill their abusers during an ongoing confrontation (Browne 1987; Maguigan 1991). Most typically, battered women kill when their abusers are attacking them; they kill when they think that they (or their children) are going to die. In other words, battered women tend to kill their abusers in situations "that would entitle a defendant to a self-defense instruction under the law of most jurisdictions" (Maguigan 1991, 382).

Domestic violence can be deadly. Each year, approximately 1,500 women are killed by their male partners and approximately 860 men are killed by their female partners (Federal Bureau of Investigation 1993). Of these homicides, approximately two-thirds are men killing their female partners and one-third are women killing their male partners (Browne and Williams 1990).

When a battered woman kills her abuser, many people continue to believe that, in the typical scenario, the woman gets up on the stand, tells the jurors she's been beaten, cries a few tears, and gets acquitted. However, the vast majority of battered women who kill their abusers are convicted or take a plea. Studies indicate that 70 to 80 percent of battered women charged with killing their abusers are found guilty or plead guilty to some charge; this means that only 20 to 30 percent are found not guilty (Browne 1987; Ewing

1987; U.S. Bureau of Justice Statistics 1995). When battered women are acquitted, their cases often make the news; unfortunately, they are newsworthy because acquittals in these cases happen so infrequently.

It has been difficult to get accurate information about the lengths of sentences for convicted battered women because so many of these women are not identified as being battered (nor, until recent years, have these statistics been tracked). What we do know, based on years of work with incarcerated battered women, is that our country's jails and prisons are filled with battered women. Many are serving very long prison sentences.[3]

Although this chapter focuses on battered women who kill, it is important to remember that battered women get arrested for a wide array of crimes. In some situations, battered women are forced by their batterers to commit crimes. In these situations the batterer threatens to do, or actually does, violence to a woman and/or her children if she fails to comply with his wishes, including performing criminal acts (e.g., passing bad checks, driving the getaway car, selling drugs for him). Battered women also get arrested when their children are hurt or killed by their abuser. In these cases, a woman is charged with a crime based on her "failure to protect" her children. The abuser does the actual violence to the child and typically the woman "fails" to intervene or "fails" to get assistance after the child is hurt or killed. Other battered women get charged with parental kidnapping when they flee from their abusers and take their children with them, usually because the children are being physically or sexually abused by the batterer.

Myths, Stereotypes, and Misconceptions: Problems for Battered Women Charged With Crimes

While public discourse about battered women charged with crimes has increased during the last ten years, the persistence of misunderstandings and misconceptions about battered women in general, and specifically about battered women defendants and their legal defenses, causes serious problems for battered women. These mistaken beliefs come into the courtroom because they are held, to a lesser or greater extent, by all the "actors" in a legal case: judges, defense attorneys, prosecutors, and jurors—all of whom bring their own biases and beliefs into any trial. These myths and misconceptions can impair a defense attorney's ability to properly defend a battered woman client and are often exploited by a prosecutor at trial.

To make matters even more difficult, there is no one concrete set of stereotypes to which all people ascribe. Often people have accumulated a mixture of beliefs about battered women and their legal defenses, some based on fact and others not. Obviously, if the myths and misconceptions are not countered during the trial—which they often are not—the situation can be very problematic for the woman facing the charges.

These myths, misconceptions, and stereotypes are often used against battered women defendants at trial despite the fact that they usually have little *direct* bearing on the legal issues at hand. The beliefs about battered women are communicated subtly *and* openly, deliberately *and* unconsciously, via innuendo, an attitude, the physical stance or the tone of voice of a defense attorney, prosecutor, judge, or witness, and they tend to draw the jury's attention to moral or social questions rather than legal ones.

For example, as we will discuss shortly in greater detail, one of the most common myths is that battered women can—and should—leave their abusers. Does a woman lose her right to act in self-defense because she has been beaten in the past? Legally speaking, of course not. But what happens when jurors believe the defendant *should* have left her abuser? Her moral right to self-defense is diminished in their eyes; jurors often feel it is the battered woman's fault that the incident happened—that by staying with the batterer

she assumed the risk of further abuse. The thinking goes, "She knew what was coming and chose to stay. Who cares if during the incident she thought she was going to die? She was morally wrong for staying."

Sometimes, to discredit the defendant herself and her legal defense, the prosecutor will introduce a method of reasoning that deliberately exploits these myths and encourages moral judgments about the woman. The prosecutor will encourage the jurors to ask themselves a set of questions about the woman: Can we really believe this woman was abused? After all, she doesn't seem like a "real battered woman." She never called the police, did she? (Or, she called 15 times, but never followed through and pressed charges.) She never went to a battered woman's program, did she? (Or, she went to a program and went back home to him; the abuse couldn't have been that bad.) Even if we believe she was beaten, didn't she really consent to or assume the risk of further abuse by "refusing" to leave her abuser, thereby diminishing her "right" to defend herself? Don't you think that she probably hit him as much as he hit her? She wants you to think that she was reasonable in her belief that she had to defend herself, but she's fundamentally unreasonable, isn't she? What's reasonable about staying with a man who hurts her?

Generally, the myths and misconceptions that often end up being harmful to battered women charged with crimes have to do with (1) a belief that battered women can and should leave their abusers; (2) a belief that if the woman on trial does not fit the person's stereotype of a battered woman, she is not a "real battered woman"; and (3) a belief in the mutuality of abuse (that women are just as violent as, or even more violent than, men).

Can't—and Shouldn't—Battered Women Just Leave Their Abusers?

One of the most prevalent, and relentless, misunderstandings about battered women's lives is that they can (and should) just leave their abusers. The belief is widespread that battered women can simply walk away from their abusers and, if they do, they will be safe. When battered women are charged with crimes, many jurors (and, unfortunately, some defense attorneys) believe that the woman should have, and easily could have, just gotten out of the relationship and thus would have avoided the situation that led to the crime. (If she had only left sooner, she would not have had to defend herself. Or, she should have left her abuser and not "let him" coerce her into criminal activity.) It is also easy for jurors to conclude that the abuse "could not have been that bad" or else the woman would have left her abuser. Or jurors believe that battered women are "sick" or "crazy" for staying with abusers, that battered women instigate or provoke all the violence, or that they are masochistic.

In reality, leaving is the most dangerous time for many battered women (Mahoney 1991).[4] Many battered women who find themselves charged with a crime have tried to leave at least once in the past, which led to an escalation of the violence. Battered women are not sick, "crazy,"[5] or masochistic; they are doing the best they can in a difficult situation. For many battered women charged with a crime, their actions were a reasonable response to a very unreasonable situation (i.e., being beaten by someone who says he loves you).

If jurors believe that a woman could easily have left an abusive relationship and been safe, that the abuse could not have been that severe, that the woman provoked the violence, or that she is "sick," it becomes impossible to see beyond these victim-blaming beliefs to understand what a battered woman's life was really like. They view the woman as if she has equal power to the man, and they seem to want to believe that leaving would actually result in safety.

Unfortunately, increased awareness about battering and programs to assist battered women sometimes cut both ways for battered women defendants. Many jurors think that because "so much" money is going to-

ward support programs that any woman can simply call one of these programs, leave her batterer, and be safe. While some women can (and want to) leave their batterers and choose to utilize programs to achieve this end, many women do not know about the programs or the programs cannot offer the services they need in order to provide real safety for them and their children. Some overburdened and underfunded programs have to turn away many women and their children. Other programs are not accessible to battered women because of geographic or other obstacles (lack of transportation to the program, no TTY telephone for deaf battered women, no ramps for women in wheelchairs, no understanding of or programming for lesbian battered women), because they are not culturally appropriate (do not have any staff who speak the woman's language or do not have the type of food a woman and her children are used to eating), or because they do not offer the types of services the woman needs at the time. If a woman on trial did not contact a battered woman's program, prosecutors will often use this fact to try to show that the defendant was not "really a battered woman," even though only a small number of abused women actually use shelter programs.

Is She a 'Real Battered Woman'?

In recent years, increased knowledge about battering and its effects has led to the creation of some new, rigid stereotypes about battered women. The actual stereotype of a "real battered woman" may vary from community to community and from person to person. One of the stereotyped images of a "real battered woman" is that of a timid, literally beaten-down (white) woman who cowers in the corner; ideally, she has tried to get outside help and has done nothing "wrong" (i.e., has never fought back, is very passive, never uses drugs, never drinks, never yells, is a fabulous mother to her kids, is nice). At least that is the image of the "good battered woman," who is also assumed to be the "real battered woman." And to the extent that any battered woman "deserves" our sympathy and compassion, it is the "good battered woman."

Maybe, just maybe, a juror can understand why a "good battered woman" would have to defend herself (or be forced into other criminal activity). But if the woman on trial does not match the juror's image of a "good battered woman" (if she drinks, uses drugs, is aggressive in any way), the juror is not likely to be sympathetic or understanding of her circumstances and will probably discount or disbelieve any testimony about the history of abuse. Prosecutors often take advantage of jurors' rigid stereotypes of "good battered women" and bring in all sorts of information to try to discredit the defendant and "prove" that she is not a "real battered woman," or certainly not a "good" one.

Many jurors, judges, and attorneys have a difficult time "buying" that women who do not fit their stereotype of the "good battered woman" are actually battered, especially if the woman is feisty, a substance abuser, or aggressive in any way, be she a woman of color or a white woman. Many jurors have a difficult time believing that some women of color are "real battered women," and women of color are often more severely "punished" for not fitting the stereotype of a "real battered woman" (Allard 1991; Ammons 1995; Richie 1996; Walker 1988). Unfortunately, in cases where jurors refuse to believe that the defendant is a "battered woman," she usually fares very poorly at trial.

Aren't Women as Violent as (or Even More Violent Than) Men?

Because of intense media interest in and news coverage of any woman who has used violence, even in self-defense, many people seem to think that a massive increase has occurred in violence against men by their women partners. In recent years, numerous articles have claimed that feminists deliberately exaggerate the extent of violence against women in order to justify getting large grants from the federal government (Hoff Somers 1994, 203; Young 1995a). These articles argue that violence against women is not as big a problem as many have claimed and that much, or even most, partner violence is perpetrated by women against their male partners (Dershowitz 1994; Young 1995b).[6] Almost as common is the belief that most domestic violence situations really involve "mutual abuse" by the parties involved. These authors claim that women are really the violent ones (the "real batterers") and that men (the "real victims") are just too embarrassed to come forward to say that they've been beaten (Cose 1994). Others think that any compassion toward battered women who kill (the granting of clemency to incarcerated battered women) condones the use of violence, gives other women "permission" to use violence against their partners, and encourages them to use violence as a means of settling differences (Associated Press 1990; Iseman 1991). Still others blame feminism in general and argue that women are now acting much more like men and are using more violence just like their male counterparts. They argue that feminism has given rise to a massive increase in female criminality.

Prosecutors will often try to portray the woman on trial as the real abuser and try to get the jurors to believe that the final incident was "simply" an extreme example of her violence toward him. Or, they will try to show that the parties engaged in mutual abuse and that this time the woman "simply got the better of him." In many of these cases, there is no evidence that the women ever used violence against their partners, except in self-defense. In cases where there have been past incidents of violence by the woman, especially if they are documented (e.g., the man took out a protection order against her or she called the police to help her and she ended up getting arrested), this information is often brought in at trial to try to show that the woman was the initial aggressor and therefore not entitled to defend herself. Of course, it is also used to show that she is not a "real battered woman."

If jurors believe these claims, they are going to have a difficult time believing a woman who says she was severely beaten and defended herself. Instead they'll believe that the homicide or assault was merely an extension of her "usual" violence. They are likely to disbelieve her accounts of the abuse (especially if the abuse is not documented in court or hospital records, which, for many women, is the case). Or, they might even believe that she experienced abuse but provoked the violence or that the violence was mutual. If, based on this thinking, she was not a "real battered woman," then she was at least morally, if not legally, culpable for the violence that occurred.

Expert witnesses can be particularly helpful in explaining that a woman, even if she has fought back in the past, can still be a battered woman. They can also provide jurors with necessary contextual information to more fully evaluate the battered woman's use of violence and the batterer's use of violence, especially given the major qualitative differences in partner homicides committed by men and women (Wilson and Daly 1992) and in most forms of partner violence. Men, especially batterers, tend to kill when they think they are going to lose their partner, as when she threatens to leave or actually does leave ("If I can't have you, no one will"). Women tend to kill their partners after being subjected to physical violence and coercive control, when they think they are going to die or get extremely hurt (and I mean *physically* hurt or killed; many men claim they "will die" if their partner leaves them, but they are not talking about being physically fearful for their own lives). Unfortunately, the public discussion about women who use violence often takes place without the necessary contextual information, including these qualitative differences based on gender

(Renzetti 1995; DeKeseredy and Schwartz 1998). Batterers use violence and other tactics, such as intimidation, isolation, economic control, personal power, and sexual abuse, to control their partners (Pence and Paymar 1993). Women who defend themselves, fight back, or use violence under other circumstances rarely use these other tactics to control their partners (Das Dasgupta 1996).

Confronting the Myths, Misconceptions, and Stereotypes

Confronting these stereotypes at the trials of battered women is challenging and difficult. They are often not even identified as an issue (especially by defense attorneys who sometimes share the same beliefs). Nor are there easy legal tools that attorneys can use to counteract these stereotypes, especially because so many of the stereotypes come into trials covertly and indirectly. An attorney can sometimes address stereotypes when prospective jurors are being questioned (during *voir dire*). If the woman herself testifies at the trial, she may have an opportunity to explain her reality, and her testimony can counter many of the myths and stereotypes. But often jurors are unwilling to find any battered woman credible and simply do not "buy" her version of the events.

Jurors come to trials full of their own biases, and it is often difficult to change them in the course of that one trial, given the tenacity of victim-blaming myths about battered women. If an expert on battering and its effects testifies, this witness can be a key educator of the jury. The expert can do much to address many of the misconceptions and replace them with more accurate perceptions and a better understanding of a battered woman's experiences. But because jurors are all over the map in terms of their beliefs and knowledge bases, it is extremely difficult to discern the best method to appropriately and effectively counter the myths and stereotypes held by any one person.

Defending Battered Women Charged With Crimes: Legal Issues

There is no "battered woman's defense" or "battered woman syndrome defense."[7] Yet the *perception* that such a defense exists is shared by many members of the legal community, including defense attorneys and the general public. They think that when a battered woman is charged with a crime, she has to prove that she is a battered woman or that she has "battered woman syndrome" and that once this is proven she will be acquitted. But there is no jury instruction that says, "Ladies and gentleman of the jury, if you find that Ms. X is a battered woman (or has battered woman syndrome), then you must find the defendant not guilty of the crimes for which she has been charged." Rather, evidence about battering and its effects is introduced (when appropriate) to support legal defenses that already exist, such as the defenses of self-defense or duress.

We have heard from some defense attorneys who, when they discover they "have one of those battered women's cases," immediately try to find an expert witness (which, if based on sound reasoning, is generally an excellent idea). However, when asked what defense they plan to use and what the goal and purpose of presenting expert testimony are, many of these attorneys have no answers. They have not thought through their theory of the case, what defense they plan to use, or how the evidence (including, potentially, an expert witness) will support that defense— the kind of preparatory thinking and case development they do in all their other cases. Instead, many attorneys think they simply need an expert to prove their client was a battered woman. They forget to think about the actual defense they plan to use at trial and how evidence about battering might be relevant to that defense.

Because of this ongoing misperception that there is a separate defense for abused women, many cases continue to be presented by defense teams or considered by judges and jurors as though new, unique legal rules apply (or should apply). Traditional concepts of criminal law continue to be discarded or oddly twisted, and, as discussed earlier, myths and misconceptions about battered women are often exploited by prosecutors. In some cases, women have had to first "prove" that they are a "real battered woman" or that they are "suffering from battered woman syndrome." Then, and only then, can they move ahead with trying to prove that they acted in self-defense or under duress. The prosecution concentrates on "proving" that the woman isn't a "real battered woman" and utilizes this "fact" to show the jury that the woman could not really have acted in self-defense or been coerced into committing a crime, reasoning that, because she's not a "real battered woman," none of her actions were justified. The central issue becomes whether the defendant is a "real battered woman" or "has battered woman syndrome" and not, as it should be, the elements of the crime and her defense. Battered women should not be held to higher legal standards than other defendants; they should not have to prove that they fit into a narrowly described "box" of being a "real battered woman" before being able to present their defenses. Testimony about the abuse (by the expert witness or other witnesses, including the defendant herself) should be part of the evidence presented to help inform the factfinders (the judge or the jury) about the social context in which the incident occurred so that they can fully and fairly evaluate the case. This evidence should support an already established defense (e.g., self-defense or duress).

Most battered women's advocates do not, generally, advocate for new, special, or different laws or defenses for battered women. Rather, it is our goal to make sure that battered women, like all defendants, be able to successfully introduce any and all relevant evidence to support their defense claims and that all battered women defendants get a vigorous and complete defense. We do not argue that "because she was battered she should be acquitted." Rather, we believe that because a battered woman's experiences of violence are usually relevant to her defense claim, the jury should be able to hear about them in order to better assess her defense.

In the late 1970s and the early 1980s, when expert witnesses started testifying in trials of battered women, they generally testified about "battered woman syndrome." Definitions of this varied, but they were usually based on the early work of Lenore Walker, a psychologist who specialized in studying battered women and did much pioneering work on their behalf. In Walker's early definitions of "battered woman syndrome," she wrote that they exhibit "learned helplessness" (an increasing inability to protect themselves) and experience at least two "cycles of violence" (Walker 1979, 1982). More recently, "battered woman syndrome" has been equated with posttraumatic stress disorder or defined as meeting "the diagnostic criteria for posttraumatic stress disorder (PTSD)" (Walker 1994, 70).

Given the court's general lack of respect for the "soft sciences" such as psychology and sociology, the use of medical-sounding terminology ("syndrome") was, in the early years, very helpful in getting expert testimony about the effects of battering into the courtroom; it helped demonstrate the scientific validity of the proffered expert testimony. The use of the term "battered woman syndrome" also became a convenient way to describe a set of characteristics common to many, but not all, battered women (Parrish 1996). But for years, many battered women's advocates—and increasingly, researchers and attorneys—have expressed concerns about using the term to describe the experiences of battered women (Schneider 1986, 1993). It stigmatizes and pathologizes battered women and can create the false perception that battered women suffer from a mental disease or defect, have a "malady," or

have something terribly wrong with their psychological makeup. It also implies that the consequences of battering are purely psychological, failing to acknowledge the other effects of being battered, such as the physical, economic, social, and other practical consequences. And the term suggests that all women who experience abuse react in the same way and suffer from a common "syndromic" malady (Dutton 1993).

The term "battered woman syndrome" is too limiting. It does not adequately describe the experiences of battered women. Many activists, expert witnesses, and attorneys have discarded the term in favor of the more accurate and more inclusive term "battering and its effects." Mary Ann Dutton, a forensic psychologist with extensive experience working with battered women, has done an excellent analysis of why "battered woman syndrome" is no longer an adequate term. She argues that it does not sufficiently reflect the breadth and nature of knowledge developed over the past 20 years concerning battering and its effects since

> the knowledge pertaining to battering and its effects does not rest on a singular construct, as the term 'battered woman syndrome' implies. (Dutton 1996, 17)

Dutton also argues that the term is imprecise and, therefore, misleading. Equating battered woman syndrome with posttraumatic stress disorder (PTSD) is also problematic, as not all battered women experience PTSD (Dutton 1993, 1996; Stark 1995). Obviously, just because a woman does not have PTSD does not mean she was not battered, nor does it mean that she did not act in self-defense.

Although battered women share some common characteristics and experiences, their situations and the ways in which they respond to these situations can vary dramatically. What women specifically do to try to reduce, resist, cope with, and escape from their abuser's violence varies from individual to individual and may also change over time for any one woman. The reactions of service providers to whom battered women turn for help also vary, as does the degree of helpfulness of any particular intervention. Rigid definitions, and the accompanying stereotypes these definitions often produce, can be problematic for battered women charged with crimes, especially if the woman does not "fit" neatly into the rigid definition.

When jurors hear testimony that the defendant "had battered woman syndrome," they often cannot reconcile this information with the woman's defense. For example, in cases involving self-defense or duress claims, the defendant seeks to help the jury understand the *reasonableness* of her actions, given the circumstances of her situation. But if jurors believe she has "battered woman's syndrome," it can be difficult for them to reconcile her "mental problems" with her claim of reasonableness. The defendant wants to show why her actions were normal, reasonable responses to a highly *unreasonable* situation (being beaten by a partner). The use of the "syndrome" terminology can shift the focus of inquiry away from "Did the woman act in self-defense?" to "Is the woman a battered woman or does she have 'battered woman syndrome'?"

The term "battered woman syndrome" is still used by some expert witnesses today and, in some circumstances, their testimony continues to be helpful to some battered women. It is also important to note that the term is deeply embedded in case law, some statutes, and much of the literature and is still used by some attorneys and judges as well. Because of this situation, it is certainly not advisable to completely eliminate the term and replace it with another. But, over time, as the field of domestic violence has developed, many have found that talking about "battering and its effects" is more accurate and complete and that expert testimony on battering and its effects more fully encompasses the range and complexity of battered women's experiences.

Conclusion

While we have seen some progress in the efforts to understand and defend battered women defendants during the past 15 years, persistent myths and misconceptions about the women and their experiences remain. Fortunately, more attorneys and expert witnesses have learned how to mount thoughtful (and accurate) defenses for battered women. Yet, battered women charged with crimes continue to face many difficulties, and even some new and different problems they did not necessarily face earlier. New educational, advocacy, and legal efforts are needed to counter the many problems battered women defendants continue to face today.

Discussion Questions

1. How would you describe the commonly held image of the "real battered woman"? What does she look like in most people's minds? How do most battered women charged with crimes deviate from this image?

2. Why is a self-defense strategy more appropriate in the defense of a battered woman charged with murdering her abusive partner than the use of battered woman's syndrome?

3. What do you think would be the most effective ways to educate the public about the reality of the lives of battered women charged with crimes and the difficulties they face in court?

Endnotes

1. See Ann Jones, *Women Who Kill* (1996), for an excellent discussion of Francine Hughes's case and the media's reaction to her acquittal (e.g., a *Time* magazine article titled "A Killing Excuse" noted that "an array of women have managed to walk away unpunished after killing their husband or

even former husbands"; Jones notes that this "array" referred to three women—see pp. 281–295.

2. Additionally, Francine Hughes did not use a self-defense defense; she used an insanity defense at her trial and claimed she was temporarily insane when she set her husband on fire. Battered women rarely use this defense in homicide trials, and those who do seldom prevail.

3. A recent study suggests that in partner homicides men tend to get more lengthy sentences than their female counterparts; the sentences of men averaged over 16 years, while women (excluding women sentenced to death) received an average sentence of six years (U.S. Bureau of Justice Statistics 1995). It is important to note that men and women typically kill for very different reasons. Men tend to kill because their partners are planning or trying to leave them; women usually kill in defense of their own lives or the lives of their children. Therefore, comparing the length of sentences based on gender is actually like comparing apples and oranges. The fact that women generally received shorter sentences is not because women are treated leniently (as some commentators argue), but rather because the reasons men and women use violence are so different.

4. A study by the U.S. Bureau of Justice Statistics (1991b) reports that separated or divorced women were 14 times more likely than married women to report having been a victim of violence by a spouse or ex-spouse. Although separated or divorced women made up 10 percent of women in the study sample, they reported 75 percent of the spousal violence.

5. This is not to say that battered women do not have any mental health problems. Some do. When this is the case, these issues need to be considered at trial.

6. These claims that women are as violent as or more violent than men are not new.

See, for example, Jones's (1996, 300–303) discussion of the "battered-husband bandwagon" during the late 1970s.

7. Possible exceptions are Rhode Island and Arkansas. See *McMaugh v. State* (612 A2d 725, RI 1992) stating that "when the issue of battered woman's [sic] syndrome is raised as a defense in a criminal trial, we hold that . . . the defendant will be required to prove the existence of the condition as an affirmative defense." See also Arkansas Code, Sec. 5-2-607(a)(3) (1997) stating that a person is justified in using deadly physical force if he or she reasonably believes that the other person is "imminently endangering his or her life or imminently about to victimize the person . . . from the continuation of a pattern of domestic abuse."

References

Allard, S. 1991. "Rethinking Battered Woman Syndrome: A Black Feminist Perspective." *UCLA Women's Law Journal* 191–207.

Ammons, L. 1995. "Mules, Madonnas, Babies, Bathwater, Racial Imagery and Stereotypes: The African-American Woman and the Battered Woman Syndrome." *Wisconsin Law Review* 1003–1080.

Associated Press. 1990, December 25. "Celeste Clemency Decision Triggers Praise, Criticism." News Messenger.

Browne, A. 1987. *When Women Kill.* New York: Free Press.

Browne, A. and Williams, K. November, 1990. *Trends in Partner Homicide by Relationship Type and Gender, 1976–1987.* Paper presented at the Annual Meeting of the American Society of Criminology, Baltimore, MD.

Cose, E. 1994, August 8. "Truths About Spouse Abuse." *Newsweek* p. 49.

Das Dasgupta, S. 1996. *Violence by Women—A Critical View.* Unpublished paper.

DeKeseredy, W. S. and Schwartz, M. D. 1998. *Woman Abuse on Campus: Results From the Canadian National Survey.* Thousand Oaks, CA: Sage.

Dershowitz, A. 1994, July 21. "Wives Also Kill Husbands—Quite Often." *Los Angeles Times.*

Dutton, M. 1993. "Understanding Women's Response to Domestic Violence: A Redefinition of Battered Woman Syndrome." *Hofstra Law Review* 21, 1191–1242.

——. 1996. *The Validity and Use of Evidence Concerning Battering and Its Effects in Criminal Trials: A Report Responding to Section 40507 of the Violence Against Women Act.* Washington, DC: U.S. Department of Justice.

Ewing, C. 1987. *Battered Women Who Kill.* Lexington, MA: Lexington Books.

Federal Bureau of Investigation. 1993. *Crime in the United States, 1992.* Washington, DC: U.S. Department of Justice.

Hoff-Sommers, C. 1994. *Who Stole Feminism: How Women Have Betrayed Women.* New York: Simon and Schuster.

Iseman, D. 1991, January 6. "Clemency: The Decision Heard 'Round the World'." *Youngstown Vindicator.*

Jones, A. 1996. *Women Who Kill.* Boston: Beacon Press.

Maguigan, H. 1991. "Battered Women and Self-Defense: Myths and Misconceptions in Current Reform Proposals." *University of Pennsylvania Law Review* 40:379–486.

Mahoney, M. 1991. "Legal Images of Battered Women: Redefining the Issue of Separation." *University of Michigan Law Review* 90:1–94.

McNulty, F. 1980. *The Burning Bed.* New York: Harcourt Brace Jovanovich.

Parrish, J. 1996. "Trend Analysis: Expert Testimony on Battering and its Effects in Criminal Case Analysis." *Wisconsin Women's Law Journal* 11:75–173.

Pence, E. and Paymar, M. 1993. *Education Groups for Men who Battered: The Duluth Model.* New York: Springer.

Renzetti, C. M. 1995, April. *The Challenges to Feminist Theory Posed by Lesbian Battering and Cross-cultural Research.* Paper presented at the conference on Reframing Domestic Violence: Moving From Private to Public Solutions, Simmons Institute for Leadership and Change, Boston, MA.

Richie, B. 1996. *Compelled to Crime: The Gender Entrapment of Battered Black Women.* New York: Routledge.

Schechter, S. 1982. *Women and Male Violence.* Boston: South End Press.

Schneider, E. 1986. "Describing and Changing: Women's Self-defense Work and the Problem of Expert Testimony." *Women's Rights Law Reporter* 9:191–122.

——. 1993. "Feminism and the False Dichotomy of Victimization and Agency." *New York Law School Law Review* 38:387–399.

Stark, E. 1995. "Representing Woman Battering: From Battered Woman Syndrome to Coercive Control." *Albany Law Review* 58:973–1026.

U.S. Bureau of Justice Statistics. 1991a. *Special Report: Women in Prison.* Washington, DC: Author.

——. 1991b. *Female Victims of Violent Crime.* Washington, DC: Author.

——. 1995. *Spouse Murder Defendants in Large Urban Counties.* Washington, DC: Author.

Walker, L. 1979. *The Battered Woman.* New York: Harper and Row.

——. 1982. "Beyond the Juror's Ken: Battered Women." *Vermont Law Review* 7:1–14.

——. 1988. *Legal Self-defense Issues for Battered Women of Color.* Paper presented at the Advanced Feminist Therapy Institute, Seattle, WA.

——. 1994. *Abused Women and Survivor Therapy: A Practical Guide for the Psychotherapist.* Washington, DC: American Psychological Association.

Wilson, M. and Daly, M. 1992. "Who Kills Whom in Spouse Killings? On the Exceptional SES Ratio of Spousal Homicides in the United States." *Criminology* 30:189–215.

Young, C. 1995a, April 6. "Crime Against Women Is Horrific, but Hyping the Threat Is Misguided." *Philadelphia Inquirer.*

——. 1995b, October 23. "Domestic Violence Isn't a One-way Street." *Philadelphia Inquirer* p. A13. ✦

17
Perspectives on Women in Prison

Barbara Owen

Women's incarceration rates have increased in recent years. This chapter discusses the unique circumstances of incarcerated women, reviewing current research on women's imprisonment and addressing several important issues. First, the chapter examines how many women are in prison and why they are there. Then it examines the characteristics of imprisoned women and what prison is like for them. Finally, there is a consideration of the special needs of imprisoned women and how these needs might be met.

For decades, the problem of women in prison has been invisible to the public eye. Although "B" movies have provided sultry images of "women behind bars," serious policy and research attention has focused on male prisons. In the mind of the public, the problems of crime and prison are male problems. Women as criminal offenders and as prisoners are often only an afterthought in public discourse and public policy. To be sure, both crime and prisons are markedly different for men and women. Overall, women tend to be less "criminal" and certainly less violent than men. Men tend to commit more crime, and their crimes are generally more serious and more violent than the crimes committed by women. Male prisons also tend to be larger, more numerous, and generally more violent. Concern about women in prison often takes a back seat to the seemingly overwhelming problems of male crime and imprisonment.

However, in the last decade the issue of women in prison has become more visible.

One explanation for this new visibility lies in a startling fact: Since the 1980s, the rate of growth in women's imprisonment has far outstripped the rate of growth in men's imprisonment. This enormous growth has prompted many criminologists to examine the rise in women's imprisonment from several perspectives. In this chapter, these perspectives are presented by posing some basic questions about women in prison:

- How many women are in prison?
- Why are these women in prison?
- Who is in prison? What do we know about this population?
- What is the prison experience like for women?
- What do women in prison need? What can be done about these problems?

In answering these questions, we need to look at several sources of information. First, we will examine data that tell us how many women are in prison. To make sense of these numbers, we then need to look at public policy and criminological theory. Second, we will look at research conducted throughout the country that describes some of the characteristics of women in prison. Then we will examine my research that describes the concept of "prison culture" among women, which allows us to picture the everyday life of women in prison. Finally, the chapter offers some suggestions of ways in which these problems can be addressed.

How Many Women Are in Prison?

As we begin the twenty-first century, one fact of women's imprisonment continues to startle those who study, work, and live in prison: The numbers of women in prison continue to increase, at rates surpassing those of men. In less than two decades, the number of women imprisoned in the United States tripled. In 1996, over 127,000 women were incarcerated in United States jails and prisons: nearly 75,000 in state and federal prisons, with another 52,000 in local jails. In California alone, the female prison population rose dramatically from 1,316 in 1980 to almost 11,000 in 1997. During 1996, Texas incarcerated about 10,000 women, New York prisons held just under 4,000, and Florida, over 3,000.

How can we begin to make sense of these numbers? To think about these increases, we first must look at crime patterns among women. Studies consistently show that women generally commit fewer crimes than men and that their offenses tend to be less serious. Bloom (1996), Chesney-Lind (1997), Gilfus (1992), and Pollock-Byrne (1990) argue that women's patterns of criminal activity differ from men's both in the type and the amount of crime committed (see also chapter 13 in this volume). A major gender difference is the low rate of violent crime committed by women. The offenses for which women are arrested and incarcerated are primarily nonviolent property and drug offenses. When women do commit acts of violence they are most likely against a spouse or partner and in the context of self-defense (Browne 1988; U.S. Bureau of Justice Statistics 1994). As Barbara Bloom and I have written, the increasing role of drug offenses has been accompanied by a decreasing role of violence in the imprisonment of women (Owen and Bloom 1995a). In 1991, 32.2 percent of the female prison population was incarcerated for a violent offense, compared to 41 percent in 1986 and 49 percent in 1979 (BJS 1994). The national 1991 figures show that almost 70 percent of the women were sentenced for a nonviolent crime; almost 30 percent were sentenced for property offenses, with a full 33 percent for drug offenses and 6 percent for public order offenses (BJS, 1994).

The experience of the state of California is instructive. California, which has seen huge increases in women's imprisonment, has experienced a decline in state prison admissions of women for violent offenses and huge upswings in drug-related prison admissions. In 1992, only 16 percent of the women ad-mitted to California state prisons were incarcerated for violent offenses, compared to 37.2 percent in 1982 (Bloom, Chesney-Lind, and Owen 1994). Nationwide, the trend is the same: In 1994 the Bureau of Justice Statistics found that about one in three women were serving time for a drug offense as compared to one in eight in 1986. The Bureau of Prisons (Klein 1993) reports that almost 64 percent of their female population is incarcerated for drug-related offenses. This compares to only 26 percent of the 1981 female federal prison population being held for drug offenses.

In addition to gender differences between male and female crime, researchers have found that women's arrest and incarceration rates vary by race (Chesney-Lind 1997) . In her study of the "triple jeopardy" that women in prison face as a result of race, class, and gender, Barbara Bloom (1996) argues that women of color are somewhat more likely than white women to be arrested for crimes against persons and are more likely to be sentenced to jail or prison. Research on the racial makeup of U.S. prison populations and incarceration patterns clearly shows growing racial disparities in punishment for both men and women (Mann 1993; see also Gilbert, this volume). However, research and discussion about racial disparity in the criminal justice system have overwhelmingly centered on men.

Why Are These Women in Prison?

If the crime rate among women was also increasing radically, these increasing numbers would make sense. But here is the puzzle: Crime rates among women have not increased as rapidly as the increasing rates of imprisonment. Again, the experience of California gives a good example. According to the data from a statewide task force that examined issues concerning imprisoned women, neither population increases nor a rise in the crime rate fully accounts for the huge increase in the incarceration rate of women there. Using data collected by the California Department of Corrections (1995), this task force found that the rate of new admissions of women to the state's prison system for felony offenses increased from 2.9 per 100,000 California population in 1980 to 11.3 in 1991, an increase of 289 percent. In contrast, the rate of new admissions for men increased from 44.8 (per 100,000 California population) in 1980 to 113.5 in 1991, an increase of 153 percent. (SCR 33 1994).

As discussed in our article (Bloom et al. 1994), a rising crime rate does not explain the increases in the female prison population. How can we explain the fact that between 1980 and 1997, the number of women incarcerated in California increased from 1,316 to 11,000? We suggest this explanation:

> The increasing incarceration rate for women in the State of California, then, is a direct result of short-sighted legislative responses to the problems of drugs and crime—responses shaped by the assumption that the criminals they were sending to prison were brutal males. Instead of a policy of last resort, imprisonment has become the first-order response for a wide range of women offenders that have been disproportionately swept up in this trend. This politically motivated legislative response often ignores the fiscal or social costs of imprisonment. Thus, the legislature has missed opportunities to prevent women's crime by cutting vitally needed social service and educational programs to fund ever-increasing correctional budgets. (p. 2)

It is important to emphasize that individual behavior alone cannot fully make sense of these dramatic increases. It is a misguided "war on drugs" and the accompanying mandatory sentencing for even the most minor drug offense that accounts for these ever-increasing numbers (Bloom et al. 1994). Quite simply, the war on drugs has become a war on women, and it has contributed to the explosion in women's prison populations. In addition to increased prosecution of drug offenses, two other factors account for the increasing population: more severe and punitive responses to these crimes and the lack of viable treatment and alternative community sanctions for women (Bloom et al. 1994).

Many criminologists believe that the theory of economic marginalization best explains why women commit crimes and are sent to prison. Specifically, the work of Chesney-Lind (1997) and Steffensmeir (1982) supports this assumption about female criminality: In its various shapes and sizes, female criminality is based on the need for women, excluded from conventional institutions, to survive under conditions not of their own making. In this view, the criminality of women reflects the conditions of their lives and their attempts to struggle for survival. Often marginalized outside of conventional institutions, many women conduct this struggle outside legitimate enterprises. The story of women in prison reflects their status in society—a status that reflects ingrained racism and sexism, the subtle devaluation of women and girls, and the open toleration of sexual and domestic abuse in a male-dominated society. Women's prison, perhaps even more than its male counterpart, is a place, by and large, for people who have no place in conventional worlds, a place for those whom no one wants, or a place for women for whom there is no place else to go (Owen 1998).

Many criminologists argue that women's lives must be understood in terms of patriarchy, a system of social control based on unequal power between men and women in society. The lives—and the needs—of women are often seen as subordinate to those of men. Under patriarchy, women have fewer opportunities than men, and they are often subjected to personal and sexual oppression and to unequal and unfair treatment within the criminal justice system. Thus, the study of imprisoned women must be framed through the lens of patriarchy and its implications for the everyday lives of women.

It may well be that the rising number of women in prison is a measure of society's failure to care for the needs of women and children who live outside the middle-class protection afforded by patriarchy. This increasing number reflects the cost of allowing the systematic abuse of women and children, the problem of increased drug use, and a continuing spiral of marginalization from conventional institutions. Currie (1985) sees that the lack of adequate economic and social supports for women and children in society is a significant contributor to rising crime rates. The poverty of their lives on the street and the lack of educational opportunity and economic advantage make crime a reasonable choice for some women, with subsequent imprisonment a predictable outcome for some proportion of female offenders (Owen 1998).

Who Are These Women?

Criminologists conduct representative surveys to assess the characteristics of individuals in prison populations. To find out more about women who are in prison, Barbara Bloom and I looked at existing surveys and conducted our own in California's women's prisons. In 1994, we surveyed a representative sample of about 300 women in the four California prisons through face-to-face interviews (Owen and Bloom 1995a, 1995b). To begin this study, we looked at surveys conducted by the Bureau of Justice Statistics (1991b, 1994), the American Correctional Association (1990) and the Federal Bureau of Prisons (Klein 1993) and summarized these leading studies in our article, "Profiling Women Prisoners: National Surveys and a California Sample" (Owen and Bloom 1995a). Information from these prior surveys was similar to what we would soon find. Based on a comprehensive national survey of women in all state facilities, the Bureau of Justice Statistics found that women inmates

largely resemble male inmates in terms of race and ethnic background and age. However, women are substantially more likely than men to be serving time for a drug of-

fense and less likely to have been sentenced for a violent crime. (1994, 1)

These descriptions remain accurate even as the number of women in prison continues to surge upward.

Demographic Characteristics

Nationally, the best source of statistics on the prison population is the Bureau of Justice Statistics (1991a, 1994), which surveys prisoners in state correctional facilities across the country. The most current BJS survey (1994), based on 1991 data, found that women in prison were most likely to be black, unemployed at the time of arrest, and never married. With a median age of 31 in 1991, the female prison population was somewhat older than those imprisoned in 1986. In the federal system, women were more likely to be somewhat older, with an average age of 36, and were more likely to be white than women in state prisons (Federal BOP 1991).

In the California sample, we also found that African-American and Hispanic women were disproportionately represented in the prison population. Although few measures of social and economic class are presented in these studies, most criminologists find that poor people are much more likely to become imprisoned than individuals from the middle, upper, and propertied classes (Reiman 1990). In our California study, fewer than half the women were employed at the time of their arrest, and only about half had completed high school. About one-fifth said they had been on some form of public assistance in the year prior to their arrest.

Physical and Sexual Abuse

In the 1991 national surveys, an estimated 43 percent of women in prison reported previous physical or sexual abuse. Nationwide, violent offenders were more likely to have previously experienced this abuse (BJS 1994). The BJS data show that almost half of the women had experienced abuse by intimates. Sexual abuse, usually involving violence, was most likely to have occurred in this sample. The 1990 American Correctional Association (ACA) survey found that 50 percent of the women reported a history of physical abuse, with 35 percent reporting sexual abuse. This abuse was likely to be at the hands of husbands or boyfriends. Our California study also found that physical, sexual, and emotional abuse is a defining experience for the majority of women in California prisons, with 80 percent of the women interviewed reporting some kind of physical, sexual, or emotional abuse. With the exception of sexual assault, most women indicated that they had been harmed by family members and other intimates.

Substance Abuse Histories

As we have seen, substance abuse plays a key role in the imprisonment of women and contributes to the increasing numbers of women prisoners. In the national studies, over one-third of all female prisoners interviewed in 1991 reported having been under the influence of some drug at the time of their offense. Around 40 percent reported daily drug use in the month before their offense. Almost one-quarter of the 1991 sample reported committing their crime to get money to buy drugs (BJS 1994).

In our California study, we asked a variety of questions about substance abuse. Alcohol was the most often mentioned substance, with three-quarters of the sample saying they began to drink before they were 18 years old. Over half of the women said they had used some form of cocaine or heroin at some time in their lives. About 60 percent said they had begun using drugs before they were 18 years old. Slightly fewer than half of those interviewed said they had used a needle to inject drugs at some time in their lives.

Drug use contributes to criminality and aggravates existing personal and social problems (see Mancuso and Miller, this volume). Many researchers (Anglin and Hser 1987; Inciardi, Lockwood and Pottinger 1993)

argue that drug use is tied to criminality, oftentimes as a result of the emotional and psychological traumas caused by abuse and prostitution, as well as living on the street (Miller 1986) and "in the life" (Rosenbaum 1981).

Family History

Another aspect of the experience of women in prison is a family history with the criminal justice system. In our California study, almost three-quarters of the women reported having family members who had been arrested. In terms of jail or prison, 63 percent reported having relatives who had done time. About half of the women interviewed said their husbands or other partners had a history of imprisonment; 25 percent said their husbands were currently imprisoned.

What Is the Prison Experience Like?

Up until now, we have only been discussing statistics. I wanted to know more about the lives of women in prison beyond these numbers. In 1992, I began to visit a new prison, the Central California Women's Facility (CCWF), trying to answer this simple question: How do women in prison do their time? To address this basic question, I conducted a qualitative case study, employing techniques of intensive interviewing, active observation, and a feminist perspective in collecting my data. To start this study, I first read three important books about the prison culture of women. These classic studies of the female prison, written by Giallombardo (1966), Heffernan (1972), and Ward and Kassebaum (1965), gave me a good basis for a close examination of the contemporary world of the female prison. These studies described a prison culture that is remarkably stable over time. As these classic studies found more than 30 years ago, the culture of the women's prison continues to be a world based on three basic foundations: personal relationships with other prisoners, connections to family and loved ones in the free community (or "on the street" in the language of the prison), and commitments to preprison identities.

The Central California Women's Facility, holding over 4,000 women in mid-1995, is the largest prison for women in the world. It is a complex world, populated not only by several thousand women prisoners but by hundreds of staff and prison managers. All attempt to negotiate its complexity and determine their place in the prison community. Like most experiences for women, imprisonment and women's subsequent response to this world is indeed a gendered experience. Just as women's offense patterns seem to be tied to differences between men and women, so is their prison social organization. The facts of their lives as women and girls, the pervasive influence of patriarchy, and the limitations created by economic and social marginalization combine with the stigmatization of criminality to contribute to the context of their offense patterns and their imprisonment (Owen 1998)

At CCWF, I found that three additional components shape contemporary prison culture. First, the size of the prison and its growing population have a profound impact on the day-to-day life of the thousands of women held there. Second, the huge influx of substance-abusing women has changed the nature of the prison population. Many women in prison have committed no crime except use and possession of drugs—or they have committed petty theft to support this drug use. These first two factors combine to create a large, crowded prison that is not equipped to deal with the problems and issues presented by thousands of women. Third, although clearly secondary to the dominant issues of personalized relationships, race and ethnic identities provide a subtext to prison life. Minority women are disproportionately represented in the U.S. prison population, with the percentage of African-American women incarcerated growing at accelerated rates. In 1991, African-American women made up about 40 percent of the female prison population; by 1995, this population had grown to 48 percent. The percentage of Hispanic and Latina women is also growing at a somewhat slower rate (BJS 1994, 1997).

Prison sociologists look at how prisoners "do their time" in terms of prison culture. *Prison culture* emcompasses a description of the ways in which prisoners define their experience in prison, how they learn to live in prison, how they develop relationships with other prisoners and the staff, and how they change the way they think about themselves and their place within the prison and the free world. At CCWF, this prison culture was based on a subtle negotiation of time and place, individual identity, and personalized relationships inside and outside the prison community. Here, four elements of this negotiation are discussed: becoming prisonized, learning the prison codes, dealing with family relationships inside and outside prison, and negotiating "the mix." These elements of prison life shape struggle and survival in the modern prison for women (Owen 1998).

Becoming Prisonized

In CCWF, over half the women in prison are first-timers. These women have had little experience with incarceration and must learn the rules and roles of the prison culture. For first-time prisoners, coming to any prison can be frightening and filled with apprehension. Vanessa, a white-collar, first-time offender, describes coming to CCWF from a county two hours away:

> And it's just when I saw those gates, I said, oh my God I'm going to prison. And it finally set in that I was actually going to be here. And we drove through them and I looked around and I said there's no way out of here, they are going to keep me here as long as they want to.

Once a prisoner gets off the bus, she is "processed" into the prison population. Vanessa tells us how she was introduced to the routine and impersonal handling that characterizes the modern prison:

> Being processed was like an assembly line. Each person had a job to do, you go in there, you weren't a person anymore, you weren't human anymore, they could care less. About 42 of us came in together. They threw us all in the same room, and we four of us, shower together, it was awful. We were in orange jump suits, with no underwear. For some girls it was that time of the month and one girl had to keep a pad on with a jump suit with no panties on. That's just the way it was. And they don't care. The phrase is always, 'Welcome to the real world.'

Once processed, women discover that prison is filled with uncertainty. To manage this uncertainty, they attempt to learn about their new community; they begin to negotiate routines and strategies that allow them to accommodate. Donald Clemmer (1940) called this process of learning how to do time *prisonization*, a process of becoming socialized into the behaviors, values, and worldview of prison life. Learning about the prison comes through interaction with other prisoners. These relationships are a critical aspect of this new socialization process. As one woman explained, "Some women are way out of their territory here, they need help from someone who knows what is happening."

Newcomers are likely to stumble through their first weeks or months in the prison, as they begin to learn "how to do their own time." One critical aspect of the prisonization process is establishing a new prison identity. As in male prisons, being respected and having a good reputation with other prisoners is important to the women of CCWF. For old-timers, their past behaviors and being known as an "Original Gangster," or "O.G.," are sufficient. Newcomers, on the other hand, may have to prove themselves in the subtle stratification system.

Learning the Prison Code

Women adjust to prison in many ways. These adjustments may change over time, taking on one form of accommodation at the beginning of a sentence, evolving to a second in the middle, and perhaps adjusting to still a third form at the end. One woman may become highly prisonized during her sentence, taking on prison-defined ways of acting and feeling, while another may maintain her preprison identity and not become attached to the values and culture of the prison. Yet another may become so involved in her prison life that "the streets" seem far away.

The diversity of the population in this prison and the complexity of the many backgrounds brought together contribute to a prison culture that itself is diverse and complex. One way of learning how to adjust to the struggle of imprisonment is through an allegiance to the prison code. The prison code is a set of values that outlines the conduct of a prisoner who has few attachments to outside values and is fully immersed in the prison community. Among male prisoners, common values include "Don't be a snitch or informer," "Be loyal to convicts," and "Do your own time." Most old-timers or O.G.s still adhere to these rules.

Although the male prison code seems to be more rigid and based on supermasculine values, there is some overlap between the prison code of male prisoners and that of female prisoners. Toni, a 48-year-old woman who has served almost 20 years, made the following comment:

> I still go by the code. I won't have a position where I have to work next to an officer. Now people tell [inform to staff]: they don't have common sense; they think they have street knowledge and don't realize that it is different than prison knowledge.

One aspect of the prison code involves teaching newcomers, or "youngsters," the rules of prison life. Toni tells us how things have changed today:

> Well, when I first came, I didn't even know how to act. So many youngsters come to prison and [they think] they are going 'to kick it on the yard.' Youngsters want to be noticed, to put their stuff out . . . they can be loud and obnoxious . . . I used to tell them [the rules, the code], like not to tell on nobody, but I have given up doing that. Years ago, you just didn't tell; I was taught the old way. It's not like the old days. I learned from the old school, in the 60s. The convicts stuck together, if you went down, you just took it—you didn't bring nobody down with you. 'Do your own time,' that was the rule.

Handling Personal Relationships: Families Inside and Out

As women adjust to their imprisonment, they develop friendships and other forms of relationships with other prisoners. One common type of relationship is the prison family or the "play family." Play families are a significant part of the social organization in women's prisons. A woman often learns how to do her time through interaction with these social units, becoming prisonized into the ways of behaving, feeling, and thinking. All previous studies of womens' prisons have found that women in prisons organize in these familylike arrangements, replicating common gender roles on the street. At CCWF, these families developed out of complicated emotional relationships, sometimes based on practical or sexual ties (Owen 1998). Families have social and material responsibilities, such as providing friendship and support; celebrating birthdays and holidays; providing food, cigarettes and clothes; and taking care of members' possessions when they are transferred out of the unit (Owen 1998). Divine talks about the types of families she has observed over her three prison terms:

> There are about five people here who called me "Moms" on the street. I would say this is my play family. Almost everybody is involved in them in one way or another. It could just be two people or a bunch. It is just like the family on the streets—you start depending on them. Then there is the loose-knit family. That is just what you call each other, but you don't really care that much about each other. All families do not have women who play the male role—some are based on couples, some on friendship.

Another way women in prison are different than men in prison is in the degree of attachment to family and friends outside. About 80 percent of women in prison are mothers, with three-quarters having children under age 18. Lord (1995), a prison warden in New York, has stated that while men in prison "do their own time," women "remain interwoven in the lives of significant others, primarily their children and their own mothers" (Lord 1995, 266). Women in prison are tied to the lives of their children during their imprisonment, some through close contact with phone calls, letters, and visits, others through emotional attachments unrealized in actual contact. For most mothers in prison, being separated from their children is the most painful part of their prison term. Many women do not see their children because of the distance, expense, and other hardships traveling to the prison may cause. Maria, a first-timer serving a short drug-related sentence, describes how missing her children affects her:

> Missing them is the hardest thing [about doing time]. I have not seen them since I have been locked up because I do not trust anyone to bring my children here. I have letters and pictures to keep me going. The first 15 months were hard, but the next 10 will be easy because I know I will get out to the gate and see them.

Connections to the free world can make it much harder to "do time," particularly for those who have a long time to serve. Divine made the following observation:

You cannot do your time in here and out on the streets at the same time. That makes you do hard time. You just have to block that out of your mind. You can't think about what is going on out there and try to do your five, 10 [years] or whatever in here. You will just drive yourself crazy.

Negotiating the Mix

A key element in surviving prison life is negotiating an aspect of prison culture known as *the mix*. In its shortest definition, the mix is a part of prison culture that can bring trouble and conflict with staff and other prisoners. It is the "fast life" or *la vida loca*, the crazy life, lived while "running the yard" in prison. Becoming involved with the mix can lead to violating the prison rules, developing negative relationships with other prisoners that lead to fights, and generally getting in trouble while in prison. A variety of behaviors can put one in the mix: same-sex relationships, known as "homo-secting"; involvement in drugs; fights; and "being messy," which means making trouble for yourself and others. As Mindy tells us, "The mix is continuing the behavior that got you here in the first place." For the vast majority of the women at CCWF, "the mix" is generally something to be avoided. Most women want to stay out of trouble and do their time in their own way. The great majority of women at CCWF serve their sentences, survive the mix, and return to society, resuming their lives in the free community.

For many women, prison life becomes a time for reflection on the trajectory of their lives. As one woman said, "Coming to prison was the best thing that ever happened to me. I know I would be dead if I hadn't been sent here. It has made me stop and think about what I was doing to myself and my kids." As Blue, ending a long sentence for kidnapping, tells us:

I probably would have been dead if I had not come to prison. I was living too fast and I was too young to be living that fast. I should have been already getting my degree

from college, and I should have been getting my life together where I had my own apartment and my own job. Instead I came to prison.

These feelings notwithstanding, it is important to emphasize the damage of imprisonment, as conveyed in these comments by Morgan, serving a long term for violence in and out of prison:

Prison makes you very bitter and you become dehumanized. I've been in prison since I was 17, I have been abandoned by my family members, and anyone else who knew me out there. Being in prison forces you to use everything that you have just to survive. From day to day, whatever, you know it's very difficult. It's difficult to show compassion, or to have it when you haven't been extended it.

As this brief summary of the data and my prison ethnography suggest, imprisonment affects a disproportionate number of women of color and those marginalized by circumstances of family background, personal abuse, and destructive individual choice. Women in prison represent a specific failure of conventional society—and public policy—to recognize the damage done to women through the oppression of patriarchy, economic marginalization, and the wider-reaching effects of such short-sighted and detrimental policies as the war on drugs and the overreliance on incarceration as social control. The story of the women in prison, however, is not hopeless. Many women have survived circumstances far more damaging than a prison term, and most will continue to survive in the face of insurmountable odds (Owen 1998).

What Are the Program and Treatment Needs of Women in Prison?

Along with many other criminologists, including Pollock-Byrne (1990), Chesney-Lind (1997), and Morash and Bynum (1996),

Barbara Bloom and I have thought about solutions to these problems (Owen and Bloom 1995b). These solutions challenge assumptions about the criminality and disposability of these women. This chapter concludes with a discussion of solutions. What do women in prison need in order to stay out of prison and avoid the kinds of behavior that lead them there? What can be done inside prison and outside as well? Four areas of intervention can provide innovations both inside and outside prison fences.

Community Interventions

Given the less serious nature of much female crime, appropriate community sanctions and treatment should be developed and implemented for female offenders. These community-based programs should include vocational training, substance abuse treatment, and other programs that facilitate productive and self-sufficient lives. When the personal histories of women in prison are examined, it is clear that opportunities exist for intervention early into their criminal and substance-abusing lifestyle outside prison fences. Community-based programs would be economically efficient as well as more logical in terms of providing intervention rather than after-the-fact sanctions.

Economic Self-Sufficiency

Most women in prison have few employment skills and inadequate education. Upon release, the majority must support themselves and their children. The need for economic self-sufficiency is apparent to even the most casual observer. Women in prison must gain the skills and training necessary to this end. Although substance abuse treatment and other counseling, as well as improved parenting and family reunification, are also critical in addressing these problems, economic self-sufficiency is the cornerstone to success after imprisonment.

Substance-Abuse Treatment

The data is clear: Drug-related crime is the single most significant cause of the imprisonment of women. Substance abuse acts as a multiplier for other high-risk or criminogenic behavior. In-prison drug programs and community-based treatment programs are an absolute necessity. These programs should be grounded in a "continuum of care," including institutional assessment and aftercare upon release into the community.

Family and Personal Issues

There is also a critical need for family based-interventions that address parenting, family reunification, family violence, and other personal concerns. Prison programs need to address these family issues, especially in light of the importance of children in the lives of imprisoned women. Individual and group counseling are also needed to address a wide variety of personal and emotional issues; the need for counseling dealing with physical, sexual, and emotional abuse is particularly acute. The overrepresentation of women of color also requires sensitivity to cultural and ethnic implications in service provision.

Conclusion

This chapter describes women's imprisonment from many perspectives. In examining the accelerating rate of women's imprisonment, we found a complicated interaction among issues of patriarchy, public policy, and individual behavior that helps account for these dramatic changes in the female prison population. In detailing the dimensions of this expanding population, we examined the demographic characteristics and personal histories that describe women in prison. In the section on female prison culture we saw the ways women confront their imprisonment and attempt to make a life behind prison walls. Finally, we closed with a discussion of prison programs and how the problems of imprisoned women can be effectively addressed both in prison and in the community. This information can be used to think about the issue of imprisoned women, in terms of both the problems of individuals and, most important, the problems of society.

Discussion Questions

1. Female prison populations have risen dramatically in the last two decades. What factors account for this rise? Which of these factors are related to individual behaviors? Why? Which of these factors are related to societal or structural factors? Why?

2. This chapter provided many details on demographic characteristics and personal histories of imprisoned women. Choose three of these details and discuss how they relate to criminal offending and resulting incarceration.

3. Choose one element of prison culture and discuss how it shapes the way women in prison "do their time."

4. The chapter suggested approaches to solving the problems of women in prison. In your view, which programs would show the most promise? How? What other kinds of programs are also needed? Beyond programs that deal with individual behavior, what kinds of changes should be made in society?

References

American Correctional Association (ACA). 1990. *The Female Offender: What Does the Future Hold?* Washington DC: St. Mary's Press.

Anglin, M. and Hser, Y. 1987. "Addicted Women and Crime." *Criminology* 25(2):359–394.

Bloom, B. 1996. *Triple Jeopardy: Race, Class and Gender as Factors in Women's Imprisonment.* Ph.D. dissertation, Department of Sociology, University of California-Riverside.

Bloom, B., Chesney-Lind, M., and Owen, B. 1994. *Women in California Prisons: Hidden Victims of the War on Drugs.* San Francisco: Center on Juvenile and Criminal Justice.

Browne, A. 1988. *Assaults Between Intimate Partners in the United States.* Washington, DC: Testimony before the United States Senate, Committee of the Judiciary.

——. 1991a. *Prisoners in 1990.* Washington DC: U.S. Department of Justice.

——. 1991b. *Special Report: Women in Prison.* Washington DC: U.S. Department of Justice.

——. 1992. *Women in Jail in 1989.* Washington, DC: U.S. Government Printing Office.

——. 1994. *Women in Prison.* Washington DC: U.S. Department of Justice.

——. 1997. *Characteristics of Correctional Populations in the United States, 1995.* Washington DC: US Department of Justice.

California Department of Corrections. 1995. *Characteristics of Felon New Admissions and Parole Violators Returned with a New Term.* Offender Information Services Branch, State of California, Sacramento, CA.

Chesney-Lind, M. 1997. *The Female Offender: Girls, Women and Crime.* Thousand Oaks CA: Sage.

Clemmer, D. 1940. *The Prison Community.* New York: Holt, Rinehart and Winston.

Currie, E. 1985. *Confronting Crime.* New York: Pantheon.

Giallombardo, R. 1966. *Society of Women: A Study of a Women's Prison.* New York: John Wiley & Sons.

Gilfus, M. 1992. "From Victims to Survivors: Women's Routes of Entry and Immersion into Street Crime." *Women and Criminal Justice* 4(1):62–89.

Heffernan, E. 1972. *Making It in Prison: The Square, the Cool, and the Life.* New York: John Wiley & Sons.

Inciardi, J. A., Lockwood, D., and Pottinger, A. 1993. *Women and Crack Cocaine.* New York: Macmillan.

Klein, S. 1993. " A Profile of Offenders in State and Federal Prisons." In *Female Offenders: Meeting the Needs of a Neglected Population.*

Laurel, MD: American Correctional Association.

Lord, E. 1995. "A Prison Superintendent's Perspective on Women in Prison." *The Prison Journal* 75(2):257–269.

Mann, C. R. 1993. *Unequal Justice: A Question of Color*. Bloomington: Indiana University Press.

Miller, E. 1986. *Street Women*. Philadelphia: Temple University Press.

Morash, M. and Bynum, T. 1996. *Findings From the National Study of Innovative and Promising Programs for Women Offenders*. East Lansing: Michigan State University, School of Criminal Justice.

Morash, M., Haarr, R., and Rucker, L. 1994. "A Comparison of Programming for Women and Men and U.S. Prisons in the 1980s." *Crime and Delinquency* 40(2):197–221.

Owen, B. 1998. *In the Mix: Struggle and Survival in a Women's Prison*. Albany: SUNY Press.

Owen, B. and Bloom, B. 1995a. "Profiling Women Prisoners: Findings from National Survey and a California Sample." *The Prison Journal* 75(2): 165–185.

——. 1995b. *Profiling the Needs of California's Female Prisoners: A Needs Assessment*. Washington DC: National Institute of Corrections.

——. 1997. *Profiling the Needs of Young Female Offenders*. Final Report to Executive Staff, California Youth Authority.

Pollock-Byrne, J. 1990. *Women, Prison and Crime*. Pacific Grove, CA: Brooks/Cole.

Reiman, J. 1990. *The Rich Get Richer and the Poor Get Prison*. New York: McMillan.

Rosenbaum, M. 1981. *Women on Heroin*. New Brunswick, NJ: Rutgers University Press.

State Concurrent Resolution 33 Commission (SCR33), California State Legislature. 1993/4. *Final Report on Female Inmate and Parolee Issues*. Sacramento: California Department of Corrections.

Steffensmeir, D. 1982. "Trends in Female Crime: It's Still a Man's World." In B. R. Price and N. Sokoloff, eds., *The Criminal Justice System and Women*. New York: Clark Boardman.

U.S. Bureau of Justice Statistics. 1990. *Prisoners in 1989*. Washington DC: U.S. Department of Justice.

Ward, D. and Kassebaum, G. 1965. *Women's Prison: Sex and Social Structure*. Chicago: Aldine-Atherton. ✦

18
Gender and Policing

Susan L. Miller

W*hat kinds of issues do women face in policing today? How have women made a difference in law enforcement? How does gender affect policing philosophies and activities? How do race, class, ethnicity, gender, and sexual orientation interact within this masculinist occupation? How do police perform their social control role when potential situations they encounter are characterized by inequitable gender-power relations? How have women embraced the latest trend in law enforcement, community policing? Although this chapter cannot provide an exhaustive review, discussion, and analysis of all these questions, it does address several key topics: women's entrance into the male world of policing, police interactions with minorities and hate crimes (racism, sexism, homophobia), and community policing, gender, and policing styles.*

Women's Entrance Into Policing

The female police officer duo of Cagney and Lacey first appeared in a television movie (and later in a weekly series) in 1981. Differing from shows (such as *Charlie's Angels*) in the euphemistically named "jiggle era," when women cops were portrayed as male sex objects as they ran around in tight revealing clothes and high stiletto heels, *Cagney and Lacey* introduced Americans to a more feminist type of officer (D'Acci 1994). At the same time, working women could identify with the two detectives because they faced many of the same challenges, such as

marriage problems, dating problems, and alcoholism. Cagney and Lacey were presented as strong, brave, physically competent heroic women who could handle a "man's" job, yet were feminine enough to squelch any allegations about their sexuality.

Unlike earlier prime-time women officers, and also different from traditional portrayals of women in society at large, Cagney and Lacey

> . . . were in-control protagonists who solved their own cases (both mentally and physically), were rarely presented as 'women in distress' and were virtually never rescued by their male colleagues. . . . Christine Cagney, a single woman, had an ongoing sex life in which she often pursued men who interested her. Similarly, Mary Beth Lacey, a married woman, was cast as a sexual initiator with her husband, Harvey. Mary Beth was also the breadwinner of the family, while Harvey, an often unemployed construction worker, cooked and took care of the house and their two children. (D'Acci 1994, 5)

Historical Context

The entrance of women into the masculine-dominated occupation of policing has not been smooth; in fact, Cagney and Lacey probably could not have been introduced to the viewing public with such success prior to the 1980s. A decade earlier, women were still battling for inclusion into the ranks of patrol officer. It took the passage of the Equal Opportunity Act of 1972 (which extended the provisions of Title VII of the 1964 Civil Rights Act to state and local governments prohibiting discrimination based on gender) to help establish women's equal employment opportunities (Martin 1992). Legislative and executive action, as well as judicial decrees, were necessary to address discrimination in eligibility criteria, selection standards, and assignment and promotion practices. The Equal Employment Opportunity Commission (EEOC) was enacted to oversee the act's enforcement. These actions, in tangent with executive orders, affirmative action activities, challenges in federal courts, and the overall climate following the riots of the 1960s and the burgeoning women's movement, lent support to the atmosphere of greater inclusion of women in traditionally male professional spheres (Martin 1992). Thus, an individual's sex was no longer a valid qualification for the job, and women were able to hit the streets as armed patrol officers with equal responsibilities to those of male officers.

The 1970s also introduced research that examined women's patrol performance. These evaluations revealed that women were equally as capable as men police officers in performing police duties (Bartlett and Rosenblum 1977; Bentell Associates 1978; Bloch and Anderson 1974; Kizzoiah and Morris 1977; Pennsylvania State Police 1973; Sherman 1992; Sichel et al. 1978).Prior to the governmental and judicial action in the 1970s, women had been constrained to roles dealing with "women, children, and typewriters" (Milton 1972). Men resisted the inclusion of women in policing because females were viewed as weaker, both physically and emotionally, and thus unable to handle the job or to exercise authority on behalf of the state. Also, men feared the risk of physical danger if they relied on women for backup in crisis situations. In addition, in our rigid gender-role based society, it was seen as "unmanly" for men to rely on women. If women became patrol officers, men's self-image would be compromised and the male subculture would be threatened (Martin 1980). Because crime fighting is perceived as the quintessential macho element in police work, women were seen as simply not up to the job.

Police forces typically comprised a homogenous occupational group with strong loyalty and subculture bonds to which women need not apply. Male officers were concerned that their informal norms would be threatened by women's presence and that they would have to curtail inappropriate language and topics such as sports, women, and sex (Martin 1992).

> Women who 'talk like truckdrivers' also upset the men by blurring the distinctions between the sexes that enable men to be men. The presence of women raised the specter of bonds of sexual intimacy between officers that compete with the demands of loyalty to the group. (Martin 1992, 287)

Concern was also raised over how citizens would respond to the introduction of female officers. It was feared that the uniform and the symbolic power it conveys would not be enough to engender cooperation and that female officers would not be able to gain citizen compliance or establish their authority:

> In a society where women are viewed as objects to be dominated rather than authority figures to be feared and obeyed and where they are not used to exercising power over men, male officers fear that male citizens' denial of male officers' authority will 'rub off' on the police in general. Yet the alternative, a woman exercising authority over men, is also threatening to male officers' identities. (Martin 1992, 287)

More recent research has indicated that women may offer alternative ways of doing police work by stressing interpersonal communication skills (Belknap 1996). These abilities are associated with the de-escalation of conflict. Grennan (1987) found that more so than male officers, female officers did not interpret conflict situations as personal altercations that challenge their position or abilities. Rather, the socialization women receive that promotes nurturing might contribute to women's equally successful skills in handling violent confrontations.

Adaptation to a Resistant Occupation

> . . . women give up some of their femininity to do this job. How many women do you know that go to work prepared to kill?. . . It goes back to home training; how many

mothers give orders to fathers? (Martin 1992, 294)

Women entering masculinist traditions have to negotiate their place within the organization. Policewomen "just decide whether they desire to accept the traditional subordinate role of females in policing, and in doing so, limit their potential career status" (Berg and Budnick 1986, 317). Susan Martin (1979), in a study of female police officers in Washington, D.C., found that the women adapted their behavior to match their comfort with the environment: POLICEwomen identified with male officers and adopted male characteristics, while policeWOMEN emphasized her femininity rather than replicating the masculine nature of police work. However, women officers who resist working solely with "women, children, and typewriters" and who embrace valued male skills of policing are seen as POLICEwomen who identify with the policemen's culture by adopting tough, aggressive, street-oriented policing styles to gain acceptance (Martin 1980). However, rather than achieving acceptance, these women face defeminizing name-calling (such as "bitch" or "dyke") by men (as well as from traditional policeWOMEN) for discarding more traditional gender roles (Martin 1980).

Other officers, characterized by Martin as policeWOMEN, adopt a deprofessionalized occupational style, "tend to accept the stereotypic sex roles of 'pet' or 'seductress,' emphasize 'being a lady' on and off the job, welcome or tolerate the protection of males, display little initiative or aggressiveness on street patrol, and seek non-patrol assignments and personal acceptance" (Martin 1995, 394). A third type of female officer reflects those women who strive for a more balanced occupational style that maintains femininity while succeeding in the job (Martin 1995). They are critical of both styles of POLICEwomen and policeWOMEN, feeling that both reinforce stereotypes and harm all female officers.

Regardless of which occupational style women officers adopt, male officers "continue to treat women officers as sexual targets and mistrust them as patrol officers" (Martin 1995, 394).

Accommodation to a sexualized working environment may depend, in part, on the interactive effects of gender and race (Martin 1994), in which racism further divides women:

> White women have ample contact with white men and the potential for increased power by association with one of them. But they have limited their influence by internalizing an image of helplessness and allowing themselves to be 'put on a pedestal.' In contrast, due to racism, black women have experienced far less protection and a far greater element of fear based on white hostility, physical separation, and intimidation. (Martin 1994, 384)

Thus Hurtado (1989) contends that "white women experience 'subordination through seduction' while black women face 'subordination through rejection'" (as quoted in Martin 1994, 384). At the same time, however, men of color "fit" into traditional police roles and expectations because they are viewed as "physically strong, streetwise, and masculine" (Martin 1994, 386) and do not threaten the police culture in the same way that women do (Pike 1991). The compounding effects of the multiple statuses of an officer's race, gender, and sexual orientation contribute to even more heightened ambiguity in negotiating gendered spaces and social interactions in policework (see Messerschmidt 1993).

At the same time, some inroads have been achieved in the hiring and promotion of nonwhite female officers, although the majority of women police officers are still concentrated at entry level patrol positions. According to 1986 statistics, while minority women make up only 3.5 percent of all police officers, they make up 40 percent of women officers. By 1986 in departments serving 50,000 residents or more, white women were 5.3

percent of the force and nonwhite women were 3.5 percent. Women also gained some supervisory positions: in 1978 only 1 percent were supervisors, while by 1986, 3.3 percent were. The percent of minority women who were supervisors increased from one-fifth in 1978 to almost one-third of all female supervisors by 1986 (Martin 1990).

What remains noteworthy, however, is that the presence of women disturbs the informal distribution of rewards—no longer does everyone compete equally. When women benefit from being female and are exempt from certain assignments, or are given favorable assignments, men often react with hostility. Rather than confront their male supervisors, however, they direct their anger at the female police officers (Martin 1992). Thus, although women have gained some increased access to police positions, they often still endure a chilly reception once they achieve some success.

Diversity and Law Enforcement Issues

Ever since the Rodney King beating involving more than 20 LAPD officers was captured on videotape, increased attention has been paid to issues relating to racism, sexism, and hate-bias crimes. This interest is revealed in three ways:

1. Adoption of state statutes that expand the scope of the law and severity of punishment for hate crimes as well as police-initiated efforts to focus attention on such offenses;

2. Emphasis on multiculturalism and diversity in the community and police interactions with these diverse groups of residents with the police, and in particular, domestic violence victims;

3. Diversity within the force itself (such as hiring gay or lesbian officers).

Police Interactions With Minorities

The federal Hate Crime Statistics Act of 1990 defines *hate crimes* as "crimes that manifest evidence of prejudice based on certain group characteristics" and includes data collection goals that cover crimes based on race, religion, sexual orientation, and ethnicity. The federal Violence Against Women Act allowed women to file civil suits for damages if they can prove that violent offenses committed against them were gender motivated, but the U.S. Supreme Court struck down this provision in 2000.

Many new legislative pieces rest on police officers' definition and determination that a hate-bias crime has occurred, as well as their interpretation and response to such incidents. Martin (1995) has explored Baltimore County, Maryland's approach to hate crimes and argues that the program encourages specialized police attention that affirms community values, rather than actually controlling crime more effectively. In her discussion of the social construction of hate crimes, she presents the paradox police face. They must

> simultaneously protect the fundamental civil rights of citizens to be free from attacks based on their ethnic or other identity; allow for the constitutionally protected right of persons to express their opinions, including expressions of bigotry; and maintain order and peace in the larger community. (Martin 1995, 322–323)

Yet police efforts are stymied (in both defining and responding to hate crimes) because perpetrator motivations are often unclear, incidents might be a result of mutual conflict or provocation, definitions of bias are confusing, and community consensus over the acts is lacking. At the same time, these police efforts of social control supply a symbolic feature: "It makes law available to the traditional 'underdog' racial and ethnic groups for whom the availability of the law has long been limited or uncertain" (Martin 1994; see also Black 1976). These efforts are important, given the long history of police insensitivity to ethnic groups. This undertaking has far-reaching ramifications: If citizens feel more respect and understanding from police, they may be more likely to come forward with information to help solve crimes. In turn, with new training in place, recalcitrant officers may become more sensitized to the diverse constituencies they serve (see Schusta et al. 1995 for excellent discussions of multicultural law enforcement approaches).

The Rodney King beating incident and the Jeffrey Dahmer incident both illustrate issues related to police prejudice and insensitivity as well as selective enforcement. In Los Angeles, the comments recorded on the Mobile Digital Terminals in officers' squad cars showed a link between sexist attitudes and violence as officers voiced their desire to control and abuse female citizens. For example, the Christopher Commission (1997) quoted some computerized communications records:

> You won't believe this . . . that female called again said suspect returned . . . I'll check it out then I'm going to stick my baton in her.

> . . . female huh . . . well, just slap that silly broad senseless.

> Did you check your fruits [gay men] at the park . . . I figured how to get rid of them . . . I'm sending in a bunch of naked girls, that will scare them away.

In Milwaukee, the police failed to protect a citizen because of the assumptions they made about the young man's sexual orientation and lifestyle. Serial killer Jeffrey Dahmer, while still on probation for child sexual abuse, lured a 14-year-old Laotian boy to his apartment. He drugged, tortured, and sexually abused the boy, who managed to escape, naked and bleeding from his rectum (see Kappeler, Sluder, and Alpert 1994). Police, dispatched via a neighbor's complaint, dismissed the emergency medical personnel and returned the boy to Dahmer's apartment. Later, Dahmer killed the boy. It is likely that if police had responded with more

knowledge and less prejudice to the earlier incidents, this murder might have been preventable. These examples vividly demonstrate the dangers and misuse of selective enforcement and prejudice, fueled by a cavalier disregard for even basic human dignity that police should accord to each citizen.

Police and Diversity

To actively recruit officers who reflect the populations they serve, as well as create strategies to address perceived homophobia in hiring practices, some progressive police chiefs actively recruit gay men and women to the police force. Preliminary findings from an attitudinal study of gay and lesbian police officers reveal that officers in a large urban police department formed an association to help in developing the department's recruitment program for openly gay officers, to educate heterosexual officers, to provide support for other gay and lesbian police officers, to assist in dispelling fears held by members of the gay and lesbian community at large about police officers, and to improve police-community relations (Miller, Forest, and Jurik 1997). In this same study, gay and lesbian officers already working in the department were asked whether they bring any unique abilities, skills, and life experiences to the job of policing. Their responses are revealing:

> I believe if gay or lesbian officers have a political consciousness and understand the dynamics of homophobia and bigotry, they can bring a certain sensitivity and patience to the job. (lesbian officer)

> Being a minority you see both sides of the coin. And if you work in the gay community, citizens will explain more to you than they would to a straight cop. (gay male officer)

> I believe that knowing how a society can push you aside and not care about you helps especially when dealing with lower income families and minorities. (lesbian officer)

As an out gay cop I know firsthand the feeling of being oppressed and victimized. (gay male officer)

Citizens expect the police to enforce the law fairly and impartially, protecting all citizens regardless of race, sex, sexual orientation, ethnicity, or religion. Do police officers from minority groups recognize oppression and discrimination more easily since they themselves are from oppressed groups, as some scholars suggest (Maghan and McLeish-Blackwell 1991; Miller, Forest, and Jurik 1997)? Future research should endeavor to query heterosexual, gay, and lesbian officers in exploring this question, as well as conducting surveys of citizens.

Community Policing

The newest trend in policing today is captured under the generic rubric of *community policing*. Some police scholars suggest that the impetus behind community policing is reminiscent of its nineteenth century roots, when police officers were more intimately and informally connected to the communities they served. Essentially, community policing encourages "the personal touch," in which police emphasize proactive problem solving, improving the nature of police-citizen encounters, and responding to the needs identified by residents (Rosenbaum 1988; Skogan 1990). Thus, a major role reorientation is introduced, resting on the ability of an institution long characterized by bureaucratic rigidity (Rosenbaum and Lurigio 1994) and hypermasculine space (Messerschmidt 1993) to implement significant philosophical and organization change. By rejecting the model of the efficient, aloof professional or the macho crime fighter, community policing aims to build closer ties between police and residents through ongoing, frequent, informal noncriminal contact. This approach emphasizes a spirit of trust, cooperation, familiarity, and appreciation between police and community residents. In our society, these traits are typically associated with female gender roles and attributes.

Yet as a masculine paramilitary occupation, policing has overwhelmingly rejected "feminine" virtues and voices; the criminal justice and legal system overall is viewed by many as operating with a uniquely masculine voice—a detached and impersonal one that emphasizes the *traditional* over the *relational* (Miller 1999). Given the ideological preoccupation with masculinity in policing, any behavior that suggests femininity, weakness, or subjectivity is suspect and denigrated in police subcultures. Officers who express care and connection beyond superficial niceties have been trivialized or dismissed as too emotional for proper policing. Ironically, these very traits were used to historically justify the exclusion of women as police officers, but, today the ideal community police officer displays a social worker orientation, a style that traditionally has been beyond the purview of acceptable police action.

This situation raises some interesting questions: How can this alternative style be accepted by the police, since for it to be adopted, "feminine" traits must be appropriated as masculine traits and reshaped to appear as powerful and desirable? What happens if some men only "pretend" to personify this new breed of officer, particularly if they think doing so is tied to promotion? Do women police officers bring a "different voice" to policing than their male counterparts? Can a more feminine style of policing be introduced in a way that both men and women will embrace this approach and not fear the consequences of "doing policing" in this transformed style?

Gender structures organizational environments, providing powerful processes of control in work organizations (Acker 1990). Kanter's (1977) work suggested that differences in how women are treated in organizations are the consequence of a masculine organizational structure, rather than of traits related to the worker being a man or a woman. Her conceptualization, however, ignores the unique effects of sexism experienced by women and such other influences as race, class, and sexual orientation (Zimmer 1986; see also Martin and Jurik 1996 and in this volume for excellent discussions of this topic). More recent research finds organizations to be gendered, not gender neutral (Cockburn 1991; Martin and Jurik 1996). In fact, Acker (1990) explains that

> advantage and disadvantage, exploitation and control, action and emotion, meaning and identity, are patterned through and in terms of a distinction between male and female, masculine and feminine. (p. 146)

Gender, therefore, does not stand alone or in addition to ongoing social processes within organizations, but rather is an inextricable part of these processes (Connell 1987).

Conclusion

While this chapter doesn't resolve the salient issues surrounding gender and policing, it offers some philosophical and policy-related questions to pursue in future research. There is some good news: Childhood socialization experiences that have traditionally disadvantaged women in police work may be changing. For decades, girls have been less likely to use firearms or to play on contact sports teams, activities that could correlate with such police subcultural values as the controlled use of violence, teamwork, and group loyalty (Martin 1992, 300)—although not everybody agrees that these traits are desirable, given the peaceful qualities associated with developing community policing models. Additionally, girls have traditionally been encouraged to be sweet, dainty, and passive and not physically assertive (Martin 1980). However, some scholars suggest that our social definitions of what is acceptable masculine and feminine behavior is being challenged and thus undergoing some changes. We are seeing a greater emphasis on girls' participation in athletics and in having an intellectual life and career. Conversely, boys and men are being admonished to break free of the cultural constructions of masculinity and to be more sensitive and expressive. Martin (1992) argues that many children now see their father actively participate in domestic work and their mother work full-time outside of the home. Other factors, such as rising education standards and evidence of citizen respect for female officers, may also help ease transitions (Moyer 1992), so the police force is more welcoming for nontraditional officers. Younger officers may also be more interested in crime prevention activities and community empowerment issues.

Despite structural and cultural changes, however, progress is slow. First, despite the fact that involvement of fathers in child rearing has increased in recent years (Rix 1990), reasons remain to accept the unambiguous conclusion that men tend not to rear children because they "don't want the job" (Polatnik 1983). Second, in cases where men take on previously designated women's work, such as with the new genre of community policing approaches, they may end up disproportionately rewarded for their "egalitarian" efforts because their contributions are evaluated as "novel" for males to adopt, whereas women's efforts go unrecognized and unrewarded because the work is seen as "natural" for them to perform and perform well. Finally, will achieving a critical mass of women on the force make a difference? According to Guinier et al. (1994), increasing the number of women in the legal profession has not necessarily transformed the law. If selection, training, and professional socialization follow the same rigid male models, it may matter little how many women are added to the ranks of police departments.

Clearly, many unresolved questions remain to be explored in future research, as well as controversial issues to be examined within the area of gender and policing. As more women make inroads into the policing occupation and challenge the rigidity of past gender roles associated with policing, all police officers will benefit from innovative and creative alternatives to macho mindsets and inflexible police behavior.

Discussion Questions

1. Why were women excluded from the male occupation of policing? How did women ultimately break into patrol?

2. In what ways might female officers police differently than male officers? What style might be less threatening to men, and why? How is discrimination compounded for nonwhite women?

3. What are the advantages of diversifying police departments?

4. How are the new community policing efforts reminiscent of early policing efforts? Why would this "social work" style be perceived as negative by some police officers today?

5. How are gender roles and socialization experiences changing the factors that may have traditionally disadvantaged women in policing? What remains to be done?

References

Acker, J. 1990. "Hierarchies, Jobs, and Bodies: A Theory of Gendered Organizations." *Gender & Society* 4:139–158.

Bartlett, H. W. and Rosemblum, A. 1977. *Policewoman Effectiveness*. Denver: Civil Service Commission and Denver Police Department.

Belknap, J. 1996. *The Invisible Woman: Gender, Crime, and Justice*. Belmont, CA: Wadsworth.

Bentell Associates. 1978. *The Study of Police Women Competency in the Performance of Sector Police Work in the City of Philadelphia*. State College, PA: Bentell Associates.

Berg, B. and Bubnick, K. 1986. "Defeminization of Women in Law Enforcement: A New Twist in the Traditional Police Personality." *Journal of Police Science and Administration* 10:110–120.

Black, D. 1976. *The Behavior of Law*. New York: Academic.

Bloch, P. and Anderson, D. 1974. *Policewomen on Patrol: Final Report*. Washington, DC: Urban Institute.

Christopher Commission. 1997. Appendix in D. J. Champion, and G. E. Rush, *Policing in the Community*. Upper Saddle River, NJ: Prentice Hall.

Cockburn, C. 1991. *In the Way of Women: Men's Resistance to Sex Equality in Organizations*. Ithaca, NY: International Labor Relations Press.

Connell, R. W. 1987. *Gender and Power: Society, the Person, and Sexual Politics*. Stanford, CA: Stanford University Press.

D'Acci, J. 1994. *Defining Women: Television and the Case of Cagney & Lacey*. Chapel Hill, NC: University of North Carolina.

Grennan, S. 1987. "Findings on the Role of Officers' Gender in Violent Encounters with Citizens." *Journal of Police Science and Administration* 15:78–85.

Guinier, L., Fine, M., Balin, J., Bartow, A., and Stachel, D. L. 1994. "Becoming Gentlemen: Women's Experiences at One Ivy League Law School." *University of Pennsylvania Law Review* 143(1):1–109.

Hale, D. C. and Bennett, C. L. 1995. "Realities of Women in Policing: An Organizational Cultural Perspective." In A. V. Merlo and J. M. Pollock, eds., *Women, Law, and Social Control*. Boston: Allyn and Bacon.

Hurtado, A. 1989. "Relating to Privilege: Seduction and Rejection in the Subordination of White Women and Women of Color." *Signs* 14:833–855.

Kanter, R. M. 1977. *Men and Women of the Corporation*. New York: Basic Books.

Kappeler, V. E., Sluder, R. D., and Alpert, G. P. 1994. *Forces of Deviance: Understanding the Dark Side of Policing*. Prospect Heights, IL: Waveland.

Kizzoiah, C. and Morris, M. 1977. *Evaluation of Women in a Policing Program: Newton, Massachusetts*. Oakland, CA: Approach Associates.

Maghan, J. and McLeish-Blackwell, L. 1991. "Black Women in the Correctional Employment." In J. B. Morton, ed., *Change, Challenge and Choices: Women's Role in Modern Corrections*. Laurel, MD: American Correctional Association.

Martin, S. E. 1979. *Women on the Move? A Report on the Status of Women in Policing*. Washington, DC: Police Foundation.

——. 1980. *Breaking and Entering: Policewomen on Patrol*. Berkeley: University of California Press.

——. 1990. *On the Move: The Status of Women in Policing*. Washington, DC: Police Foundation.

——. 1992. "The Changing Status of Women Officers: Gender and Power in Police Work." In I. Moyer, ed., *The Changing Roles of Women in the Criminal Justice System: Offenders, Victims, and Professionals*. Prospect Heights, IL: Waveland.

——. 1994. " 'Outsider Within' the Station House: The Impact of Race and Gender on Black Women Police." *Social Problems* 41(3):383–400.

——. 1995. " 'A Cross-Burning Is not Just an Arson': Police Social Construction of Hate Crimes in Baltimore County." *Criminology* 33(3):302–326.

Martin, S. E. and Jurik, N. C. 1996. *Doing Justice, Doing Gender: Women in Law and Criminal Justice Occupations*. Thousand Oaks, CA: Sage.

Merlo, A. V. and Pollock, J. M. 1995. *Women, Law, and Social Control*. Boston, MA: Allyn and Bacon.

Messerschmidt, J. W. 1993. *Masculinities and Crime: Critique and Reconceptualization of Theory*. Lanham, MD: Rowman and Littlefield.

Miller, S. L. 1989. "Unintended Side Effects of Pro-Arrest Policies and Their Race and Class Implications for Battered Women: A Cautionary Note." *Criminal Justice Policy Review* 3(3): 299–317.

——. 1999. *Gender and Community Policing: Walking the Talk*. Boston: Northeastern University Press.

Miller, S. L., Forest, K. B., and Jurik, N. C. 1997. "Diversity in Blue: Lesbian and Gay Police Officers in a Masculinist Occupation." Paper presented at the Annual Meeting of the American Society of Criminology. San Diego, CA.

Milton, C. 1972. *Women in Policing*. Washington, DC: Police Foundation.

Moyer, I. (ed.) 1992. *The Changing Roles of Women in the Criminal Justice System: Offenders, Victims, and Professionals*. Prospect Heights, IL: Waveland.

Pennsylvania State Police. 1973. *Pennsylvania State Police Female Trooper Study*. Harrisburg, PA: Pennsylvania State Police Headquarters.

Pike, D. L. 1991. "Women in Police Academy Training: Some Aspects of Organizations Response." In I. Moyer, ed., *The Changing Roles of Women in the Criminal Justice System: Offenders, Victims, and Professionals*, 2nd ed. Prospect Heights, IL: Waveland.

Polatnik, M. R. 1983. "Why Men Don't Rear Children: A Power Analysis." In J. Trebilcot, ed., *Mothering: Essays in Feminist Theory*. Savage, MD: Rowman and Littlefield.

Rasche, C. E. 1995. "Minority Women and Domestic Violence: The Unique Dilemmas of Battered Women of Color." In B. R. Price and N. J. Sokoloff, eds., *The Criminal Justice System and Women: Offenders, Victims, and Workers*. New York: McGraw-Hill.

Rix, S. E. (ed.) 1990. *The American Woman 1987–88: A Report in Depth*. New York: W. W. Norton.

Rosenbaum, D. P. 1988. "Community Crime Prevention: A Review and Synthesis of the Literature." *Justice Quarterly* 5:323–395.

Rosenbaum, D. P. and Lurigio, A. S. 1994. "An Inside Look at Community Policing Reform: Definitions, Organizational Changes, and Evaluation Findings," *Crime Delinquency* 40:299–314.

Schusta, R. M., Levine, D. R., Harris, R. R., and Wong, H. Z. 1995. *Multicultural Law Enforcement: Strategies for Peacekeeping in a Diverse Society*. Englewood Cliffs, NJ: Prentice Hall.

Sherman, L. J. 1975. "Evaluation of Policewomen on Patrol in a Suburban Police Department." *Journal of Police Science and Administration* 3: 434–438.

Sherman, L. W. 1992. *Policing Domestic Violence: Experiments and Dilemmas*. New York: Free Press.

Sichel, J., Friedman, L. N., Quint, J. C., and Smith, M. E. 1978. *Women on Patrol: A Pilot Study of Police Performance in New York City*. Washington, DC: National Institute of Law Enforcement and Criminal Justice.

Skogan, W. G. 1990. *Disorder and Community Decline: Crime and the Spiral of Decay in American Neighborhoods*. New York: Free Press.

Zimmer, L. E. 1986. *Women Guarding Men*. Chicago: University of Chicago Press. ✦

19
Femininities, Masculinities, and Organizational Conflict: Women in Criminal Justice Occupations

Nancy C. Jurik
and Susan E. Martin

This chapter reviews women's changing work roles in the U.S. criminal justice system. It discusses how gender, race, class, and sexual orientation frame and organize work. Upper-middle-class women reformers entered criminal justice in the nineteenth century as specialists to save poor, immigrant women and children. They hoped to reform corrupt and ineffective criminal justice practices by establishing women's prisons and police bureaus. In the 1960s, when women in the system demanded the same assignments as men, men resisted women's move into police patrol work and prison security duties. Women represented efforts to supplant punitive crime control models with service and community relations models. Women's integration has accompanied efforts to reform and professionalize agencies and workers. However, barriers to reform remain. Although professionalization has advanced women workers, ideals of professionalism still reflect middle-class, white men's behavior.

Over the past three decades, women have moved into formerly all-male criminal justice (CJ) jobs in police patrol work and secu-

rity positions in men's prisons. Women's advancement in these fields is the outcome of two waves of arduous struggles to overcome the resistance of male colleagues and supervisors. Today, women are still far from achieving full equality in policing and corrections.

In the mid-nineteenth century, upper-middle-class women volunteers and reformers entered CJ fields to work with "fallen" women and children and to improve the moral fabric of society. They argued that their innate womanly dispositions enabled them to work more effectively with women and children. Thus, women gained entry into CJ fields by emphasizing their "natural" differences from men and by seeking only specialized positions performing clerical chores or supervising women and children (Rafter 1990; Schulz 1995). They were excluded from positions that involved the supervision of men.

In the late 1960s, following social movements, socioeconomic changes, and legal and CJ organizational reforms, women demanded integration into all aspects of policing and corrections. Women and their supporters emphasized that apparent differences between men and women are learned, not inborn. They argued that, with proper training, women could perform as well as men in any field. Their efforts met strong resistance from men, who cited women's natural or learned physical inferiority. In response, many advocates argued that women had unique job talents (e.g., communication or mediation skills) that offset any weaknesses. Ironically, these arguments are similar to those of nineteenth-century CJ reformers who emphasized women's natural differences from men. However, rather than accept specialized slots, as their nineteenth-century counterparts did, they demanded the same tasks as men.

In both eras, women's advancements fueled and were fueled by broader debates about the mission and scope of CJ organizations, the true nature of work in policing and corrections, and the meaning of gender in society. This chapter focuses on the relationship between competing models of policing and corrections work and U.S. women's employment struggles in those fields. We examine how gender as well as class and racial/ethnic relations affect struggles over CJ work opportunities and changes in the definitions of policing and corrections work. Conceptually, we do not view gender as a fixed role or individual attribute. Instead, we see it as a dynamic but enduring social construction of difference. We show how gender, race/ethnicity, and class are fundamental organizing features of CJ organizations and the jobs within them.

The first section of this chapter outlines our approach to the study of women's progress in traditionally male CJ fields. Then we review women's entry into policing and corrections, sources of resistance to women's progress, women's coping strategies, and organizational changes that have both fostered and hindered women's advancement.

Analyzing Women's Struggles in Criminal Justice Occupations

Women's struggles in traditionally male CJ occupations are usually explained through a gender-role approach that treats gender as a psychological attribute. Individuals learn roles through childhood socialization and societal reinforcement as adults. Gender-role training teaches women to be passive, nurturing, expressive, physically weak, and economically and emotionally dependent on men. Men learn that they should be more aggressive, independent, rational, and physically capable than women. Women learn to aspire to different jobs and to perform differently from men in similar jobs (Parsons and Bales 1955). Men also learn to view women as inferior and to dominate them in the home and workplace; women work in subordinate and support positions. Women who enter traditionally male CJ jobs thus experience "role conflict," wherein the duties of their status as women conflict with those of

police or correctional officers (Peterson 1982; Wilson 1982).

Despite the usefulness of gender-role theory, it has several important limitations. Race and ethnicity, class, sexual orientation, and other behavioral differences within gender categories are not easily explained by a framework built around one masculine role and one feminine role (West and Fenstermaker 1993). Moreover, gender-role theory underestimates the extent to which gender permeates human organizations. It fails to recognize that men's domination is also facilitated by organizational hierarchies, rules, and practices that reflect gender inequality.

Because men control powerful positions, they are able to base rules and regulations (e.g., performance evaluations) on their experiences and behavior (Acker 1990; Morash and Greene 1986; Zimmer 1987). The concept of gender role also distracts from understanding the interwoven but ever-changing character of gender and social organization throughout history (Connell 1987).

In contrast, we analyze gender as an ongoing social construction (Lorber and Farrell 1991; Martin and Jurik 1996). People construct or "do" gender through routine social interactions (West and Zimmerman 1987). Social interactions also construct and reaffirm racial and ethnic, sexual-orientation, and class differences (Connell 1993; Messerschmidt 1993; West and Fenstermaker 1995). Jobs are organized around expectations about the gender, sexual orientation, race/ethnicity, and class of those who do them. Accordingly, work becomes a resource for doing gender as well as for other social differences. For example, the social control functions and perceived danger of police and corrections work have led to the association between competence in these jobs and culturally dominant notions of masculinity. Thus, the successful handling of danger and administering of social control offer specific men an opportunity to construct their masculinity in ways that conform to dominant social expectations. Not surprisingly, the presence of women officers tarnishes the association of police or corrections work and masculinity.

Of course, the interactions that produce social differences do not occur in a vacuum. They are framed and constrained by historical and contemporary social, political, and economic climates. Different historical periods are characterized by varying ideas about race and ethnicity, sexual orientation, class, and socially appropriate gender behavior (Connell 1993; Foucault 1979; Omi and Winant 1994; Thompson 1993). At any point in time, there are competing and conflicting images of socially appropriate masculine or feminine behaviors. Some images are more widely accepted and socially powerful than others. Robert Connell (1987) uses the terms "hegemonic masculinity" and "emphasized femininity" to refer to culturally idealized forms of gender in particular historical periods. These forms are extolled in the media and by other societal institutions (churches, schools).

Hegemonic masculinity in contemporary Western industrialized societies is characterized by gainful employment, authority, control, aggressiveness, heterosexism, uncontrollable sexuality, and subordination of women. Emphasized femininity complements hegemonic masculinity and is defined as including sociability, fragility, compliance with men's desires, sexual receptivity, marriage, housework, and child care. Individuals are pressured to conform to culturally dominant images of gender-appropriate behavior for their sex category. However, they do not always succumb to these expectations (West and Zimmerman 1987). Ideals of socially appropriate masculinity and femininity vary across nations, races and ethnicities, social classes, ages, sexual orientations, and even day-to-day situations (Messerschmidt 1993), although images of masculinity and femininity offer individuals the opportunity to reinterpret or resist social expectations.

Existing societal institutions, including work organizations, are structured in ways that reflect culturally dominant images and power relations of gender, class, and race/ ethnicity (Acker 1990). In occupations held mostly by men, notions of effective job performance usually correspond to the culturally dominant notions of masculinity for the social class of job incumbents. For example, physicians and lawyers are expected to conform to dominant notions of middle class masculinity that include the rational manipulation and control of ideas. On the other hand, working class men's occupations often expose them to physical demands and danger. In these occupations, competence is defined in terms of physical strength, courage, and aggressiveness (Martin and Jurik 1996). A man who fails to demonstrate these qualities may be degraded by male coworkers as a "sissy" or "homosexual."

In contrast, occupations held mostly by women often involve tasks that are extensions of their domestic responsibilities; thus, competence is defined in terms of nurturing and supportive qualities. Working-class white women and women of color are assigned harsh, "dirty" service jobs (nurse's aid, housekeeper), while middle-class white women perform the cleaner professional service work (librarian, administrative assistant) (Collins 1991; Wilke 1988).

Over time, transformations have occurred in hegemonic masculinity and emphasized femininity that affect both the nature of jobs and who is in them. Connell (1993) argues that since World War II, hegemonic masculinity has changed from an emphasis on control through personal violence to an emphasis on technical expertise. The enormous growth of school and university systems and the number of "professional" occupations with claims to specialized expertise are aspects of this change.

Increases in demands for women's paid labor and awareness brought about by the second wave of the feminist movement in the 1960s and 1970s also changed culturally dominant ideals of femininity. Feminist goals such as women's rights to paid employment, equal pay for equal work, and jobs in all occupations became accepted; paid work and career pursuits became more compatible with culturally emphasized femininity (Ryan 1992).

Changes in CJ occupations, including the alteration of women's roles in them, are a part of this larger social-historical context. Expansion of opportunities in policing and corrections also reflect transformation in CJ organizations, such as bureaucratization, professionalization, and reform efforts. In turn, these organizational changes were stimulated by societal-level struggles and transformation. Racial/ethnic, class and gender relations and identities were central issues framing social struggles and change.

The History of Women in Policing and Corrections

Upper-middle-class women first entered the CJ system as volunteers and reformers. Early in the nineteenth century, upper-middle-class women sought to reform and train women inmates for "respectable" jobs such as domestic workers in Christian homes. Many of these activists had been involved in abolitionist, temperance, and suffrage movements. By resocializing "fallen women" to meet upper-middle-class Christian ideals of femininity, reformers hoped to bring about a moral reordering of society (Freedman 1981; Heidensohn 1992). Before and after the Civil War, freed African-American women also became activists working to "uplift their race" (Perkins 1981). They were often excluded from white women's activist groups (Amott and Mathaei 1996).[1]

By the end of the Civil War, upper-middle-class-women activists had moved beyond jails and prisons to encompass virtually all activities that placed government agencies in contact with women and children (Schulz 1995). In 1870, reformers demanded separate prisons for women. They envisioned institutions that would exemplify a home-like, feminine atmosphere of rehabilitation (Freedman 1981; Rafter 1990). Women also worked to establish the modern juvenile justice system that would serve as a "protective parent" for wayward youth, especially girls from lower-class immigrant families (Rafter 1990).

In the 1880s, women gained paid employment as jail matrons in new, large city police departments. Women presented themselves as specialists to work with women and children. In 1910, Alice Stebbins Wells became the first sworn woman police officer (Schulz 1995). With help from social reformers outside policing, women established separate police bureaus.

Class and race as well as gender shaped the relations of male and female police. Women's bureaus had higher educational standards, different uniforms, lower pay, and lower physical requirements. In contrast to the predominantly working-class, ethnic profile of policemen, policewomen were upper middle class, professionally oriented, and often college educated. Criminal justice work was also racially segregated. Young African-American women were hired to work with women and children of their own race. Like white female officers, they were also of middle-class origins (former teachers, ministers' wives) (Schulz 1995). Class differences reinforced the desires of both men and women to have a gender-segregated force.

Through the 1920s, policewomen remained formally separate from men. Their numbers grew slowly, but duties and pay were restricted. Their early successes were linked to the goals they shared with police reform movements. They sought to end corrupt police practices and to upgrade and professionalize personnel. They also emphasized a social service or crime prevention model, rather than a crime control model of policing (Appier 1992; Martin and Jurik 1996). The social-service and crime-prevention model, with its emphasis on community relationships and communication skills, was more compatible with culturally dominant images of femininity.

Like policing, nineteenth and early twentieth century corrections was characterized by competing organizational models of punishment and rehabilitation. Reformers sought to incorporate rehabilitative goals and duties into prison routines. These goals called for correctional officers with communication, conflict diffusion, and service skills. Rehabilitative correctional models were more compatible with culturally dominant ideals of femininity, whereas punishment models emphasized masculine powers of physical coercion and aggressiveness as methods for inmate control (Cressey 1966).

For a time, women reformers succeeded in transforming the corrections field. By the end of the nineteenth century, women ran many institutions that housed female inmates. Women's prisons were cottagelike structures with homey atmospheres and rehabilitative programming that disseminated middle-class ideals of feminine domesticity (Rafter 1990).

The struggle to create women's prisons across the United States continued through the 1920s. These prisons inspired reformers who advocated rehabilitation in men's prisons (Freedman 1981). However, by the 1920s, although most states had enacted laws that supported rehabilitation, the pressures of rapid industrialization, economic depression, and increasing inmate populations overwhelmed the best rehabilitative intentions (McKelvey 1977). More punitive models of control predominated over rehabilitative models.

As innovative programs of early women's prisons stagnated, women's work roles in corrections ceased to expand (Freedman 1981). From the 1930s to the 1970s, women worked as security and counseling staff and as administrators in juvenile and women's prisons; they held clerical positions in all institutions and worked as parole and probation officers to supervise women and juveniles. Women seldom supervised male inmates (Rafter 1990). The continuation of women's prisons came at the cost of becoming more like men's prisons—i.e., institutional warehouses. Women inmates and prison matrons became second-class citizens in a correctional system planned around the needs of men's prisons. Women staff worked long hours for low pay and little recognition (Morton 1991).

Women's inroads into policing also slowed in the 1930s. The crime control model almost totally obscured the crime prevention model (Appier 1992; Martin and Jurik 1996). The crime-control model, which advocated centralized control and a military-style command structure fostered by the FBI, firmly reinforced male working-class culture and values in police departments. In particular, it reaffirmed the superiority of the masculinist virtue of using force to overcome resistance (Appier 1992). Less visible was a shift in the content of actual police work toward the order maintenance and service tasks of the job (Walker 1983). For the next 40 years, a few policewomen feigned assignments to detective, vice, and crime lab units, but most worked as juvenile specialists or as secretaries.

This brief history of women in policing and corrections reveals the importance of gender, class, and race/ethnicity in defining and organizing the CJ system. Criminal justice work was a resource for both constructing and reaffirming gender, class, and racial/ethnic differences. Early twentieth-century policewomen and prison matrons were highly educated and from native-born, middle-class families. Policemen were less educated and from foreign-born, working-class families. Men emphasized the crime-fighting and control dimensions of CJ jobs; women focused on extending nineteenth-century, middle-class feminine virtues to "fallen" women and children. Women wanted crime prevention and rehabilitation to be the focus of CJ work. Although they emphasized their natural feminine differences from men, the intensity with which those differences were institutionalized was also due to the class and racial/ethnic differences between male and female CJ workers at the time. As is the case today, CJ system controls at that time focused on immigrants, persons of color, and the poor. Although men and women of color worked in the system, CJ workers were primarily white. Thus, gender, class, and race and ethnicity organized nineteenth- and early twentieth-century CJ work.

The social class and career goals of women entering policing in the 1950s and 1960s were more similar to those of policemen. Consequently, they began to seek a wider array of assignments and promotional opportunities (Schulz 1995).

Women's Modern Integration Into Policing and Corrections

The 1960s began a period of change in women's policing and corrections work. In a 1961 lawsuit in New York City, policewomen gained the right to compete in a promotional process previously closed to them (Martin and Jurik 1996). In 1968, Betty Blankenship and Elizabeth Coffal of the Indianapolis police department were the first women assigned to patrol (Milton 1972). In 1972, the metropolitan police of Washington, D.C., assigned over 100 women to patrol duties. Since then, the representation of women in all types of law enforcement agencies (including sheriffs' departments and the FBI) has increased; women have been integrated into patrol and virtually all other police activities (Martin and Jurik 1996). In 1950, women were only 3.8 percent of all full-time police officers, but by 1993, that figure had risen to 8.8 percent (U.S. Department of Justice 1997). These successes led to the demise of separate women's bureaus.

In the 1970s, women also sought security positions in men's prisons. In 1977, Diane Rawlinson, a college graduate in correctional psychology, brought a class action suit challenging Alabama's height and weight restrictions and a regulation that prevented female officers from "continual close proximity" to inmates in men's maximum security prisons (Jacobs 1983). The Supreme Court invalidated the height and weight restric-

tions but upheld the "no contact rule," arguing that women guards' vulnerability to rape would weaken prison security (*Dothard v. Rawlinson* 1977). Some have suggested that the paternalistic ruling in this case was influenced by the dangerous situation in Alabama prisons (Jacobs 1983). Nevertheless, subsequent courts refused to uphold the no contact rule and, by 1978, 33 states and many cities had assigned women to security posts in men's prisons (Jurik 1985).

Between 1978 and 1988, the number of women correctional officers assigned to men's prisons more than doubled (Morton 1991). As of 1994, women made up 24 percent of correctional officers in county jails, 18 percent in state prisons, and 11 percent in federal prisons (Maguire and Pastore 1994). The most recent available estimates indicate that women are about 13 percent of correctional officers in men's prisons (Morton 1991).

Through the end of the twentieth century, women in policing and corrections battled legal, organizational, and interpersonal barriers. Although most formal restrictions have been removed, women today continue to face numerous informal barriers. Women's opportunities and barriers since the 1970s can best be understood by examining their historical context.[2]

The Social Context of Women's Advancements in Criminal Justice Fields

The expansion of women's work within policing and corrections was part of a number of changes that occurred in CJ agencies. Throughout the nineteenth and early twentieth centuries, sporadic attempts to rid the CJ system of inefficiency, corruption, and brutality were ineffective. However, social unrest and activism in the 1960s and 1970s triggered social changes that, in turn, stimulated dramatic shifts in CJ organizations.

Post-World War II prosperity obscured a growing dissatisfaction with social and economic inequality in the United States. However, in the mid-1950s, the civil rights movement raised public consciousness about racial inequality. Growing inner-city poverty and racial segregation fueled a series of urban riots. The sexual revolution, increased labor force participation of women, and continuing gender inequities led to a second wave of the feminist movement. Growing dissatisfaction with the Vietnam War stimulated student democracy movements and antiwar protests. There were also movements demanding increasing rights for lesbian, gay, and disabled citizens among others (Martin and Jurik 1996).

In several highly publicized cases, police responded ineptly and brutally to protests and urban unrest. Exposures of police corruption further aroused public concern (Reuss-Ianni 1983). Within prisons, inmate riots sparked an inmate rights movement and suits challenging arbitrary use of force and inadequate prison services (Jurik and Musheno 1986). Courts began to scrutinize and intervene in prison administration (Collins 1991).

These events joined with public concerns about rising urban crime rates to encourage expansion and scrutiny of CJ organizations. In 1967, a presidential commission recommended that CJ agencies form an integrated system for improving the coordination of police, courts, and corrections. The commission called for upgrading CJ personnel by raising educational standards, providing better training, recruiting more men of color, recruiting more women, and widening women's work assignments. The Law Enforcement Assistance Administration (LEAA) was established to provide funds for CJ training, college degree programs, and technology for detecting and fighting crime. In the late 1960s, prisons and police departments recruited more men of color for front-line staff positions, but many agencies resisted hiring women until the late 1970s (Martin and Jurik 1996).

Legal Change and Women's Criminal Justice Opportunities

The civil rights and women's movements also led to significant legal changes that rippled through the CJ system. Title VII of the Civil Rights Act of 1964 prohibited discrimination on the basis of race, religion, creed, color, sex, or national origin with regard to hiring, compensation, and privileges of employment in the private sector. The Equal Employment Opportunity Act of 1972 extended the 1964 act's provisions to state and local governments, including police departments and prisons. Exceptions to these laws were allowed if gender was a necessary or *bona fide* occupational qualification (BFOQ) for that particular enterprise. However, rulings in class-action suits largely eliminated BFOQ exclusions of women from CJ jobs. The Crime Control Act of 1974 included a provision that required the termination of federal funding to CJ agencies that could not demonstrate their implementation of equal opportunity guidelines. This law and numerous suits alleging both racial and sex discrimination induced police and correctional agencies to voluntarily increase their hiring of and range of assignments for women (Feinman 1986).

During the 1980s, sexual harassment was recognized as a form of sex discrimination prohibited by Title VII of the Civil Rights Act of 1964. Courts recognized two types of harassment: *quid pro quo* harassment, which involves an explicit demand for sexual favors in exchange for a job reward or avoidance of job punishment, and hostile environment harassment, which is an ongoing pattern of hostile or harassing behavior as a condition of work (Erez and Tontodonato 1992; MacKinnon 1978, 1995). Both legal changes and court rulings encouraged the hiring of women and men of color in CJ agencies.

Women and Criminal Justice Organizational Changes

Criminal justice reforms in the 1960s and 1970s included increased formalization of organizational practices by creating written policies and rules. Reforms also encouraged the upgrading of educational and training credentials of line staff. This organizational bureaucratization and staff professionalization promoted the hiring of white women and persons of color. In addition to policies that directly mandated the hiring of men of color and women, these reforms facilitated such hiring *indirectly*. Bureaucratization encouraged the adoption of universal criteria for hiring and promotion that conformed to legal standards. Such formalization and routinization challenged the informal, aribtrary, and particularistic criteria (i.e., the buddy system) that had previously disadvantaged white women and men and women of color.

Reforms also promoted modifications in organizational goals and definitions of staff competence that challenged traditional links between masculinity and CJ job performance. By calling for policing and corrections to incorporate human relations/treatment concerns into their work routines, CJ reforms challenged an older organizational emphasis on control through physical intimidation and coercion. This discourse links job competence to working-class ideals of masculinity. By emphasizing control through verbal communication rather than physical coerciveness, CJ commissions and administrators strengthened the link between police and correctional job performance and culturally dominant notions of middle-class masculinity. To a lesser degree, by deemphasizing physical coerciveness, they also made CJ work more compatible with emphasized femininity.

Policymakers and reform-minded CJ administrators hoped that men of color and women would be particularly sensitive to the needs and problems of prisoners and citizens, especially the growing number of prison inmates and inner-city residents who were racial/ethnic minorities. They believed that more highly educated men of color and women would relate to inmates with a more communicative and less hostile style than that of the predominantly white, less-educated (read working-class) male staff of past decades. Women were expected to exert a calming effect on male citizens and inmates (Kissel and Katsampes 1980; Sherman 1975).

The reform and bureaucratization of CJ agencies represented an attempt to replace an ethos of control through physical and interpersonal dominance with a professional era of accountability, rule-bound behavior, and technology of control. Line staff were to be held accountable for the use of force; citizens and inmates were to have access to grievance procedures to protect against excesses of CJ authority. In practice, these new rules were not always applied, but their existence promoted a new organizational discourse to frame police and corrections work (Britton 1995; Marquart and Crouch 1985; Reuss-Ianni 1983).

These changes altered the class as well as gender and race composition of CJ line staff. Accordingly, there was dissension even among male officers (Jurik and Musheno 1986; Owen 1988). Higher standards for CJ personnel increased the percentage of those in police and corrections agencies with college degrees. Many agencies tied hiring and promotions to having a degree. Men of color and any women who had taken advantage of increased educational opportunities in the 1960s provided a ready pool to meet these higher educational standards and to fill vacancies created by the retirement of World War II veterans in the 1960s and 1970s. Given the changing ethos in CJ agencies, the entry of a "new breed" of officers presented serious challenges to white, working-class male subcultures in these agencies (Hunt 1984; Jurik and Musheno 1986; Marquart and Crouch 1985; Messerschmidt 1993; Reuss-Ianni 1983). Some line officers denigrated reform-oriented male administrators and staff as paper-pushing bureaucrats who were "soft on crime." Such criticism often included challenging the manhood and heterosexuality of administrators. The implication was that "real men" were out in the streets fighting crime or facing tough inmates in prisons, not in the stationhouse or office (Hunt 1984, 1990; Jurik 1985). In turn, some new and college-educated officers became disillusioned with the entrenched, militaristic hierarchies in CJ organizations (Jurik et al. 1987; Talarico and Swanson 1982).

Organizational Change and Resistance to Women

The fact that many of the newer, more educated staff were also women heightened the resentment from veteran ("old boy") line staff. Jennifer Hunt (1984, 1990) describes how many street patrol officers viewed women as in league with administrators. Despite evidence that most police work consists of routine service chores, order maintenance, and paperwork, some patrol officers continue to define their jobs as action-oriented, violent, and risky. These men view policing as a dirty job that sometimes entails corruption, and they see success in these realms as evidence of true masculinity. They believe that rule-oriented colleagues and administrators seek to feminize the profession by focusing more on communication, service, and paperwork skills. They also believe that women have higher moral standards than men and will report the corruption associated with police "dirty work." Like administrators, women are outsiders who threaten work-group solidarity. Figuratively and literally, women represent the feminization of policing.

Similar tensions occurred during periods of correctional reform (Jurik 1985; Jurik and Musheno 1986). Women correctional officers were symbolic of "getting soft" on inmates and sacrificing officer rights for inmate rights. Women symbolized a treatment approach that in the eyes of many long-term male guards downgraded the prestige of their job (Jurik 1985).

Many male staff and supervisors in policing and corrections resisted women's presence through a variety of interactional tactics. These tactics included outright hostility, physical and verbal harassment, exclusion of women from informal work cultures, gossip about or sexualizing of encounters with women, and subtle methods of reminding women of their difference (such as apologizing for telling sexual jokes or commenting on a woman's appearance) (Jurik 1985; Martin 1980; Pollock 1995; Zimmer 1986; Zupan 1992). Often, male officers were overly protective of women and took over when there was a threat of violence. In other instances, men tried to frighten women by "setting them up" or not providing backup in potentially dangerous situations (Martin 1980; Zimmer 1986).

Women entrants into male-dominated CJ jobs were highly visible "token" symbols of all women (Jurik 1985; Kanter 1977; Martin 1980). Their performance was closely scrutinized; one woman's failure proved that no woman could succeed. Many men stereotyped female colleagues and pressured them to behave as incompetent "little sisters," "seductresses," overachieving and manlike "iron maidens," or "mothers" in whom they could confide (Jurik 1985; Kanter 1977; Martin 1980). Many women felt that they had to perform their job according to one of two extremes: (1) conforming to emphasized femininity, which included accepting men's protection, or (2) "acting tough" and emulating working-class ideals of masculinity. Women who acted tough and refused male protection were still viewed by men as suspect; they were devalued as unfeminine or as lesbians (Brewer 1991; Jurik 1988). Macho CJ cultures were intolerant of homosexuality in the work group; they read it into the behavior of women who did not conform to emphasized femininity or who were not receptive to sexual advances. Women labeled as lesbians faced social isolation and additional danger from male coworkers who withheld backup in dangerous situations.

Race/ethnicity also differentiated the hostilities that women experienced. Women of color often experienced a combination of racial and sexual harassment. Black women were plagued by a convergence of sexist and racist stereotypes that included the sexually promiscuous "Jezebel," the "Mule" who does the dirty work that white women will not do, or the "uppity black woman" who does not know her place (Collins 1991; Davis 1981; Martin and Jurik 1996). Black women were rarely offered protection by white male colleagues. Sometimes black officers provided additional protection and support; at other times, black men showed resentment for women's encroachment on their space or anger at women's rejection of their sexual advances (Maghan and McLeish-Blackwell 1991; Martin 1994). Thus, many male officers "did gender" in ways to highlight women's difference and inferiority.

Organizational-Level Barriers to Women

An even greater hindrance to women's success than interactional hostilities have been organizational-level barriers. These barriers have sometimes stemmed from overtly discriminatory policies and practices and, at other times, from lack of proactive policies to integrate women into policing and corrections. Inadequate academy and informal training, restrictions on work assignments, ill-fitting uniforms, inadequate women's toilet facilities, subjective performance standards based on masculine qualities that may be irrelevant to the job, and lack of adequate maternity leave and sexual harassment policies have been some of the organizational barriers women faced (Jurik 1985; Martin 1980; Zimmer 1986). In addition, legal requirements that discrimination claims must be based on either race *or* gender grounds have posed considerable dilemmas for women of color who experience both

forms of disadvantage (Belknap 1991). Although the CJ reforms opened opportunities for women to integrate into policing and corrections, many organizations have lacked sufficient commitment, plans, and resources to implement recommended changes (Felkenes, Peretz, and Schroedel 1993; Jurik 1985; Jurik and Musheno 1986; Martin 1990).

As in the 1920s and 1930s, the past three decades have exhibited continued tensions between crime control and crime prevention policing models. Police departments have significantly increased the number of women, men of color, and college-educated officers. They have routinized, bureaucratized, and promoted the use of advanced technology in police work. However, growing poverty and violence in inner cities, public fear of crime, and "get tough" on crime political rhetoric work against large-scale transformation of police routines. Informal organizational cultures continue to emphasize macho images of police as militaristic crime fighters (Appier 1992; Heidensohn 1994). Within this framework, women are morally threatening and physically problematic coworkers.

Some police departments were faced with consent decrees that required affirmative action hiring and training plans; others adopted voluntary affirmative action plans. Both strategies have increased the hiring of women in policing, especially women of color (Martin 1991). However, because many plans did not address the promotion and daily treatment of women, little changed in those realms (Felkenes et al. 1993).

Since the 1980s, community policing has become a new version of the crime prevention model of policing. It seeks to link police and the public in the production of crime control and public safety. This model of policing calls for officers to proactively identify and solve recurrent problems in the community. Thus, officers need sharp analytic and interpersonal skills. This model arouses opposition from male officers who see it as another effort to feminize policing. The extent to which community policing models have actually been implemented is unclear

(Manning 1984). Recently, several cases of police brutality suggest that relations between police and citizens, especially citizens of color, remain strained (see Miller, this volume).

Although women correctional officers generally have received a positive reception from male inmates, a few federal lawsuits have presented formidable organizational barriers. Male inmate suits charged that women officers' presence in housing and washrooms violated prisoners' rights to privacy. In early suits, rulings supported women's equal employment claims but also required prisons to accommodate inmate privacy (e.g., screens in showers). The decline of political climates favorable to inmate claims led later court rulings to support women's employment rights with few, if any, accomodations for inmate privacy (Bernat and Zupan 1989; Collins 1991; Maschke 1996). Despite this change, for several years supervisors continued to use old rulings to justify restrictions on women's work assignments (Jurik 1988).

Rising public fear of crime yielded increasingly more and longer prison sentences for convicted criminals. State budgetary crises limited the resources available to fund prison rehabilitative programs amidst rapidly growing inmate populations. Attacks on rehabilitation beginning in the 1970s from both the political left and right converged with economic shortfalls to sharply curtail rehabilitative efforts. In the 1980s, most states removed rehabilitation mandates from their legal codes (Hawkins and Alpert 1989).

Although the rehabilitation model declined in the United States, it was replaced by a human service approach to corrections work (Johnson 1987). Like rehabilitation, the service model challenges traditional punitive correctional styles. The discourse of correctional service dictates that while correctional officers must handle security demands, they must also provide inmates with basic human services. In some states, job titles changed from "correctional security officer" to "correctional service officer" (Jurik 1985). Correctional service officers are ex-

pected to follow bureaucratic rules and use communication and conflict diffusion skills to handle inmates. Thus, the service model is still more compatible with emphasized femininity than the strictly punitive model was.

Although many states spent significant portions of their budgets to build new prisons, exploding inmate populations of the 1980s and 1990s produced dangerous overcrowding. Such danger bolstered old masculinized discourses that emphasized physical strength and verbal aggressiveness at the expense of service provision (Belknap 1996; Britton 1995; Jurik 1985).

Although an ethos of force and danger pervades contemporary police and corrections organizations, rival discourses of human service, community relations, conflict diffusion, and technical expertise continue to challenge the association between working-class masculinity and officer competence (Johnson 1987). Pressures from federal laws, threats of further litigation, and progressive administrators and line staff have led most agencies to institute sexual harassment and pregnancy leave policies. Although women still receive a narrower range of duties than men do, formal restrictions on work assignments have largely been abolished. Experienced and new women officers report that the overt hostilities of male coworkers and supervisors have subsided significantly since the 1970s and early 1980s (Dene 1992; Heidensohn 1994; Martin 1990; Walters 1993). Nevertheless, women remain grossly underrepresented in the supervisory and administrative ranks of policing and corrections (Martin 1990; Morton 1991).

Women's Responses and Strategies

The strains of surviving in CJ agencies have resulted in high rates of work-related stress and turnover for women (Bartol et al. 1992; Cullen et al. 1985; Jurik 1988; Martin 1990; Morash and Haar 1995; Poole and Pogrebin 1988). Nevertheless, many women continue to establish themselves as competent officers.

Research is equivocal as to whether CJ women adopt the same attitudes and behavioral styles as men or exhibit their own unique work styles (Heidensohn 1994; Jurik 1988; Jurik and Halemba 1984; Worden 1993; Zimmer 1986; Zupan 1992). Some research suggests that gender as well as racial/ethnic behavioral differences among officers are reduced by pressures from the work organization, work-group cultures, and job demands (Jacobs and Kraft 1978; Jenne and Kersting 1996; Wright and Saylor 1991; Zupan 1986).

Women CJ workers worldwide feel pressured to demonstrate their competence by conforming to working-class masculine performance norms (Heidensohn 1994; Holdaway 1997; Jurik 1985; Seagram and Stark-Adamec 1992). Lesbian and gay police officers feel pressure to remain closeted and to emulate macho police behavior in order to be perceived as competent (Miller, Forest and Jurik 1997). In contrast, some women attempt to preserve their feminine self-images by conforming to emphasized femininity and accepting men's protection while on the job (Martin 1980; Zimmer 1986).

Research suggests that many women try to "strike a balance" and develop strategies that mediate between cultural dichotomies of masculinity and femininity (Jurik 1988). Women adopt modified and innovative styles that incorporate elements of both hegemonic masculinity and emphasized femininity in their work (Zimmer 1986). Research identifies significant variations *both across and within gender groups* (Martin and Jurik 1996). Although constrained by societal, organizational, and peer-group pressures, individuals have the capacity to innovate and create new work styles that defy simple gender dichotomies (Johnson 1987; Martin and Jurik 1996; Miller et al. 1997). Women and men who regard their social status as marginalized in some way (e.g., as women, persons of color, lesbians, and gay men) believe that their position gives them a heightened sensitivity to the problems of street and prison clientele (Maghan and McLeish-Blackwell 1991; Miller et al. 1997; Zimmer 1986; see also Miller, this volume).

Regardless of the accuracy of such difference claims, women display a wide heterogeneity of work styles and little solidarity. Class, race and ethnicity, education, sexual orientation, and length of experience diversify work adaptations and foster tensions among women on the job (Cuadrado 1995; Lanier 1996; Van Voorhies et al. 1991). For example, black women often experience racism at the hands of white women as well as men. Such experiences, plus concerns about encouraging discrimination against the men of their own race, often discourage black women from organizing with white women to complain about sexual harassment and discrimination (Belknap 1991; Martin 1994; Owen 1985). Some research suggests that white women respond to work barriers in a more individualistic fashion than do black women, who tend to exhibit a more collective consciousness (Martin 1994). Lesbian officers may experience hostility from heterosexual women (Miller et al. 1997). Lesbians who are also women of color often feel rejected by the very groups with whom they should identify.

Rarely have women CJ line staff attempted to organize collectively for social change (Martin and Jurik 1996). When they have, frightened supervisors and administrators have discouraged them and promoted further divisions among women across racial and sexual-orientation boundaries (Jurik, 1988; Martin, 1994). Still, Frances Heidensohn (1992) has observed an increasing amount of networking among U.S. policewomen in recent years. Networks also have been developed by women correctional administrators (Morton 1991).

Instead of focusing on collective organizing, most writers have called for heightened efforts by CJ administrators to establish policies that will promote equal work opportunities (Lovrich and Stohr 1993; Porgrebin and Poole 1997; Zimmer 1989). However, reliance on future administrators may not be the best strategy for promoting women's future advancement.

Conclusion: Women and Criminal Justice Professionalism in the Future

Women first entered policing and corrections as specialists, using their natural feminine virtues to "rescue" poor women and children. In the 1960s and 1970s, social transformations, CJ system organizational changes, and changing cultural ideals of femininity led women to demand more complete integration into CJ fields, particularly in areas involving the control and supervision of men. Men fiercely resisted, but a new ethos of CJ reform and professionalization generated a work discourse favorable to women's inclusion.

Because it emphasized communication and mediation over forceful coercion, the professionalization-reform model has been embraced by many women CJ workers and their supporters as a discourse that is supportive of women, or that is at least gender-neutral (Heidensohn 1992). These women rely on professional models of conduct to mediate between images of feminine incompetence and working-class masculine competence, and they draw on reform discourses about the importance of good communication skills, team building, and conflict diffusion to justify women's place in policing and corrections work (Jurik 1988).

However, professionalism and bureaucratic rationality are not entirely gender-neutral; they are closely associated with culturally dominant views of elite white masculinity as the essence of rationality, objectivity, and emotionless affect (Kaschak 1978; Vega and Silverman 1982). Women are viewed as being more emotional and less objective than men (Pogrebin and Poole 1997). The professional model also fails to challenge institutionalized images and structures of work designed around male workers with no child care responsibilities. Thus, women's child care responsibilities are seen as detrimental to most policing and correctional officer jobs (Martin and Jurik 1996).

Neither is professional imagery neutral with regard to race or ethnicity. Professional ideals include notions of proper demeanor, dress, and speech that reflect white, middle-class standards (Young 1990). Under the guise of professionalism, women may be told that they cannot wear makeup. African-American men and women may be told to restyle their hair to emulate white middle-class standards of appearance (Maghan and McLeish-Blackwell 1991).

The transformation of corrections and policing into professional occupations mirrors Robert Connell's (1993) description of the transformation of hegemonic masculinity from being interpersonally and physically aggressive (read working class) to wielding control through technical expertise. The use of increasing technology in CJ fields offers mixed support for women. Women's technical expertise (their ability to operate guns or sophisticated computer technology) is still viewed as more limited than men's.

Professionalism may also fail to challenge nonviolent but still oppressive forms of social control of CJ inmates, suspects, and staff. Michel Foucault (1979) argued that the societal shift away from corporal forms of punishment was not to punish less, but to punish better through more efficient and sophisticated forms of surveillance. Many have attacked treatment/service and crime prevention/community policing innovations as simply widening and intensifying social control nets in our society (Cohen 1985). In fact, surveillance technology is increasingly directed at CJ personnel and other workers (e.g., drug testing).

Criminal justice professionalism has increasingly focused very narrowly on raising the educational credentials and accountability of individual line staff rather than on promoting larger structural changes or organizational accountability of CJ agencies. Much of CJ reform discourse has focused on ending CJ abuses by removing problematic, "nonprofessional" line staff, thus overlooking enduring organizational problems that foster corruption and brutality (Jurik and Musheno 1986). In response to a continuing lack of meaningful participation and control over their work, officers in both policing and corrections have formed unions. Although some CJ unions have opposed affirmative action plans and protected the privileges of senior, white male officers, seniority agreements have also slowly eroded arbitrary restrictions on women's work assignments (Martin and Jurik 1996; Zimmer 1986).

By undermining masculinist discourses of force, reforms have facilitated women's advancement in traditionally male CJ occupations. However, the reform ethos also presents barriers to women. Especially in the face of continued demands in the 1990s to get tough on crime and lock up more criminals, the human service and community relations sides of CJ occupations have receded. Resources and efforts for innovative officer training programs, community and inmate services, and means to foster the full integration of women and minority men have been curtailed. Certainly, there will be even less room for significant restructuring of work routines to accommodate women's differential family responsibilities and physical abilities. Recent court and voter attacks on affirmative action policies suggest that the mere continuation of existing programs is in question.

Aptly, Connell (1993) has argued that managers and technocrats are not openly hostile toward women and "do not directly confront feminist programs, but instead underfund or shrink them in the name of efficiency and voluntarism" (p. 615). Today's ideal professional strives for organizational universalism, rather than "special rights" for women or other social groups (Connell 1993; Young 1990).

The challenges faced by women CJ professionals of the future are formidable. However, the inroads that women have already made should provide considerable momen-

tum for continued advances. Women must work to network with each other and share work problems and strategies. Moreover, increased worker awareness of problems that crosscut gender, racial/ethnic, sexual-orientation, and class boundaries is essential for the advancement of all CJ workers. Networks and alliances must be fluid and sensitive to both differences and similarities among CJ workers. Finally, workers must also develop more critical insights into the problems that oppressive forms of social control pose for CJ staff and clients alike.

Discussion Questions

1. How have women's work roles in the CJ system changed over the course of U.S. history?

2. What part did CJ reforms play in women's changing work roles in the nineteenth and early twentieth centuries and then in the 1960s to the present?

3. What is meant by the social construction of gender? How does this approach differ from the gender-role perspective in explaining barriers to women in CJ work?

4. Discuss three ways in which work in the CJ system provides a resource for doing gender.

5. How has CJ work also been organized along the lines of race and ethnicity, class, and sexual orientation?

6. Discuss interactional and organizational-level barriers to women CJ workers.

Endnotes

1. Women in Britain also entered CJ work as reformers to save "fallen" women. Their establishment of separate bureaus and prisons for women parallels that of U.S. women. They experienced similar periods of stagnation between the 1930s and 1960s (Heidensohn 1992).

2. As in the United States, women in Canada, Britain, and Europe have made consider-

able inroads into policing and corrections fields. They face similar informal restrictions on work assignments (Brewer 1991; Dene 1992; Heidensohn 1994; Holdaway 1997). In some countries, women police remain isolated in separate police bureaus where they handle women and children offenders and victims (Dos Santos 1997; Natarajan 1996).

References

Acker, J. 1990. "Hierarchies, Jobs and Bodies: A Theory of Gendered Organizations." *Gender and Society* 4:139–158.

Amott, T., and Matthaei, J. A. 1996. *Race, Gender and Work: A Multicultural Economic History of Women in the United States.* Boston: South End Press.

Appier, J. 1992. "Preventive Justice: The Campaign for Women Police, 1910–1940." *Women and Criminal Justice* 4:3–36.

Bartol, C., Bergen, G., Volckens, J., and Knoras, K. 1992. "Women in Small-Town Policing: Job Performance and Stress." *Criminal Justice and Behavior* 19:240–259.

Belknap, J. 1991. "Women in Conflict: An Analysis of Women Correctional Officers." *Women and Criminal Justice* 2:89–116.

——. 1996. "Policewomen, Policemen, or Both? Recruitment and Training Implications for Responses to Woman Battering." *Journal of Contemporary Criminal Justice* 12:215–234.

Bernat, F. P., and Zupan, L. L. 1989. "An Assessment of Personnel Processes Pertaining to Women in a Traditionally Male Dominated Occupation: Affirmative Action Policies in Prisons and Jails." *The Prison Journal* 69:64–72.

Brewer, J. D. 1991. "Hercules, Hippolyte, and the Amazons—or Policewomen in the RUC." *British Journal of Sociology* 42:231–247.

Britton, D. M. 1995. *Controlling Sex, Controlling Violence: Cross-gender Supervision in Men's and Women's Prisons.* Unpublished doctoral dissertation, University of Texas at Austin.

Cohen, S. 1985. *Visions of Social Control.* London: Polity Press.

Collins, W. C. 1991. "Legal Issues and the Employment of Women." In J. B. Morton, ed., *Change,* *Challenge and Choices: Women's Role in Modern Corrections.* Laurel, MD: American Correctional Association.

Connell, R. W. 1987. *Gender and Power: Society, the Person and Sexual Politics.* Palo Alto, CA: Stanford University Press.

——. 1993. "The Big Picture: Masculinities in Recent World History." *Theory and Society* 22: 597–623.

Cressey, D. 1966. "Contradictory Directives in Complex Organizations: The Case of the Prison." In L. Hazelrigg, ed., *Prison Within Society.* New York: Doubleday.

Cuadrado, M. 1995. "Female Police Officers: Gender Bias and Professionalism." *American Journal of Police* 14:149–172.

Cullen, F. T., Link, B. G., Wolfe, N. T., and Frank, J. 1985. "The Social Dimensions of Correctional Officer Stress." *Justice Quarterly* 2:505–533.

Davis, A. Y. 1981. *Women, Race and Class.* New York: Random House.

Dene, E. 1992. "A Comparison of the History of the Entry of Women Into Policing in France and England and Wales." *The Police Journal* July, pp. 236–242.

Dos Santos, M. C. M. 1997. "Gender Under Construction by/in the State: The Case of Women's Police Stations in Sao Paulo, Brazil." Paper presented at the Annual Meeting of the American Sociological Assocation, Toronto, Ontario, Canada.

Erez, E. and Tontodonato, P. 1992. "Sexual Harassment in the Criminal Justice System." In I. Moyer, ed., *The Changing Roles of Women in the Criminal Justice System.* Prospect Heights, IL: Waveland Press.

Feinman, C. 1986. *Women in the Criminal Justice System.* New York: Praeger.

Felkenes, G. T., Peretz, P., and Schroedel, J. R. 1993. "An Analysis of the Mandatory Hiring of Females: The Los Angeles Police Department Experience." *Women and Criminal Justice* 4: 31–63.

Foucault, M. 1979. *Discipline and Punish: The Birth of the Prison.* New York: Vintage.

Freedman, E. 1981. *Their Sisters' Keepers: Women's Prison Reform in America, 1830–1930.* Ann Arbor: University of Michigan Press.

Hawkins, R. and Alpert, G. P. 1989. *American Prison Systems: Punishment and Justice.* Englewood Cliffs, NJ: Prentice Hall.

Heidensohn, F. 1992. *Women in Control? The Role of Women in Law Enforcement.* New York: Oxford.

———. 1994. " 'We Can Handle It Out Here.' Women Officers in Britain and the USA and the Policing of Public Order." *Policing and Society* 4: 293–303.

Holdaway, S. 1997. "Policing Women Police: Constraint and Opportunity in an English Constabulary." Paper presented at the Annual Meeting of the British Society of Criminology, Belfast, Northern Ireland.

Hunt, J. 1984. "The Development of Rapport Through Negotiation of Gender in Field Work Among Police." *Human Organization* 43:283–296.

———. 1990. "The Logic of Sexism Among Police." *Women and Criminal Justice*, 1:3–30.

Jacobs, J. B. 1983. *New Perspectives on Prisons and Imprisonment.* Ithaca, NY: Cornell University Press.

Jacobs, J. B., and Kraft, L. 1978. "Integrating the Keepers: A Comparison of Black and White Prison Guards in Illinois." *Social Problems* 25: 304–318.

Jenne, D. L., and Kersting, R. C. 1996. "Aggression and Women Correctional Officers in Male Prisons." *The Prison Journal* 76:442–460.

Johnson, R. 1987. *Hard Time: Understanding and Reforming the Prison.* Belmont, CA: Wadsworth.

Jurik, N. C. 1985. "An Officer and a Lady: Organizational Barriers to Women Working as Correctional Officers in Men's Prisons." *Social Problems* 32:25–38.

———. 1988. "Striking a Balance: Female Correctional Officers, Gender-Role Stereotypes, and Male Prisons." *Sociological Inquiry* 58:291–305.

Jurik, N. C. and Halemba, G. J. 1984. "Gender, Working Conditions and the Job Satisfaction of Women in a Nontraditional Occupation: Female Correctional Officers in Men's Prisons." *Sociological Quarterly* 25:551–566.

Jurik, N. C., Halemba, G. J., Musheno, M. C., and Boyle, B. V. 1987. "Educational Attainment, Job Satisfaction, and the Professionalization of Correctional Officers." *Work and Occupations* 14:106–125.

Jurik, N. C. and Musheno, M. C. 1986. "The Internal Crisis of Corrections: Professionalization and the Work Environment." *Justice Quarterly* 3:457–480.

Kanter, R. M. 1977. *Men and Women of the Corporation.* New York: Basic Books.

Kaschak, E. 1978. "Sex Bias in Student Evaluation of College Professors." *Psychology of Women Quarterly* 2:235–243.

Kissel, P. and Katsampes, P. 1980. "The Impact of Women Corrections Officers on the Functioning of Institutions Housing Male Inmates." *Journal of Offender Counseling Services and Rehabilitation* 4:213–231.

Lanier, M. M. 1996. "An Evolutionary Typology of Women Police Officers." *Women and Criminal Justice* 8:35–57.

Lorber, J. and Farrell, S. A. 1991. "Preface." In J. Lorber and S. A. Farrell, eds., *The Social Construction of Gender.* London: Sage.

Lovrich, N. P. and Stohr, M. K. 1993. "Gender and Jail Work: Correctional Policy Implications of Perceptual Diversity in the Work Force." *Policy Studies Review* 12:66–84.

MacKinnon, C. 1978. *Sexual Harassment of Working Women.* New Haven, CT: Yale University Press.

———. 1995. "Sexual Harassment: Its First Decade in Court." In B. R. Price and N. J. Sokoloff, eds., *The Criminal Justice System and Women.* New York: McGraw-Hill.

Maghan, J. and McLeish-Blackwell, L. 1991. "Black Women in Correctional Employment." In J. B. Morton, ed., *Change, Challenge and Choices: Women's Role in Modern Corrections.* Laurel, MD: American Correctional Association.

Maguire, K. and Pastore, A. L., eds. 1994. *Sourcebook of Criminal Justice Statistics 1993.* Washington, DC: U.S. Department of Justice, Bureau of Justice Statistics.

Manning, P. K. 1984. "Community Policing." *American Journal of Policing* 3:205–227.

Marquart, J. W. and Crouch, B. M. 1985. "Judicial Reform and Prisoner Control: The Impact of *Ruiz v. Estelle* on the Texas Penetentiary." *Law and Society Review* 19:557–586.

Martin, S. E. 1980. *'Breaking and Entering': Police-women on Patrol*. Berkeley: University of California Press.

——. 1990. *On the Move: The Status of Women in Policing*. Washington, D.C.: The Police Foundation.

——. 1991. "The Effectiveness of Affirmative Action: The Case of Women in Policing." *Justice Quarterly* 8:489–504.

——. 1994. " 'Outsider Within' the Stationhouse: The Impact of Race and Gender on Black Women Police." *Social Problems* 41:383–400.

Martin, S. E. and Jurik, N. C. 1996. *Doing Justice Doing Gender: Women in Law and Criminal Justice Occupations*. Thousand Oaks, CA: Sage.

Maschke, K. J. 1996. "Gender in the Prison Setting: The Privacy-Equal Employment Dilemma." *Women and Criminal Justice* 7:23–42.

McKelvey, B. 1977. *American Prisons: A History of Good Intentions*. Montclair, NJ: P. Smith Publishers.

Messerschmidt, J. 1993. *Masculinities and Crime*. Lanham, MD: Rowman and Littlefield.

Miller, S. K. F., and Jurik, N. 1997. "Diversity in Blue: Lesbian and Gay Police Officers in a Masculinist Occupation." Paper presented at the Annual Meeting of the American Society of Criminology, San Diego, CA.

Milton, C. 1972. *Women in Policing*. Washington, DC: Police Foundation.

Morash, M. and Greene, J. 1986. "Evaluating Women on Patrol: A Critique of Contemporary Wisdom." *Evaluation Review* 10:230–255.

Morash, M. and Haar, R. 1995. "Gender, Workplace Problems and Stress in Policing." *Justice Quarterly* 12:113–140.

Morton, J. B. 1991. "Pregnancy and Correctional Employment." In J. B. Morton, ed., *Change, Challenge, and Choices: Women's Role in Modern Corrections*. Laurel, MD: American Correctional Association.

Natarajan, M. 1996. "Towards Equality: Women Police in India." *Women & Criminal Justice* 8: 1–18.

Omi, M. and Winant, H. 1994. *Racial Formation in the United States: From the 1960s to the 1990s*. New York: Routledge.

Owen, B. A. 1988. *The Reproduction of Social Control: A Study of Prison Workers at San Quentin*. New York: Praeger.

Parsons, T. and Bales, R. 1955. *Family, Socialization, and Interaction Process*. Glencoe, IL: Free Press.

Perkins, L. 1981. "Black Women and Racial 'Uplift' Prior to Emancipation." In F. Steady, ed., *The Black Woman Cross-Culturally*. Cambridge: Schenkman.

Peterson, C. B. 1982. "Doing Time With the Boys: An Analysis of Women Correctional Officers in All-Male Facilities." In B. Price and N. Sokoloff, eds., *The Criminal Justice System and Women*. New York: Clark Boardman.

Pogrebin, M. R. and Poole, E. D. 1997. "The Sexualized Work Environment: A Look at Women Jail Officers." *The Prison Journal* 7:41–57.

Pollock, J. M. 1995. "Women in Corrections: Custody and the 'Caring Ethic'." In A. V. Merlo and J. M. Pollock, eds., *Women, Law and Social Control*. Boston: Allyn & Bacon.

Poole, E. and Pogrebin, M. 1988. "Factors Affecting the Decision to Remain in Policing: A Study of Women Officers." *Journal of Police Science and Administration* 16:49–55.

Rafter, N. H. 1990. *Partial Justice: Women in State Prisons, 1800–1935*. New Brunswick, NJ: Transaction.

Reuss-Ianni, E. 1983. *The Two Cultures of Policing: Street Cops and Management Cops*. New Brunswick, NJ: Transaction.

Ryan, B. 1992. *Feminism and the Women's Movement: Dynamics of Change in Social Movement Ideology and Activism*. New York: Routledge.

Schulz, D. M. 1995. *From Social Worker to Crimefighter: Women in United States Municipal Policing*. Westport, CT: Praeger.

Seagram, B.C. and Stark-Adamec, C. 1992, October. "Women in Canadian Urban Policing: Why Are They Leaving?" *The Police Chief*, pp. 120–128.

Sherman, L. J. 1975. "Evaluation of Policewomen on Patrol in a Suburban Police Department." *Journal of Police Science and Administration* 3: 434–438.

Stacey, J., and Thome, B. 1985. "The Missing Feminist Revolution in Sociology." *Social Problems* 32:301–316.

Stohr, M. K., Lovrich, N. P., and Mays, G. L. 1997. "Service v. Security Focus in Training Assessments: Testing Gender Differences Among Women's Jail Correctional Officers." *Women and Criminal Justice* 9:65–85.

Talarico, S. and Swanson, C. R. 1982. "Police Perceptions and Job Satisfaction." *Work and Occupations* 9:59–78.

Thompson, E. P. 1993. *The Making of the English Working Class*. New York: Pantheon Books.

U.S. Department of Justice. 1997. "Law Enforcement Management and Administrative Statistics, 1997." Bureau of Justice Statistics. Web address: www.ojp.usdoj.gov/bjs/abstract/lemas97.htm.

Van Voorhies, P., Cullen, F. T., Link, B. G., and Wolfe, N. T. 1991. "The Impact of Race and Gender on Correctional Officers' Orientation to the Integrated Environment." *Journal of Research in Crime and Delinquency* 28:472–500.

Vega, M., and Silverman, L. 1982. "Female Police Officers as Viewed by Their Male Counterparts." *Police Science* 5:31–39.

Walker, S. 1983. *The Police in America: An Introduction*. New York: McGraw Hill.

Walters, S. 1993. "Changing the Guard: Male Correctional Officers' Attitudes Toward Women as Coworkers." *Journal of Offender Rehabilitation* 20:47–60.

West, C. and Fenstermaker, S. 1993. "Power, Inequality and the Accomplishment of Gender: An Ethnomethodological View." In P. England, ed., *Theory on Gender/Feminism*. New York: Aldine.

———. 1995. "Doing Difference." *Gender and Society* 9:8–37.

West, C. and Zimmerman, D. H. 1987. "Doing Gender." *Gender and Society* 1:125–151.

Wilke, J. R. 1988. "Marriage, Family Life, and Women's Employment." In A. H. Stromberg and S. Haress, eds., *Women Working*. Mountain View, CA: Mayfield.

Wilson, N. K. 1982. *Women in the Criminal Justice Professions: An Analysis of Status Conflict*. In N. H. Rafter and E. A. Stanko, eds., *Judge, Lawyer, Victim, Thief*. Boston: Northeastern University Press.

Worden, A. 1993. "The Attitudes of Women and Men in Policing: Testing Conventional and Contemporary Wisdom." *Criminology* 31:203–242.

Wright, K. N. and Saylor, W. G. 1991. "Male and Female Employees' Perceptions of Prison Work: Is There a Difference?" *Justice Quarterly* 8:505–524.

Young, I. M. 1990. *Justice and the Politics of Difference*. Princeton, NJ: Princeton University Press.

Zimmer, L. E. 1986. *Women Guarding Men*. Chicago: University of Chicago Press.

———. 1987. "How Women Reshape the Prison Guard Role." *Gender and Society* 1:414–431.

———. 1989. "Solving Women's Employment Problems in Corrections: Shifting the Burden to Administrators." *Women & Criminal Justice* 14:349–361.

Zupan, L. 1986. "Gender-related Differences in Correctional Officers' Perceptions and Attitudes." *Journal of Criminal Justice* 14:349–361.

———. 1992. "The Progress of Women Correctional Officers in All-Male Prisons." In I. Moyer, ed., *The Changing Role of Women in the Criminal Justice System*. Prospect Heights, IL: Waveland Press. ✦

CPSIA information can be obtained at www.ICGtesting.com
Printed in the USA
LVOW03s0310080815

R9879200003B/R98792PG448895LVX2B/1/P